An in-depth look at the committee that is generally regarded as the most powerful in the House. Professor Manley's study, covering the period from the New Deal to the Nixon administration, emphasizes both the internal relations of the Committee and the Committee's relations with the House, the Senate, the President, and pressure groups. The author carefully examines the policy-making process in the Committee, whose financial and social policy decisions affect most Americans and many foreigners.

Special attention is paid to Committee Chairman Wilbur D. Mills and to the policy-making process involving issues in the areas of taxation, social security (Medicare), and international trade. Chairman Mills's role in the organization and functioning of the Committee is nearly legendary; he is certainly one of the most prominent and influential congressmen in modern times.

THE POLITICS OF FINANCE

The
Study of
Congress
Series

THE POLITICS
OF FINANCE

The House Committee
on Ways and Means

JOHN F. MANLEY
The University of Wisconsin, Madison

LITTLE, BROWN AND COMPANY · BOSTON

To Susan, John, and Laura

Foreword

The Study of Congress is sponsored by the American Political Science Association with the support of a generous grant from the Carnegie Corporation. The project was first conceived by a small group of scholars and congressmen (the latter led by Chet Holifield, D-Calif., and Thomas B. Curtis, R-Mo.) who held a series of discussion meetings on Congress with financial aid from the Philip Stern Family Fund. These discussions led to an agreement to seek support for a comprehensive study of Congress. A formal proposal was prepared by Evron M. Kirkpatrick, Executive Director of the American Political Science Association, and Donald G. Tacheron, Associate Director, which resulted in the grant by the Carnegie Corporation.

The Study of Congress gave political scientists an opportunity to cover ground in one concerted thrust which they might individually inch over in a decade. Such an opportunity was unprecedented, and it increased the urgency and importance of the basic questions: What should be the target of the study? Who should do it? How should it be done?

Reform of Congress is always in the air. Congress is criticized, even by its own members, because, as a representative body, it mirrors the weaknesses as well as the strengths of the represented. Moreover, it is powerful; almost alone among the national legislatures, it has withstood domination by the Executive and has remained the coordinate branch the Founding Fathers meant it to be. What Congress does matters very much, here and abroad, and for that reason one is tempted to try to change it, to alter some procedure or structural arrangement in order to increase one's influence on the legislative product.

Nevertheless, reform is not the target of this research project. Congress does change, but slowly, adaptively in things that matter,

vii

and seldom according to blueprint. Structure and procedure are not neutral; they are used to work the will of those who control them. Moreover, alterations in them often have unforeseen consequences. This is more likely to be true when structure and rules, and to whose benefit they work, are imperfectly understood. The Study of Congress began, therefore, with a modest admission and an appropriate resolution: there are large gaps in what political scientists know about Congress and the Study would try to fill in as many as it could.

Each of the studies which make up the Study of Congress has been undertaken by a scholar already deeply immersed in the subject. The research in each case promises to produce a book, a monograph, or one or more scholarly articles. Each man is free to recommend changes in the organization and procedures of Congress, but there will be no "official" list of recommendations by the Study of Congress itself. The purpose of the Study is to produce original research studies of Congress. Like other research enterprises, the usefulness of this one will be determined by the people who use it.

The Study of Congress Series presents associated studies designed to tell interested people as much as possible about how Congress works. It provides analytical descriptions of Congress, its subsystems, and its relations with its environment. The series fills in research blanks and suggests relevant variables for future research. It provides some basis for stating the functions performed by Congress for the political system, evaluating the performance, and pointing out alternative structural arrangements and modes of action which realistically seem to be open to Congress. Until these tasks are completed, our lists of congressional reforms are little more than statements of personal preference.

Through the House Committee on Ways and Means is funneled a great deal of the most significant legislation that Congress is called upon to pass — tax policy, medicare and social welfare issues, and problems of reciprocal trade and tariff control. John F. Manley's comprehensive study of this important committee is the fifth volume in the Study of Congress Series. Strongly influenced by Fenno's landmark research on the House Appropriations Committee, the author also draws extensively upon Barnard's inducements-contributions theory and the exchange theory of Homans and Blau. Interviews with Committee members (thirty in all) form the core of his data. Theory and data are imaginatively blended to explain recruitment to the Committee, why congressmen value their membership, integration, and other Committee norms. In a central chapter he examines Chairman Wilbur Mills in operation and analyzes his crucial role in the Committee, on the floor, and in conference committee activity with the Senate. He deals in subsequent chapters with the Committee's relationships with the rest of the House membership; interactions with the Senate, especially Finance Committee members; and executive-legislative relations. Throughout the book, interview data are supported by a careful review of public records extending back to 1933 and an intensive use of roll call votes. The end product demonstrates anew the importance of committee-centered research as a means of understanding the workings of Congress.

Ralph K. Huitt
Robert L. Peabody

Acknowledgments

This book would not have been written without the assistance of two friends and colleagues, H. Douglas Price and Richard F. Fenno, Jr. Both men gave me countless hours of their time; equally important was their moral support. My hope is that the results in some way approximate the help they extended.

My thanks are also due to Ralph K. Huitt, one of the truly unselfish men in the political science profession, and to Robert L. Peabody, who helped in many ways. Representatives Thomas B. Curtis, Dante Fascell, and Hale Boggs opened their offices to me and in so doing greatly eased the difficulty of research in Washington. Two professional staff members of Ways and Means who went out of their way to assist me were Richard Wilbur and David West. Gary Hymel, legislative assistant to Representative Boggs, gave far more than he received while I was in the Boggs office.

Lewis A. Froman, Jr., a colleague on the Congressional Fellowship program, Frank Munger, my advisor, Randall B. Ripley and Nelson W. Polsby, fellow Washington researchers, all contributed much to this novice's attempt to explore national politics. My graduate assistant, Jacques De Puy, was extremely helpful, and Mrs. Anne Filippone did her usual superb job in typing the manuscript.

Financial support for the study was provided by the American Political Science Association's Congressional Fellowship program, the Brookings Institution, the University of Wisconsin Graduate Research Committee, and, most significantly, the APSA Study of Congress. This book could not have been written without the assistance of the members of the House Ways and Means Committee. For putting up with repeated demands on their time, my thanks.

Anyone who writes a book calls upon his family for sacrifices, and I am no exception. This book's dedication to them is a measure of their contribution to it. Final responsibility for the content of this study unhappily rests with me.

John F. Manley

Table of Contents

I   Introduction   1

SCOPE. THEORY AND METHOD.

II   Recruitment and Attractiveness   15

THE COMMITTEE IN THE CONTEXT OF THE HOUSE. RECRUITMENT:
THE DEMOCRATS. RECRUITMENT: THE REPUBLICANS. EFFECT OF RE-
CRUITMENT ON THE COMMITTEE. ATTRACTIVENESS. CONCLUSION.

III   Integration and Exchange:
The Internal Relations of Ways and Means   59

RESTRAINED PARTISANSHIP. MILLS AND BYRNES: THE RECIPROCATION
OF ESTEEM. SOCIALIZATION: PERPETUATION OF NORMS THROUGH
EXCHANGE.

IV   Wilbur D. Mills   98

MILLS AS INSTRUMENTAL AND AFFECTIVE LEADER. MILLS: INFLUENCE
AND EXCHANGE. MILLS: THE SWING VOTE. CONCLUSION.

V   The Committee and the House   151

I. MAJORITIES: 1933–1968. II. HOUSE-COMMITTEE RELATIONS: DE-
PENDENCE AND INDEPENDENCE. PASSING COMMITTEE BILLS. CONCLU-
SION.

VI   The Committee and the Senate   248

WAYS AND MEANS—SENATE RELATIONS. CONFERENCE COMMITTEE DE-
CISIONS. CONSERVATIVE CONTROL OF THE CONFERENCE. THE JOINT
COMMITTEE ON INTERNAL REVENUE TAXATION. CONCLUSION.

VII   The Committee and the Executive:
      Interest Aggregation   322

THE ROLE OF CONGRESS. EXECUTIVE-LEGISLATIVE INTERACTION. COM-
PENSATORY REPRESENTATION. REVENUE-GAINING PROPOSALS. CONCLU-
SION.

Conclusion   380

Appendix I: Persons Interviewed   385

Appendix II: Roll Call Votes   387

Index   389

List of Tables

2.1 Democratic Appointments to Ways and Means, and
Medicare, 1961–1965   28

2.2 Party Unity Scores of Ways and Means Democrats and All
Democrats, 1951–1966   30

2.3 Support for a Larger Federal Role, Ways and Means
Democrats and All Democrats, 1957–1966   31

2.4 Support for a Larger Federal Role, Ways and Means
Republicans and All Republicans, 1957–1966   41

2.5 Party Unity Scores of Ways and Means Republicans and
All Republicans, 1951–1966   42

3.1 Executive Session Participation, Medicare and Excise
Tax Reduction, 1965   74

4.1 Task and Socioemotional Leadership in the Ways
and Means Committee   102

4.2 Members' Estimates of Their Bargaining Position with
the Chairman   133

5.1 Index of Party Likeness, Ways and Means and the House,
All Roll Call Votes, 1933–1964   159

5.2 Roll Call Votes Lost by the Ways and Means Committee,
1933–1964   161

5.3 Roll Call Votes on Which the Conservative Coalition Has
Appeared, Ways and Means Bills, 1933–1964   162

5.4 Index of Party Likeness, Ways and Means Committee
Voting, 1940–1946   175

5.5 Index of Party Likeness, Ways and Means and the House,
Bipartisan Bills, 1940–1946   176

5.6 Index of Party Likeness, Ways and Means and the House,
Partisan Bills, 1940–1946   179

5.7 Index of Party Likeness, Ways and Means and the House,
Mixed Bills, 1940–1946   180

5.8   Index of Party Likeness, Major Bills, 1953–1960   201
5.9   Index of Party Likeness, Major Bills, 1961–1964   208
5.10   Bills Amended or Defeated and Type of Rule, 1947–1965   221
5.11   Ways and Means Members' Responses to Pressure Group
       Question   236
6.1   Major Revenue-Raising Bills, 1947–1966   273
6.2   Major Revenue-Reducing Bills, 1947–1966   274
6.3   Comparison of Revenue Loss Under House and Senate
       Versions of 1954 Revenue Act   275
6.4   Comparison of 1964 Revenue Act as Passed by House and
       Reported by the Senate Finance Committee   276
6.5   Revenue Effects of House and Senate Revenue Bills,
       1947–1966   278
6.6   Level-Cost of Social Security Bills, 1950–1967   280
7.1   Revenue-Reducing and Revenue-Gaining Proposals of
       Treasury in Capital Gains Area, 1963   363
7.2   Revenue-Losing Proposals of Treasury and Ways and Means
       Action (Individuals and Corporations)   366
7.3   Testimony on Minimum Standard Deduction   367
7.4   Testimony on Tax Treatment of Older Persons   369
7.5   Revenue-Raising Proposals, Testimony, and Ways
       and Means Action   370

List of Figures

2.1 Party Unity and Disunity in the House of Representatives
on Roll Call Votes, 1956–1967   17

2.2 Percentage of House Roll Calls on Which the Conservative
Coalition Appeared and Won, 1957–1967   18

2.3 House Support for a Larger Federal Role and Opposition
to Cutting Federal Spending, 1957–1967   20

2.4 Man-Years Service of Ways and Means Democrats, by
Region, 1947–1966   37

5.1 Party Control of House of Representatives, 1933–1968   156

5.2 Southern and Non-Southern Democrats in the House,
1933–1968   157

5.3 Number of Votes Needed by Non-Southern Democrats for
Absolute Majority of the House, 1933–1968   158

THE POLITICS OF FINANCE

CHAPTER ONE

Introduction

"The student of committees," writes K. C. Wheare, "has to make a choice. Either he can try to hack his way through the jungle on foot or he can try to get a bird's eye view of the terrain from the air. If he chooses the first alternative, the most he can hope for is to clear a portion of his territory; if he chooses the second, the most he can hope for is to produce a rough sketch-map of the whole area." [1]

The decision to clear the portion of congressional territory occupied by a single committee, the House Committee on Ways and Means, was made shortly after the appearance of a path-breaking study of the House Appropriations Committee by Richard F. Fenno, Jr.[2] Ways and Means, which handles more nationally significant legislation than most other committees, was then, as it is now, in the news. But little was known about the Committee except that it had virtually complete control over the Kennedy Administration's desire to cut federal taxes; that it had, for years, refused to report out a medicare bill; and that, in foreign policy, the Committee was the first — and most crucial — hurdle for the monumental Trade Expansion Act. Political scientists had, as Fenno notes, failed to treat committees as discrete units for analysis despite the aged generalization about committee power and autonomy.[3]

[1] *Government by Committee: An Essay on the British Constitution* (London: Oxford University Press, 1955), p. i.
[2] "The House Appropriations Committee as a Political System: The Problem of Integration," *American Political Science Review*, LVI (June, 1962), 310–24. See also Richard F. Fenno, Jr., "The Comparative Analysis of Congressional Committees," unpublished paper read at Ann Arbor, Michigan, 1964.
[3] There are, of course, exceptions, but not until Fenno did committee studies reach the take-off stage. For earlier studies see Albert C. F. Westphal, *The House Committee on Foreign Affairs* (New York: Columbia University Press, 1942); Robert K. Carr, *The House Committee on Un-American Activities, 1945–1950* (Ithaca: Cornell University Press, 1952); Ralph K. Huitt, "The Congressional

1

The decision to concentrate on one committee rests, then, on the importance of the policy areas that come under the jurisdiction of Ways and Means (tax, social security, and trade legislation) and on the inattention heretofore given individual congressional committees. An intensive examination of the Ways and Means Committee could greatly illuminate the inner workings of the congressional legislative process and, more generally, lead to a better grasp of the place of Congress in national policy-making. These objectives — a clearer understanding of how the internal legislative process works in the areas considered by Ways and Means and a stronger understanding of the interaction between Congress and other political participants in three major policy areas — are the purpose, the value, and the problem of this book.[4]

SCOPE

To analyze the internal relations of the Ways and Means Committee as well as the Committee's relations with other major participants in the policy-making process — in three policy arenas — the almost infinite amount of data that could, in theory, be collected had to be brought within finite proportions. This was done in two familiar ways: first, by limiting the time span of the study and, second, by imposing specific theoretical controls on the questions explored within each general area of interest.

An historical study of the Ways and Means Committee could, no doubt, be of great value to American history and to political science. Ways and Means, first established for a brief time in 1789, became a permanent fixture of the House in 1795 and a formal standing committee in 1802. Its job, until 1865, was to consider most appropriations and revenue bills, including one of the classic partisan is-

Committee: A Case Study," *American Political Science Review*, XLVII (June, 1954), 340–65; Charles O. Jones, "Representation in Congress: The Case of the House Agriculture Committee," *American Political Science Review*, LV (June, 1961), 358–67; Nicholas A. Masters, "Committee Assignments in the House of Representatives," *American Political Science Review*, LV (June, 1961), 345–57.

[4] Woodrow Wilson wrote the first comprehensive account of the place of committees in the legislative process. See his *Congressional Government* (Cleveland: World Publishing Co., 1956). It is interesting that in 1833, fifty years before Wilson wrote his book, Thomas Hamilton (and no doubt others) recognized the power of committees in Congress. Quoted in James Sterling Young, *The Washington Community, 1800–1828* (New York: Columbia University Press, 1966), p. 202. Wilson's book was, however, the first major analysis of the power of committees in Congress.

sues in American history, the tariff. In 1865 the Committee lost control over appropriations bills to the newly created Committee on Appropriations but it continued to consider revenue bills, the most significant of which was the tariff. In the nineteenth century, the jurisdiction of the Committee was so broad that, as one historian writes, "It seemed like an Atlas bearing upon its shoulders all the business of the House." [5] For much of this period the chairman of Ways and Means was also de facto majority leader of the House, and six Presidents had once served on the Committee.[6]

But such an historical study is outside the purview of this book. To give a modicum of historical depth to the present study but mainly to investigate Committee behavior under a variety of conditions, important questions about the Committee are explored using data from the New Deal onward; by no stretch of the imagination can this book be considered a history of the Committee even for the relatively brief 1933–1968 period. Indeed, for most purposes the data are drawn from the post-World War II years, a time span that has the advantage of including every possible combination of party control of Congress and the presidency.

THEORY AND METHOD

The second way in which limitations were placed on this study was through the interplay of broad theoretical interests, specific hypotheses, and the research experience itself. The study began with some rather general interests derived from diverse theories (mostly sociological in origin), and a key decision-making unit of the House of Representatives. It continued for six years, during which time — largely as a result of the research process — much of the early theory and many of the early hypotheses were jettisoned. New theoretical interests and hypotheses were developed along with the research; similarity between the original research design and the final product is virtually nonexistent.

[5] DeAlva S. Alexander, *History and Procedure of the House of Representatives* (Boston: Houghton Mifflin, 1916), p. 234.
[6] Madison, Jackson, Fillmore, Polk, Tyler, and McKinley. For historical material on Ways and Means see Neil MacNeil, *Forge of Democracy* (New York: David McKay Co., 1963), *passim*. Walter Kravitz, "A Brief History of the House Ways and Means Committee," Library of Congress, Legislative Reference Service, May 14, 1964. Walter Kravitz, "A Brief History of Appropriation Committees and Procedure in Congress Before 1867," Library of Congress, Legislative Reference Service, April 18, 1963. Remarks of Hon. Robert L. Doughton, *Congressional Record*, May 2, 1940, pp. 2636–39.

To illustrate how the intermingling of theory and research set the parameters of the study and defined its content, the research strategy and the theory will be discussed separately but, as we mentioned, they were far from separate during the study.

RESEARCH STRATEGY. A brilliant essay by Homans compares the research of some industrial sociologists to that of some social psychologists.[7] His description of the research strategy of the industrial sociologist is almost exactly the strategy that led to this book.

Industrial sociologists spend most of their time in field research, studying social organizations firsthand. Their major obstacle is establishing rapport with their subjects. Therefore, they tend to rely on participant observation and nondirective interviewing. Armed more with a set of what Homans calls "mental pigeonholes" than with a list of hypotheses to test, the industrial sociologist is engaged in an "experiment of light," intended to reveal something new in a relatively uncharted area, rather than an "experiment of proof" that, at a later stage of research, demonstrates what one is already pretty sure of. A *conceptual scheme*, not a fully developed model and not a single hypothesis, orients the industrial sociologist to his data. The participant observer or field researcher may prepare a paradigm to satisfy some supporting foundation but he knows that what is left between the lines and arrows may well be crucial. Confronted by the "softness" of some of the data he collects, he takes solace in their richness if not in their susceptibility to statistical manipulation. Once he learns which variables to test he tests them, but the learning process is no less vital to the total scientific enterprise than the testing process.[8]

The important methodological feature of this study is that most of the time was spent in field research and quasi-participant observation. Although I worked for two members of the Committee I never became a full-fledged participant observer. Access was obtained to certain verbatim transcripts of executive sessions but I never attended a closed meeting of the Committee. Hence the research was merely "quasi" participant observation.

Because attendance at the executive sessions was precluded, heavy

[7] George Caspar Homans, *Sentiments and Activities* (New York: Macmillan, 1962), pp. 259–68.
[8] For a general discussion see Severyn T. Bruyn, *The Human Perspective in Sociology: The Methodology of Participant Observation* (Englewood Cliffs, N.J.: Prentice-Hall, 1966).

reliance had to be placed on two sources of information: interviews with the participants in which they would tell me what happened, what their perceptions of the Committee members were, and how they thought the Committee worked; and informants, mainly staff members, who let me see the Committee through their eyes and assisted me in a variety of ways. Months were spent gaining and utilizing access to both sources of data.

Because of the lack of research on congressional committees when this study began, the general ignorance about the Ways and Means Committee, and the absence of any dependent variable of over-powering interest,[9] it was inevitable that the "theory" and the mental pigeonholes used in this study would develop during the course of research. If such a process seems inordinately sloppy compared to the theory-hypothesis-test model of, say, physics, some comfort may be derived from the fact that it appears to be fairly common among studies of social organizations.[10] As Becker says:

> Sociologists usually use this method when they are especially interested in understanding a particular organization or substantive problem rather than demonstrating relations between abstractly defined variables. They attempt to make their research theoretically meaningful, but they assume that they do not know enough about the organization *a priori* to identify relevant problems and hypotheses and that they must discover these in the course of the research. Though participant ob-

[9] James S. Coleman recalls that at the start of his research on the adolescent society some colleagues observed that he had no dependent variable. He remarks: "I think this will be characteristic of such studies [of social systems]; in contrast to most social research, they will have no single dependent variable. The difference is analogous to the difference between (1) finding the coefficients of a regression equation to account for the variance in a dependent variable and (2) finding the coefficients of a system of simultaneous equation which link together a number of variables. It is quite obvious that the latter research will appear less focused than the former, for it attempts to lay out the structure of relations in a system rather than to explain the variance in a single variable." See Coleman's "Research Chronicle: The Adolescent Society," *Sociologists at Work*, ed. Phillip E. Hammond (New York: Basic Books, 1964), pp. 190–91.

[10] See, for example, William Foote White, *Street Corner Society* (Chicago: University of Chicago Press, 1955), pp. 279–358; Anselm Strauss et al., *Psychiatric Ideologies and Institutions* (New York: Free Press, 1964), chap. 2; Barney G. Glaser and Anselm L. Strauss, *The Discovery of Grounded Theory* (Chicago: Aldine Publishing Co., 1967), chap. 5, pp. 148–50 on Evans-Pritchard; Howard S. Becker, Blanche Geer, Everett C. Hughes, and Anselm L. Strauss, *Boys in White* (Chicago: University of Chicago Press, 1961), chap. 2; W. Richard Scott, "Field Methods in the Study of Organization," ed. James G. March, *Handbook of Organizations* (Chicago: Rand McNally, 1965), pp. 261–304.

servation can be used to test *a priori* hypotheses . . . this is typically not the case.[11]

If one grants the value if not the absolute necessity of participant observation research on organizations such as congressional committees then the difficulties of this approach as well as its potential have to be recognized. Access is one problem but much more serious is the danger that the field researcher may become more of an artist than a social scientist. What distinguishes the participant observer of Congress from the journalist? On Capitol Hill there is great similarity between their methods. For access, few political scientists can compete with reporters who spend years in daily contact with leading congressmen. And few observers would dispute that at least some reporters get a very good "feel" for the Congress, though perhaps not as good as that of a first-rate participant observer such as the late Congressman Clem Miller.[12]

Three characteristics of the participant observer-political scientist seem particularly important in distinguishing him from the non-social scientist observer. The participant observer is primarily interested not in a running account of current events or in collecting intriguing anecdotes about important personalities, but in the pattern of relationships in the social system. His ultimate objective is and must be generalization, not skill at storytelling. Second, he does have some theoretical notions, however crude, guiding his research, even though these notions undergo considerable change over time. Third — and most important — his generalizations have to rest on as much empirical evidence as he can gather and, whenever possible, this evidence is presented in quantified form.

At some time in the research on Congress the methods of the experimentalist and the participant observer may have to merge if, in

[11] Howard S. Becker, "Problems of Inference and Proof in Participant Observation," *American Sociological Review*, XXIII (December, 1958), 652–53. Merton puts it well: "With a few conspicuous exceptions, recent sociological discussions have assigned but one major function to empirical research: the testing or verification of hypotheses. The model for the proper way of performing this function is as familiar as it is clear. The investigator begins with a hunch or hypothesis, from this he draws various inferences and these, in turn, are subjected to empirical test which confirms or refutes the hypothesis. But this is a logical model, and so fails, of course, to describe much of what actually occurs in fruitful investigation. It presents a set of logical norms, not a description of the research experience." Robert K. Merton, *Social Theory and Social Structure*, rev. ed. (Glencoe, Ill.: Free Press, 1957), pp. 102–03.
[12] See his perceptive *Member of the House* (New York: Scribner's, 1962).

truth, generalization is the goal of both. The real point made by Homans is not that he defends the value of industrial sociology, which he does, but that he calls for the erasure of the differences between the two approaches:

> This is as much as to say that the industrial sociologist, on his way to the ultimate goal, will move from a study of the social system as it is exemplified in single groups toward a study of the system as it is exemplified in many groups, including groups changing in time, just as the social psychologist will move from a study of single equations toward a study of a system of equations. The methods and ideas of the two will converge as they approach the goal from different directions. For the industrial sociologist this means that his methods must become more quantitative.[13]

Nothing short of this, it seems, will lead to much progress in the study of congressional behavior.

This account of the Ways and Means Committee is a case study of one committee, and its findings cannot be generalized to other committees. But wherever possible hypotheses drawn from "hard-to-get" data are tested by "hard" data and an attempt is made to generalize about the Committee and its behavior over the past few decades. As many participant observation studies show, there is no inherent conflict between studying human organizations closely and generalizing about them, even though in many instances it is hard to measure precisely how all the influences on behavior fit together.

THEORY. The theoretical orientation of this study began with the writings of the systems theorists and functionalists, especially David Easton, Talcott Parsons, and Robert Merton. It moved to the literature on small groups when "grand" theory, as Merton discusses it,[14] proved too grand to be of much specific help, and came to rest heavily on the inducement-contribution theory of Barnard and similar notions in the exchange theory of Homans and Blau. With few qualms about making intellectual raids into a number of sometimes conflicting camps, and with a decided bias in favor of letting theory shape research and vice versa, the inducement-contribution view of the Committee came after a good deal of research had been done.

[13] Homans, *op. cit.*, p. 266.
[14] Merton, *op. cit.*, pp. 4–10. Easton, of course, rejects functionalism out-of-hand but there are many similarities between his aims and those of Parsons.

(Like Fenno, I have found an eclectic approach most useful in this kind of research,[15] but unlike him I have not attempted to analyze the Senate in the same framework used for the House. The Senate is relevant in this study only as it directly affects an understanding of the House.)

The systems theory of Easton provided a sensitivity to the relationships between the Committee, its environment, and the policy decisions made by the Committee.[16] Hence the attempt to view the Committee as the central unit in a decision-making process involving a number of other groups and individuals.

Easton's desire to relate part to whole was reinforced by Parsons and the functionalists. More important, functionalist literature provided some clues to what to look for while studying the part, not in following the basic logic of functional analysis, which sees the part as meeting certain needs of the whole. Certain key concepts in the work of Parsons and his associates — integration (originally stressed by Fenno), value consensus, differentiation of function, socialization, sanction, norms, adaptation, collectivity-orientation, interdependence of parts — became the initial foci of the study.[17] These defined the substance of the study in the early stages and, though covering a wide territory, helped transform the territory into manageable size.

But systems theory and functionalism, as is well known, are not without their problems. Their utility as general orientations toward data is also their main weakness.[18] In a sense they provide a road map with the principal cities and points of interest clearly marked but without the routes linking one place to the other. Systems theory and functionalism, rich in concepts but poor in hypotheses, are first and foremost general theories designed for general problems. My problem was a series of what Dahrendorf calls "riddles of experi-

[15] Richard F. Fenno, Jr., *The Power of the Purse* (Boston: Little, Brown, 1966), p. xviii.

[16] David Easton, "An Approach to the Analysis of Political Systems," *World Politics*, IX (April, 1957), 383–400. Also see his *A Framework for Political Analysis* (Englewood Cliffs, N.J.: Prentice-Hall, 1965), and *A Systems Analysis of Political Life* (New York: John Wiley, 1965).

[17] Talcott Parsons and Edward A. Shils, eds., *Toward a General Theory of Action* (New York: Harper Torchbooks, 1962); Talcott Parsons, *The Social System* (New York: Free Press, 1964); Marion J. Levy, Jr., *The Structure of Society* (Princeton: Princeton University Press, 1952); A. R. Radcliffe-Brown, *Structure and Function in Primitive Society* (New York: Free Press, 1965).

[18] On this point see Merton, *op. cit.*, p. 9. Easton would disagree, but in my judgment many of the problems with functionalism are also problems for systems theory.

ence," [19] and more was needed than systems theory or functionalism could contribute.

The literature on small groups provided the distinction between instrumental leadership and socioemotional leadership.[20] Apparently in many groups the goal-oriented problems are handled by one man while the affective problems arising from group interaction are handled by another. The relevance of this distinction to my study turned out to be, somewhat unexpectedly, that one man, the Chairman, plays both roles, and in a much more complex way than a simple dichotomy between instrumental and affective leadership allows.[21] The work of Homans and French and Raven on small groups also suggested methods of looking at Ways and Means and hypotheses that might be relevant for the study of a congressional committee.[22]

To understand — and to explain — the behavior of Committee members, three very simple questions seem necessary.

1. What satisfactions does the Committee provide its members?
2. What are the demands of Committee membership?
3. How do the satisfactions relate to the demands?

Systems theory, functionalism, and small group studies all say something about these questions. But none makes the rewards and costs of membership in organizations their basic concern. The conclusion was reached that at best these theories were useful for de-

[19] Ralf Dahrendorf, "Out of Utopia: Toward a Reorientation of Sociological Analysis," in *Sociological Theory,* ed. Lewis A. Coser and Bernard Rosenberg, 2nd ed. (New York: Macmillan, 1964), pp. 219–20. In fairness to Merton, it should be noted that Dahrendorf completely distorts Merton's view of the relationship between theory and research.

[20] Robert F. Bales and Philip E. Slater, "Role Differentiation in Small Decision-Making Groups," Talcott Parsons et al., *Socialization and Interaction Process* (London: Routledge & Kegan Paul, 1956), pp. 259–306. Sidney Verba, *Small Groups and Political Behavior* (Princeton: Princeton University Press, 1961), pp. 142–43.

[21] On the dangers of lifting findings from the small group laboratory and applying them to natural groups see James D. Barber, *Power in Committees* (Chicago: Rand McNally & Co., 1966), chap. 1.

[22] George C. Homans, *The Human Group* (New York: Harcourt, Brace & World, 1950). Although Homans' theory is applicable to small groups and Easton is attempting to design a theory for society as a whole, it is interesting to see how very similar much of their work is. See especially pp. 90–92 in Homans. John R. P. French, Jr., and Bertram Raven, "The Bases of Social Power," *Group Dynamics,* ed. Dorwin Cartwright and Alvin Zander, 2nd ed. (Evanston, Ill.: Row, Peterson & Co., 1960), pp. 607–23.

scribing or conceptualizing the problem; for *explanation* a different
approach was necessary.

If, for example, the question is the type of integration characteristic of Ways and Means, the "explanation" can be couched in terms
of how different roles fit together into a functional whole, a primary
concern of Parsons. But all this does is substitute one problematical
concept for another. To explain integration in terms of roles, why
individual members take the roles they do must be explained. Riddles of the group conceived in sociological terms in the final analysis
must be explained in psychological terms if the chain of using one
undefined term to explain another is to be broken.[23]

Most helpful in breaking this chain have been the inducement-
contribution theory of Barnard and, as mentioned previously, the
exchange theory of Homans and Blau. Both theories are explicitly
meant to answer the three questions central to explaining Ways and
Means: what are the inducements or incentives associated with membership on the Committee, what are the costs of being on Ways and
Means, and what is the relationship between the benefit and the
cost.[24] In Chapter Three we utilize this perspective — which is essentially psychological — in explaining the internal operations of Ways
and Means.

The final question is the problem of change. Equilibrium models
are sometimes attacked because they give undue attention to the
problems of stability, consensus, and integration at the expense of
instability, dissension, and disintegration in social systems.[25] If a

[23] This is recognized by Homans: "I came to the conclusion, though I could
demonstrate it even to my own satisfaction in only a few cases, that the ultimate
explanatory principles in anthropology and sociology, and for that matter in history, were neither structural nor functional but psychological: they were propositions about the behavior of men as men." *Sentiments and Activities, op. cit.,* p.
29. Although Parsons considers role as the most significant unit of social structure he observes that: "The actual operation of this structure of roles . . . is
. . . possible in the last analysis only because the component personalities are
motivated to act in the requisite ways and sufficient gratification is provided
enough individuals. . . ." Parsons and Shils, *op. cit.,* pp. 24–25.

[24] Chester I. Barnard, *The Functions of the Executive* (Cambridge: Harvard
University Press, 1966), chap. 11. See Homans, "Social Behavior as Exchange,"
American Journal of Sociology, LXIII (May, 1958), 597–606; and his *Social
Behavior: Its Elementary Forms* (New York: Harcourt, Brace & World, 1961).
Peter M. Blau, "A Theory of Social Integration," *American Journal of Sociology,*
LXV (May, 1960), 545–56; and his *Exchange and Power in Social Life* (New
York: John Wiley, 1964).

[25] Dahrendorf, *op cit.,* pp. 222–25. For a treatment of this question in functionalism see Pierre L. Von Den Berghe, "Dialectic and Functionalism," *American Sociological Review,* XXVIII (October, 1963), 695–705.

researcher tends to see his problem in terms of an equilibrium model he may present an accurate picture of the subject at one point of time, but he runs the risk of overlooking or deemphasizing the conflicts that lead to changes in organizational behavior. As Mead asks: "How can you present order and structure in society and yet bring about the changes that need to take place, are taking place? How can you bring those changes about in orderly fashion and yet preserve order?" [26]

In coping with this problem either or both of two things may be done: (1) deny that there is any inherent bias toward stability in systems theory or functionalism; and (2) study organizations at different times to see if conflict prevails at one time and harmony at another. Both are done in this study. Easton makes a very persuasive argument that, put simply, there are no insuperable barriers to analyzing change or conflict in systems theory terms.[27] And in this study of Ways and Means change and stability, conflict and harmony, consensus and dissensus are treated as merely two sides of the same coin. All are present simultaneously but in different proportions in all social systems.

Ways and Means is examined over a fairly long time and a number of issue areas to see if the Committee in one context and at one time is the same in another context and time. By doing this, it is hoped that the metronomic behavior of the Committee, which veers toward conflict under certain circumstances and consensus under others, is sufficiently detailed to put appropriate qualifications on the generalizations.

DATA. The most important source of data on the functioning of the Committee was the interview. Off-the-record interviews with the members were conducted in two series, first in 1964 and again in late 1967 and early 1968, with occasional interviews in between. For reasons of rapport, the members were promised anonymity, and normally no notes were taken during the interview. Quotes are based on notes made immediately after each interview. Altogether thirty members of the Committee were interviewed (eighteen Democrats, twelve Republicans).[28] For the Democrats, the interview time ranged from

[26] Anselm Strauss, ed., *The Social Psychology of George Herbert Mead* (Chicago: University of Chicago Press, 1956), p. 18.
[27] See, especially, *A Framework for Political Analysis, op. cit.*, chaps. 6, 7, 8. For Almond's response see Gabriel A. Almond, "A Development Approach to Political Systems," *World Politics*, XVII (January, 1965), 183–214.
[28] See Appendix I for a list of those interviewed.

five minutes to more than four hours, with an average of almost two hours per man. For the Republicans, it ran from sixty-five minutes to more than six hours, with an average of about two and one-half hours per man. Based on a very conservative estimate, about sixty-five hours were spent in actual interviews with the members.

In addition to interviews with Ways and Means members, eight of the fifteen members of the Senate Finance Committee were interviewed in 1965. Senator Lee Metcalf, a former member of Ways and Means who was later appointed to Finance, was also interviewed at this time. Many more hours were spent interviewing and discussing the Committee with knowledgeable members of the staff.

Outside Congress, interviews were conducted with persons in the Treasury Department and the Department of Health, Education and Welfare, all of whom regularly attend Committee executive sessions. The sheer size of the lobbying community involved in Ways and Means legislation precluded much systematic interviewing of lobbyists. Talks were held from time to time with a few journalists who regularly cover Ways and Means.

From June through December 1967 I served as an assistant to House Democratic Whip Hale Boggs, who is also a member of the Committee, and interviewed House Speaker John W. McCormack and House Majority Leader Carl Albert. This position also provided an invaluable opportunity for participant observation research on the House generally, and enabled me to chat with members of the Committee on the House floor. These informal discussions are not included in the calculations of interview time except in some cases where the interview was actually conducted on the floor. Some of the observations about House-Committee relations in Chapter Five are based upon the Whip office experience.

Another major source of data was the public record. House floor debates on slightly over one thousand bills considered from 1933 through 1966 were read.[29] This material contained information on such questions as patterns of relationships between the House and the Committee; what happened during Committee consideration of the bills; and House members' perceptions of the Senate, interest groups, lobbyists, staff, different issues, and administrations. Committee reports and hearings yielded data on many of the same questions.

[29] My graduate assistant, Mr. Jacques DePuy, separated the major from the minor bills for me for the 1933–1947 period. I read the debates on the major bills.

Standard secondary sources (newspapers and periodicals) were used, but only the *Congressional Quarterly* was used extensively.

The public record also provided the data for a roll call analysis of all the record votes taken on Ways and Means bills since 1933. A statistical analysis of these votes (248 roll calls were involved) was made to test hypotheses about Committee solidarity on the floor, the changing nature of party voting on Ways and Means bills, variations in regional voting behavior, and the like. Roll call analysis, though by no means the most significant part of the study, permitted a precise analysis of some aspects of Committee and House behavior in the areas of trade, tax, and social security.

The public record was used to make a systematic analysis of the floor debates in the House and Senate over a ten-year period (1958–1968) on all conference reports called up for consideration by the two bodies. This shed light on the politics of conference committees between Ways and Means and Finance and the response of each body to the work of its conferees, and also helped check generalizations about the policy-making role of the House and Senate that were made on the basis of certain "hard" measures of output.

Finally, transcripts of the executive sessions on three bills considered in 1965 — medicare, excise tax reduction, and tourist duty exemption — served as a way of checking the accuracy of some of the interview data (e.g., that membership participation is highly concentrated in a small number of members) and — perhaps most significant of all — alleviated some of the uneasiness that necessarily accompanies complete reliance on interview information.

ORGANIZATION. We begin this study by analyzing the members of Ways and Means: how they are recruited to the Committee, what attracts them to it, what their dominant political characteristics are, and what kind of Committee one would expect to find if all one knew about it were what kind of men become members. Chapter Two serves as preparation for an intensive look at the internal operations of Ways and Means. Chapter Three is focused on how the members see and do their job, the roles played by various members, what committee membership demands of them, and what they get from the Committee. Chapter Four is devoted to the Chairman since 1958, Wilbur D. Mills, and we attempt to describe and analyze the way Mills runs the Committee, the sources of his influence in the Committee, and the nature of the limitations on this influence.

Chapters Five, Six, and Seven deal with the connections between the Committee and the House, Senate, and executive branch, respectively. We include no separate chapter on interest groups or lobbyists because they are considered as essential for understanding the Committee's relations with the House, Senate, and executive. Hence a good deal of the discussion in all three chapters deals with group and individual demands in tax, trade, and social security legislation. In a final section we summarize the major findings.

CHAPTER TWO

Recruitment and Attractiveness

THE COMMITTEE IN THE CONTEXT OF THE HOUSE

American political parties wage vigorous if nonviolent battles over who should man the central posts of government; once this question is settled by elections, the elected partisans in theory carry the battle into government, where it centers around how best to handle the problems of foreign and domestic affairs. But if something akin to live ammunition is used in the electoral process it appears to some observers that only blanks are fired in the post-electoral battle over policy. As election day nears the parties come alive; once the hoopla of the campaign is over, the parties, great at electioneering mechanics, systematically fall apart as mechanisms for government. As a result, the indictment reads:

> We oscillate fecklessly between deadlock and a rush of action. Congress fails to act on crucial long-term problems; inevitably crisis comes, and the President uses his emergency powers. The Senate kills a bill to control harmful drugs; then a drug causes babies to be born without limbs; the Senate passes the same bill unanimously. Congress slashes vital foreign aid appropriations, then passes mammoth arms bills with little debate and without a single dissent.[1]

The key to the fecklessness of the American policy-making process, according to the critics, is Congress. In the House of Representatives, which is the major barrier to party government, the only vote that is certain to be completely partisan is the election of the Speaker. Having split neatly on this vote the parties tear themselves as well as each other up for the remainder of the session. On many important is-

[1] James MacGregor Burns, *The Deadlock of Democracy* (Englewood Cliffs, N.J.: Prentice-Hall, 1963), pp. 324–25.

sues, the critics claim, basic differences between the parties are scarcely noticeable, and on too many crucial issues intraparty differences determine the outcome.

Party regularity in Congress, frequently conspicuous by its irregularity, strikes many political scientists as incongruous, others as puzzling, and some as an intolerable institutional flaw. If, they argue, the parties are to offer some choice to the electorate over alternative sets of policies and give the electorate an opportunity to pass judgment on the actions of those elected, then the differences between the parties must be accentuated, exposed, and somehow enforced on those who call themselves Democrats or Republicans. The congressional parties, in this view, are the great befuddlers of American politics, confused and confusing, whose individual weakness makes Congress a negative force standing in the path of progress (and the president). In the hyperbole of one leading critic, "The party in Congress is like a Mexican army; everyone in it takes care of himself. When the enemy appears he may fight, run, or parley as he thinks best. This is the kind of army that can be overwhelmed by one man assisted by a boy beating a dishpan." [2]

Graphic evidence for the extent of party agreement in the House that tends to support the position of the party critics is presented in Figure 2.1. Even using a weak definition of a party vote, i.e., a majority of one party opposing a majority of the other, in only five of the past twelve years did the House vote along party lines on a majority of the roll calls. In six of these years a majority of the votes were bipartisan, and in one year the votes split 50–50. Notice, however, how close the partisan and bipartisan votes are: the mean percentage of bipartisan roll calls during this period is 52 per cent, party vote 48 per cent. Still, critics like Schattschneider can point out that the normal roll call in the House is not a partisan vote, not even by a weak test.

These data include all roll call votes in the House and they necessarily hide voting patterns on really controversial bills. On most controversial issues the key question facing those responsible for

[2] E. E. Schattschneider, *Party Government* (New York: Farrar & Rinehart, 1942), p. 196. For a perceptive analysis of some of the leading critics of American parties see Austin Ranney, *The Doctrine of Responsible Party Government* (Urbana, Ill.: University of Illinois Press, 1962). See also Stephen K. Bailey, *The Condition of Our National Political Parties* (New York: Fund for the Republic, 1959); E. Pendleton Herring, *The Politics of Democracy* (New York: W. W. Norton, 1965); and Herbert Agar, *The Price of Union* (Boston: Houghton Mifflin, 1950).

FIGURE 2.1
PARTY UNITY AND DISUNITY IN THE
HOUSE OF REPRESENTATIVES ON ROLL CALL VOTES, 1956–1967

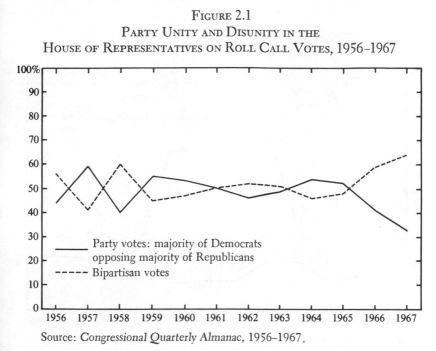

Source: *Congressional Quarterly Almanac, 1956–1967*.

passing legislation, i.e., the House Democratic leadership, is how to deal with intraparty splits. If a majority of Republicans vote with a majority of southern Democrats this coalition can defeat measures supported by the rest of the Democrats. In a sense, the real test of party voting in the House is the extent to which the "conservative coalition" appears and, when it appears, how often it defeats the majority of Democrats and minority of Republicans.

Figure 2.2 presents the data on the conservative coalition from 1957 to 1969. Reviewing all House roll call votes, we find that the conservative coalition voting pattern, defined as a vote on which a majority of voting southern Democrats agrees with a majority of voting Republicans contrary to a majority of the Democrats, appears on only a small minority of votes. From 1957 to 1969 the mean percentage of its appearance was 17, with a range of 11 per cent in 1964 to 25 per cent the following year. But Figure 2.2 also shows that when the coalition appears it wins: in seven of the eleven years it won a clear majority of the votes on which it appeared. In its worst year, 1965, the coalition also occurred most often (25 per cent of the votes); the coalition's weakness in 1965 and 1966 is attributable

FIGURE 2.2
PERCENTAGE OF HOUSE ROLL CALLS ON WHICH THE
CONSERVATIVE COALITION APPEARED AND WON, 1957–1968

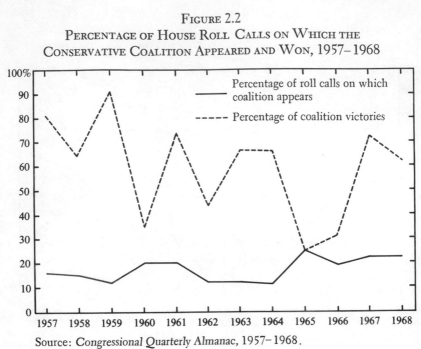

Source: *Congressional Quarterly Almanac, 1957–1968.*

to the large influx of northern Democrats as a result of the 1964 Johnson-Goldwater election. In 1967 the House returned to "normal" and the coalition won 73 per cent of the time it appeared.

The importance of the conservative coalition to the House is dramatized because it appears on many of the most important issues the House decides. In 1967, the coalition won on such issues as barring Adam Clayton Powell from the House, repealing the twenty-one day rule that had taken considerable delaying power away from the Rules Committee in the 89th Congress, cutting foreign aid, cutting rent supplements to the poor, cutting funds for Appalachia, and granting states more control over the allotment of funds for education. The coalition is by no means supreme in the House, just as its appearance is by no means the rule, but it does occur on a good many issues and, when it does, it usually prevails.[3]

3 Some House members — especially Republicans — vigorously deny that a conservative coalition exists in the sense of any organized or formal cooperation between Republicans and southern Democrats. It does appear that when Judge Smith was leading the southern Democrats and Charles Halleck was the Republican leader the contacts were more direct, but direct or indirect, the fact re-

Figures 2.1 and 2.2 give a rough overview of how the House of Representatives structures itself on the issues it decides by roll call votes. Both sets of data tend to confirm the view of those who criticize the parties in Congress for their loose structure. It is as true today as it was when Lowell compared British and American parties that party voting in Congress palls in comparison to other national legislatures.[4]

Still, the fragmentation of parties in Congress, though upsetting to party purists, is only part of the picture. The parties in Congress are clearly much more distinct than the tweedledum-tweedledee simile indicates. At a very general level the two parties in the House differ greatly on the proper federal role in American life. Figure 2.3 shows that the House Democrats, on selected votes, are much more likely to support a larger federal role or oppose cutting federal spending than are the Republicans. More detailed roll call studies of the House that take into account a number of factors which are associated with voting behavior (e.g., constituency, region, nature of issues) consistently show that the party affiliation of the members is very important, though not all-important, in explaining how the members vote.[5]

In the House, therefore, the two parties agree — and disagree — on a wide variety of issues. Absolute party voting is rare, and on the majority of roll calls one party does not line up consistently against the other. But on a sizable number of votes (never less than 36 per cent of roll calls since 1956), a majority of Democrats is in opposition to the Republicans. Without denigrating the importance of the conservative coalition, even when the Democrats lose a number of southerners to the Republicans it is still possible for the remaining

---

mains that the coalition exists. Whether it operates by conscious design or happenstance is irrelevant for our purposes, but my guess is that it is a lot more deliberate than some Republicans think.

[4] A. Lawrence Lowell, "The Influence of Party Upon Legislation in England and America," American Historical Association, *Annual Report*, 1901.

[5] Julius Turner, *Party and Constituency* (Baltimore: Johns Hopkins University Press, 1951), p. 23; Duncan MacRae, Jr., *Dimension of Congressional Voting* (Berkeley: University of California Press, 1958), *passim*. MacRae's study is part of the "University of California Publication in Sociology and Social Institutions," Vol. 1, no. 3. Turner's is part of "The Johns Hopkins University Studies in Historical and Political Science," ser. 69, no. 1. See also Lewis A. Froman, Jr., *Congressmen and Their Constituencies* (Chicago: Rand McNally & Co., 1963), chap. 7; David B. Truman, *The Congressional Party* (New York: John Wiley, 1959), pp. vi–vii; David R. Mayhew, *Party Loyalty Among Congressmen* (Cambridge, Mass.: Harvard University Press, 1966), *passim*.

FIGURE 2.3
HOUSE SUPPORT FOR A LARGER FEDERAL ROLE AND
OPPOSITION TO CUTTING FEDERAL SPENDING, 1957–1967

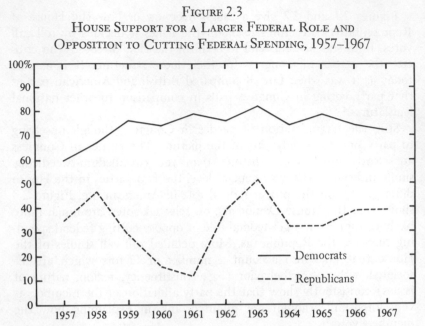

Source: *Congressional Quarterly Almanac*, 1957–1967. In 1960 *CQ* changed its measure from opposition to moves to cut federal spending to support for a larger federal role. 1957–1959 votes are opposition to economy moves.

Democrats to hold together and defeat the coalition (sometimes with the aid of a few Republicans, sometimes with the aid of some southerners who "take a walk"). And, as a recent study shows, the importance of party identification in the House far transcends the question of how often the party members ballot against one another.[6]

The same tendencies toward party cohesion, disintegration, and conservative coalition that characterize the House are also found in the Ways and Means Committee. On some issues the Committee breaks nicely along party lines; on some the Committee is not at all partisan; and on some, such as medicare, a bipartisan conservative coalition controls the outcome. Ways and Means is by no means a perfect microcosm of the House but it is subject to and reflective of the same forces that affect policy-making in the House generally. Because the Committee reflects the diversity of opinion in the House it would be too much to say that the way the Committee splits

[6] Randall B. Ripley, *Party Leaders in the House of Representatives* (Washington: Brookings Institution, 1967), chap. 6.

causes the same distribution of voting in the House, but there is certainly a relationship between the two. In most cases, it is not too much to say that as the Committee goes so goes the House. Thus the decision-making processes in the Committee and decision-making by the House are inextricably linked.

A second matter is the relationship between the norms governing the legislative process — the "style" of the process — and the substance or outputs of the process. How do the members of Ways and Means and Congress as a whole make decisions? Amicably or bitterly? Through accommodation and compromise or through unbridled majority rule? By a rap of the gavel or negotiation?

Questions about the style of decision-making in Congress are interesting because of both the history of the House and the connection between style and substance. In the nineteenth century House, partisan and personal fights were common. Punches were thrown, raucous debate was common, and when personal relationships broke down completely knives were drawn.[7] Unlike the "cocoon of good feeling"[8] that envelops contemporary members of the House (with occasional exceptions) the House in the nineteenth century was more congenial to Davy Crockett (a three-termer) than to a Philadelphia lawyer.

Historical interest aside, it is obvious that the way of doing things may profoundly affect what is done. A highly partisan committee may be so because it deals with highly partisan issues, but underlying and exaggerating the partisanship may be bitter animosities, grievances over the way the chairman runs the committee, and long feuds that affect the way the committee articulates its policy differences. Such a committee, if it loses the respect of other House members, may have difficulty keeping its bills intact on the floor. (An examination of the House Banking and Currency Committee might prove worthwhile in this regard.) And almost certainly such a committee will pay little heed to the policy suggestions of the minority.

The committee that operates with accommodation and consensus utmost in mind, that does its job with a minimum of disruptive conflicts, that is able to resolve the tensions that necessarily accompany the legislative process is more likely to enjoy the respect of the House. Its bills may have an easier time passing and, most important, the

---

[7] Nelson W. Polsby, "The Institutionalization of the U.S. House of Representatives," *American Political Science Review*, LXII (March, 1968), 166–68.

[8] Clem Miller, *Member of the House*, ed. John W. Baker (New York: Scribner's, 1962), p. 93.

substance of its bills will bear the mark of the minority. Ways and Means fits this style of decision-making, and this has enormous consequences for public policy.

RECRUITMENT: THE DEMOCRATS

If the House of Representatives has a claim to a unique position and role in American national government it stems from Article I, section 7, of the Constitution, which provides that all bills for raising revenue shall originate in the House. If the Committee on Ways and Means has a claim to a special place within the House it rests on the House's delegation of its power over the origination of revenue bills to the Committee. To understand the political behavior of the Ways and Means Committee it is necessary to appreciate how this peculiarly significant jurisdiction affects both the kinds of problems the Committee must resolve and the type of member who is attracted and assigned to Ways and Means.

The Committee's jurisdiction over revenue bills gives it a distinctive position among House committees and it also requires the Committee to handle some of the most important, controversial, and potentially partisan issues coming before Congress: tax bills, the reciprocal trade program, social security legislation, and the national debt. Because these issues are of prime importance to the Democratic and Republican parties and have historically generated intense party conflicts, it is not surprising to find partisanship built into the Ways and Means Committee through the recruitment process. Truly surprising is the degree to which partisanship is muted in the day-to-day operation of the Committee.

In 1967, at the death of John Nance Garner, Speaker John W. McCormack recalled how Garner, 35 years earlier, had helped him get elected to the Ways and Means Committee.[9] In his eulogy, McCormack touched upon some factors that were involved in his transfer from two minor committees to Ways and Means; the interesting thing about McCormack's experience is that today, with an almost entirely different membership in the House, the same factors operate for Democrats who aspire to Ways and Means.

1. *The role of the party leadership:* McCormack was recruited by Speaker Garner for service on Ways and Means, which reveals the intense interest of party leaders in who gets on the Committee and

---

[9] *Congressional Record,* November 7, 1967 (daily edition), p. H 14704.

who does not. When the second-term representative from Boston went "with trepidation" to ask Garner's help in moving to the Judiciary Committee, he was told that he was scheduled to go on Ways and Means. McCormack, surprised at this, replied: " 'Well, Mr. Garner, I do not mind running and being defeated if at the outset I have a chance of winning. But,' I said, 'I do not want to run just knowing I am going to be defeated, and if you will blow your nose at me I will go out and be a candidate.' "

"Well, he blew his nose. So I did."

2. *The role of state delegations:* Garner told McCormack: "You go and tell Billy Connery to send out a letter from the delegation for you." "The first delegation that met and unanimously endorsed me for election to the Ways and Means Committee was the Texas delegation. I knew that was due to John Garner — to Jack Garner, as we called him — and Sam Rayburn." Getting the support of the Massachusetts delegation was the first step after being tapped by the leadership; getting support from other state delegations was the second.

3. *Personal style of the candidate:* ". . . I did not know the Democratic leader knew I was a Member of the House for the first two years. Apparently they did. I was one of those who wanted to learn my rules of parliamentary law and, although not completely unheard, I conducted myself so that I was not aware the leadership knew I was actually a Member of the House during my first two years. I went in to see John Garner . . . and I went to see him with trepidation. . . ."

4. *Status and attractiveness of Ways and Means:* "Of course, that was beyond my fondest dreams or ambitions, to get on the Committee on Ways and Means, with actually only one full term of service." His lack of seniority and the place of Ways and Means in the committee hierarchy of the House made McCormack's election unlikely without unusual assistance from party leaders. For some reason, he was selected as a protege of the leadership who assigned him to one of the most influential committees in the House.

Implicit in McCormack's story is that he impressed the party leaders in his first term as someone with whom they could work on the issues considered by Ways and Means. He must have appeared to them as a good party man, a regular, a "comer" in the House who knew his place but had enough ambition to want to improve it. His deference to them along with his appreciation for an unexpected windfall made it unlikely that once assigned to Ways and Means he would become an uncooperative ingrate who, having zoomed ahead of his peers in the House, would arrest his career after such a promising start. If this estimate is speculation McCormack's subsequent behavior is not. Seven years later the second-termer left the Committee to become Majority Leader under the newly elected Speaker, Sam Rayburn.

It is not difficult to imagine why party leaders — today as in the 1930's — have an active interest in who goes on Ways and Means. Year in and year out the Committee handles legislation that is vital to the administration's foreign and domestic policy, and it is the party leader's job to get this legislation through the House. The Reciprocal Trade Act, which until 1962 was the heart of American foreign trade policy; social security legislation, the great welfare accomplishment of the New Deal; medical care for the aged, a cornerstone of the Democratic party's program since the Truman years; national debt bills, allowing the government to borrow money to offset unbalanced budgets; tax bills, the basic source of funds for running the government and vitally related to the productivity of the entire economy — all are Ways and Means bills, all must begin or end in the Committee, and all are issues on which the presence of party mavericks on Ways and Means could be disastrous.

The jurisdiction of Ways and Means, then, is enough to generate leadership concern about who is recruited to the Committee. But there is another reason too. When the House revolted against Speaker Cannon in 1910–1911 one of the powers he lost, which has been denied to his successors, was the power to appoint members to committees. The Democrats placed this power in the hands of the Democratic members of the Ways and Means Committee. (House Republicans established a separate committee on committees.) The Speaker, then, if he is to exert any influence over the vital committee assignment process, has to work through and with the Ways and Means Democrats. Committee assignments are vital to the leadership in two ways. First, to the degree that the leadership affects assignments it has an important resource for doing favors for individual members, for rewarding members for past favors, and for establishing bonds with members that may provide some leverage in future legislative situations. Second, committee assignments are vital to the policy for which the leadership is responsible. If the House Education and Labor Committee falls into the hands of a conservative coalition and pigeonholes important bills, the leadership can, if it is influential with the Ways and Means Democrats, stack the committee with members who are safe on such bills. If the House Rules Committee delays or kills important legislation the leadership can, with the help of the Ways and Means Democrats, thwart the coalition by filling vacancies with members acceptable to it. If the foreign aid program is endangered in the Foreign Affairs Committee the leadership can stack Foreign Affairs with pro-foreign aid Democrats, but only if the Ways and Means Democrats cooperate. That in the past decade or so the Education and Labor Committee was packed with liberals, the Rules Committee with administration Democrats, and Foreign Affairs with pro-foreign aid members is evidence of leadership concern with who goes on Ways and Means, leadership influence over the recruitment process, and its subsequent relations with the Committee. By affecting who goes on Ways and Means the leadership affects who goes on other committees and, through this indirect but remarkably effective means, what legislation is reported to the House.

Additional evidence for the salience of Ways and Means to the Democratic leaders and their active participation in filling vacancies on the Committee comes from both the leaders and the Committee members. The leaders were unanimous on their role in the recruitment process and thirteen of the eighteen Democrats interviewed mentioned the leadership as playing an important part in their successful candidacies. In at least six known cases, as with McCormack, the leadership took the initiative by asking the members to go on Ways and Means, and in the others the members made a call on the leadership first or second priority in their campaign for the Committee. One member, a freshman, learned one night that the Ways and Means member from his area was planning to retire, and lost no time seeking the seat. "Next morning at 9 o'clock I was in the Speaker's office telling him I wanted Ways and Means. He almost fell off his chair." He also told the Speaker (Rayburn at the time) to watch him, see how he did, and when the next vacancy occurred he would seek his support. Another member, explaining why he was attracted to Ways and Means, cited the Committee's importance and Rayburn's request that he go on it: "That's about it. I said 'Mr. Speaker, consider it done.' "

According to conventional wisdom on Capitol Hill, a third reason why the party leaders have been involved in Ways and Means elections — in addition to the general importance of the issues and the committee on committees role of Ways and Means — is that on three issues in particular, the trade program, the oil depletion allowance, and medicare, the leadership has had to make sure that the Democrats are "all right."

The conventional wisdom states that the party leaders would not let a Democrat on Ways and Means unless he was for the trade program, against cutting the oil depletion allowance, and for medicare. But if the conventional wisdom is correct, orthodoxy on these issues was enforced in indirect, informal ways. Sixteen Democratic members commented on the role of issues in their assignment to the Committee and eleven of them did not recall being asked directly about how they stood on anything. The general feeling of the members, however, is that on the trade issue their position was well known, and that, more generally, they had been in the House long enough so the leadership knew that they were "reliable" men. It appears that on the trade issue once the leadership let it be known that no protectionist-oriented Democrat could get on Ways and Means the rest was automatic: no protectionist need apply, and none did.

The views of three members on international trade were checked. One told Rayburn, "I'm probably the best man on this issue you'll ever have on that committee"; the second was told by the chairman of Ways and Means that although he couldn't go along with the administration on everything he could on trade and this was the important issue; and the third told the leadership that he had always followed the liberal trade philosophy of Cordell Hull. Although the recruitment process did not work perfectly on the trade issue (one Democrat from an import-sensitive state, Aime Forand from Rhode Island, did get on and deviate from his colleagues) it was very nearly perfect, as shown by the voting record of the Committee Democrats throughout the 1957–1967 period.

The evidence for direct leadership activity on the oil depletion allowance is even less clear than it is on trade. It is generally believed that Rayburn would not let anyone on Ways and Means who would vote to cut the 27½ per cent allowance given to the oil industry, a provision that has become the symbol of tax loopholes and the cause célèbre of liberal tax reformers,[10] but not one member who got on

10 The depletion allowance permits the owner of an oil well to deduct 27½ per cent of his gross income from the well for tax purposes, up to an amount not in excess of 50 per cent of his net income from the property. If the gross income from a property is $100,000 the deduction is $27,500. If, however, the net income was $40,000 he can take only $20,000. See one of the leading critics of tax loopholes, Philip M. Stern, *The Great Treasury Raid* (New York: Random House, 1963), p. 322.

In 1969, eight years after Rayburn's death and with a substantially different

the Committee under Rayburn could recall being asked if he supported the oil depletion allowance. But if Rayburn did not normally interview the members on the oil question he did allow the perpetuation of the widespread belief that no depletion reformers need apply, and this was sufficient. One of his closest associates said unequivocally: "Rayburn had two things. One was trade. He was 100 per cent for international trade. And the second was the depletion allowance for oil and gas. These were the two." And when Richard Bolling wanted a way to turn down Rayburn's request that he go on Ways and Means he found that all he had to do was point out that he would vote to reduce the depletion allowance.

The oil industry had much more influence than the support, tacit or explicit, of Rayburn. Republican appointments to Ways and Means had resulted in bipartisan opposition in the Committee to cutting depletion so that even if some Committee Democrats were inclined to cut the allowance the issue would never be raised in a serious way. Also, Democrats are elected to the Committee in the Democratic caucus, which means that to get the votes of members from oil states the candidate for Ways and Means may have to be either safe on the issue or not inclined to be a crusader on it. Thus one member who had a close race in getting on the Committee was asked about his views on depletion when he sought support in the Texas and Oklahoma delegations. He was able to reply that although he had no oil in his district he did have coal, he was jealous of the 27½ per cent given oil, and he hoped they would help him raise the coal allowance up to oil's level. He was also told that everyone who went on Ways and Means had made a commitment on oil; in the face of this, he answered, his vote didn't matter anyway.

The clearest case of packing Ways and Means to ensure a policy outcome is medicare. When medicare came to a vote in 1960 the Committee rejected it 17–8. All ten Republicans were joined in the coalition by seven of the fifteen Democrats. Six of the seven were southerners and one was from Kentucky. To pack the Committee the leadership had to replace anti-medicare votes by pro-medicare votes and ensure that if any pro-medicare Democrats left the Committee they were replaced by members equally committed to the program. As Table 2.1 shows, every pro-medicare Democrat who left the Committee after 1960 was replaced by a pro-medicare Democrat,

---

Committee membership, Ways and Means voted to reduce the depletion allowance to 20 per cent.

TABLE 2.1
DEMOCRATIC APPOINTMENTS TO WAYS AND MEANS, AND MEDICARE, 1961–1965

Anti-medicare vacancies

Member	Stand on medicare Pro	Stand on medicare Con	Replaced by
Harrison (Va.)	x		Jennings (Va.)
Ikard (Texas)		x	Thompson (Texas)
Frazier (Tenn.)	x		Bass (Tenn.)

Pro-medicare vacancies

Member	Replaced by	Stand on medicare Pro	Stand on medicare Con
Bass (Tenn.)	Fulton (Tenn.)	x	
O'Brien (Ill.)	Rostenkowski (Ill.)	x	
Forand (R.I.)	Burke (Mass.)	x	
Machrowicz (Mich.)	Griffiths (Mich.)	x	
Green (Pa.)	Rhodes (Pa.)	x	
Metcalf (Mont.)	Ullman (Ore.)	x	

Others: Two Democrats, Landrum (Ga.) and Vanik (Ohio), were appointed in 1965 when the number of Democrats on the Committee was increased from 15 to 17. Vanik supported medicare and Landrum had earlier indicated that he would vote to report it from Committee.

and two of the three departing anti-medicare Democrats were replaced by pro-medicare men. The one exception, Clark Thompson
(Texas), had doubts about medicare but was inclined to vote it out
of the Committee anyway. In the relatively brief period of five years
a 17–8 majority against medicare was transformed into a 13–12 pro
medicare majority even if Thompson did not vote right. Leadership
influence over who was elected to the Committee, the conversion of
Boggs who switched his 1960 position after he became Democratic
Whip in 1962, plus the leadership decision to increase the number of
Democrats on the Committee from fifteen to seventeen ensured a
positive Committee vote on medicare in 1965.[11]

This evidence, though persuasive, is only indirect support for
leadership intervention on behalf of medicare, but because at least
two members were asked by Speaker McCormack about medicare
and all but two of the replacements were well-known supporters of
medicare, it seems clear that the opinion of most that no anti-
medicare Democrat could win a Ways and Means seat after 1960 was
correct. Such a rule could not have operated without clear-cut leadership endorsement; without such a rule the conservative coalition in
Ways and Means might not have been broken on medicare.

Because of the size of the Committee's jurisdiction, its importance
to the party, and the role of the leadership in the recruitment process,
the Democrats elected to Ways and Means are generally "good" party
men. "To get on Ways and Means," one member said, "you have to
be pretty much in favor of the Administration, what the Administration wants."

To test this hypothesis and to present data on the general party
orientation of those who make it to Ways and Means, the party
unity scores of the members were compared with the overall score of
Democrats. Table 2.2 shows the results for twenty-four Democrats
elected to Ways and Means since 1951. Nineteen of the twenty-four
had higher party unity scores than the average Democratic member
of the House; only five fell below the Democratic average; four of
them were from the South. In addition, three of the four Democrats
first elected to Ways and Means in 1949 had very high party unity
scores although *Congressional Quarterly* (CQ) did not compute the
average for all Democrats. Boggs of Louisiana scored 87 per cent,

---

[11] Events inside the Committee led to a solid Democratic vote to report medicare in 1965.

Table 2.2

PARTY UNITY SCORES OF WAYS AND MEANS DEMOCRATS AND
ALL DEMOCRATS, 1951–1966 [a]

Member	State	Party unity score, two years preceding appointment (mean %)	Party unity score, all Democrats (mean %)
Eugene Keogh	N.Y.	90	80
Frank Karsten	Mo.	85	77
A. S. Herlong	Fla.	64	77
John Watts	Ky.	72	68
Al Ullman	Ore.	94	72
James Burke	Mass.	80	72
Clark Thompson	Texas	83	71
Martha Griffiths	Mich.	84	71
Pat Jennings	Va.	78	71
George Rhodes	Pa.	90	72
Dan Rostenkowski	Ill.	85	72
Phil Landrum	Ga.	62	71
Charles Vanik	Ohio	87	71
Richard Fulton	Tenn.	78	71
Walter Granger	Utah	89	80
Burr Harrison	Va.	56	80
Eugene McCarthy	Minn.	85	77
Frank Ikard	Texas	72	77
T. Machrowicz	Mich.	97	69
James Frazier	Tenn.	80	70
William Green	Pa.	59	68
Lee Metcalf	Mont.	90	68
Ross Bass	Tenn.	85	71
Jacob Gilbert	N.Y.	88	67

SOURCE: *Congressional Quarterly Almanac*, 1951–1966.

[a] Percentage of partisan roll calls (majority of one party opposing majority of other) on which a representative voted with a majority of his party.

Combs of Texas 95 per cent, and Carroll of Colorado 91 per cent. The fourth Democrat, Stephen Young of Ohio, went on Ways and Means in 1949 after having served in the House in an earlier period for which no scores are available. Thus, of the twenty-seven Democrats elected to the Committee over the past twenty years for whom scores are available, twenty-two clearly fit the designation of party regular as measured by the party unity index and five do not.

Party regularity for House Democrats is usually accompanied by a generally liberal stand on the scope of the federal role in American society. Members elected to Ways and Means, as Table 2.3 shows, are "liberals" on this question. Of the sixteen Democrats elected to the Committee since CQ began compiling the federal role index, only one (Frazier, Tenn.) did not support a larger federal role more

TABLE 2.3
SUPPORT FOR A LARGER FEDERAL ROLE, WAYS AND MEANS
DEMOCRATS AND ALL DEMOCRATS, 1957–1966 [a]

Member	State	Support for larger federal role, two years preceding appointment (mean %)[a]	Democratic support for larger federal role (mean %)
John Watts	Ky.	76	63
Al Ullman	Ore.	100	74
James Burke	Mass.	83	74
Clark Thompson	Texas	75[b]	74[b]
Martha Griffiths	Mich.	100[b]	74[b]
Pat Jennings	Va.	83	78
George Rhodes	Pa.	94[c]	78[c]
Dan Rostenkowski	Ill.	94[c]	78[c]
Phil Landrum	Ga.	80	74
Charles Vanik	Ohio	94	74
Richard Fulton	Tenn.	94	74
James Frazier	Tenn.	53[d]	60[d]
William Green	Pa.	71	63
Lee Metcalf	Mont.	92	63
Ross Bass	Tenn.	94	78
Jacob Gilbert	N.Y.	96	75

SOURCE: *Congressional Quarterly Almanac*, 1957–1966.
[a] During 1957–1959 CQ rated congressmen on their support for moves to limit federal spending or their opposition to such moves. For these years the opposition score is treated as equivalent to support for a larger federal role. Support for a larger federal role is the percentage of selected roll calls on which the representative voted to increase the size of the federal role.
[b] Elected to Ways and Means in 1962 but scores based on 1959–1960.
[c] Elected to Ways and Means in 1964 but scores based on 1961–1962.
[d] 1957 only.

than the average Democrat in the two years preceding election, and ten exceeded the average Democrat's liberalism by at least ten points.

On these data, we may base three initial generalizations about Democratic recruitment to Ways and Means: (1) party leaders take an active interest in who goes on the Committee and they have an important say in the recruitment process; (2) party regulars are elected to Ways and Means; and (3) the members selected over-represent their party's liberalism prior to appointment. As with many generalizations, however, the subtleties overlooked and the deviant cases may reveal more about the nature of the process than the generalizations.

Take the first generalization about the role of party leaders. It is easy to exaggerate their actual control of the assignment process and to miss some of the most important aspects of political recruitment, as does one student of Congress who states: "Democratic vacancies on Ways and Means are filled by election by the party caucus which ratifies the choice of the party leadership which is thus able to exercise influence over tax and other legislation reported by that committee." [12] It is not quite so simple. A number of factors intervene between party leaders and Ways and Means assignments. These factors limit the party leaders' influence but, perhaps more important, they permit the leaders to avoid settling contests for Ways and Means (contests which may result in a number of disaffected losers) as long as the process does not turn up members who deviate too far from the criteria the leaders think are essential for members of Ways and Means. Party leaders often find it in their interest to do little more than accept the results of other phases of the recruitment process.

One intervening variable is the same state "rule" that gives certain states an enforceable claim to representation on Ways and Means. Since 1947 the Democrats have filled vacancies on the Committee with men from the same state in 62 per cent of the cases (eighteen of twenty-nine cases).[13]

As McCormack said, his state delegation was less important in his campaign for Ways and Means than the backing of Garner and Rayburn, but recruitment sometimes takes place almost entirely within the state delegation with the party leaders playing a secondary role.

For example, when William Green of Pennsylvania died in 1963 the Pennsylvania delegation backed the candidacy of George Rhodes, the most senior Pennsylvania member who wanted to go on Ways and Means, against the claims of other states. The New Jersey delegation, in particular, desired the seat but decided not to press the matter to a vote in the party caucus. (Shortly thereafter the Ways and Means Democrats, acting as the Committee on Committees, awarded New Jersey the unusual distinction of having a second member on the Appropriations Committee.) Dan Rostenkowski of Illinois was elected to the Committee in 1964 after the death of Thomas J. O'Brien, the former sheriff of Cook County who for many years was the leader of the Chicago Democrats in the House. Rostenkowski

[12] George B. Galloway, "Leadership in the House of Representatives," *Western Political Quarterly*, XII (June, 1959), 433.

[13] It is not surprising that most of the states that failed to keep one of their Democratic members on the Committee are either small states or have small Democratic delegations: N.C., Ga., R.I., Colo., Mo., Ohio, Utah, Minn., Mont., Va., and in 1967 Texas as a result of a ratio change.

was elected to Ways and Means unanimously by the party caucus only after he deflected a mild challenge from another Illinois Democrat, Roman Pucinski, and received the support of Chicago Mayor Richard J. Daley who canvassed the other Chicago congressmen and found that Rostenkowski had most support. And in 1967, when members from both Texas and New York left the Committee but a change in the Committee's ratio provided only one seat for these areas, the leadership took a hands-off approach to the contest and endorsed neither candidate. The New York delegation unanimously endorsed a liberal, Jacob Gilbert, and Texas nominated one of its senior conservative members, Omar Burleson, a prominent figure in the informal organization of southern Democrats in the House, the "Boll Weevils." Conservatives in the House, plus some liberal Democrats who preferred Burleson, almost won, but Gilbert got the seat by a narrow 115–113 vote in the caucus.[14] In a contest between two large state delegations the leadership did not take sides because, as one of them said in an interview, "There are three states which because of the size of their delegations have men on: New York, California, and Texas. We usually just accept whoever they nominate." In other words, the leaders let the large delegations pick their representatives on Ways and Means.

The importance of state delegations in recruitment does not mean that the party leaders and partisan factors are totally inoperative. When Frank Ikard of Texas left Ways and Means in 1961 to become an executive of the American Petroleum Institute, it appeared that Walter Rogers, also of Texas, might try to get on the Committee. Rogers, for several reasons, was unacceptable to the leadership and Clark Thompson was persuaded to exert his seniority within the delegation to block him. Although Speaker Rayburn never took the matter up directly with Thompson it was clear to those involved that the leadership was behind the move.

Evidence of leadership activity can also be seen in the Rostenkowski case. Speaker McCormack made sure that Rostenkowski was safe on medicare by asking him about it, and the leadership indicated to the Illinois delegation that it should pick a candidate without too much delay in order to avoid a challenge to Illinois' claim to the seat, feeling that vacillation could spark a counterclaim from another delegation.

The same state "rule" does not make the leaders irrelevant; rather it

[14] Richard L. Lyons, "Liberal Narrowly Wins Ways and Means Post," *The Washington Post*, January 18, 1967, p. A1.

enables them to avoid intraparty battles and lets other processes make, or appear to make, important decisions. In this way, the leaders reap the benefit of circumspect support while the target of complaints from disappointed members becomes the impersonal same state rule.

Members may go on Ways and Means with varying degrees of leadership support. In the case of A. Sydney Herlong (Fla.), Speaker Rayburn acquiesced without a fight. Herlong, a shade too conservative for Rayburn's tastes, got on the Committee in 1955 after A. S. Camp of Georgia died the year before. Carl Vinson, the Georgia delegation leader, wanted a Georgian to replace Camp but confronted by Herlong's popularity among the Democrats neither he nor Rayburn prevailed. Herlong, running in the Democratic caucus where popularity can be important, had deliberately ingratiated himself with his Democratic colleagues by, among other things, bringing dozens of them to his Florida district (with the assistance of the local chamber of commerce).

And it is possible for a member with overt leadership support to be defeated in the party caucus, though this event is atypical. Even Rayburn, generally acknowledged as a very powerful Speaker, was beaten in a Ways and Means contest when Burr Harrison (Va.) was elected over the Speaker's choice, Winfield Denton (Ohio). The most recent case of the leadership's candidate being rejected by the caucus was in 1963, when W. Pat Jennings (Va.) ran against Phil Landrum (Ga.).[15]

In January 1963, the Democrats caucused to fill two vacancies on Ways and Means. A lively contest had developed for one of the seats between Landrum, backed by Speaker McCormack and the leadership, and Jennings, who was supported by many liberal Democrats. Jennings won.

Many factors were involved in this contest. Landrum's conservative record and coauthorship of the controversial Landrum-Griffin labor law repelled the liberals. It was feared that if elected to Ways and Means he might help delay the administration's medicare bill, which the Committee had refused to report out. Jennings, in addition to being from the same state as one of the departed members, was considered more liberal than Landrum, although the latter reportedly

[15] The most detailed story of the Landrum-Jennings contest is by one of the key liberal participants, Richard W. Bolling, *Defeating the Leadership's Nominee in the House Democratic Caucus* (Indianapolis: Bobbs-Merrill Co., 1965). Publication #91 of the Inter-University Case Program. See also *Congressional Quarterly Weekly Report*, January 18, 1963, p. 46.

had given assurances that he would not vote to keep the medicare bill in Committee (raising the question of whether the liberals truly thought Landrum would help block medicare or merely found medicare a good issue to use against him).

Another issue in the conflict between the liberal Democrats opposing Landrum and the party leadership was the question of permanently enlarging the House Rules Committee. Two years earlier Rayburn had won a close vote temporarily increasing the size of the Rules Committee after Rules had blocked a number of bills desired by the liberals. When the time came to enlarge the Rules Committee permanently, Rayburn was dead and Speaker McCormack apparently had made a deal with the Georgia delegation led by Carl Vinson; in return for Georgia's votes on packing Rules (only two Georgians had voted with Rayburn in 1961), McCormack would support Landrum for Ways and Means. Whether or not there was an explicit agreement between Vinson and McCormack it sounded, as Richard Bolling has written, "like an accommodation Speaker McCormack might make." [16] In any event McCormack, Vinson, and Landrum lost. A footnote to this story is that in 1965 Landrum was elected to the Committee unanimously after demonstrating more liberal inclinations by guiding the administration's antipoverty bill through the House. His support for a larger federal role also indicated increasing liberalism: 33 per cent in the 86th Congress, 61 per cent in the 87th Congress, and 80 per cent in the 88th Congress before he went on Ways and Means. [17]

The general tendency of Committee Democrats to be liberal party regulars before election to the Committee ignores the fact that the makings of a conservative coalition are built into the recruitment process for Democrats. It is true that the great majority of Democrats on Ways and Means are both liberal and regular; but it is just as true that, over the years, a few have been conservatives and, on some crucial votes, have joined the ten Republicans in a 13–12 conservative coalition. That this happens only to a limited degree on the Committee will be explained shortly; that it can happen at all on such crucial party issues as medicare is explained by the politics of recruitment.

On Ways and Means, unlike some other congressional committees, the Democrats have made a deliberate attempt to represent all the

[16] Bolling, *op. cit.*, p. 5.
[17] *Congressional Quarterly Weekly Report*, January 18, 1963, p. 46; and *Congressional Quarterly Almanac*, 1959–1964.

major geographical regions of the country, a practice which ensures
that the conflicts inherent in the party are represented in the Committee. The reasons for this policy are (1) Ways and Means deals with
national issues; and (2) the Committee Democrats act as the Committee on Committees, with each member responsible for one zone,
so every geographical section with Democrats in the House must
have a representative on Ways and Means. Of course, areas with
many Democrats in the House feel entitled to representation on the
Committee and have the votes to be represented.

The South, which is entitled to representation on the Committee
both because Ways and Means is a national committee and because
southern Democrats must have spokesmen on the Committee on
Committees, sometimes sends to Ways and Means men who are
more likely to dissent on questions of national policy than to agree
with their northern brethren. If — and when — they dissent, as on
medicare, they can, even though outnumbered by regular Democrats,
join with the Committee Republicans in a majority coalition.[18]

Since 1947 there have never been less than four southern Democrats on Ways and Means ("South" defined as the eleven states of
the Confederacy). For sixteen of the twenty years from 1947 to 1967
there were, of fifteen Democrats on the Committee, six or seven from
the South. If the South's total man-years on Ways and Means is compared with other regions (Figure 2.4), the Democratic side of the
Committee looks most southern indeed.[19]

Recruitment to the Committee on Ways and Means, therefore,
clearly makes a conservative coalition inside the Committee possible.
But because differences between the policy inclinations of individual

[18] Interestingly, McCormack might have inadvertently strengthened the conservative coalition thirty years ago. Before he went on the Committee in 1933
there were no clear-cut zones for Committee on Committees business. Since he
had no one to speak for him on committee assignments when he came to Congress, he thought it would be a good idea if the Ways and Means Committee
set up zones with each member handling committee requests for all the Democrats in his zone. He was instrumental in persuading the Committee to do this
and, it appears, in strengthening the South's claim to representation on Ways
and Means. Thus "rationalization" of the Committee on Committees was probably dysfunctional for party unity on issues.

[19] Figure 4 is derived by adding up the total number of years served on the
Committee by each man in each region. Regions are as follows: *South:* Va.,
N.C., S.C., Ga., Fla., Ala., Miss., La., Tenn., Ark., Texas; *East:* Me., N.H., Vt.,
Conn., Mass., R.I., N.Y., Pa., N.J., Del.; *Border:* Ky., Md., Mo., Ok., W. Va.;
Midwest: Ill., Ind., Iowa, Kan., Mich., Minn., Neb., N.D., S.D., Ohio, Wisc.;
Far West: Mont., Wyo., Colo., N.M., Ariz., Utah, Id., Wash., Ore., Calif.,
Nev., Alaska, Hawaii.

FIGURE 2.4
MAN-YEARS SERVICE OF WAYS AND MEANS DEMOCRATS, BY REGION, 1947–1966

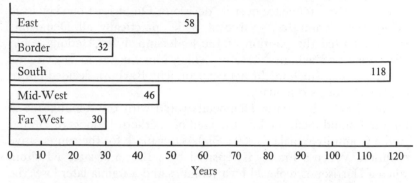

southerners on the Committee are great, the appearance of the coalition and its voting strength are much less impressive than might be inferred from the fact that five to seven southerners serve on the Committee at any time. The coalition on Ways and Means is not powerless, but if all the southerners were hard-rock conservatives it would be unbeatable. A world of difference distinguishes Hale Boggs of Louisiana, who supported Democratic administrations on most issues, from A. Sydney Herlong of Florida, a conservative who sometimes voted with the Committee Republicans. Most important, the southerners who have gone on the Committee in the past few years have usually been moderates or liberals, at least on the key issue considered by the Committee. Liberal House Democrats, under the leadership of the Democratic Study Group (DSG), an informal organization of over one hundred liberal Democrats, blocked the election of Phil Landrum in 1963 in favor of Pat Jennings largely because Jennings was considered more liberal than Landrum. In 1967 the liberal wing of the party succeeded in preventing a southerner from getting on the Committee when Gilbert was elected over Burleson. And two years earlier a conservative Democrat from Tennessee, James B. Frazier, was replaced by another Tennessee Democrat, Richard Fulton, who had the support of the DSG, had campaigned for Congress in favor of medicare, and had even voted for civil rights bills.

Another countervailing force to the conservative coalition is that, except for Herlong and .Harrison, most southern Democrats elected to Ways and Means since the 1940's have been protégés of the House leadership. Wilbur Mills, Hale Boggs, Frank Ikard of Texas —

and probably others — were all close to Rayburn, as was Clark Thompson who went on the Committee shortly after Rayburn's death. These men, though all southerners, gave Rayburn access to the Committee and influence over its decisions. On at least one key issue before the Committee, reciprocal trade, practically all Democrats have supported the position of the leadership. Even Herlong could allay some of Rayburn's fears by telling him he was in favor of reciprocal trade, which might help explain why Rayburn decided not to oppose Herlong's candidacy.

Since 1960, when seven Democrats voted with the Republicans to kill the Forand medicare bill, the kind of southern Democrats elected to the Committee makes 1960 a high-water mark for the conservative coalition. When a Frazier is replaced by a Bass and later a Fulton, when a Harrison is replaced by a Jennings and Virginia later loses the seat completely to a Vanik of Ohio, and when a Gilbert defeats a Burleson, a series of individual changes in the Committee add up to a body very different from the one that killed medicare by more than 2–1 in 1960, and opposed it 3–2 in 1962. The new committee in 1965 reported a medicare bill far more generous than the original administration proposal by a vote of 17–8, an exact reversal of 1960. Ways and Means, for reasons peculiar to itself, is not likely to become as liberal and as partisan as the House Education and Labor Committee, but it would be a gross error to downgrade the secular changes in the Committee wrought by changes in the recruitment process.

RECRUITMENT: THE REPUBLICANS

Compared to the Democratic members of Ways and Means the Republicans are remarkably homogeneous: all, with one possible exception, are from the conservative wing of the party. Moreover, at no time in recent memory has this not been true. The party of Robert Taft, not John Lindsay, is represented on the minority side of Ways and Means.

Republican members of the Ways and Means Committee, when asked what factors were important in their assignment to the Committee, replied in a way that would please the most ardent supporters of programmatic parties for the United States. One Republican member declared that:

> It's hard to generalize. There are a lot of factors — region, seniority. Then of course there are certain key issues that you want to be sure a member is pretty much a party-line type of

member. You want to be sure that he will go along with the party on certain things, you want to be sure he's safe on some things. On Ways and Means we get people who all fall within pretty much the same general philosophical area.

"Of course," said another Republican, "we want a man who can take the heat if the going gets rough. You don't want a member who will fold. You want a guy who will follow the party line — not on every little detail but on most important things." A colleague agreed: "You don't want a lightweight on the Committee. You want a man who will go along with the party." Accentuating the indeterminacy of the future, a Republican Committee member declared: "What if something comes up a year from now that they [party leaders] aren't thinking about now? What they want is a solid party man, a team player, a real Republican. I was with the party on everything but things that affected my district." Another linked his appointment to his party regularity:

I know several members who perhaps have more ability than I who would *never* get on Ways and Means simply because somewhere along the line they have become disliked by some people. One word describes it better than all the others: *co-operation*. I have been cooperative. That doesn't mean I've always voted with the leadership but I've never opposed them out of spite. Cooperation.

A Republican candidate for Ways and Means need not always vote with the majority of his party but he must not be seen as an unreliable maverick who has little or nothing in common with the majority of his party colleagues. Asked if good party men get on Ways and Means, one member said: "This depends on what a party man means. It's hard to say. To the extent that we don't want renegades we want party men. We do have to present a front and a renegade would not be — he's someone who makes a career of being a deviant."

Associated with party regularity for House Republicans is a generally conservative position on questions of public policy. One Republican member explained another's appointment to the Committee by referring to his good conservative voting record ("Broyhill has a good conservative ACA [Americans for Constitutional Action] rating"), and a second member declared, "We on the Republican side are quite conservative so we'd want someone who was conservative. I won't mention any names but there are four or five House Republi-

can liberals who probably wouldn't want to get on Ways and Means
— Sy Halpern, for example." One of the leading Republicans on the
Committee summed up:

> Now when you get down to the individual, I think we want
> conservative people. And appropriately so. Taxes are not
> something that lends to experimentation. You want to go
> slow, you could knock the whole economy into a cocked hat
> with experimentation. So we put conservatives on and as a
> matter of fact this used to be true for the Democrats too. I
> think a Republican would have to be on the moderate side of
> conservatism and not on the liberal side of conservatism.

One Republican member of Ways and Means, who also sits on
the Republican Committee on Committees, was quite explicit about
what both he and his Committee on Committees colleagues look for
when considering appointments to Ways and Means. "We look to
see that he hasn't supported all the giveaways." In this man's judgment:

> You don't want, and the executive committee would never
> accept, some members. Ogden Reid would never get on. Fino
> wouldn't have but he has done a complete 180 degrees so he
> could now. You have to have someone who is able to stand
> up to socialism, resist the pressure toward welfarism.

What makes this man's opinion unusually significant is that he was
probably correct when he claimed that his standards for Ways and
Means assignments were shared by a majority of the executive committee of the Committee on Committees. The executive committee,
in effect a subcommittee of the Committee on Committees, is composed of and dominated by senior Republicans from states with large
Republican delegations in the House [20] — conservative party regulars
almost to the man.

The voting records of the Committee Republicans before they get
on Ways and Means indicate their image of themselves and their
fellow Committee members is correct. Conservative Republicans, as
measured by support for a larger federal role, are assigned to Ways
and Means. Table 2.4 shows that of the eleven Republicans for whom
scores are available, only one supported a larger federal role more
than the average House Republican. If anything, Republicans who
go on Ways and Means are more conservative than the average Re-

---

[20] Nicholas A. Masters, "Committee Assignments in the House of Representatives," *American Political Science Review*, LV (June, 1961), 349–50.

TABLE 2.4
SUPPORT FOR A LARGER FEDERAL ROLE, WAYS AND MEANS
REPUBLICANS AND ALL REPUBLICANS, 1957–1966

Member	State	Support for larger federal role, two years preceding appointment (mean %) [a]	Republican support for larger federal role (mean %)
Jackson Betts	Ohio	25	39
Herman Schneebeli	Pa.	0 [b]	17 [b]
Harold Collier	Ill.	22	24
Joel Broyhill	Va.	22 [c]	24 [c]
James Battin	Mont.	35	40
Bruce Alger	Texas	5	39
Albert Bosch	N.Y.	29	39
John LaFore	Pa.	39	38
Walter Mumma	Pa.	26	38
Stephen Derounian	N.Y.	0	17
Barber Conable	N.Y.	10	36

SOURCE: *Congressional Quarterly Almanac*, 1957–1966.
[a] During 1957–1959 CQ rated congressmen on their support for moves to limit federal spending or their opposition to such moves. For these years the opposition score is treated as equivalent to support for a larger federal role.
[b] 1960 only.
[c] Appointed in 1964 but score based on 1961–1962.

publican member of the House. Table 2.5 confirms the related hypothesis that "good" party men, as measured by CQ's party unity index, are assigned to Ways and Means. In only two cases since 1951 Republicans going on the Committee have not scored higher on party unity than the average for all House Republicans. In addition, party unity scores are available for four Republicans appointed since 1947, although no House average was computed, and of these three were very high (91 per cent, 96 per cent, 88 per cent) whereas one was relatively low (71 per cent). Thus of the twenty-four Republicans appointed to the Committee over the past twenty years, fifteen had high party unity scores, two registered lower than the average Republican, one averaged 71 per cent, and six had no CQ score (three were freshmen members of the House when appointed to the Committee; one man had a year's service in the House).

Thus, the formal Republican party leaders in the House, like their Democratic counterparts, exert a considerable amount of influence over which members fill seats on Ways and Means. The late Republican leader Joseph W. Martin states in his autobiography, "In the four years that I served as Speaker no Republican went on an im-

TABLE 2.5
PARTY UNITY SCORES OF WAYS AND MEANS
REPUBLICANS AND ALL REPUBLICANS, 1951–1966

Member	State	Party unity score, two years preceding appointment (mean %)	Party unity score, all Republicans (mean %)
Tom Curtis	Mo.	84	82
Jackson Betts	Ohio	94	66
Herman Schneebeli	Pa.	80[a]	70[a]
Harold Collier	Ill.	85	72
Joel Broyhill	Va.	78	72
James Battin	Mont.	73	72
Antoni Sadlak	Conn.	75	82
Howard Baker	Tenn.	79	82
Bruce Alger	Texas	78	66
Albert Bosch	N.Y.	84	66
John LaFore	Pa.	89	71
Walter Mumma	Pa.	94	71
Stephen Derounian	N.Y.	95	73
Barber Conable	N.Y.	70	69

SOURCE: *Congressional Quarterly Almanac*, 1951–1966.
[a] 1960 only.

portant committee without my approval." [21] And the Republican leader sits as nonvoting chairman of the Committee on Committees.

But — again like their Democratic counterparts — their actual involvement and influence vary with different situations, they too sometimes find it advisable to let others make the selection, and it is possible for them to get beaten. At times, state delegations play a key part in Republican assignments to Ways and Means. When Thomas A. Jenkins of Ohio left the Committee in 1959 the Ohio delegation selected Jackson Betts for Ways and Means and Betts, somewhat against his will, agreed to go on the Committee. A similar process took place when the Pennsylvania seat on Ways and Means was vacated by the death of Walter Mumma in 1961. The delegation met, selected its man, and appointed him to the Committee against the wishes of some New England Republicans who wanted one of their men to get the position. In both cases the key decisions were made in the state delegations.

Both cases, however, involved states that have large Republican

[21] Joseph W. Martin (as told to Robert J. Donovan), *My First Fifty Years in Politics* (New York: McGraw-Hill, 1960), p. 181.

delegations in the House with considerable voting power in the executive committee of the Committee on Committees. No ironclad rule guarantees a state that it will always have a member on Ways and Means. In fact, the same state rule is more of a rule for Democrats in the House than it is for Republicans. Democrats followed the same state rule in 62 per cent of the cases since 1947, whereas the Republicans have followed it in only 44 per cent of the appointments (eleven of twenty-five cases). The pattern of appointments for both parties is similar, however, in that Ways and Means seats tend to switch among small states or large states with few party members, and are retained by the powerful delegations.[22]

In some cases the operation of the same state rule may bring to Ways and Means members who are acceptable to but not preferred by the Republican leaders. Within the delegation, prize appointments such as Ways and Means are determined by seniority. Normally the most senior members do not want to leave the committee on which they have built up seniority, but if they are willing to shift they can preempt junior members. When Noah Mason of Illinois left the Committee in 1963 he was succeeded by Harold Collier, also of Illinois. Collier rested his claim to Ways and Means on the seniority he had accumulated and, because he was acceptable on ideological grounds and to the delegation, the leadership concurred in his appointment. It is clear, however, that the party leaders would have preferred Collier to stay on the Interstate and Foreign Commerce Committee where he had risen to the fifth position, and let Collier's Illinois colleague, John Anderson, have the Ways and Means seat. In another recent case, Joel Broyhill of Virginia left his ranking position on the District of Columbia Committee as well as a senior position on the Post Office and Civil Service Committee to go on Ways and Means. Again seniority was the key factor and the leadership bowed to it, after ascertaining that Broyhill was "right" on medicare. (An AMA lobbyist had suggested to Broyhill that he try for Ways and Means in the first place.)

Like the leaders of the House Democratic party, the actions of the Republican leaders are limited despite Joe Martin's observation that he exercised a great deal of control over committee assignments. And, in at least one case, the Republican leadership has shared with the

[22] Republican state delegations that won more contests than they lost are: N.Y., Ohio, Calif., Pa., Ill., and the deviant case of Texas. Republicans put two Texans on the Committee during this period in part as a gesture to the South. Losing Republican state delegations are: Minn., N.J., Neb., Iowa, Ind., Wash., W.Va., Conn., Tenn., Mo., Mont.

Democratic leadership the embarrassment of having their candidate
for Ways and Means flatly rejected in favor of another man. In 1965
Gerald R. Ford, fresh from his victorious campaign against the in-
cumbent Republican leader, Charles Halleck, went down to defeat
in his effort to get an easterner assigned to the Committee.[23] James
F. Battin (Mont.) defeated Charles Goodell (N.Y.), a leader of the
Republican bloc that helped Ford topple Halleck.

Battin's winning coalition included the votes of three large delegations: California, Illinois, and Pennsylvania. He was close to James
Utt (a member of Ways and Means who doubled as the California
representative on the Committee on Committees) who wanted another westerner on Ways and Means and who was attuned to the
voices of some business interests that did not want Goodell to succeed. The votes of Illinois were directed by Leslie Arends who, with
a seconding speech from Battin, had just been reelected as the party's
whip to the chagrin of those Republicans (Goodell and others) who
had defeated Halleck.[24] Luckily, Battin was on the Foreign Affairs
Committee and if he left it for Ways and Means then James Fulton
of Pennsylvania, who wanted to return to Foreign Affairs after having been on it previously, could fill the vacancy. In a classic example
of implicit bargaining in the House, without a word between them,
Fulton supported Battin for Ways and Means. Fulton then returned,
happily, to Foreign Affairs and Goodell remained, unhappily, on the
Education and Labor Committee.

Both Democratic and Republican party leaders, then, are influential in the assignment process for Ways and Means, but they operate
in a context of factors that affect Ways and Means recruitment. Normally the entire process works so that the majority views within each
party are represented in the Committee. To the extent that these
views are in conflict it is to be expected that the Committee will
divide along similar, if not identical, lines.

EFFECT OF RECRUITMENT ON THE COMMITTEE

CONFLICT. The kinds of men who are recruited to Ways and
Means and the processes through which they are recruited indicate

[23] Richard L. Lyons, "House GOP Hands Ford Rebuff on Committee Jobs,"
The Washington Post, January 20, 1965, p. A8.
[24] On the Ford-Halleck fight and Arends' victory see Robert L. Peabody, *The
Ford-Halleck Minority Leadership Contest, 1965* (New York: McGraw-Hill,
1966). Eagleton Institute Case #40.

that members of the Committee are expected by their respective parties to *disagree* on important issues of public policy. They are recruited to Ways and Means in large part because they identify with their party and may be expected to continue identifying with it when Ways and Means takes up major bills that each party ranks high on its list of priorities. The importance of party and ideological factors in Ways and Means assignments should not be underestimated: party conflict on the Committee is not something to be avoided but, on the contrary, is positively fostered by the recruitment process. If the Ways and Means Democrats and the Republicans ever start reaching a consensus on the major policy issues considered by the Committee they will, in the absence of a corresponding shift in the parties as a whole, be failing to perform the functions for which they were assigned to the Committee.

Republicans appoint conservative party regulars to Ways and Means; liberal party regulars are elected to the Democratic side; after medicare became an issue, no Democrat who would not vote to report it stood much chance of going on Ways and Means; for the Republicans, the contrary was true; for much of the post-1933 period the Democrats put reciprocal trade liberals on the Committee; the Republican contingent was the heart of protectionism in Congress; [25] and in economic orientation the Republicans have a bias against government intervention, the Democrats a bias for it.

RESTRAINED CONFLICT. But the recruitment process is not completely unidirectional in its effect on Ways and Means; it is, rather, ambivalent. The Ways and Means Committee does not normally perform its functions, partisan though they may be, in a Hobbesian atmosphere; part of the reason it manages partisan conflict without too much internal strife lies in the ambivalence of the recruitment process.

Four factors affecting the internal relations of the members are: (1) the legislative style of the men who serve on Ways and Means; (2) the significance of prior service in the House before a member goes to the Committee; (3) the probable consequences for the Committee of having members who are from safe seats and normally spend many years on the Committee; and (4) the role of the chairman and ranking Republican in recruiting Ways and Means members.

[25] Raymond A. Bauer, Ithiel de Sola Pool, and Lewis A. Dexter, *American Business and Public Policy* (New York: Atherton Press, 1963), chap. 2.

1. In recounting his election to Ways and Means, Speaker Mc-
Cormack remarked that during his first two years in the House he
was not completely invisible, just almost so. He said little, studied
much, and was somewhat diffident in his relations with his seniors.
His style, in other words, conformed to general House norms for
freshmen; the party leaders were aware of his existence and approved
of the way he conducted himself.

McCormack's style as a freshman contains the essential ingredients
of a successful House career. The public image of some House members and their image among their peers differ greatly; master politicians and masters of personal relations occupy positions in the
House but so do masters of the political and personal gaffe. When
the latter get up to speak, the more tactful of the former divert their
attention or have business elsewhere; the less tactful conduct a barely
audible but intensive critique of their unfortunate colleagues. Anyone within earshot shares the confidence of the House kibitzer; at
times the undercurrent of animosity must reach the target's ears,
though it may be hard to tell from his reaction.

If the target of the gratuitous commentary is a rather engaging
person but just a little foolish the House kibitzer is caustic but good-
natured in his remarks; if the target is offensive the kibitzer and his
audience are severe. That this happens in a group of four hundred
and thirty-five is not surprising but it does reveal that in the House,
as in organizations generally, there are certain accepted ways of
doing things that, if violated, cost the transgressor prestige and influence with his peers.

The normative structure of the House makes it extremely unlikely
that members who violate basic norms will advance to a top committee such as Ways and Means. Protocol in the House is not elaborate,
but it is helpful to have a tolerant attitude toward those with whom
one disagrees, to respect and defend the right of others to hold views
contrary to one's own, and to show empathy toward other members
and their problems. From these general categories stem such norms
as avoiding personal references in debate, refraining from gratuitous
revelations and comments that might be embarrassing to others, and
a proclivity for bargaining and accommodation, which permit the
legislative process to run smoothly. Conflicts of opinion and clashes
of interest are everyday affairs, but no one respects the man with no
mind of his own — the "hack." The norms require a certain style in
battle — strong but not strident, serious but not destructive.

Within such an organization the ideologue who cannot contain his fervor, or the man who is so fired with his vision of the truth that he brooks no dissent, are unlikely to do very well. Congressmen, of course, respect men who can answer questions but they resent the answer man who cannot wait to get the microphone, rarely misses an opportunity to speak, and regularly lectures his colleagues on what is right and wrong for the nation. Such an approach is a sure way to snatch defeat from the jaws of victory.

Ways and Means members are, in general, pragmatic in their outlook on politics, patient in their pursuit of objectives, unbending on few things, and inclined to compromise on all but the most basic issues. They perceive themselves as reasonable, moderate men. Some of them link these characteristics to their success in getting on the Committee, and the obeisance paid to these qualities supports the mild conflict found in the Committee.

Not every member commented on this aspect of the Committee, but enough did to construct at least a facsimile of the self-image of the Committee members. Three members, two Democrats and one Republican, observed that the characteristics of their opponents for Ways and Means helped them get on the Committee. One man's opponent was "somewhat disliked," inclined to go off "half-cocked" occasionally, overly fond of publicity, and if nominated by the state delegation would be opposed by some Democrats simply because they disliked him, thus endangering the state's hold on the seat. Another man recalled that he was tapped for Ways and Means by Speaker Rayburn because the man from his state who wanted Ways and Means was unacceptable to the Committee chairman and others. His opponent, whom he liked, was nevertheless "compulsive," a man who could not "contain" himself and so would not be right for Ways and Means. This man compared his rival for Ways and Means to Phil Burton (D., Calif.), a fairly well-known liberal then serving in the House. In his judgment, Burton had the same difficulty containing himself as his rival had, and would never get on Ways and Means. The Republican had two contestants in his delegation for Ways and Means but he received the delegation's support because compared to them he was "uncontroversial." One of them, he feels, was not well liked and the other was a member of the Tuesday-to-Thursday club who worked harder at his law practice than at being a congressman.

Rayburn, according to one Democratic member, preferred quiet, reasonable men for Ways and Means, men who were not crusaders on particular issues. He explained that on oil depletion Rayburn knew "I wouldn't be a radical . . . that I would be in favor of some study and moderate reform of the depletion allowance. What Rayburn was interested in," he declared, "was your temperament. He knew I'd be reasonable." In this view everyone on Ways and Means is a moderate because "they screen out those members who would play for publicity and make a lot of noise."

One man, who feels Rayburn kept him off Ways and Means because one of his first speeches in the House was an attack on tax loopholes, including the oil depletion allowance, admitted that by the time he got on Ways and Means he had "toned down" his public position on oil. A Republican who received support for his appointment to Ways and Means from an influential member from an oil state who forgot to check the candidate's views on oil depletion, was later asked by the man if he had publicly gone on record against the depletion allowance. As long as he had not, and as long as he would be willing to take a "reasonable" approach to the question, the oil-state Republican could support him. The backer with oil in his district and votes to cast in the Committee on Committees said that no crusader — "like Phil Burton" — could get on Ways and Means and that the man he supported, even though a commitment was neither asked nor given on the oil question, was one of the most "solid" Republicans in the House.

The appointment of Bruce Alger (Texas) to the Committee in 1959 is the deviant case that proves the rule. Once on the Committee, Alger's style, if not his ideology, was so out of line with Committee norms that a senior Republican tried — mostly in vain — to get him to calm down. The danger of putting someone like Alger on Ways and Means was manifest in 1964 when a Republican effort to expand social security benefits lost by one vote — Alger's. By liberalizing accepted social security benefits the possibility of financing medicare out of the social security tax would have been reduced, if not eliminated. But Alger, who could not bring himself to vote for any increase in social security, voted with the pro-medicare majority and tipped the balance against the Republican motion. As a friend of Alger's said, in a perfect exposition of the ethos of Ways and Means: "He would have been better on Education and Labor where the cleavage was sharper and the issues were clearer, more black and white." After Alger was defeated for reelection in 1964 one of the leading Republicans on the Committee was asked if Alger would get back on Ways and Means should he return to Congress. The Republican hastily pointed out that one could claim reappointment only if bumped from the Committee due to a ratio change, not if one failed to be reelected and later returned to the House.

Thus, extremely controversial men who fight what their colleagues believe are lost causes, or who are unshakably committed to objectives alien to the interests of other members, who demonstrate by the way they pursue their goals that they cannot be relied on to engage in reasonable compromise, or who become widely disliked for whatever reasons have little chance of becoming members of Ways and Means. This does not mean that every member of the Committee is a paragon in the House, hardworking and highly respected, but it does mean that men who are consumed by, let us say, the need for tax reform and fail to push their ideas in accepted ways, do not, except in rare cases, get on the Committee. Dedicated liberals and dedicated conservatives do get on the Committee but they tend to see the legislative process as a long-term affair in which a good working relationship with other members is not only a more pleasant way to do business but is essential to doing business at all. As one liberal put it, "I'm for tax reform but politics is the art of the possible. If you go after oil depletion head-on you'll get no place. You have to be subtle, indirect, devious." His approach to legislative affairs, not Alger's, is typical of Ways and Means.

2. Another factor that both heightens partisanship but also helps ensure that only certain kinds of members are appointed to the Committee is tenure in the House. For the twenty-eight Democrats first elected to the Committee since 1947 the average number of years spent in the House prior to election was 7.4. No freshman Democrat made it to the Committee and only three members were elected early in their second term: James A. Burke (Mass.), Richard Fulton (Tenn.), and John Carroll (Colo.). The average Republican served only 4.7 years in the House before appointment and, contrary to the Democratic practice, the Republicans placed four freshmen on the Committee: Herman Schneebeli (Pa.), George Bush (Tex.), James Utt (Calif.), and Victor Knox (Mich.), the latter two in the 83rd Congress when the Republican victory opened up five seats on Ways and Means.[26] Thus the Republican party requires a shorter apprentice period than the Democrats and is more apt to put a freshman on the Committee, but for both parties a number of years' service in

[26] Data compiled from the *Congressional Directory*, 1947–1967, and from relevant volumes of the *Congressional Record*, 1947–1967.

the House is usually a prerequisite for assignment to Ways and Means.

The apprentice period enables party leaders to get an impression of the men who aspire to important committees. During this period members prove themselves to be "good" party men with the qualities recruiters rank high for membership on Ways and Means. In some cases this means little more than party regularity but in others it involves more than a solid record of support for the party. It may mean that a man has proved himself personally, as did the Democrat who said, "I was around here so long that they knew whether I was a son of a bitch or whether I was the kind of guy they wanted." A man who gets on the Committee, one Democrat felt, has been in the House "long enough to win his spurs," and, it might be added, to demonstrate that he is the sort of person who is not waiting for the opportunity to dig his newly won spurs too far into the depletion allowance.

The apprentice period gives the party leaders time to determine how members feel about such issues as oil and mineral depletion allowances, free trade, medicare, and tax reform. The apprentice in this period impresses or fails to impress his colleagues. One Republican appointed early in his House career said, "Not to toot my own horn, but I had worked hard as a freshman and had a reputation as someone who did his homework." "I had a lot of assignments," declared a second Republican in discussing his early House years, "and I think I proved myself as a benefit to the party. I would go out to speak for the party." One argument Joel Broyhill used in getting on the Committee was that after several years of working in the Post Office and District of Columbia Committees he deserved some reward. Thomas B. Curtis of Missouri was asked to go on Ways and Means in his second term by Dan Reed of New York, the ranking Republican. Curtis had demonstrated skill in cutting President Truman's budget in his first term and impressed Reed as the sort of member who should be on Ways and Means. Unfortunately for Reed, he did not ask Curtis about his views on foreign trade and Curtis later broke with his mentor by supporting a liberal trade program.

During the apprentice period, the two parties distinguish good party men from less reliable men, identify the policy orientation of members, and form judgments about the caliber of individuals. To get on the Ways and Means Committee members must pass through this testing period and if they emerge as loyal party supporters, as safe on the major issues coming before the Committee, and as reasonable men to whom no one has strong objections they may have a chance at being considered for the Committee. This part of the recruitment process, therefore, leads to the recruitment of partisans but partisans with a difference: men who have shown some ability to get along well with their fellow legislators and who, typically, practice the legislative art of accommodation.

3. Most members of the Committee, as indicated by the fact that they have some seniority before appointment to it, hold safe seats (defined as 55 per cent or more of the vote). Of the twenty-eight Democrats first elected to the Committee since 1947 only four failed to receive more than 55 per cent of the vote in the election immediately preceding their shift to Ways and Means. Twenty-four Republicans have been appointed to the Committee since 1947. Five of them did not break the 55 per cent mark but nineteen did.[27]

The safeness of seats is perceived by some congressmen as an insulating factor that may allow a member to take an unpopular stand in defense of a party position without endangering his political career. This adds one more guarantee that the party's position on key issues will be maintained. But because most members have safe seats has additional consequences for Committee behavior. It allows those members who want to to devote their energy and time to mastering the complex subject matter of the Committee, an essential task if the Committee is to hold its own against the expertise of the executive branch, not to mention against the Committee's own staff. In addition, having members from safe Democratic and Republican areas provides the opportunity for the Committee to develop a bipartisan core of members who make the Committee their career, a vital feature of Ways and Means that is described more fully in Chapter Three. A stable membership, as Fenno points out, provides opportunities for a stable leadership group to develop, for the development of a set of norms for the regulation of internal Committee behavior, for the evolution of informal techniques of conflict resolution, and time for new members to learn and internalize Committee

---

[27] Electoral statistics are taken from Richard M. Scammon, ed., *America Votes* (Pittsburgh and New York: University of Pittsburgh Press and the Macmillan Co., 1956–1962), vols. 1–5. When no data were available in Scammon, computations were made from the returns reported in relevant volumes of the *Congressional Directory*, and from the *Congressional Quarterly Weekly Report*.

norms.[28] These opportunities are not guaranteed by having members
who spend many years on Ways and Means, but without some degree of stability few lasting patterns of relationships among the
members can be developed and passed on to newcomers.

4. The recruitment process is safeguarded against party and personal deviants by the veto powers of the Committee's chairman and
ranking Republican. Chairman Mills has helped some of the current
members to get on the Committee, usually in quiet ways, while remaining publicly noncommittal. He is consulted by the party leaders
on Ways and Means assignments and, rather than veto members, his
influence is exercised by sitting down with them and "working it
out." In at least one instance, that of Phil Landrum in 1963, what
Mills and the leadership worked out did not prevail in the party
caucus, but in most cases the recruitment problem of Ways and
Means is decided before the party caucus votes.

The ranking Republican on Ways and Means, John Byrnes, also
has remained publicly aloof from contests over Ways and Means
seats. However, he is notified of potential nominees before the final
decision is made by the Republican Committee on Committees. This
courtesy notification symbolizes that the ranking Republican does
check the flow of members to the Committee, a custom that has had
important consequences for public policy. As one Republican critic
of the ranking member's power told Clapp: "Why should the ranking member of Ways and Means on the Republican side have the
power to prevent anyone supporting the Republican President's position on reciprocal trade from getting on his committee just because
he does not happen to agree with that position?" And, in reply, a
conservative Republican argued: "I think it was perfectly proper to
select only people who opposed President Eisenhower on reciprocal
trade for assignment on Ways and Means because I think they represented the majority Republican sentiment in the House." [29]

Mills and Byrnes both are in a position to affect appointments to
their Committee, and both have done so. Both men are professional
members of the Ways and Means Committee who have spent most
of their adult lives on the Committee. They work very closely together, they get along well, and they may be expected to prefer

[28] Richard F. Fenno, Jr., "The House Appropriations Committee as a Political
System: The Problem of Integration," *American Political Science Review*, LVI
(June, 1962), 315.
[29] Charles L. Clapp, *The Congressman* (Washington, D.C.: The Brookings
Institution, 1963), pp. 195–96.

members for the Committee who fit their image of a responsible legislator. No direct evidence has been obtained on whom they have supported or opposed for membership on Ways and Means so the importance of their role in recruitment must remain a matter for speculation. We do know that they get involved and because of their involvement their activities reinforce the other factors that screen out undesirable candidates. With Mills and Byrnes involved in the recruitment process certain members of the House have one more reason for not attempting to get on Ways and Means, and the Committee has one more safeguard against irreconcilable conflict.

ATTRACTIVENESS

The only way I can interpret what I want to be is power. I don't know what I'd do with it when I got it but I want it where I can reach out and use it when I want it.
Ways and Means Democrat

Becoming a member of Ways and Means, Speaker McCormack recalled years later, was "beyond my fondest dreams or ambitions . . . with actually only one full term of service," accurately describing the feeling of most members who join the Committee. Ways and Means is at the top of the committee hierarchy in the House, perhaps the most desirable of all the committees. It is highly attractive to most of those who seek it; it is sought after by many more members than it has openings; it is an elite group to Republicans and Democrats alike.

This attractiveness raises several questions. What effect does the unique attractiveness of the Committee have on the men who strive to become members and succeed? How do they perceive the Committee? What attracts them to it? What attitudes and inclinations do they bring with them to the Committee? Is the way the Committee works affected because its members want to join it very badly and, once on it, see themselves as members of an elite subsystem of the House?

It is plausible to argue that a man's behavior in a group depends heavily on whether or not the group is attractive to him. If initially he is strongly attracted to the group and, perhaps, has to invest much time and effort to attain membership, his behavior will probably be different from any he might indulge in if his membership is accidental, unimportant, or if he is dragooned into becoming a member.

At a minimum, members find more saliency in a highly attractive group, they are more conscious of being members, and they are probably more willing to respond to the demands of group membership than if the group were of secondary importance to them. Attractiveness is considered so important by some students of small groups that they put it at the center of their treatment of cohesiveness.[30]

If Committee members are strongly attracted to it for whatever reasons, they will be predisposed to conform to the norms of the Committee and to behave in such a way that they do not endanger the continuation of the Committee as an attractive organization. If they are attracted by the Committee's status, power, and prestige, the members have a stake in perpetuating these values, and they will tend to avoid behavior that threatens the status and reputation of the Committee.

How ATTRACTIVE IS WAYS AND MEANS? Objectively and indirectly measured, Ways and Means is one of the most desirable committees in the House. One study, by John E. Eberhart, compared the attractiveness of House committees by comparing 4,841 committee appointments from 1914 to 1941 using five criteria: (1) length of service in the House when appointed; (2) length of service on the committee; (3) the holding power of a committee; (4) the drawing power of a committee; and (5) a combination of drawing power and holding power. Ways and Means placed first, followed by Appropriations and Rules in that order.[31]

A more recent study by Miller and Stokes compares committees from the 80th to the 88th Congress and finds that the status of Ways and Means depends somewhat on which measure is used.[32] If the holding power of the committee is the standard used then Ways and Means, which has lost no members to another House committee in the last twenty years, ranks first among committees. When other factors are included, such as the proportion of freshmen among new members, Rules stands ahead of Ways and Means, and the ranking is Rules, Ways and Means, and Appropriations.

[30] For a discussion see Dorwin Cartwright and Alvin Zander, eds., *Group Dynamics*, 2nd ed. (Evanston, Ill.: Row Peterson, 1960), pp. 69–92. See also Leon Festinger, Stanley Schachter, and Kurt Back, *Social Pressures in Informal Groups* (Stanford: Stanford University Press, 1963), pp. 164–65.

[31] Cited in George B. Galloway, *Congress at the Crossroads* (New York: Thomas Y. Crowell, 1946), p. 90.

[32] Warren E. Miller and Donald E. Stokes, *Representation in Congress* (Englewood Cliffs, N.J.: Prentice-Hall, forthcoming).

In any event, both studies confirm that the Ways and Means Committee is a prime committee. However, although most members were strongly attracted to the Committee a few were virtually compelled to go on it by the circumstances surrounding their appointment. Clark Thompson of Texas would have preferred to remain on the Agriculture Committee but he reluctantly agreed to be elected to Ways and Means in order to block a member from going on the Committee. Cecil King of California was on the Merchant Marine and Fisheries Committee before Speaker Rayburn contacted him about going on Ways and Means to block Jerry Voorhis, a Californian, who was reportedly persona non grata to Committee Chairman Robert L. ("Muley") Doughton (D., N.C.).[33] And in a third case, Lee Metcalf (Mont.), who was co-opted for Ways and Means by Rayburn, initially wanted to remain on the Education and Labor Committee and the Interior Committee, the latter's subject matter being more directly related to Montana than that of Ways and Means.[34] Of the thirty Ways and Means members interviewed for this study, five either had little interest in going on the Committee or had serious reservations about it. The others sought membership on the Committee willingly and, for the most part, enthusiastically. The great majority of Committee members were strongly attracted to it, had to campaign hard to get on it, took pride in having waged a successful campaign, and considered Ways and Means to be the prime committee in the House.

The Committee attracts members for a variety of reasons. One former member, afraid that he might be defeated for Congress some day, thought Ways and Means would provide good on-the-job training in tax law if he ever had to resume his law practice. Another man cited his constituency interests and how closely they paralleled the Committee's jurisdiction ("I got more congratulatory telegrams from home after I was elected to Ways and Means than I did after I won election to Congress"). Two Democrats saw Ways and Means as a position from which they could lead their state delegations in the House, and one observed that the Committee is a good springboard for higher public office. Two more members mentioned that they had had some economics in college, another man had specialized in tax law before coming to Congress, and one lifelong businessman was

[33] Note how Voorhis's story of what happened conflicts with the one presented here. Jerry Voorhis, *Confessions of a Congressman* (Garden City, N.Y.: Doubleday, 1947), pp. 72–73.

[34] Masters, *op. cit.*, p. 351.

attracted by the business subject matter of the Committee and his desire to keep taxes from becoming onerous.

Fully two-thirds of those interviewed, however, did sound a common theme: they were attracted to the Committee because of its importance, power, and prestige. This comment, from a Democrat, is atypical only by his surprise that anyone would ask such a question:

> Who wouldn't be attracted to it? It's the top committee in the House of Representatives. The entire revenue system is locked into the Committee. Everything that has anything to do with our entire economic system, the revenue aspect of it, is locked right into that Committee. This means trade too. And if that's not enough there's the power of appointing other members to committees. . . . That itself isn't enough to attract a man to Ways and Means, unless he's a sadist or something and wants to fix somebody, but it's another factor that's attractive. It's the fountainhead of the economic structure.

A Republican, asked the same question, replied, "Power!" He then described it in stream of consciousness fashion with such metaphors as "guts of government," "queen committee," "center of the House," "key committee." One member claimed that he wanted to go on Ways and Means even before he was elected to the House. Another member was asked if he ever thought about leaving Ways and Means for another committee: "Are you kidding! Why leave heaven to go to hell? There's no committee in Congress, including Appropriations, that's as important as Ways and Means. Why step downward once you have reached the top?"

"Why step downward once you have reached the top?" fairly summarizes how the typical member of Ways and Means sees his committee. Other committees are recognized as important, but none can compete with Ways and Means. "Prestige-wise, of course, Ways and Means is best. I think if you ask anyone they'd say the same thing. Oh, they may say their committee is as important but if you took a secret ballot you'd find Ways and Means first." "I was attracted to Ways and Means," said a second Republican, "because I knew it would have a lot of political prestige for me." A Democrat grew reflective, asked assurances that he would not be quoted and whispered, "It was the prestige more than anything. It's the first committee in the House. The prestige was the thing." "I assume, and I think I'm correct in this," said another Democrat, "that it's the most important committee in the House, it's the top committee."

Almost as interesting as why the members were attracted to the Committee is that, with the single exception of the man who mentioned an interest in tax reform, no member cited specific policy objectives that he wanted to promote as a reason for desiring Ways and Means, and the one who was interested in specifics was kept off the Committee for several years. The closest a member would come to citing specific policy interests was keeping taxes from becoming onerous; typically, no one talked of desiring Ways and Means in order to promote international trade, to reform the Revenue Code, to revamp social security, to help the economy of his district, to get a bill enacted into law, to stimulate economic growth through fiscal policy, to raise the duty on imported leather or lower it on Chinese gooseberries. Typically, the members were attracted to the Committee simply because it is the Committee and, said one member, mainly because it is the Committee on Committees, not a means to specific objectives. To some extent the members were attracted to the Committee as an end in itself, as a pinnacle in the House, and as the capstone of their legislative careers.

What is known about the kind of member who is recruited to the Committee seems to indicate that the members did not recall specifics because there were no specifics. Their reasons for wanting a seat on Ways and Means were: the Committee's prestige; its control over vital questions; for Democrats, its committee assignment function; and its role in expanding personal influence in the House or even in running for higher office. The reasons were not, in short, policy oriented, though many cited the wide scope of the Committee's jurisdiction. They were attracted to the Committee simply because of its importance, power, and prestige. The Ways and Means aspirant may not know what he wants to do with power but he knows Ways and Means has it, and he wants Ways and Means.

Because burning policy interests do not characterize those who are attracted to the Committee, because the members have shown that they are reliable on issues but are not "crusaders," because the committee assignment function attracts some Democrats as much if not more than the issues handled by Ways and Means, and because nearly all members are strongly attracted to the Committee, we can see why, in the words of a senior Democrat, "It's a battleground but without the goriness usually associated with a battleground." It is not that the members do not care enough about issues to fight for them, they do. It is not that party conflict in the Committee is unheard of, it is not. It is just that all members have in common membership on an elite committee whose interests may supersede the interests of the party, and party conflict, when it is required, is conducted according to certain rules that guard the ultimate position of the Committee from impairment.

CONCLUSION

Some of the most important features of recruitment to the Ways and Means Committee act to make it a bastion of party conflict in the House of Representatives: manned by liberal Democrats with strong ties to their party and by conservative Republicans with equally strong party ties. However, the ideal of party conflict — if it can be called an ideal — can be thwarted by the opportunity for a conservative coalition to gain a majority of votes in the Committee and frustrate certain objectives. Safeguards against the conservative coalition have been erected in the recruitment process to Ways and Means and these safeguards — though not perfect — do incline the Committee to split along party lines on at least some of the major issues it considers.

Decision-making in Ways and Means is determined by a number of informal factors in the recruitment process, plus the attractiveness of the Committee, resulting in a Committee composed of members who are bound to disagree on general issues but equally bound to manifest this disagreement in particular ways.

In addition, the kind of members who get on Ways and Means are likely to take a pragmatic approach to the issues coming before the Committee. Literally hundreds of issues are decided by the Committee other than such general questions as whether or not a medical care program should be financed out of social security taxes. On these issues — which are not well publicized and in which party interest is tenuous or completely nonexistent — the members of Ways and Means may be expected to be accommodating to one another and prone to compromise and reaching a consensus. And even on the basic issues there probably will be some bipartisan agreement on the way programs ought to work and a good deal of nonpartisan cooperation in solving related problems.

CHAPTER THREE

Integration and Exchange: The Internal Relations of Ways and Means

> *You see, we differ in tariffs and currencies and all them things, but we agree on the main proposition that when a man works in politics, he should get something out of it.*
>
> Boss Plunkitt

> *There is harmony on the Committee because of all the back-scratching that goes on.*
>
> Former Committee Staff Member

The contrast between the internal relations of the House Education and Labor Committee and the Committee on Ways and Means vividly illustrates the wide variability between House committees and the analytical task of this chapter.

Education and Labor *Democrat*	*Ways and Means* *Republican*
It's a very discouraging Committee. You can't get a resolution praising God through that Committee without having a three day battle over it. . . . It's about the most difficult Committee around. Our executive sessions are the most exciting things you ever saw.	We try to write the best legislation we can in a non-partisan way — more so than any other committee. . . . We work in a nonpartisan way. Sure, there are philosophical differences but they never become the partisan legislative fighting that they do on other committees.[1]

Parts of this chapter first appeared in John F. Manley, "The House Committee on Ways and Means: Conflict Management in a Congressional Committee," *American Political Science Review*, LIX (December, 1965), 927–39.

[1] Quoted in Richard F. Fenno, Jr., "The House of Representatives and Federal

59

If there is a trace of enjoyment in the excitement of being a member of the Education and Labor Committee the statement by the Ways and Means Republican demonstrates much pride: he and his colleagues, despite philosophical differences, try to write "good" legislation without the partisan legislative fighting that erupts in some committees. Why is Ways and Means like this?

The question is complex, and so, necessarily, is the answer. In essence, the answer developed in this chapter centers around a particular view about social and political relationships, which stems from the work of Talcott Parsons, Chester I. Barnard, George C. Homans, and Peter M. Blau.

Following Parsons, the analytical problem posed by the internal relations of the Ways and Means Committee can be divided into three parts: (1) problems associated with tasks (instrumental interaction); (2) problems of personal gratifications and interpersonal relations (affective interaction); and (3) problems of internal differentiation (integrative problems).[2] When the question of how the Committee members are motivated to deal with these problems [3] is posed in this way the inducement-contribution theory of Barnard, known as "exchange" theory in the work of Homans and Blau, may be employed to develop some answers.

Exchange theory, as Barnard makes clear, involves a view of human nature that emphasizes the self-interest and egoism of individuals. "The contribution of personal efforts which constitute the energies of organizations," Barnard writes, "are yielded by individuals because of incentives. The egotistical motives of self-preservation and of self-satisfaction are dominating forces; on the whole, organizations can exist only when consistent with the satisfaction of these motives, unless, alternatively, they can change these motives." [4] Thus, ex-

---

Aid to Education," *New Perspectives on the House of Representatives*, ed. Robert L. Peabody and Nelson W. Polsby (Chicago: Rand McNally, 1963), pp. 197–98.

[2] Talcott Parsons and Edward A. Shils, eds., *Toward a General Theory of Action* (New York: Harper Torchbooks, 1962), pp. 208–09.

[3] Talcott Parsons, *The Social System* (New York: The Free Press, 1964), p. 27.

[4] Chester I. Barnard, *The Functions of the Executive* (Cambridge, Mass.: Harvard University Press, 1966), p. 139. It is interesting to note how heavily Parsons relied on Barnard when called upon to show how his general sociological theory pertains to organization theory. See Talcott Parsons, "Suggestions for a Sociological Approach to the Theory of Organization — I," *Administrative Science Quarterly*, I (June, 1956), 63–85. Another leading organizational theorist who owes a large debt to Barnard is, of course, Herbert A. Simon. See his

change theory focuses on the rewards and costs that form the basis of human interaction.

In this view of human nature, and in the propositions that stem from it, the theory of Parsons and Barnard is basically similar to that of Homans and Blau. In an essay on functionalism, Gouldner expressed the key assumptions of exchange theory. "Specifically, I suggest that a norm of reciprocity, in its universal form, makes two interrelated, minimal demands: (a) people should help those who have helped them, and (b) people should not injure those who have helped them." [5] All four men are concerned with the rewards and costs of social behavior. As Homans writes in discussing functionalism, "Any statement explaining an institution as being 'functional' or 'dysfunctional' for men could readily be translated with no loss of meaning into one that said it was 'rewarding' or 'punishing.'"[6] It is true that Barnard and Homans stress the psychological aspects of behavior, whereas Parsons and Blau are more concerned with the sociological, but for analyzing Ways and Means this difference — though important — is not critical. To understand and explain a group such as Ways and Means the sociology of the group can be approached through the psychological needs and satisfactions of the individual members. Any other approach, in fact, would seem to run the risk of accentuating a few variables at the expense of other factors that are equally significant to the functioning of the group.

To illustrate the focus of exchange theory, the popular definition of the term "norm" used by Homans in his earlier work is compared to that of his later writing on exchange theory. In 1950, Homans defined a norm as "an idea in the minds of the members of a group, an idea that can be put in the form of a statement specifying what the members or other men should do, ought to do, are expected to do, under given circumstances." [7] From an idea stipulating a behavioral "ought" Homans in 1961 defined a norm as "a statement made by some members of a group that a particular kind of quantity of be-

---

Administrative Behavior, 2nd ed. (New York: Free Press, 1957), *passim*. Also see James G. March and Herbert A. Simon, *Organizations* (New York: John Wiley, 1958), pp. 84–88.

[5] Alvin W. Gouldner, "The Norm of Reciprocity: A Preliminary Statement," *American Sociological Review*, XXV (April, 1960), 171.

[6] George C. Homans, *Sentiments and Activities* (New York: Free Press of Glencoe, 1962), pp. 33–34. Homans, of course, prefers the latter formulation.

[7] George C. Homans, *The Human Group* (New York: Harcourt, Brace & World, 1950), p. 123. Fenno, for one, adopts this meaning of norm from Homans. See Richard F. Fenno, Jr., *The Power of the Purse* (Boston: Little, Brown, 1966), p. xxi.

havior is one they find valuable for the actual behavior of themselves, and others whom they specify, to conform to. The important thing is not that the behavior is conformity but that it is valued." [8] Exchange theory, in other words, directs attention to the things men find valuable in social relationships (rewards) and to the relationship between rewards and costs. As Blau puts it, "Human beings tend to be governed in their associations with one another by the desire to obtain social rewards of various sorts, and the resulting exchanges of benefits shape the structure of social relations." [9]

Because role theory is not used in the view of Ways and Means taken here, the meaning given to integration differs somewhat from that used by Fenno in his study of the Appropriations Committee. He defines integration as "the degree to which there is a working together or a meshing together or mutual support among roles and subgroups. Conversely, it is also defined as the degree to which a committee is able to minimize conflict among its roles and its subgroups, by heading off or resolving the conflicts that arise." [10] No attempt is made here to analyze the internal relations of Ways and Means in terms of roles or subgroups. Rather, the focus is on the individual members of the Committee, what they get out of membership on Ways and Means, and what it costs them by way of contributions to the Committee. The advantages of couching this focus in role terms are not apparent; moreover, it is felt that the utility of role theory for building typologies is not matched by its value as a help in explaining behavior, and, therefore, little systematic use of role theory is made in the present study. Integration here means a sufficient imbalance on the side of rewards compared to costs so that the members of a group — regardless of internal differences — are motivated to do what is necessary to ensure the perpetuation of the power and prestige of the group.

The Ways and Means Committee can be thought of as a group that makes certain kinds of demands on its members. It costs mem-

[8] George C. Homans, *Social Behavior: Its Elementary Forms* (New York: Harcourt, Brace & World, 1961), p. 116. See also George C. Homans, "Social Behavior as Exchange," *American Journal of Sociology*, LXIII (May, 1958), 597–606. For a critique of Homans see S. N. Eisenstadt, *Essays on Comparative Institutions* (New York: John Wiley, 1965), pp. 23–25.

[9] Peter M. Blau, *Exchange and Power in Social Life* (New York: John Wiley, 1964), p. 18.

[10] Richard F. Fenno, Jr., "The House Appropriations Committee as a Political System: The Problem of Integration," *American Political Science Review*, LVI (June, 1962), p. 310.

bers something to belong to it and members receive rewards from it in exchange for certain kinds of behavior. It is crucial that the members make linkages between the Committee as a reward-producing group and the way in which they comport themselves; that is, they must identify the Committee and its well-being as important to the realization of their own objectives, and they must be aware that the continuation of these rewards is partially dependent upon how they as members behave. In Barnard's terms, members of organizations must be induced to make contributions to the organization; in Blau's words, members of organizations exchange valuable "things" with group members in return for things they value.

In this chapter the internal decision-making process of Ways and Means is described — in particular, how the Democrats and Republicans subordinate party and policy differences to what they consider to be a good job on Ways and Means legislation — and the internal relations of the members are explained in terms of the rewards that accompany different forms of behavior. A characteristic of Ways and Means that is of overriding importance — restrained partisanship — is explained by reference to the costs and benefits of Committee membership to the members. The Committee functions as it does because important incentives are to be protected and gained by keeping internal conflict within certain clearly defined and widely understood bounds.

RESTRAINED PARTISANSHIP

Party disagreement is abundant within the Ways and Means Committee (see Chapter Five for an account of party impact). Minority reports by Republican members and motions to recommit bills on the House floor frequently accompany the major bills reported by the Committee. Since Wilbur Mills of Arkansas became Chairman in 1958 the minority report-recommittal motion combination has been the pattern on the following major bills: [11]

1. Trade Agreements Extension Act of 1958.
2. Trade Expansion Act of 1962.
3. Revenue Act of 1962.
4. Revenue Act of 1963.
5. Medicare, 1965.

[11] For the Committee report and votes on these bills see: (1) Committee on Ways and Means, *Trade Agreements Extension Act of 1958*, H. Rept. 1761 to accompany H.R. 12591, 1958, pp. 55–87. *Congressional Record*, June 11, 1958,

Not every bill reported by Ways and Means is the subject of intense partisan disagreement, of course, but a number of the more important ones are. The primary question of this chapter concerns the nature of the decision-making process within the Committee that occurs with members who are bound to disagree over fundamental issues of public policy.

Party-line or near party-line splits within the Committee, a deeply divided Committee before the House, general differences in ideological orientation, and members placed on the Committee because they will be inclined to disagree with members of the other party might indicate that conflict dominates the Committee's internal processes as it does the Education and Labor Committee. It does not. The forces leading to partisan conflict in the Committee are tempered by a vital integrative norm governing the behavior of members in executive session: *the norm of restrained partisanship.*

The norm of restrained partisanship means that partisanship should not interfere with a thorough study and complete understanding of the technical complexities of the bills under consideration. Members may disagree over what decisions the Committee finally should make, but there is a firmly rooted consensus on *how* they should go about making them. Those members who attend the protracted meetings, and attendance varies greatly, go through a laborious process of illuminating the implications of arcane tax, tariff, debt, and social security proposals. Proposed legislation is pondered line by line with the assistance of experts from the executive agencies, the House Legislative Counsel's Office which helps draft the technical language, the tax staff of the Joint Committee on Internal Revenue Taxation, and at times by Library of Congress experts. The decision-making process varies somewhat from issue to issue but, with the aid of a battery of "technicians," it generally is marked by caution, methodical repetition, and, most important, restrained partisanship.

pp. 10881–82. (2) Committee on Ways and Means, *Trade Expansion Act of 1962,* H. Rept. 1818 to accompany H.R. 11970, 1962, pp. 83–104. *Congressional Record,* June 28, 1962, pp. 12089–90. (3) Committee on Ways and Means, *Revenue Act of 1962,* H. Rept. 1447 to accompany H.R. 10650, 1962, pp. B1–B28. *Congressional Record,* March 29, 1962, pp. 5431–32. (4) Committee on Ways and Means, *Revenue Act of 1963,* H. Rept. 749 to accompany H.R. 8363, 1963, pp. C1–C28. *Congressional Record,* September 25, 1963, pp. 18118–19. (5) Committee on Ways and Means, *Social Security Amendments of 1965,* H. Rept. 213 to accompany H.R. 6675, 1965, pp. 243–57. *Congressional Record,* April 7, 1965 (daily edition), pp. 7181–82.

Some Committee members think that Ways and Means decides most issues on a partisan basis, but a Democrat states the preponderant view:

> Most of the time we go along up to a certain point and then a sharp party vote will come. On the tax bill [Revenue Act of 1964] we went along for a long time without party votes, working very well, then the Republicans lined up at the end against it. There's very little partisanship up to a point, when the political factors come in, and then a partisan vote comes.

"We've never had," a high-ranking Republican argued, "the attitude on Ways and Means — and some committees are like this — that because we oppose the bill or technique philosophically we are going to do everything we can to keep all the inequities, all the problems, all the flaws in, and then use these on the floor. No, we've never done that; well, 'never' may be too strong but generally no." One member, a Democrat, concluded that the Committee is as bipartisan as any committee in the House. "I always say that on Agriculture you couldn't get anyone to agree on anything, and on Ways and Means they don't disagree on anything. That's not completely true, of course, because we do disagree on some things but most of the time we get along pretty well. It's as bipartisan a committee as you have in the House." The member who claimed that the Republicans try to perfect the legislation and hold their real feelings toward it in abeyance explained:

> I think the most important factor here is experience. We get men with some experience on Ways and Means. Some members think that fighting Democrats from morning to night is the most important thing in the world. They say if a Democrat's for it I'm against it. But the members of Ways and Means aren't like this. If there's a big issue sure we fight it out but then we go on to something else.

"We may not *vote* together," said a Democrat, "but we get along well."

These attitudes toward the work of the Committee express in different ways the norm of restrained partisanship and can be supplemented by the public expressions of members. Two examples, of many, may be given. In January 1963, Al Ullman of Oregon, the eighth-ranking majority member of the Committee, told a group of freshman congressmen how the Committee gets along without formal rules to guide its procedure:

> On the Ways and Means Committee, while we generally follow the rules of the House, there is a pretty much unwritten code of procedure in the committee and an esprit de corps that allows the committee to function without a formal rules (*sic*), as my friend, Tom Curtis, can elaborate upon, I am sure. But it works very effectively. The committee has the most complex legislation to handle of any other committee in the House. I am amazed at what we do get done without a formal set of rules, and the caliber of legislation that comes out of that committee; meticulously done, thoroughly considered.[12]

In a very different kind of situation, his floor statement opposing the 1963 tax bill, John Byrnes of Wisconsin, the ranking Republican member of Ways and Means, told the House about the way they marked up the legislation:

> We tried to come up with as good a bill as we could. And I say to the Speaker it was not done on a partisan basis — and that has been confirmed by the chairman. It was done on a bipartisan basis, up until the last few days. When they had almost all the drafting completed and perfected, then they said, "Now we don't need your help any more, boys; we will put the steamroller to work." But up until then it was on a bipartisan basis.[13]

Before the party steamroller was revved up, in other words, the Committee had spent months working in a generally bipartisan atmosphere that became partisan only when the members faced the question of whether an $11 billion cut in taxes should be made without some firm safeguards against increased federal spending. The parties split on this question, with the Republicans supporting a motion to recommit that would have tied the cut to expenditure controls. All ten Committee Republicans voted for recommital; all fifteen Democrats opposed Byrnes's motion. On final passage the voting line-up was identical: the Committee Republicans voted against the bill and the Democrats supported it.[14]

[12] *Transcript of Seminars for New Members of the 88th Congress* (Washington, D.C.: *Congressional Quarterly*, 1963), p. 20.
[13] *Congressional Record*, September 25, 1963, p. 18113.
[14] *Ibid.*, pp. 18118–19. Republican opposition to the tax cut evaporated after President Johnson proposed a budget $200 million less than that suggested by

It is important to realize that restrained partisanship is an ideal. As such, it is not always attained. Moreover, the members recognize that although the degree of partisanship varies by issues, on most fundamental questions they will probably divide along party lines. "It's done without regard to party even though everyone knows that when we get right down to the shank party lines are going to be drawn." In this sense, Ways and Means is a very partisan committee indeed. Still, the members contend that given the political questions they face they do a good job, and they identify a good job with a nonpartisan one.

Despite the consensus on the importance of restrained partisanship the members may be exaggerating the degree of nonpartisan decision-making in the Committee. It is impressive, therefore, that a Treasury Department official who has worked closely with Ways and Means for several years believes that it is a

> partisan committee in the sense that you get a lot of partisan voting. But while you get a lot of party votes the members discuss the bill in a nonpartisan way. It's a very harmonious committee, the members work very well and harmoniously together. Sure, there is partisanship but they discuss the issues in a very nonpartisan way.

Or a staff member, who has been with the Committee for years, stated:

> Of course, many decisions, both the tentative ones and the ones on draft language, are made with no formal votes taken. It's just passed or rejected and everyone is satisfied. I think you will find that Ways and Means is a partisan committee, there are usually minority views. But partisanship is not that high when they discuss the bill and legislate. About 95 per cent of the time the members deliberate the bill in a nonpartisan way, discussing the facts calmly. Then toward the end Byrnes and the Republicans may get partisan. But an awfully large part of it is nonpartisan.

Or a former staff member said:

> Ways and Means is a partisan committee and then again it is not partisan. Take tax bills, for example. Everyone knows, including Republicans, that you can't do too much with the

---

the Republicans as the level of spending that would justify tax reduction, a development for which, rightly or wrongly, the Republicans claimed credit.

tax code. You can tinker here and there but it's different from
Powell's Education and Labor Committee where the *issues*
are real fundamental clashes between party philosophies. You
don't get these real hot emotional issues on Ways and Means.
On medicare, of course, it's different and a lot of blood is
spilled. But on most things the members get along real well.

Or an official of the Department of Health, Education and Welfare
who feels that Ways and Means is a partisan committee, that the
members are not amateurs at being partisan politicians, "But it's
never so partisan that they are sloppy." They are restrained partisans.

Thus the dualism uncovered in the recruitment process to Ways
and Means is complemented by a dualism in the legislative style of
the Committee. A senior Democrat expressed the paradox: "You've
seen how these committees wrangle. We don't rankle and wrangle
like the rest of them. And we have wrangling issues too! We keep it
in hand."

Why and how does Ways and Means "keep it in hand"? The answer lies in the inducements associated with membership on the
Committee, the most important being that which attracted the members to the Committee in the first place: status and prestige in the
House. Membership on Ways and Means makes one a member of
the House elite; it gives one a share in the Committee's prestige; it
places members above their peers in the House. The members therefore are induced to follow the norms that ensure the perpetuation of
the Committee's stature, especially the norm of restrained partisanship.

If there were no other rewards to Ways and Means beyond membership — and there are several — the Committee members would
derive great satisfaction from the fact that they have "arrived" in the
House of Representatives. Asked if the members cooperate to protect
the Committee's status and to write sound legislation, a Democrat
responded: "Yes, yes! I'm sure that that's behind a lot of it. It may
not be a conscious thing but that's exactly what we do — Republicans too." "We all respect the dignity of the position we occupy. And
while it may be an unspoken thing, no one says anything about it, we
all know it's there." "When we come to the floor," a third Democrat
stated, "it's not a bunch of irresponsible renegades, it's Mills and
Byrnes. These are responsible men." A Republican expressed the
same feeling: "Being on Ways and Means gives me stature and respect. We are a powerful committee and a prestigeful one. The
House is jealous of the Committee. Many members say our bills

can't be amended because we know it all, we're the experts. They are jealous." Another member concluded that Republicans and Democrats have a spirit of cooperation, adding, "We are members of the 'club' now." Ways and Means is a "real blue-ribbon committee. When a man gets on Ways and Means you know he's got something on the ball. The work is interesting. It's sometimes called the primary committee."

These statements give a sense of what membership on the Ways and Means Committee means. In essence, the members feel:

> Ways and Means is looked up to. You stand a little above the other members and are looked up to. You're a cut above them and it's a good feeling. It's a close-knit committee. Apart from Appropriations, I'd say Ways and Means is the closest-knit committee there is. It's not close-knit in the sense that we meet and say grace or pray together, or drink together, or party together. But when you get into that hallowed hall over there and look out . . . I can't describe it actually but you're a cut above.

No one expressed the strong sense of group identification better than a former staff member who drew a rather bizarre analogy between the Committee and a group of animals on an island during a forest fire. "There may be some predators there but for the moment they are all in it together. It's the same way on the Committee. There's a predatory relationship between Republicans and Democrats but for a time, while they are in Committtee, they all have an equal interest in maintaining the image of the Committee."

The norm of restrained partisanship is rooted in these attitudes toward the Committee. Members of Ways and Means have serious disagreements over policy but they also have shared attitudes and perceptions of the status of the Committee and what they must do to maintain that status. The norm is followed even when the issue is such a highly partisan one as medicare.[15] During the 1965 executive session on medicare a Republican commented on the way the Committee was handling the bill: "I think there is almost an unwritten rule, the members don't say so but it's there, which keeps things from becoming too partisan and political. It's different from any other committee — there's a feeling of cooperation and respect on the part of the members on both sides." An examination of 3,453

[15] See Chapter 4, pp. 118–21.

pages of the executive session transcripts on medicare turned up no evidence to contradict this observation.

The main link between the legislative style of the Committee and its status and prestige in the House is most members' awareness that without the norm of restrained partisanship the reputation of the Committee, which they enjoy regardless of party, may be impaired or destroyed. Their reputation in the House as Committee members depends on how they perform their legislative chores. If they cannot contain conflict inside the Committee, as they often cannot, then they feel that conflict should be articulated in a way that does not imperil the long-run standing of the Committee in the House.

A Democratic Committee member claimed that all the chairmen under whom he has served have emphasized the prestige of the Committee and the need to preserve it. "Dan Reed said on a couple of occasions that we have this respect and we ought to enjoy it and keep it. He said, 'There are twenty-five members on this Committee and I want all of them to get reelected.' Mills has said a couple of times, 'Let's keep this inside the Committee. Let's not let the House think we have a snake pit over here.'" The Republicans who compared Ways and Means to a fraternity contrasted the Committee with another House committee, "We are all concerned with how the Committee looks to outsiders and if there's a lot of bickering the Committee doesn't look good. Take Banking and Currency for example after Patman took over. He's arbitrary and the committee's prestige has sunk way down. We know that to be an effective committee we must be reasonable."

But maintaining the Committee's reputation involves more than preventing the House from thinking Ways and Means is a snake pit. It involves a professional approach to legislation. "The House says here are a bunch of smart guys, we won't tamper too much with what they do. The Ways and Means Committee has a reputation of being a well-balanced, level-headed group and the House respects this." A second Republican commented:

> I've always had the feeling, sensed that the members pretty
> much know that if you are going to do a thing then the way
> the Committee suggests is probably as good as you can get.
> They know that we have been through it, *dug* into it, and
> that if you have to have the bill or program then it's probably
> as good a way as you can get. They know we've been con-
> scientious. Some committees, of course, no. Agriculture, and
> here personality is important — there's a personality factor

there. . . . If you are going to do something I think members know that our way is probably best.

"On our committee," said a third minority member, "we have a responsibility to the House, we have to do the best job we can. Our subject matter is very important and complex and we just have to work in a responsible way."

The nature of the Committee's subject matter supports the norm of restrained partisanship and is closely related to the special character of Ways and Means. Members often mention the extreme complexity and intricacy of revenue bills and the national significance of the legislation they consider. This perception of the subject matter inclines them to act in a "responsible" way, by which they mean being "conscientious," "thorough," "careful," and "studious." "We deal with the most complicated, technical subject in the Congress, in the country for that matter, and we have to be thorough on Ways and Means," according to a Democrat. A Republican said simply, "You just don't mess around with taxes, it can create millionaires or paupers." Another Republican thinks that, "What we try to do is draft the best bill we can." And, in the argot of House Republicans, "every part of it may have serious consequences on the individual initiative of our free enterprise system."

A particularly revealing manifestation of the Committee's dual jurisdiction occurred when a member said, "Relations with the Democrats are personally good but we are clearly and deeply split over issues. We have our policy and they have theirs." Later in the interview he concluded, without seeing any conflict between the views, "partisanship is not too high on Ways and Means — taxes, trade, and social security should not be settled on a partisan basis," which shows clearly how the Committee's subject matter helps support the commitment to the norm of restrained partisanship. Another member made the point succinctly: "It's the *issues* that are partisan, not the members."

Ways and Means members, in brief, are acutely aware of the importance of the bills that they must consider, which buttresses the norm against letting "political" considerations dominate the decision-making process. Wilbur Mills, at the end of his first year as Chairman, summed up the Committee's general approach to legislation:

> . . . The nature of the measures falling within the jurisdiction of the Committee on Ways and Means is such that this committee must always proceed with the utmost caution, re-

sponsibility, and prudence. Taxes, tariffs, social security, and
fiscal legislation are matters which intimately and personally
affect the lives of every American, and in all these areas our
committee must act with the highest degree of responsibility
bearing in mind that these are sensitive and vital areas of
action.[16]

The ethos and objective of Ways and Means is restrained partisanship and prudent, cautious, professional, and responsible law-making.
The Committee members have a stake in perpetuating this kind of
committee and reap important incentives from being perceived in the
House as members of this kind of committee.

Data on House perceptions of Ways and Means are, of course,
hard to come by short of a survey of the House members, but much
can be inferred from the fact that the House regularly considers Committee bills under a closed rule.

Virtually all major bills reported to the House by the Committee
are debated on the floor under a closed rule that precludes all floor
amendments save those offered by Ways and Means. When the
House votes whether to grant a closed rule to a Ways and Means
bill, it is in a sense a vote of confidence in the Committee. The Committee is widely thought (and expected) to be the master of its
esoteric subject matter, and in exchange for this expertise the House
voluntarily gives up its right to amend Ways and Means bills — or,
as the vocal opponents of closed rules say, the House "gags" itself.
This expectation helps to explain why the Committee is noted for
time-consuming diligence and induces members to follow the norm
of restrained partisanship. In the words of a Democrat, "It'd be sui-
cide if you ever tried to write a tax or social security bill on the floor.
We sit in there surrounded by experts to keep us from going off on a
tangent so you can imagine what would happen on the floor. We
cooperate to write a good bill partly because of the closed rule. We
get consensus."

It is expected that the Committee will perfect the bill and polish
it till it is almost technically perfect. This takes time and a school-
room environment, and it is in this kind of atmosphere that the
members like to pursue their labors. "The average congressman," a
Republican explained, "can't understand what we deal with and you
just can't open it up on the floor. We try to report well-rounded
packages of legislation, the best bills we can. We compromise a lot to

[16] *Congressional Record*, August 22, 1958, p. 19311.

get a good bill we can report out." "We go to school every time we sit in that committee," a Democrat said. The autonomy that members of Ways and Means enjoy does not mean, as seen in Chapter Five, that the House has little or no influence over the decisions reached by the Committee, but it does engender attitudes and values that are the cement of restrained partisanship and that make *some* members define their roles as professional students of legislation with a responsibility to study, sift, weigh, and bargain until they reach a satisfactory reconciliation of the competing demands placed upon them.

We should here distinguish between the Committee as a formal organization of twenty-five members and the Committee as a working group. Attendance and participation in the executive sessions varies widely from member to member, with the Republicans being more consistent in attendance than the Democrats. The variability in attendance is in part due to the absence of subcommittees. Ways and Means does its work in plenary sessions, not through subcommittees. This practice works against decentralized decision-making while it relieves the members of the time-consuming burden of attending both subcommittee and full committee meetings.

Members give a number of reasons to support the absence of subcommittees. They feel that the bills considered by Ways and Means are of such great national significance that no one wants to rely on a subcommittee's judgment; the Committee is small so plenary meetings are easy to manage; they may spend months working on one bill and if a subcommittee marked it up first the full Committee would want to go over it again, thereby wasting time; it would be hard to get members to attend lengthy subcommittee meetings; all the members are equal and subcommittees would introduce inequality of influence into the Committee; the "historic tradition" of the Committee is not to use subcommittees;[17] and, as a Democrat said of the subject matter of the Committee, "What if they had a subcommittee on foreign trade and one on corporations, what one would *I* go on? All the members want to know what's going on in everything."

But the absence of subcommittees does foster a highly centralized system of decision-making in which a few members — led by the

[17] Actually Ways and Means has not always done its work in plenary sessions. When it handled the Smoot-Hawley tariff bill in 1929 the Republicans wrote the bill in subgroups consisting only of Republicans. See the description of the process by the Clerk of the Committee, Clayton F. Moore, "How a Tariff Bill is Passed," *The Congressional Digest*, VIII (June–July, 1929), 164–66. Subcommittees have been used periodically in the past but primarily for study and oversight purposes, not for drafting major legislation.

Chairman — participate much more than the others. No votes are taken until the end of the mark-up (which, on a major bill, takes many weeks) and the fiction is thereby created that no decisions have been made. In reality, countless decisions have been made by the working group, but the postponement of controversial questions to the end of the process allows the subgroup to proceed without appearing to preempt the decision-making process and actually encourages the other members to stay away, safe in the knowledge that they will have the opportunity to review the tentative results, press for those things that interest them at the voting stage of the process, or attend when the Committee gets to something in which they are interested.

Table 3.1 presents the results of a participation count made on the transcripts of the 1965 executive session meetings on medicare and excise tax reduction. Confirming the results of interviews, Chairman Mills, John Byrnes, and Tom Curtis of Missouri constituted the heart of the Committee, with the Chairman as the major substantive participant. These men dominated the executive session deliberations of the Committee, and although participation is not synonymous with influence (e.g., the late Tom O'Brien of Chicago, who was an important vote because of his influence in the Illinois delegation but said little), it is clear that a small number of members carries the discussion, and Mills carries the most.

Because the subgroup is willing to do most of the Committee's work, the demands made on the other members by the Committee are lessened. It is possible for a member to enjoy all the benefits of the Committee's prestige and rarely if ever attend a Committee meeting. The subgroup cares little one way or the other; if other members want to get involved in the details of Committee business they can.

TABLE 3.1

EXECUTIVE SESSION PARTICIPATION, MEDICARE AND
EXCISE TAX REDUCTION, 1965 [a]

Member	Medicare	Excise taxes
Wilbur Mills	1731	234
John W. Byrnes	772	102
Thomas B. Curtis	837	83
Fourth Member	333	61
Fifth Member	272	55

[a] If a member made a comment on a page he was given credit for that page and the total number of pages on which his name appeared was added up. Mills's participation has been adjusted by excluding the pages on which he, as Chairman, made purely procedural remarks.

Since there are no barriers to widespread participation there is usually no resentment of those who participate the most. With an unequal distribution of the Committee burden and an equal distribution of its glory the benefits of Committee membership far exceed the costs for most of the members. And the disproportionate ratio of benefits to costs adds up to a Committee composed of members who, for the most part, like it very much.

High prestige at a low cost is not the only incentive Ways and Means has for its members. By and large, the attendance of members is more general than participation and, for those members who attend, the meetings are pleasant, if somewhat tiresome, experiences. Second, the Democratic members have the important fringe benefit of acting as their party's Committee on Committees. Third, the members can protect and promote the interests of their constituents and friends to the extent that these interests are affected by what the Committee considers. Fourth, some members like the subject matter of the Committee.

1. Affective relations inside the Committee are good. Members are in direct face-to-face contact for weeks at a time during the mark-up of a major bill. This style of deliberation is accompanied by a fairly well-defined set of norms that govern interpersonal relations.

Committee meetings are not supposed to be partisan or personal battles. Acrimony develops occasionally, perhaps more than is revealed in interviews, but on the whole the members feel that to be effective they must maintain decorum and act in a gentlemanly way. Bitter personal disputes erupt infrequently and even public conflicts that appear to be disruptive of interpersonal relations are often played out in a benign spirit. "We spar a lot but it never gets serious," according to a Republican. "We don't have knock-outs. Maybe we're a little more clubby, more closely knit than others." "Every now and then things flare up but not too often. We fight out issues but laugh about it later. It's like two lawyers who argue a case hard and then walk out arm in arm." One Republican illustrated the kind of relationships that exist behind the public record:

> Personal relations are pretty good although some acrimony does develop. Wilbur [Mills] and I have argued back and forth and then joked about it later. In fact today when I made my speech on the floor about the conference committee report on the tax bill Wilbur and I were talking and I told him

without me around he wouldn't be able to play the Great
Compromiser role. Wilbur just laughed.

When the Ways and Means Committee closes its doors to mark up
a bill, thereby closing out the press and all other "outsiders," the
rules of the game change. "In public sessions there's more politics.
Members play up witnesses and introduce them. . . . But in executive session politics is less. It's different . . . no gallery to play for, no
publicity." "Oh, for people who have rapport," said a Democrat, "and
where everything is open and above board Ways and Means can't be
beat." When asked if this includes the Republicans he said, "Yes.
The executive hearings we are having now [medicare] are just like a
conversation, just like a davenport conversation. Coffee is served. It's
very nice."

One member who replied "I love it!" when asked if he liked being
on Ways and Means, drew a comparison between the Committee
and the one he left. "Oh that was such a knock-down drag-out, it was
murder. Fighting all the time, everyday a battle. One of my colleagues just the other day said, '———— has come here from that other
place and he's just learning to be a gentleman here.' " A Republican
who views Education and Labor as in constant turmoil, said, "I don't
know what it's like on that committee, but for me I'd think it'd be a
real cross to bear."

The impulse toward a cooperative, friendly spirit in the Committee
is derived from the fact that members feel more comfortable in a low
tension environment; they prefer to disagree amicably if they can. On
those occasions when they cannot, the deviant member may be subjected to corrective measures. A senior member warned a junior member of his own party that he was losing his effectiveness by pursuing
his objectives in an overly adamant way. (It did little good.)

Thus the members of the Committee get along with each other
fairly well, and some of the time the meetings are actually enjoyable.
Although the entertainment value of most meetings is relatively low,
the members try to conduct themselves so that conflict is not high,
and in the consensus on this norm lies the support for actions designed to make the meetings as peaceful as possible. Good interpersonal relations are important benefits to some members of the
Committee, benefits not readily available on all House committees.

2. If the Ways and Means Committee decided nothing more important than the tariff on eviscerated pigeons, membership on the
Committee on Committees would make each Democrat an impor-

tant member of the House. His vote and his skill in the bargaining process surrounding committee assignments determine entire legislative careers and may even help decide the electoral fate of members. For some Democrats the Committee on Committees function of Ways and Means is the most attractive feature of the Committee and its most important incentive.

Asked what benefits he derives from being a member of Ways and Means, one member replied that, "I wouldn't overlook the political side of Ways and Means, the Committee on Committees. At the start of every Congress the dean of every delegation seeks you out and comes to you. That's not bad for a starter." "They call you 'Mister' and 'Sir' when you are on the Committee on Committees." Members "look up to me," a third Democrat said. Contacts with other House members are expanded by being on the Committee on Committees. Members get to know other House members and, most important, make their colleagues indebted to them. "When a new member comes here who does he see? Not the leadership but the members of Ways and Means. We are leaders." "*They* come to you," another Democrat said, "and that's very important. Members are always coming to me for things and when I go to them, boy, they remember." "When you're on Ways and Means the other members smile at you. They never know when they are going to ask for your support for a committee for someone in their zone. They don't go out of their way to pick a fight with you, let's put it that way."

Committee Democrats do not make assignments to other committees in a vacuum. The Democratic leadership is involved in the assignment process and although the leadership no longer participates extensively in the deliberations, as they once did according to Masters,[18] their views are taken into account. Yet all ten Democrats who commented on this point discounted the importance of the leadership in making assignments and stressed their freedom of decision. Seven indicated that the leadership has a right to designate Rules Committee membership, but with this one exception the members feel that they, not the party leaders, have the say. The Speaker's wishes are listened to but, except for Rules, not always followed.

Thus the Ways and Means Democrats feel that they have enough autonomy in allocating committee seats to see this as one of the most

[18] Nicholas A. Masters, "Committee Assignments in the House of Representatives," *American Political Science Review*, LV (June, 1961), 346. The Speaker and Majority Leader pay a courtesy call on the Ways and Means Democrats at the start of their meetings and then leave.

important things they do. For some, however, it is probably their most important Committee function. Big-city Democrats, in particular, are inclined to rank committee assignments ahead of the job of molding substantive, and sometimes boring, legislation. These members may be very significant at the voting stage of the legislative process but if they prefer the Committee on Committees role to the legislative committee role, as some of them do, their influence is not likely to be felt, save as proxy votes, when the Committee marks up bills.[19]

One big-city Democrat admitted that the tedious work of Ways and Means is just not "my cup of tea." Alluding to his initial excitement over being elected to the Committee and his subsequent disillusionment he said, "For a couple of weeks you're the biggest kid on the block and then, well, I don't know." His frustration with the lack of glamor of the Committee's normal routine turned to pique when he learned that the Committee would not provide funds to make a trip: "People talk about the powerful Ways and Means Committee. . . . I can't even get a visa to go to Falls Church."

3. "On Ways and Means if you have something in your district they will scratch your back a little. On other committees they'll say, 'well, screw you.'" This Republican's statement highlights the third source of incentive for members of the Committee on Ways and Means: the relationship between membership and the satisfaction of constituent demands.

Not every member believes that he can serve his constituents better from Ways and Means than he could from any other House committee, but most members concur that being on the Committee affords opportunities to serve their constituents. Moreover, no member's career is so intimately dependent on a committee other than Ways and Means that he risks electoral defeat simply because of his committee assignment.[20]

[19] See Blau's treatment of the question of intrinsic and extrinsic attractiveness, *op. cit.*, chap. 2.

[20] Joel Broyhill (R., Va.), appointed to the Committee in 1964, was thought to be running a grave risk in leaving the District of Columbia Committee and the Post Office and Civil Service Committee because many of his Virginia constituents are government employees who work in the District. He met the issue head-on by stressing the importance and prestige of Ways and Means and he was reelected, albeit with a somewhat smaller percentage of the vote than he received in 1962. See *The Washington Post*, October 3, 1964, p. B2. He was reappointed to the District Committee in 1965 without having to yield his seat on Ways and Means, notwithstanding the general rule that membership on the latter is "exclusive." Forcing him to give up his former committees had been a key tactic used by those who tried to keep him off Ways and Means. Once on the Committee, the general rule was waived.

During the intensive bargaining surrounding the myriad parts of a major Ways and Means bill a member can often promote or protect constituent interests by supporting a position unfavorable to the administration. Clark Thompson of Texas, for instance, proved intractable on a key section of the 1964 Revenue Act and, some people believed, the inclusion of a provision desired by the Tennessee Gas Transmission Company helped win him over. Executive department representatives may even try to lure Republican support, as evidenced by the late Howard Baker's success, in getting one of his pet proposals included in the same Act.[21] "You know, you can really do things for your constituents on the Committee," one member said with glee. "Boy, if you are a horsetrader you can really move. Exports, imports, that sort of thing."

Serving constituents from Ways and Means takes many forms. One member feels that being on a top committee enhances his access to the executive agencies. "The first thing they do is check to see what committee you are on. You get more and better service. I used to get a 'no' on everything but now I get a 'yes,' or at least sympathetic understanding." He also boasted, "When I call up Social Security they know damn well who I am. If I say I want a social security office three blocks from my office it's done. And I don't kid around — I tell them!" Dan Rostenkowski (D., Ill.), a protégé of Mayor Daley and the leader of the Chicago Democrats in the House, told his constituents after his election to Ways and Means that, "It is a most interesting assignment, but more important it places me in a position whereby I can be more effective in assisting you with your needs, both personal and legislative."[22] Shortly after his election to the Committee, George M. Rhodes (D., Pa.) could take credit for two amendments to a social security bill that were of interest to his constituents.[23] And Hale Boggs (D., La.) could take credit, via a press release, for amendments to the 1967 social security bill which would bring Louisiana millions of dollars in federal medicaid payments.

Major legislation is not the only opportunity for serving one's constituency. Ways and Means also processes so-called "members' bills,"

[21] For this provision see House, Committee on Ways and Means, *Revenue Act of 1963*, 88th Cong., 1st Sess., 1963, H. Rept. 749 to accompany H.R. 8363, pp. 45–47. It allowed the exclusion from gross income of a limited amount of capital gain received from the sale or exchange of a personal residence by a person 65 years old or over.

[22] Dan Rostenkowski, "Washington Report," July 20, 1964, p. 2.

[23] George M. Rhodes, "A Report from Congressman George M. Rhodes," July 16, 1964, p. 1.

which were described by one knowledgeable staff man as the "gravy" of the Committee. Every year time is set aside for the consideration of members' bills, which are supposed to be minor, noncontroversial pieces of legislation that ameliorate the adverse or unintended impact of some small feature in the tax laws or make some "technical" improvement in the laws that come under the Committee's jurisdiction; they are regarded as "little," of no special interest to anyone other than the members who introduced them. Typical examples are bills that alter the tariff on brooms made of broom corn, provide a credit or refund of self-employment taxes in certain cases, allow the free importation of spectrometers for universities, or continue the suspension of duties on various metals.

Committee members are asked by the staff to list bills to be considered during "members' bill time." Every member may call up a bill and if he can get the unanimous consent of his colleagues the bill will be reported to the House, called up on the floor by unanimous consent or suspension of the rules, and usually passed in a few seconds by voice vote. Sometimes bills are reported out despite objections from other members, but the general attitude is, "If it doesn't affect my district or something I'm interested in, I don't object." Executive department officials are also present during these proceedings and their views are solicited, although not always followed.

After members' bill time the Chairman will call the bills up on the House floor and they will be passed by the House. On April 30, 1964, Chairman Mills called up twelve bills.[24] Eleven passed by voice vote. One bill, providing for the free importation of soluble and instant coffee, was defeated when Spark Matsunaga (D., Hawaii) objected on behalf of the Hawaiian coffee industry. Mills had also intended to call up a bill introduced by Boggs but another Committee member, Curtis, prevented it by indicating to Mills that he would object.

Of the eleven bills passed at this time, four were introduced by nonmembers of Ways and Means. Two of the remaining seven were introduced by Republican members of Ways and Means, and five by Democratic members. All were reported unanimously by the Com-

---

[24] *Congressional Record*, April 30, 1964 (daily edition), pp. 9397–9410. Mills also tried to get a joint resolution passed at this time which would have declared bourbon whiskey a distinctive product of the United States. Representative John Lindsay killed the resolution when he objected on behalf of two female constituents whose income came from a small distillery in Mexico. Sober heads prevailed and the resolution passed the House later. For additional members' bills see *Congressional Record*, May 13, 1969 (daily edition), pp. H3545–54.

mittee and most were supported actively on the floor by the Committee's ranking Republican.

A member's bill may be killed by another member of the Committee, as in the case of the Boggs bill, or it may be killed or postponed by other members of the House, as illustrated by the coffee bill. Not every member's bill becomes law. But many do.

In 1964 Committee member Curtis took upon himself the job of unofficial objector to members' bills, which did not endear him to his colleagues. Curtis felt that members' bills had gotten out of hand, and that too many were really substantive bills favoring particular interests. They were not, he claimed, merely technical improvements in the law. Curtis's objections to these bills in the executive session became so intense that the chief of staff of the Joint Committee on Internal Revenue Taxation, Dr. Laurence N. Woodworth, was deputized to go over the bills beforehand with him and discuss the merits of various proposals. The choice of Woodworth, a professional staff member whose reputation for objectivity is strong, was shrewd but evidently was not good enough. The next year Curtis brought the entire process to a halt when he stood on the House floor and objected to every unanimous consent request made by Mills.[25] At this writing members' bills are still being processed, but Curtis's action shows what can happen when just one member decides to protest against long-established procedures.

Members' bills are important bipartisan benefits of membership on the Ways and Means Committee. They are positive incentives that emanate from the Committee and help the members meet some demands they face. They are "little" favors that are often large to individual congressmen. As one more element in the mix of incentives, they help explain why the members are willing to do certain things which the Committee requires to persist as a viable subsystem of the House. How these bills are handled, resting on unanimous consent, helps solidify the social bonds of the group just as it depends upon those bonds; the exchanges that are involved in members' bills, by helping to satisfy the members' needs, buttress the commitment to the norms that govern the Committee's handling of major bills.

[25] *Congressional Record*, October 13, 1965 (daily edition), pp. 25946–47. Curtis objected to a member's bill in Committee which had negative reports from four executive agencies. When the Committee decided to report the bill over his objection he took his protest to the floor of the House, accepting, as he put it, the "oddball role" when he felt that bills lacked merit.

As important as or more important than promoting legislation is
the ability of members to protect the interests of their constituents
and friends by killing or modifying the proposals of others. To be an
effective member of Ways and Means a man need not work feverishly
to get laws passed which will benefit his clientele if he can prevent
laws that will hurt them. Committee members make sure that nothing interrupts the "normal flow of the lumber business," they "keep
oil from being used as a whipping boy" and from being "persecuted,"
they watch over the varied financial interests of big cities like New
York and the trading interests of New Orleans, they act as surrogates
for businesses that might be affected by changes in the tax and trade
laws, and so forth. Nine members (five Democrats and four Republicans) responded to a question about whether their job on Ways and
Means was more to promote or protect constituent interests. Seven
of the nine said it was both or could not say which was more important, two said protecting interests was more important than promoting
legislation, and, significantly, none put promotion ahead of protection. It appears that on the Ways and Means Committee, although
positive activity is more likely to attract attention, the negative task
of maintaining the status quo may be just as important. What never
gets through the Committee and what is never proposed to the Committee because it would have no chance of passage is as much a part
of the Committee's job as the meticulous legislative mark-up despite
the fact that one takes the Committee months and the other takes no
time at all.

Because Committee members must be reelected every two years,
and because the Committee does permit them to serve some of the
interests of their constituents,[26] it might be thought that the members would see Ways and Means as an important electoral help.
They do not. The overwhelming response of those who were asked if
the Committee helps them get reelected was that their Committee
membership is of little value in their districts.[27] Of eighteen classi-

[26] Eleven members (eight Democrats, three Republicans) said Ways and
Means was a good committee for them in terms of their constituents. Five members (two Democrats, three Republicans) gave a mixed answer, saying Ways and
Means has some value for them vis-à-vis their constituents but they tended to
discount its importance or emphasize the negative side of the Committee. One
of them said that on balance Ways and Means was a minus.

[27] The results contrast sharply, as one would expect, with the House Public
Works Committee. Most of the members of Public Works think their com-
mittee has definite electoral benefits. See James T. Murphy, "The House Public
Works Committee" (Ph.D. Dissertation, University of Rochester, 1969), chap. 4.

fiable responses to this question, four members (all Republicans) emphasized the positive contribution of the Committee to their electoral success; fourteen (ten Democrats, four Republicans) stressed the negative side either by saying Ways and Means hurt them (three said this) or by discounting the value of the Committee. All eighteen recognized that the Committee has some value in their districts, but virtually all said its value was concentrated among the "upper stratum," "sophisticates," and, most commonly, businessmen. A fairly typical response follows:

> I don't think the people in the country know the importance of it. You go up to Joe Smith who's a steamfitter or a pipefitter and tell him you're on Ways and Means and he'll look at you, say that's nice, and what else is new? Now the ones who know are the upper stratum — the bankers, the businessmen. Tell them you're on Ways and Means and they sit right up and take notice.

Thus the electoral value of membership on Ways and Means is that it allows them to do some things for their districts, it does not hurt them in their districts, and it has advantages among the well-informed, concerned elements of their constituency. The man in the street, if he knows who his congressman is, neither knows nor cares what committee he is on. Most Committee members are, in any event, from relatively safe districts before they get on Ways and Means. The Committee provides opportunities to get some things done for some constituents, but perhaps more important Committee membership is not a liability back home. On the contrary, it is a distinct asset with segments of their constituents, it has prestige-value despite the fact that most people probably do not really understand the reasons for its prestige, and may help with campaign finance, as one member observes:

> The work takes a lot of your time and Ways and Means has no political sex appeal. You may get support from the business community, financial support, it can help you here. But it's not like Armed Services or Space. It's cold. You may get financial support. The Chamber helps those who they think agree with them, the AMA helps those who agree with them, and the AFL–CIO will do the same for their members. You get financial support because they hope you would support their side in debate. They play it up in the district but I think Ways and Means has no glamor like other committees.

"Businessmen," said a Republican, "are particularly impressed with the Committee, of course." A party leader struck near the mark when he commented that, in all likelihood, members of the Ways and Means Committee have little difficulty financing their campaigns.

4. A final incentive offered by Ways and Means is the satisfaction of participating in important decisions. The breadth of the Committee's subject matter draws some men to the Committee and stimulates some after they become members; the complexity of the Committee's subject matter cuts two ways. For some it is intriguing and challenging; for others it is the most onerous aspect of Committee life.

While discussing their likes and dislikes regarding the Committee, twenty-one members referred to the Committee's subject matter. Twenty cited the Committee's jurisdiction as an important reason for their satisfaction. One member disliked Ways and Means intensely because of the complexity and detail of the subject matter. When asked why he never tried to leave the Committee he said you just never leave a "blue ribbon" committee such as Ways and Means, especially when you are the state's representative on the Committee on Committees. This man's voice is seldom heard during the executive sessions, although his attendance record is reported to be good.

Barber B. Conable, Jr., a New York Republican who was appointed to the Committee in 1967, summed up his feelings toward the Committee which are typical of other members:

> The assignment will change my work in the House of Representatives in many ways, not all of them good. I have had to give up my other committees and to curtail less important activities. The Ways and Means Committee is so demanding that I will not be able to get back to the District so often or do as much outside political work as previously. After one week on the Committee my staff already is looking startled every time I return to the office during the day.
>
> Why would I give up relative tranquility in this way to go on a tax writing committee? I can just hear some of my friends back home ask in consternation, "Why would you want to involve yourself in controversial issues like taxes and social security, Barber, when you had such interesting work before?" The answer, I suppose, lies in the excitement of participation. On the Space Committee, although non-scientific control of policy is a democratic necessity (just like civilian control of the Defense Department), I was essentially an observer of the space program.

There is something much more *central* about Ways and Means. These twenty-five men and women actually establish the tax structure for the country, and decide what the social security benefits and payroll taxes shall be. Every cent the government raises is their responsibility. The Constitution assigns to the House the initiation of all revenue bills. The traditions of Congress are such that the House Ways and Means Committee has a unique initiating role: rarely can its bills be amended on the floor, but the rest of the House has to accept or reject its suggested legislation as the Committee has drawn it. This sort of responsibility is a magnet, and most Congressmen are drawn by it if they get the chance.[28]

Contributions to the instrumental tasks of the Committee vary greatly among the members, and participation tends to be highly concentrated in a small working group of five or six members. But any member may contribute to the discussion with few constraints on what he says or how long it takes to say it. Almost without exception the members find the Committee's work interesting, though some of them take little active interest, and challenging, though some of them expend more energy meeting the challenge than others. Because the Committee meets almost interminably, even those who prefer to let others bear the major part of the responsibility for the decisions have a feeling of participation — and of having worked hard. The rare member feels no obligation to put in an appearance at notice of a Committee meeting. Members hardly may speak once they are there but by their presence they discharge the minimal obligation of Committee membership. Thus they may claim — not without justification — that considering the many demands on their time every meeting they make is some sort of contribution to the Committee.

Attendance at the long working sessions of Committee meetings creates a group feeling that Ways and Means is an unusually hard-working Committee with unusually complicated problems that demand unusual sacrifices from the members. The more the members complain about how hard they have to work on the Committee the stronger their group identity becomes. Many take pride in the Committee's hard work even though they express mixed feelings about it.

Ways and Means, in the words of a junior Democratic member, is "the best legislative committee here, the hardest committee in the House. We go all over everything with a fine tooth comb. Mills is

[28] Barber B. Conable, Jr., "Washington Report," February 8, 1967, p. 1.

excellent — every 'i' and 't,' line by line." His sense of pride in the
Committee's work was total: "No committee works like Ways and
Means. On other committees you get a proposal, hear a few witnesses, and it's are you for it or against it? Ways and Means plows
through it." Another Democrat explained why he likes the Committee and noted that one may get too wrapped up in the work, "It's a
good committee, a hard working committee. It's interesting work. In
fact, I find myself — and this is a big danger — getting all wound up
in it, getting absorbed." He then told how former Democratic chairman Jere Cooper almost was defeated because Ways and Means demanded so much time. "It's the salt mines of Congress," he said. A
Republican agreed but noted that the craftsmanship of the Committee is impressive: "Comparing Ways and Means with my other two
committees the detail with which these technical things — which can
affect the whole economy — is amazing. It's overdone sometimes, I
have to come back here and let them carry on with all the gnats, but it
is impressive." He appended the standard paradox, "And without any
partisan battles either despite the fact that of all the committees we
are the one most apt to be partisan."

"Not that you have your name on an historic piece of legislation,"
according to another Republican, "but you can throw in an idea or
two. This makes for an exciting session because you're part of it. We
are encouraged to be of some use." This touches on a feature of
paramount importance to some Committee members: the members
feel that if they participate they can affect policy. Good suggestions,
whether from Republicans or Democrats, junior members or senior
members, get a fair hearing. "Well, it's a challenge. It's my temperament, I guess. I like to be effective by working and I can change
things and shape bills in executive session. I don't like a lot of show."
This Democrat, who takes his legislative work on Ways and Means
very seriously and who is regarded as a "comer" on the Committee,
said: "I can go through a bill and point to the places where I've had
an impact, there, there, and there." "Every bill," another Democrat
said proudly, "is a *Committee* bill." No one summed up better than a
Republican, "On Ways and Means I participate, I feel I participate.
I've sat on a lot of committees and gotten smiled at." "Normally we
can reach an agreement — 99 per cent of the time, Republicans and
Democrats alike," concluded a Democrat.

The members of Ways and Means dwelt almost exclusively on the
positive inducements of membership when asked if they like the Committee. A few members qualified these inducements — most com-

monly that the Committee's rigorous schedule reduces the amount of time for other Congressional business — but compared to the rewards of membership the negative features are inconsequential.

No systematic attempt was made to either measure or classify the rewards and costs of membership on Ways and Means, but it can be concluded that one reason the Committee retains its prestige and power, one reason the members follow the basic norm of restrained partisanship, is that for virtually every member the rewards far outweigh the costs. Moreover, most or all members are aware that there is a relationship between the way the Committee works and the benefits of Committee membership. Referring to the House floor, a Democrat observed, "We're not one of these committees that you see come out here all the time and get crapped on. We do the work in the Committee." He might have added that they do the work peacefully enough and, except for general policy matters, with relatively little partisanship or friction. "In my two and one-half years on the Committee I'd say there have been only three or four occasions that developed into a shouting match, usually involving Curtis."

The fundamental reason why the members of Ways and Means have certain normative ideas to follow is because the maintenance of the specific rewards of Committee membership depends upon conformity to the norms of the Committee. The norm of restrained partisanship, in particular, sums up the distinctive character of Ways and Means and makes it a far different kind of committee than, say, Education and Labor. Acceptance of and conformance with the norms of the Committee is the members' contribution to the Committee, a contribution made as a result of the inducements associated with Committee membership.

But the analysis of the inner workings of the Committee is still far from complete. The inducement-contribution problem has been discussed as though the Committee were internally undifferentiated, except that the variable nature of contributions to the work of the Committee has been noted. Compared to larger committees that have numerous subcommittees Ways and Means is structurally homogeneous. But two sets of relationships or exchanges are peculiarly important to the problems of instrumental interaction, affective interaction, and integration. These occur between the dominant leaders of the Committee, Wilbur Mills and John Byrnes, and between senior members of the Committee and newcomers in the course of socialization into the life of the Committee.

MILLS AND BYRNES:
THE RECIPROCATION OF ESTEEM

No inexorable law guarantees leadership to the chairmen and ranking minority members of congressional committees, but in Ways and Means the formal leaders are the real leaders as well. Mills was elected to the Committee in 1942 and became chairman in 1958. Byrnes was appointed in 1947 and ascended to the ranking member's position in 1963. Their influence is not unlimited, of course, but it has been substantial; their will has not always prevailed but there has been a strong tendency on the part of members to look to them for leadership, cues, and policy direction; their influence has varied depending on issues but has been normally strong across the board. As the two most important members of Ways and Means, Mills and Byrnes have wielded more influence than anyone else.

Their positions and policy preferences limit cooperation between them and they frequently have opposed one another on key policy matters, both within the Committee and on the House floor. Byrnes, as the accepted leader of the Committee Republicans, helps to fashion a cohesive minority bloc against the Democrats, and he frequently caucuses the Republicans to hammer out a united front — occasionally with the Minority Leader and other party leaders in attendance. Party considerations, such as the connection between the kind of unemployment compensation bill passed by the House and the November elections, are important to Byrnes, and he discusses these matters with the House leadership as well as with other Republican members of Ways and Means. From 1959 to 1965 Byrnes held one of the top House Republican leadership positions as chairman of the Policy Committee.[29]

There is, however, a good deal of cooperation and mutual respect between Mills and Byrnes; both men played prominent leadership roles before assuming their formal positions. They realize that their positions may be reversed some day and they therefore cooperate on most procedural and some substantive matters.[30] In addition to jointly

[29] For a discussion of Byrnes as a party leader see Charles O. Jones, *Party and Policy-Making: The House Republican Policy Committee* (New Brunswick, N.J.: Rutgers University Press, 1964), *passim*.

[30] For example, late in 1967 the Committee was going to have closed hearings on the tax surcharge issue. Byrnes called Mills in Arkansas, pointed out to him the advantages of open hearings for protecting the Committee from administration press releases, and was told by the Chairman to call the Committee Clerk

sponsoring some bills, usually of a noncontroversial variety, they have collaborated on certain kinds of bills on the House floor. Major bills reported to the floor of the House by Ways and Means are often the quintessence of party conflict in the House. But the easy fraternization between Mills and Byrnes even at the height of floor battles indicates the spirit with which the Committee has performed its day-to-day labors and which allows Mills to cross the aisle occasionally and ask Byrnes to round up some Republican votes.

One former staff member described the two men:

> Mills calls the shots, he runs the show. If a member would like a Committee meeting next Monday, for example, he'd have to get Mills to call it. Every once in a while Mills is questioned about hearings and witnesses but he's very good about it. He discusses these things with Byrnes. The hearings last fall [1963] on beer concentrate were Byrnes's doing. He wanted them so he and Mills arranged a date. It's quite informal. Mills and Byrnes are good friends.

He pointed out that both men have the Committee in common: "Both are dedicated and have no outside life — no hobbies, never take vacations. The Committee is their life. They take work home. They remind me of guys working in a factory who punch in and out, go home and wait for the next work day to begin."

This assessment is undoubtedly exaggerated. Byrnes, at least, plays golf from time to time. But the Committee is quite literally a large part of their lives. Many years ago both men, Mills with a law degree from Harvard, Byrnes with a law degree from the University of Wisconsin, began careers on the Ways and Means Committee. The Committee defines their major legislative tasks in the House and Committee business occupies most of their time; their identification with the Committee in their own eyes and by other members of the House is complete. Their current relationship is the product of years of evolution and accommodation and while they may not be intimate friends — both are rather aloof personalities — the reciprocation of esteem between them is a powerful factor governing their interaction. They disagree, as a more revealing House cliche goes, without being disagreeable, and the tone of their relationship permeates the Committee. Other members come and go but Mills and Byrnes have sat

---

and make the hearings open. Byrnes did and the witnesses were heard in public. See also the 1964 Social Security amendments, *Congressional Record*, July 29, 1964 (daily edition), p. 16680.

through endless hours of executive and public sessions, sometimes
breaking the tedium with a whispered pleasantry or muffled discussion of future Committee business. They often arrive at different conclusions but transitory conflicts do not shatter the basic bonds that
tie them together. They get along not by avoiding controversy but by
transforming the controversy itself, articulated and resolved under the
norms governing the clean fight, into an integrative force. This relationship, enlivened by the excitement of trying to outwit each other,
explains a good deal about the Ways and Means Committee. Asked if
Ways and Means is a partisan committee, a Democrat replied, "Hell
no. Mills and Byrnes — *close*." In all interviews conducted for this
study not one person expressed a different opinion; the great majority,
in fact, agreed that Mills and Byrnes get along very well. They get
along so well and have so much respect for one another that on different occasions each man has taken steps to help the other in his campaign for reelection.

Their personal relationship does not prevent strong disagreements
over particular policies. Nor does it remove all conflict from the
Committee. But it has reinforced the norm of restrained partisanship
on the kind of work expected of Ways and Means, and it has led to
some minor criticism of Byrnes for not being as partisan as someone
in his position should be. Their friendship and cooperation are, to
them, an important part of being full-time, professional members of
the Ways and Means Committee, and through the reciprocation of
esteem a lifetime of service on the Committee is made more than
tolerable. It is made rewarding.

SOCIALIZATION: PERPETUATION OF
NORMS THROUGH EXCHANGE

In keeping with the exchange focus of this chapter, socialization is
defined as a dynamic process through which a group, by rewarding
certain kinds of behavior and sanctioning other kinds of behavior,
perpetuates its norms, values, and roles. Although socialization is
often restricted to new members of the group, as it is here, it is a
two-part process involving experienced members as well. To the newcomer socialization involves exposure to and inculcation of the norms
and values of the group. In essence, this is an exchange in which the
newcomer is explicitly taught (or absorbs on his own) that his interests are best served by accepting and conforming to the prevailing
behavior patterns of the group. To the experienced or "socialized"

member of the group the socialization process involves his activities as a socializing agent, as is often stressed, but it also involves exchanges that maintain his allegiance to group norms. Groups face the problem of socializing newcomers but they also face the problem of socialization maintenance, i.e., of continuing to reward members for particular contributions long after their initiation to the group. A breakdown in socialization or in socialization maintenance may lead to disintegration of the group, changes in its internal relations, and, unless checked, the destruction of group solidarity.[31]

The socialization process is characterized as dynamic in this definition to introduce the notion that the content of what is passed on to newcomers and espoused by experienced members may change with new problems and demands on the group. As discussed in Chapter Five, the Ways and Means Committee has not always been the same kind of group that it is today. The Committee in the 1930's, in fact, closely resembled the Education and Labor Committee of the early 1960's in its internal operations, and although the present patterns of behavior in Ways and Means have been maintained for some years there is no assurance that the Committee will not change in its management of internal conflict.

The newcomer to Ways and Means must persuade the other members that he is a valuable member of the group to whom they should respond favorably. He does this, as Blau and others have noted, by impressing them with his conformity to the norms of the group. He does not speak at first, even when given the opportunity, or if he does participate right away he prefaces his remarks with self-deprecating comments like "as a new member. . . ." He defers to the senior members hoping that they will in turn accept him into their company. He flatters their egos and praises their expertise while struggling gamely with complexities they understand (or at least hints that he knows they understand them). He thanks the chairman for his magnanimity in allowing him time to speak even though he realizes that what he has to say may not make much sense, and when finished with his brief remarks he thanks the members for bearing with him in the trying first days they all remember. All this is done, if the newcomer is skillful at interpersonal relations, without a trace of obsequiousness and with the casual shrewdness of the "nice guy." The new member may have to disagree with his more senior colleagues early in his career on the Committee but the norms allow for

---

[31] For Parsons' treatment of socialization and social control see Parsons and Shils, eds., *op. cit.*, pp. 227–30.

this. Indeed, by disagreeing he may impress them with the independence of his judgment and convince them that he is no mere rubber stamp. If he manifests this disagreement in accepted ways (for example, without tongue-lashing the Committee on the House floor), his reputation in the group is enhanced. The newcomer does all of these things until he finds himself being courted by some new Committee member, at which point he, having been absorbed into the group, becomes a socializing agent with rewards and sanctions to apply to the new man. The norms and values of the group are passed on over the years through this process, which in stable or integrated groups takes place in a matter-of-fact way.

One interesting aspect of the socialization process is the extent to which it is self-imposed by the new members of the Committee. Freshly assigned members have been entering new groups and adjusting to new situations all their lives and know intuitively how to get along and be effective. They may not always follow the norms surrounding the behavior of newcomers, but no one has to tell them to take a back seat at first, be respectful of the more experienced members, and attempt to convince the others that they are attractive. One freshman Democrat said, "I know what I should do: keep my mouth shut. That Committee won't hear much from me for a while." "As a new member," a freshman Republican stated, "I am going to be content to sit back until I get familiar with the subject and feel at home." Another newly appointed Republican said that he would advise a newcomer to keep his mouth shut until he knew what he was talking about. "If I tried to talk a lot it would be resented, while it wouldn't be for an older member."

The norm of reticence that newcomers impose upon themselves does not mean that they cannot and do not participate in the first few weeks of their apprentice period. Junior members are neither muzzled nor immobilized; they exist in a state of animated quiescence until they have absorbed enough information to make meaningful contributions to the policy discussion. To be effective members they must appear to know what they are talking about; and this takes time on a committee like Ways and Means with its difficult issues and formidable revenue jargon. One experienced member recalled: "When I first went on the Committee I used to leave the meetings with a headache, truly a headache! The stuff was just over my head. I just kept plugging along and gradually you catch on." "Detail and technical," another veteran exclaimed, "oh, there's so much detail and it's so technical! You have to take work home and study. Everything is complicated now. Social security has become complicated, tax and tariff too."

During the apprentice period, Committee members are expected to "attend religiously, study hard, and pay attention to what the experts are saying." To become influential Committee members they must "get their lessons up." "The first thing is to sit down and keep your mouth shut. There's always an expert around and you shouldn't speak about something until you are really expert."

One committee member remembered his period of apprenticeship:

> I was sitting there one day not knowing what the —— was going on. Title 19, title 18. You sit there trying to look smart and I really felt phony. I remarked to the Chairman that this was calculus and I hadn't had arithmetic yet. He told me, "It'll come, it was the same way when I went on. What I did was go back to the original law and read up." But that takes hours of study — years! I've got all those books there, haven't opened a —— one.

During the apprentice period they are told by Byrnes: "If you want to be right 100 per cent of the time vote with the Chairman 95 per cent because that's what I do."

As a consequence of these norms and expectations, the newcomer tends to look to the senior men for leadership. "Effectiveness increases as you go up the seniority ladder and decreases as you go down it. The senior members are the most effective because they have been around the longest and know the most about the Code." Although there is no guarantee that seniority and experience will make one an effective member (of one senior man a member said, "If you want to know what a member of the Committee should *not* do look at what —— does"), a Democrat concurred:

> Leadership is pretty constant. The men who sit at the head of the table naturally lead the Committee. They are knowledgeable and have been around a long time. It's the same in any group, the Rotary or the Baptist Church. Some men are just natural leaders. Now that doesn't mean that if I have a question I can't get my oar in. There's no problem about that. But leadership is as you go up the ladder.

Then, with a smile, he concluded that "neither Rhodes nor I will

ever be fireballs on the Committee — we are too old." To quote two
more members, the first a Democrat, the second a Republican:

> Jennings is a smart member and Martha Griffiths shows a
> lot of potential. But we are all learners and beginners, the
> older members are the ones we listen to. . . .
> Byrnes and Curtis are real students, are experienced, and
> know more about it. They *should* lead the Committee. Yes-
> terday, for example, I could have spoken on the Renegotia-
> tion Act but I am quite content to let Byrnes and Curtis
> handle it. They are the experts.

Thus, the behavior of new members during the apprentice period
is partially controlled by the difficulty of rapidly accumulating expertise in the Committee's subject matter. They are exposed to the
norms of the group; they soon detect the Committee's leaders; and
they learn how to become effective members. Effectiveness, of course,
is relative, and some members never become truly influential with
their colleagues, although they may think they are. For those who
want to become influential members of Ways and Means — some
members decide that the costs of influence outweigh the rewards —
the norms that regulate the behavior of the new member and the
experienced member are clear.

SPECIALIZATION. Unlike the House Appropriations Committee,
which does its job through specialized subcommittees, there is no
norm of specialization on Ways and Means. The apprentice period
on Ways and Means also appears to be somewhat different from that
on Appropriations.[32]
Seventeen members commented on what a new member of the
Committee should do to become an effective member, and fourteen
(seven of each party) rejected specialization. This does not mean
that members of the Committee never develop special expertise in
particular areas of the Committee's subject matter. Nor does it mean
that a member cannot specialize if he wants to. If he does specialize
he may well exert considerable influence on some matters. It does
mean that, in keeping with the organizational structure of the Committee, the division of labor on the Committee is not spelled out in
any detail. The members see themselves as generalists and their job
as understanding an assortment of topics. Decision-making in Ways
and Means, is, therefore, much more dispersed than other committees

---

[32] Fenno, *Power of the Purse, op. cit.,* pp. 130–36, 166–67.

in that all members have the same opportunities for developing general expertise, but it is also much more centralized than other committees because equal opportunities coupled with unequal abilities evoke unequal contributions. As a result, a handful of members exert a disproportionate share of influence over the decisions which the Committee makes.

Because the Committee is run in such a way that any member with something to contribute may participate, the newcomer who takes his work seriously may participate right away. He is expected to familiarize himself with the questions before the Committee, which normally means a period in which he listens and studies more than he participates. Too, it is extremely unwise for the new member to show his ignorance too often, and it may be disastrous for him to speak in a knowledgeable tone and have it demonstrated that he really does not know what he is talking about. "We had a new member who came on the Committee and right away started asking too many questions and using too much time. You lose your effectiveness that way and after a while people will get up to leave and won't listen." "Avoid the thing," a senior Democrat said, "that I am always afraid of — looking foolish." "He can participate but if he's wise he'll comment only if he knows what he's talking about. He'd better not show his ignorance." A Democrat recalled his strategy as a newcomer:

> I did not participate in my first two years at all, in public hearings. I'd sit beside an older member and question him. If he didn't know, chances are he'd ask the witness. You know I'm pretty far down that table and by the time they come to me most of the questions have been asked. You've seen how Mills operates. First he takes the senior Democrat, then the Republican. We don't have any time limit. If we operated under a five-minute rule why then. . . . But it'd be stupid for me to ask the same questions all over again. I made it a point to go and talk to all of the older members, have a chat.

Still, it is legitimate and easy for a newcomer to participate if he has something to say and enough self-confidence to say it. One newcomer, a Republican, downplayed the apprentice role almost completely, "Mills is more interested in substance than who you are." In public hearings most of the good questions may be gone by the time they get to the junior members, but in executive sessions the process is more fluid. Of the new Republican who feels comfortable participating right away, an HEW staff man said, "He had a disproportionate influence from what you'd expect from a freshman Republican.

He's intelligent, doesn't talk all the time, but when he does his questions are very well received. . . . You can go through the bill and pick out four or five places that are [his]. Not major, but some weren't so minor."

Thus the early weeks on the Committee for a newcomer are days in which he observes how the Committee works. He learns that the Committee is quite informal and when he wants to speak he can. He also learns that unrestrained partisanship is as out of place as unrestrained personal attacks on other members. If he does not know beforehand, he soon learns who the effective members of the Committee are and what makes them effective. It is much better to learn the norms than to have them taught but if he has difficulty learning he may be told, as the senior Republican told a junior colleague, that he is destroying his effectiveness by being too adamant. The newcomer need not heed the warning nor be intimidated by explicit sanctions but, given the nature of the recruitment process, he is likely to be predisposed to follow the Committee norms. He is, after all, highly attracted to the group and it is unlikely that he will turn his back on those norms that determine the rewards of his membership.

In addition, the newcomer on Ways and Means sees members who work well together, who share a consensus on what the Committee should be like, who are very satisfied with the Committee as it is, and who feel that the best way to get and keep the rewards of membership is to operate as they do.

It is doubtful if any amount of incentives or any number of years' experience on the Committee could result in policy agreement between such dedicated conservatives as James Utt of California (Utt's office had a sign on a secretary's desk reading "Repeal the Income Tax") and such Democrats as former socialist George Rhodes who fondly recalls his youthful association with Aneurin Bevan and Jennie Lee, but agreement on broad policy is not necessary on Ways and Means. It is not even expected. The members are expected to cooperate to write technically sound bills, to air their disagreements in a way that does not detract from the Committee's standing in the House, and to show a decent respect for those with whom they disagree.

Coming to the Committee with, in Newcomb's words, "reward-associated attitudes," [33] Ways and Means members generally find

[33] Theodore M. Newcomb, "Varieties of Interpersonal Attraction," *Group Dynamics: Research and Theory*, ed. Dorwin Cartwright and Alvin Zander (Evanston, Ill.: Row, Peterson, 1960), p. 105.

that the group is pleasant to belong to, the Democrats find that even if they don't like the legislative business of Ways and Means the committee assignment function is important, all members can realize a number of pragmatic goals through the Committee, and some members actually get caught up in the intricacies of the Committee's subject matter. Moreover, the members derive great psychological satisfaction from membership on what is widely regarded as the top committee in the House. One Democrat who initially found the Committee disappointing was, when last seen, getting a little more interested in the work than before. And, anyway, as he put it, "Does a man enjoy a Cadillac? Suppose a guy has a Cadillac and a Ford. He likes the Ford but in the Cadillac you drive up to a hotel and they open the door."

CHAPTER FOUR

Wilbur D. Mills

> All leaders are also led; in innumerable cases, the
> master is the slave of his slaves. Said one of the
> greatest German party leaders referring to his
> followers: "I am their leader, therefore I must
> follow them."
>
> Georg Simmel [1]

Political scientists studying Congress have shown the same disinclination for the study of individual leaders as that of the profession as a whole. Whatever the reasons for avoiding an analysis of social and political processes from the perspective of an individual — and there are several good ones [2] — it is difficult to ignore, if not to discount, the extreme emphasis placed on personalities by experienced participants and observers of the congressional process. One may decide, with Fenno, to underplay references to specific individuals in an effort "to show how much generalization is possible short of a heavy reliance on personality data." [3] But those closest to the legislative process do see it in terms of individuals and personalities and, more impor-

---

Much of this chapter appeared in John F. Manley, "Wilbur D. Mills: A Study in Congressional Influence," *American Political Science Review,* LXII (June, 1969), 442–64.

[1] "On Superordination and Subordination," *Theories of Society,* ed. Talcott Parsons, Edward Shils, Kasper D. Naegele, Jesse R. Pitts (New York: Free Press, 1965), p. 542.

[2] Edinger discusses many of them. See Lewis J. Edinger, "Political Science and Political Biography: Reflections on the Study of Leadership (I)," *Journal of Politics* XXVI (May, 1964), 423–39. Among other reasons, social and economic conditions may be more important than individual leaders, the group-oriented concern of political science which may downplay individuals, the difficulties facing empirical research on leaders, and the variety of personalities which makes generalization difficult.

[3] Richard F. Fenno, Jr., *The Power of the Purse* (Boston: Little, Brown, 1966), p. xxiii.

tant, much can be learned, as evidenced by Huitt's work, by focusing on individual legislators and the contexts within which they function.[4] Whether it is Lyndon Johnson as Senate Majority Leader searching for the man who is the "key" to a particular bill, the differences between a Rayburn and a McCormack, the skill of a Judge Smith, or the Ways and Means Republican who said, "I think a book on the Ways and Means Committee would have to be a book on Wilbur Mills," strong reasons exist for looking at individuals as they operate in the legislative process. Making one man the centerpiece of a study of the Ways and Means Committee might seriously exaggerate his importance, especially if a developmental perspective on the Committee is sought, but the centrality of Mills in the public mind and to the Committee makes imperative an analysis of his relationship to the Committee.

Political scientists have shied away from individual or personality-centered studies of Congress because, first, the extreme variability of personalities stands as a barrier to generalization, and, second, it is hard to say how much of the legislative process is due to individuals and how much is due to the situational factors that affect them. Confronted by these old problems, the understandable tendency is to downplay individuals and personalities and, implicitly or explicitly, to treat the situation and the group as the primary determinants of behavior. Homans, however, warns about Durkheim's social mold theory (which overemphasized the influence of society on individuals): "Intellectually the descent into hell is easy. One false step, and logic will do the rest."[5]

Durkheim erred, according to Homans, because he thought of the individual-society dichotomy as cause and effect, not as mutual dependence.[6] Norms are the result of human interaction, but they may also be the cause of such interaction if, once established, they govern future behavior. The same kind of mutual dependence exists between individual leaders and the group. "Neither individual character structure nor the contextual configuration alone," Edinger writes, "can explain a leader's behavior, but careful analysis of their interaction —

[4] Ralph K. Huitt, "The Morse Committee Assignment Controversy: A Study in Senate Norms," *American Political Science Review*, LI (June, 1957), 313–29; "Democratic Party Leadership in the Senate," *American Political Science Review*, LV (June, 1961), 333–44; "The Outsider in the Senate: An Alternative Role," *American Political Science Review*, LV (September, 1961), 566–74.

[5] George C. Homans, *The Human Group* (New York: Harcourt, Brace & World, 1950), p. 318.

[6] *Ibid.*, p. 319.

in as many instances as possible, may reveal certain patterns and facilitate understanding." [7]

Thus, for certain analytical purposes, one may take either a group-sociological or an individual-personality approach to the study of Congress, but the two approaches may also be treated as complementary. Indeed, in the Ways and Means Committee, Mills stands out as one of the most influential committee chairmen in recent years, if not in history, and, like all leaders, he also follows. The paradox of leadership is that it always involves followmanship, and a leading House liberal once said of Mills, "He's an expert in followmanship." [8] The group that forms the base of his influence in the House and that he is most likely to follow is the Committee.

Mills's leadership is conceived not according to the traits he possesses that enable him to lead others, a view of leadership that has been rejected for many years,[9] but as a function of his relationship to his colleagues on the Committee. "There can be no leadership," as Gibb says, "in isolation, it is distinctly a quality of a group situation." [10] Our interest is in Mills as he interacts with the Committee, which, although it does not omit personality traits, does tend to stress the group-sociological side of leadership. A balance is sought and, it is hoped, achieved, between Mills as an individual leader and the nature of the group he leads, but the approach to the former is primarily through the ways in which Mills is seen by the rest of the Committee: their perceptions of his leadership, what they like and dislike about the way in which he runs the Committee, the scope and limitations of his leadership as they see it, why they respond to him in certain ways, and how it is that he is allowed to exert influence on them. More than lip service is paid to the complementarity between the individual-personality view of leadership and the group-sociological view, and much will be said about the way in which Mills sees things

[7] *Op. cit.*, p. 437.

[8] Quoted in Julius Duscha, "The Most Important Man on Capitol Hill Today," *The New York Times Magazine*, February 25, 1968, p. 78.

[9] Seligman wrote one of the obituaries in 1950. See Lester G. Seligman, "The Study of Political Leadership," *American Political Science Review*, XLIV (December, 1950), 912–14.

[10] Cecil A. Gibb, "The Principles and Traits of Leadership," *Small Groups: Studies in Social Interaction*, ed. A. Paul Hare, Edgar F. Borgatta, and Robert F. Bales (New York: Alfred A. Knopf, 1955), p. 91. Likert comments: *"To be effective and to communicate as intended, a leader must always adapt his behavior to take into account the expectations, values, and interpersonal skills of those with whom he is interacting."* Rensis Likert, *New Patterns of Management* (New York: McGraw-Hill, 1961), p. 95 (italics his).

and the reasons why he acts as he does, but more emphasis will be placed on his relationship with the Committee members than in attempting to ascertain the psychological reasons why he behaves as he does. The justifications for this emphasis are the conception of leadership just discussed and because much better data have been collected on Mills vis-à-vis the Committee members than on Mills the inscrutable personality who intrigues and frustrates those in Washington whose view is restricted to him as a particular kind of individual.[11]

MILLS AS INSTRUMENTAL AND AFFECTIVE LEADER

It is well known that studies of small groups commonly report a tendency for two types of leaders to function in groups: the instrumental or task-oriented leader and the socioemotional or affective leader.[12] Instrumental leaders are primarily concerned with realizing the goals of the group and directing the group toward the completion of its tasks. Task-oriented direction may give rise, however, to intragroup conflict and disintegrative pressures, creating a need for some way to relieve tension. The affective leader helps to cool the internal tensions and to stimulate a harmonious working atmosphere. Theoretically, the activities of the two leaders complement each other and the stable group achieves a state of equilibrium internally and in relation to its environment. Experiments with small groups have found that one man may perform both task and maintenance functions, but by and large the opposing requirements of these functions lead to a division of labor within the group.

Initial research on the Ways and Means Committee led to no evidence that the task and affective leadership functions were separated in the Committee; in fact, the evidence seemed to show that Mills was responsible for guiding the Committee's task efforts and that he was the main reason why the affective tone of the Committee was high. To test this hypothesis the members were asked two questions:

1. When you come to particularly difficult problems, does any

[11] A reporter who is very close to Mills and has studied him for ten years once observed to me, "I know Wilbur Mills better than anyone in this town, and I don't know him at all."

[12] Robert F. Bales and Philip E. Slater, "Role Differentiation in Small Decision-Making Groups," *Family, Socialization and Interaction Process*, in Talcott Parsons, et al. (London: Routledge & Kegan Paul, 1956), pp. 279–306. See also Philip E. Slater, "Role Differentiation in Small Groups," in Hare, Borgatta and Bales, eds., *op. cit.*, pp. 498–515.

member of the Committee stand out as being the one who most often comes up with a way out?

2. During the course of discussing legislation things can get rather tense from time to time. I know that this happens even in Ways and Means at times. Does anyone stand out as the peacemaker in these situations?

Table 4.1 categorizes the responses to these questions by party. The results on the task leadership question show a greater tendency among Democrats to assign this function to Mills than the Republicans. For the Republicans, Mills and Byrnes, together and in that order, are the instrumental leaders in the sense posed by the question. The results on the affective leadership question are more mixed but again Mills is more often seen as the man who stands out for Republicans and Democrats alike. Although the data are more suggestive than conclusive, the Republicans were more inclined to cite Mills as the affective leader by himself, while they linked Mills and Byrnes as the instrumental leaders.

A few members of the Committee mentioned others than Mills and Byrnes on these questions, but the overwhelming response put Mills in a class by himself, with Byrnes the runner-up. One Democrat nominated himself as the affective leader but no one seconded the nomination. Some members used the questions to talk favorably about others on the Committee, but the only qualifications on the data are that one Republican put Curtis in the task leadership category behind Mills and Byrnes, another Republican said Mills and John Watts were peacemakers, and a Democrat gave Watts some credit for task leadership. One Democrat and one Republican said

TABLE 4.1

TASK AND SOCIOEMOTIONAL LEADERSHIP IN THE
WAYS AND MEANS COMMITTEE

| | TASK LEADERSHIP | | | |
	Mills	Mills and Byrnes	No one stands out	Other and no response
Democrats	9	2	2	0
Republicans	1	4	2	0
	SOCIOEMOTIONAL LEADERSHIP			
Democrats	6	2	1	3
Republicans	4	1	1	1

there had been no tension in the Committee since they became members, and one Democrat replied that it is always tense right up to the vote. These responses are classified in the last category. The six respondents in the third category said that no one stands out as either task or affective leader because several members may perform these functions in the Committee.

These results must be greatly qualified because the complexity of leadership in the Committee far transcends the power of dichotomous questions. These questions, though useful as a starting point, are fairly crude ways of tapping general perceptions of leadership. Suggesting ways out of difficult problems, for example, is only one form of task leadership, and perhaps not the most important form at that. Acting as the peacemaker in tense situations is only one form of affective leadership, and it is probably more important to Mills's leadership that the mark of the meetings is the absence of tension, not its relaxation. Table 4.1 is more interesting for the questions it raises than for the finding that one man is seen as both instrumental and affective leader of the Committee.

The table does not show that although the members were willing to name Mills as the task and affective leader of the Committee, many members qualified their answers by commenting that the senior leaders are the dominant figures on the Committee but any member is free to participate and contribute. Leadership is both more diffuse in the Committee than the task-affective dichotomy implies, and there is a relationship between affective relations in the Committee and the way Mills performs the taskmaster function. Task leadership, in short, is more collegial in the members' eyes than the conspicuousness of Mills in the public eye might lead one to expect, and because this is true Mills also rates high as the affective leader of the Committee.

Such a finding should not be altogether unexpected. Because leadership functions are separated in some groups is no reason why they cannot be joined in others. There is no reason why the primary instrumental leader of the group cannot guide the group in performing its tasks so that he is the main reason why the job gets done, and without much tension. As Thibaut and Kelley commented:

> The dichotomous separation of task and maintenance roles may not be necessary under all conditions. If . . . there are clear norms as to what each person should do on the common task and when he should do it, instigation to conform to these norms may come from many members, and no per-

son will need to generate much hostility toward himself if he uses the norm. . . . This is an important part of the pattern of behavior referred to as "democratic" leadership. The democratic leader encourages the members to influence one another in their work on the task. . . . By group decision and participation procedures, he attempts to distribute many of the task functions among the membership at large, and in this manner is enabled to perform a maintenance role himself.[13]

Mills is a democratic committee chairman par excellence. In this way, he guides the Committee on tasks and maintains good affective relations in the process.

Seen in this light, the observation that Mills is a consensus-seeker, which is made by almost everyone who has ever looked at the contemporary Committee, takes on theoretical interest. Mills's search for a consensus in the Committee means that he is a democratic chairman of the Committee, a task leader who encourages the members to influence one another, who shares the quest for solutions with the members even though at the end of the process he may articulate and legitimate the conclusion they reach together, and a leader who directs the members along lines he may favor but who does not attempt to force his predilections on others. Mills's task leadership of the Committee, subtle and indirect, is an important source of the high esteem in which he is held by the members and helps explain why the members like the Committee as well as they do.

Several members (six Republicans, three Democrats) touched on this while discussing who suggests solutions to the Committee's substantive problems, but no one put it better than a Republican:

I don't really understand our mark-up . . . . Many times we don't have a bill. The first two-thirds is like a rudderless ship, flopping all over, anyone brings up anything on his mind. The drafters are right there, we never draft anything, they take their notes and write it up. Mills will say, "Well, I guess we can agree on this, draft it up." He gives direction, yes, but anyone can jump in. He's quick to see an idea that will have appeal in the House.

[13] John W. Thibaut and Harold H. Kelley, *The Social Psychology of Groups* (New York: John Wiley, 1959), p. 282. See also Verba's observation that in ongoing groups the development of a legitimate leadership structure replaces dual leadership. Sidney Verba, *Small Groups and Political Behavior* (Princeton: Princeton University Press, 1961), p. 171.

This metaphor recalls the comment of a Democrat in an early interview. He grew impatient with questions about leadership in the Committee and finally blurted out, "I think you are putting something in the Committee which just is not there. We don't have any leaders. It's more of an amalgamated mess." When the members say that the Committee is like a rudderless ship, loosely directed by the Chairman, or an amalgamated mess, with Mills responsible for whatever amalgamation there is, they simply express the feeling that the hand of leadership weighs lightly on them in the Committee. "When you get to the nut-cracking stage it's Mills and Byrnes. But we all participate. I do. Less than they, but if I have something to contribute, or if anyone else does, there's no problem." A Republican concurred, "I'd say the final legislation is never very far from the way Mills wanted to go, the general direction. He consults with Byrnes: 'Here we have a piece of legislation, where do we go?' They decide the general direction. Now when we get into the Committee there is general participation. A number of us give suggestions." "If the members start from points apart," a Democrat summed up, "he [Mills] puts them together to points similar. But I'd say it's *one* committee with a head."

That the members of Ways and Means tend to blur the distinction between Mills's task leadership and his affective leadership within the Committee is evident from the last-quoted Democrat. He was answering, interestingly enough, the peacemaker question, not the problem-solving question, and he depicted Mills as the peacemaker because the Chairman brings the members together on substantive issues. The close relationship between the two leadership functions became even clearer when the members talked about Mills's general style of leadership. When left free to discuss leadership and conflict in the Committee as they pleased, most of them spoke favorably of Mills's consensus-seeking style and many of them linked it in a causal way to the quality of relations among the members.

Consensus-seeking in Ways and Means is the hallmark of the decision-making process. It involves, necessarily, a willingness to bargain and compromise on the part of the Chairman, and many of the bargains and compromises are made with the Republican members of the Committee in full participation. As the Chairman, Mills decides what kinds of constraints to place on participation in public and in executive sessions, and his constraints are loose and informal. Not all of the Republicans participate at great length in the Committee's deliberations, but they know that when they want to be heard Mills will allow them ample time. By running the Committee in a democratic way Mills has earned the universal and complete approval of the Republicans for his fairness. He may not get their votes on big issues but he certainly gets their appreciation.

Mills's attitude toward the Republicans is reflected in the widely held views of one senior Republican: "I think the major reason things don't disintegrate is Mills. Chairman Mills is very fair and reasonable. I can visualize disintegration and bickering if some of the members now ever become chairman, quite frankly, but all the time I've been on the Committee the chairmen have been reasonable men."

Procedural fairness, of course, need not be accompanied by consensus decision-making, but with Mills it is. To reach a consensus in the Committee the Chairman will compromise, bargain, cajole, swap, bend, plead, amend, coax, and unite until as much of the controversy as possible is drained from the bill, and as many members of the Committee as possible support it. "Mills, although he may feel strongly about things, is not by nature an uncompromising man, you know, even on some principles he may have. . . . He likes to be a leader, to be in front of the troops, and if he sees that the troops are ahead of him then he'll circle around and make sure that he gets out in front again." Other Republicans say that if Mills "finds out my backers have a lot of votes, he'll give in, he'll compromise," "he encourages you to participate and the first 95 per cent of the approach is nonpartisan," "our committee is a little unique in that we have a chairman who doesn't let the political dominate," and:

> If we had a partisan chairman the Committee could become partisan overnight. In some ways, for political purposes, it might be better to have a partisan chairman. This would unite the minority, we could come out with our political position, and perhaps get some votes in the next election. But I don't think on our committee it should be like that.

Republican appreciation for the way Mills runs the Committee probably is heightened by their awareness that there is no absolute necessity for Mills to treat them well. In fact, a few commented: "Some committee chairmen just use their authority and ram things through. Wilbur won't do this." A second Republican refuted an erroneous popular image of the Chairman that he felt was promulgated by the newspapers:

> Although consensus is a bad term since Johnson screwed it up, he is a consensus-seeker. He never pushes things to votes,

we reach a compromise. Nothing bothers me more than to
read, as you do in the newspapers, that he's an authoritarian
— the "little authoritarian from Kensett, Arkansas." That's
not it, he's no authoritarian. The reason the tax bill is not
going through is because they have to cut expenditures. . . .
It's not that Mills is a dictator, the newspapers are all wrong.

A third Republican put the matter strongly: "Anyone who has ever
been on another committee appreciates the way Mills conducts Ways
and Means. There's almost a reverence among the members about
him because they know how it is on other committees."

Democratic members of Ways and Means are no less unanimous
in their agreement on Mills's fairness, the considerate way he treats
all members, and that, above all, he directs the Committee's task
operations with consensus uppermost in mind. Few members of
either party would disagree with the Democrat who said, "He's eva-
sive, aloof, coy, and he's not a stern oak that stands in the wind and
splits rather than bends. He'll bend in the wind." As for sensing the
strength of the winds, another Democrat expressed a common view,
"He has developed the ability, if two sides are opposed on some
issue, to sense what may bring them together in an acceptable compromise." "He *leads* the Committee, he doesn't *drive* it," summarized
the general view of the way Mills runs the Committee, as did the
comment that the Chairman has enough skill as a leader to "retreat
with dignity." "He counts the heads in the Committee and he counts
the heads in the House, he's always counting." And, while counting,
he is compromising. Questions about Mills drew the inevitable comparison, "Now you take Education and Labor, they never try for a
consensus, they battle it out. But on Ways and Means we try to reach
a consensus. . . . He always seeks a consensus and he's a genius at
getting one on complex problems."

If, as one Democrat said, "Mills loves harmony," and will sometimes "abandon his position" to get it, it is also true, as another
Democrat said, that the search for harmony is not the easiest way to
proceed: "It's long, hard, tedious work, but he seeks a consensus." In
the course of this work the Chairman, aided by the general consensus
on the norm of restrained partisanship, guides but does not continu-
ally dominate the Committee's discussion. He does participate more
than other members but much of his participation involves commenting on the comments of others, raising searching questions if not
objections about various ideas, and, most important, stepping in to
legitimize a position that the active members have arrived at under

his guidance, not under his urging. This kind of leadership requires
a flexible approach to controversies and an inclination to accommo-
date the opposing views of the members. An HEW official comments:

> Mills is an eminently successful opportunist. He does not an-
> nounce his position and force it through. He sits and listens
> to the members and knows what will go. I'd say 80 per cent
> of it is consensus, 20 per cent Mills, but certainly not 50 per
> cent Mills.

It could be argued, of course, that this is not real leadership, that
all Mills does is sense what the members will accept, fix his position
accordingly, and take a firm stand in favor of a sure thing. But this
interpretation — which is sometimes made — seriously distorts a complex form of leadership because it does not conform to a simplified
model of what leadership should be: getting other people to accept
one's position. Leadership, as Simmel says, always involves a certain
amount of followmanship. On this point, Gouldner argues that one
of the most important elements of leadership is the ability to legitimate decisions:

> It is not . . . the individual who first develops an idea or
> makes a suggestion (not the man "ahead of his time") who
> is necessarily a leader, in the sense proposed. The leader
> would be, rather, that individual who is able by his support or
> espousement of the proposal to legitimate it. He transforms it
> into something to which group members are obliged to orient
> themselves.[14]

Gouldner's description of legitimacy is precisely the kind of leadership Mills exercises in the Ways and Means Committee. Simply
because it does not involve early commitments on proposals and a
herculean effort to convince others of the soundness of his position is
no reason to discount the importance of Mills's style of leadership for
the policy decisions made by the Committee.

Perhaps the major obstacle to easy and unqualified generalizations
about the scope of Mills's leadership is that one of the prerequisites
for consensus-seeking leadership is the ability not only to be flexible
on policy but to keep one's position unclear to others. On many issues
Mills is inscrutable to the members: they don't know if he has a position or, if he does, what it is. A Democrat praised Mills: "I always

14 Alvin W. Gouldner, *Studies in Leadership* (New York: Harper & Bros.,
1950), p. 19.

said if he were a gambler he'd be the world's best poker player. He plays his cards close up. He'd sit there and you'd never know what card he had until he showed it — and maybe not then!" A Republican member confirmed this characteristic of Mills's leadership: "Wilbur sure does lead us down many paths all at the same time. We never know what he's for. . . ." Another Democrat felt that this inscrutability was part of the Chairman's strength, not a sign of weakness: "Mills is a very fine and subtle leader. He leads sometimes by taking us down one way and we think we are going that way but he's really doing it only to get us to go a different way. Man, that's real smart and shrewd leadership."

The leadership of the Chairman is, then, a subtle process in which Mills "leads but he does it by compromising." Committee members see Mills as the legitimate leader of the Committee, as the central figure on the Committee, as the man who gives the Committee direction and who shapes the decisions of the Committee. But they also see him as a shaper of decisions, not a dictator. To them he is an extremely skillful leader who responds to them in such a way that his conclusions, drawn from their discussions, become their conclusions. It appears to matter little to them if in the abstract, before the Committee goes to work, Mills would favor or oppose many of the proposals made to the Committee. On many questions they do not know where he stands and, in any event, there is no such thing as leadership in the abstract. Leadership is part and parcel of the group process and the members think that Mills is a leader without parallel. One primary reason Mills holds this position is that regardless of what his initial views "really" are he will be responsive to the views of the members, and the members know it.

Leading the Committee as he does, the Chairman helps meet the Committee's instrumental or task objectives at the same time that he helps maintain good affective relations among the members. By letting the members talk themselves out, Mills both ensures good affective tone within the group (although complaints sometimes arise that his fairness goes too far and permits some members to talk too much) and subjects administration proposals to microscopic scrutiny and critical analysis. In this way the instrumental task of perfecting the legislation is promoted and the members of the Committee are made to feel that they have an important part in shaping major public policy.

By timely suggestions that a particular line of action may be acceptable to the members, thereby resolving whatever tensions arise,

Mills is seen by the members as "powerful," "smart," "expert," "clever," and a "good synthesizer," qualities that are associated with instrumental leadership, and as "fair," "considerate," "pleasant," "patient," and the "peacemaker," qualities that go with affective leadership. Small wonder, if man's reputation is dependent upon his reputation in committee, that Mills is known as one of the most effective legislators in the House.

In some ways the Committee is jointly directed. Mills and Byrnes together, not just Mills alone, are responsible for the way the Committee goes about its business. Although Mills is the most important member of the Committee, a great many of the decisions taken by the Committee — some of them among the most important decisions the Committee makes — can be traced to Mills and Byrnes. If Mills and Byrnes disagreed over the way the Committee should function the amount of conflict in the Committee would be appreciably high. As implied, the Chairman and the ranking Republican agree on the nature of the Committee's job and how it should be done, if not on all major policy questions.

Few people outside of the Committee realize how important the Chairman–ranking Republican relationship really is. The Democrats were more inclined to reserve Committee leadership to Mills than the Republicans, but the Republicans feel that Mills and Byrnes together are the leaders of the Committee, which helps explain the partisanship in the Committee. Far from being cut off from influence in the Committee the Republicans feel that because of Mills and Byrnes they have as much say if not more than the Democrats. One Republican observed that the Committee under Byrnes would be about the same as it is under Mills. Asked why, he said, "Because we Republicans get so much in now."

Mills's efforts to reach a consensus often are directed primarily at Byrnes and the Republicans. Although only two Democrats assigned task leadership to Mills and Byrnes they were two of the most perceptive Democrats interviewed. One said he answered Mills and Byrnes to the problem-solving question, "Because they have locked arms on everything, that's why." The second Democrat said, "They get together once in a while but it's not like a group of corporations conspiring to fix prices. With them it's a conspiracy with no conspiring." He explained that, having worked together long enough to know each other's position almost automatically, they take the consensus of the Committee together. This man feels — with strong reason — that when Mills moves toward a decision, he has communicated, explicitly or implicitly, with Byrnes, and that much of what Mills does is in fact a joint proposal by Mills and Byrnes.

MILLS'S PERCEPTION OF HIS JOB. The way Mills sees the Committee's job and defines his role as chairman fits the perceptions of the other members of the Committee. Mills thinks that the Committee, in addition to reporting technically sound bills, should report bills that can pass the House, and the best means of ensuring passage in the House is through compromise in the Committee. His reputation and his committee's are at stake every time a Ways and Means bill comes before the House, and Mills tries hard to avoid defeat in the House.

Mills believes that part of the Committee's job is to examine carefully all policy proposals it actively considers. Given the complexity of tax law and fiscal policy and the need to protect the actuarial soundness of the social security system, he makes sure that the Committee is painstakingly thorough in the mark-up stage of the legislative process, that it studies the alternatives before reaching conclusions, and that it proceeds cautiously to lessen the chances of adversely affecting the economic status of the country, corporations, or individuals. The Committee must perfect bills before sending them to the House for final approval, and Mills sees no sense in spending two or three days on the House floor amending Ways and Means bills. Hence the argument that because Ways and Means Committee bills are so "intricate" and are reported only after weeks of concentrated study, no floor amendments should even be considered unless they are first approved by the Committee.

A workmanlike job on the legislation, however, is only half the task. The other half is to get enough votes in the Committee and in the House to pass the Committee's product. "As I see it," Mills has said, "our job is to work over a bill until our technical staff tells us it is ready and until I have reason to believe that it is going to get enough support to pass. Many of our bills must be brought out under a closed rule, and to get and keep a closed rule you must have a widely acceptable bill. It's as simple as that." [15]

Six years later, Mills revealed that his conception of the Committee's job had not changed. "I was always taught by Mr. Rayburn that our whole system was to settle disputes within the committees. It's a

[15] Quoted in Charles B. Seib, "Steering Wheel of the House," *The New York Times Magazine*, March 18, 1962, p. 146.

waste of time to bring out a bill if you can't pass it. I just don't like to have a record vote for the sake of having a vote." [16]

If Mills's main objective is to report sound, passable legislation the means to this end are clear. In 1967 the Chairman said that reports of his consensus-seeking were highly exaggerated. Perhaps so. But during the course of his remarks he revealed that consensus-seeking is exactly what he does in the Committee. In Mills's very practical world, compromise is the most widely accepted form of decision-making, and the perfect compromise is a consensus. As the Chairman remarked on the practical nature of the Committee's work:

> Oh yes, there is no place for just the idealist because we're dealing with very practical matters. We're living in a very practical world, we have to find practical answers; generally those answers have to be a compromise of the judgment of the 25 men on the committee, and the 435 members of the House, the members of the Finance Committee and the hundred members of the Senate. So it's a very practical world in which we live and a very practical . . . area within which we operate in the Ways and Means Committee.[17]

Moreover, Mills observed that, in his opinion, reaching a consensus in Ways and Means is not a mysterious skill which only a few can understand: you sit, listen, and in the end compromise.

> Oh, to get a consensus, I think of the Ways and Means Committee or of any other group is a relatively easy matter. If you sit and listen long enough, you don't have to talk, you can pretty well find out what the 25 members are thinking about, what their primary interests are with respect to the particular issue, how they would like the legislation dressed a little differently from the way it's introduced maybe. What particular provision might satisfy a group of the members, another provision that might satisfy another group. It's the easiest thing in the world, I think, to get a consensus.[18]

Mills himself has observed that not everything connected with a piece of legislation can be compromised. "But there're so many areas

---

[16] Duscha, *op. cit.*, p. 76.

[17] "Interview with Congressman Wilbur Mills," for "Operation Government," Westinghouse Broadcasting Company, October 11, 1967, p. 3. I am indebted to Stephen Horn of the Brookings Institution who conducted the interview for a copy of the transcript.

[18] *Ibid.*, p. 3.

of any bill that are less important than the main issue of the bill that there's always a way to change some little method of doing something." [19] Underlying this approach to the legislative process in Ways and Means is his belief that: "I think if I can get a vast majority of the membership of the Ways and Means Committee to agree upon something, that I've got a vast majority of the House agreed upon the same thing. Because our committee is a cross section of the membership of the House. Just as it is a cross section of the people of the United States." [20]

Mills's theory about the Committee as a microcosm of the House has yet to be tested, but at present the importance of his conception of legislation is that it leads him to look for a "vast majority" of the votes in the Committee. As a result, Ways and Means bills, in the words of an HEW specialist, are all "negotiated items so they aren't so partisan. Mills will work it around so that 80 per cent of the Committee will support it." A Treasury Department official agreed, "Sometimes he'll give up and settle things by party votes but he prefers not to do this." A member of the Committee's staff has the impression that Mills is "happiest when all twenty-five members agree and the House is unanimous." To achieve this end Mills will, in this man's opinion, "take a tentative position and then if he sees that the Committee is not likely to go along he'll make it clear that this isn't really what he wants anyway." Not surprisingly, the staff man also believes that the Chairman "has the most acute antennae of anyone I've ever seen. He can gauge the sentiment of the House and the Committee extremely well." Why all this? "He doesn't like to lose." Another HEW employee agrees:

> Mills wants more than anything not to have a minority report. He wants at least twenty votes and one way he does it is drop out anything controversial. I don't mean just major policy questions that may be controversial but anything. If they come across a provision and some member raises an objection, he'll drop it out. They go through it once, make tentative decisions, again, and drop out anything controversial. If Burke were chairman it might be different but Mills is amazing. If he started by saying I'm for the administration position then all the Republicans would gang up, but he doesn't do it like this.

[19] *Ibid.*, p. 4.
[20] *Ibid.*, p. 5.

Because Mills is the chairman of an enormously important committee, and because he has acquired a position of legitimate leadership to go with his formal status, many people in the Washington community enjoy trying to explain why Mills leads the Committee as he does. Some dismiss him as a man who has a built-in aversion to taking chances but others see him as a man who does not have strong feelings about any policy in particular and so is willing to hold back until the feelings of others make victory certain if policy is formulated according to the least common denominator. Mills's admirers — most notably all the Committee members but one — see him as "the most capable man in the House of Representatives." His detractors, like one House liberal, explain his influence in the House as the "myth" that he always has his Committee under control, and argue that even if he does it's because he has no real competition for leadership in the Committee.

Amidst the conflicting opinion of Mills and the reason that ostensibly explain why he is influential, the most common observation is that he will do practically anything to avoid losing a bill on the House floor. Several Committee members mentioned that Mills lost one of the first major bills he brought to the floor, which is supposed to have made the Chairman permanently cautious.

But this explanation ignores the possibility that Mills might have expected — indeed planned — his first defeat. Mills claims that his first so-called defeat was in fact part of the strategy he used to pass a controversial unemployment compensation bill.[21] By bringing a two-part bill to the floor Mills contends that he was willing to sacrifice one part in order to get the other part passed. The controversial matter drew criticism away from the other section, which on its own would have had trouble in the House. A recommittal motion extracted the controversial title and the bill passed. If this is true, Mills's humiliating loss was in truth a clever — if little-known — victory.

It would be naive not to admit the possibility that Mills's explanation of his first defeat might be a post hoc rationalization (at least one reporter who was on the scene in 1958 thinks it is), but whether it is true is irrelevant here. Even if the Chairman's first loss had no lasting impact on him, his behavior since 1958 and his view that policy disputes should be resolved in the Committee make it highly probable that the tenuity of power in the House (which is stressed

[21] *Ibid.*, p. 7.

less often than the concentration of power in the committee chairmen) is an important constraint on how he conducts the Committee. Mills is probably well aware that underneath the "cocoon of good feeling" that envelops its members the House is sentimental, even maudlin, about everything but who has power. His reputation in the House is on the line every time he commits himself to the passage of a bill. Although one defeat is not necessarily disastrous, a few defeats would rapidly display that he has lost his grip. To guard against loss Mills tries for support from both sides of the Committee table, a strategy that fits perfectly with the norm of restrained partisanship, and although he can win with just the fifteen Democrats behind him it is much more comfortable to have bipartisan support. In any event, the norm and the strategy are conducive to harmony in the Committee and to the completion of quality work on the complex legislation considered by the Committee. He tries to iron out rough spots in the interaction of members just as he tries to iron out rough spots in the bills, which is why his leadership is effective.

Case studies of two bills illustrate more concretely how the Chairman operates in practice and his effect on the policies that emanate from the Committee. The two bills, excise tax reduction and medicare, were reported by the Committee and enacted into law in 1965. Both involved major compromises stimulated by Byrnes, legitimated by Mills, and adopted with little discussion by the Committee.

EXCISE TAX REDUCTION. In 1965, after several years of extending the "temporary" wartime excise tax rates, the Committee and the administration agreed that economic and fiscal conditions (as well as the political appeal of tax cuts) warranted a large excise tax reduction. Because Byrnes and the Republicans had unsuccessfully tried to cut some excises in 1964 and the proposal was universally popular, no doubt existed that Ways and Means would report a bill cutting the rates. Congress and the administration disagreed only over how much revenue the federal government could afford to lose without raising the budget deficit to an unacceptable level.

By the time the administration made its formal proposal to the Committee in May, the tax reduction package was about twice that mentioned earlier (about $4 billion compared to $2 billion). Part of the reason behind the increase, reportedly, was a vigorous effort by the automobile industry to gain a reduction in auto excise taxes, and the argument of Dr. Gardner Ackley, Chairman of the President's Council of Economic Advisers, that (contrary to Treasury's position) a large reduction was needed to counter the depressing economic effects of increased social security taxes after the enactment of medicare.[22] As a result, the administration proposed to reduce the 10 per cent auto excise tax in stages to 5 per cent in 1967, at a cost of almost $1 billion in revenue. The question for the administration was how to keep the other 5 per cent or $1 billion from being cut by Congress.

Ways and Means took the issue up on May 19. The case for removing the auto excise altogether and at once was argued in the Committee by Martha Griffiths of Detroit. She contended that the tax should come off because the auto industry was certain to pass the saving on to the consumer by lowering car prices, that to remove other excises completely and leave 5 per cent on cars was not sensible, that removal would increase the economic stimulus of the tax reduction, and that if Ways and Means did not reduce it the Senate would.

Some used car dealers, a number of members reported to the Committee, feared that tax removal would help new car dealers but seriously injure the used car business. More potent was the argument that Treasury could not afford another billion dollar revenue loss.

Mills sided with Treasury. He countered Griffiths's contention that Ways and Means should remove the tax or the Senate would do it for them by arguing that one was never sure what action the Senate might take. To buttress this point he recalled a 1950 tax reduction bill that passed the House and, with the outbreak of the Korean War, was transformed into a tax increase bill in the Senate. After some discussion Griffiths moved that the 10 per cent tax be lifted completely, retroactive to May 15. Mills, who felt that this was too much, did not put the motion to a vote right away. Rather, he engaged Assistant Secretary of the Treasury Stanley Surrey in a colloquy to reveal what effect the Griffiths motion would have on the FY (fiscal year) 1966 deficit. Surrey replied that it would cost $1.1 billion and Treasury Secretary Henry Fowler, also in the room, noted that this would increase the deficit from $4.3 billion to $5.4 billion.

With this point made, the Chairman then asked the cost of removing the telephone excise all at once, and argued that the Committee could not stagger the telephone excise reduction and refuse to stagger the auto excise cut. Surrey quickly calculated that removing

---

[22] Rowland Evans and Robert Novak, "Inside Report," *The Washington Post*, May 25, 1965, p. A19.

the telephone tax in one shot would cost another $500 million. With the federal deficit now up to almost $6 billion Mills was ready to put the Griffiths motion to a vote. At this point Dr. Laurence Woodworth, chief of the Committee's tax staff, asked to be heard. Before Woodworth could speak a member suggested a compromise on the Griffiths proposal, but Mills recognized Woodworth before considering a compromise. Woodworth pointed out that the staff of the Joint Committee on Internal Revenue Taxation estimated that the federal deficit would be about $700 million larger than the Treasury estimate. Mills observed that Woodworth's findings were very serious and that the FY 1966 deficit might be greater than the deficit in FY 1965. Woodworth agreed. With this additional help from Woodworth, and with the observation by Eugene Keogh that in cases of conflict the Joint Committee staff estimates have usually been more accurate than Treasury's, Mills put the motion to a vote. A voice vote was sufficient to defeat the Griffiths proposal.

Immediately after the barrage from Mills and the Treasury Department, and the subsequent defeat of the Griffiths motion, Byrnes made a compromise proposal. In Byrnes's opinion there was no rationale for keeping 5 per cent of the levy on cars while all the other excises in the bill were removed. He proposed to take the tax off completely by 1969 in stages over three years to lessen the adverse effect on the deficit. The Committee's lengthy discussion of the Byrnes amendment made it clear that there was a good deal of interest in reducing the auto excise by more than Treasury proposed, even though the Committee was not willing to go as far as fast as Mrs. Griffiths desired. A number of alternatives were discussed, different combinations of repeal were explored, and finally Mills broke in. The Chairman observed that there appeared to be a "feeling" in the Committee for repealing the tax and that he was impressed with Byrnes's argument. Mills also said that if the Committee did not act on the 5 per cent the Senate would, an argument he had dismissed earlier, and he proposed a 7 per cent tax retroactive to May 15 (Byrnes had proposed 8 per cent to help the used car dealers), 6 per cent in 1966, 4 per cent in 1967, 2 per cent in 1968, and expiration January 1, 1969. The difference between Byrnes's and Mills's proposals was one percentage point in 1965. Byrnes endorsed Mills's compromise. Treasury representatives protested that it would cost $1 billion in revenue, but Mills told them they should have thought of that before proposing half a loaf for one industry. One of the Committee's car dealers applauded Mills's compromise as a "wonderful" way to remove the tax, a couple of members balked, and the compromise then carried by a show of hands.

Mills's compromise satisfied no one completely but it satisfied enough members to pass with only token opposition. Treasury lost more money than it wanted, but not all at once; Griffiths and the auto industry did not get immediate repeal, but they did get repeal; used car dealers did not get retention of the bulk of the tax, but they did get delayed reduction; the Chairman did not get what he wanted, but he did get something he could accept, defend in the House, and use as a base against the anticipated Senate adoption of the Griffiths immediate repeal amendment, which he opposed.

The Excise Tax Reduction Act of 1965, following approval by the Republican Policy Committee and a lackluster debate in the House, passed 401–6. A few days prior to the vote Mills made public a letter in which the president said he preferred his original program but if the entire auto tax was to be removed "the Ways and Means Committee program represents a prudent way of doing so." Mills, by coming up with a prudent compromise — or, more precisely, adapting the bill to Byrnes's compromise — resolved the dispute in the Committee and presided over the mere formality of victory in the House. (Ultimately the increased need for revenue as a result of the Viet Nam war led to the postponement of the reduction.)

MEDICARE. Just before the passage of the much-delayed medicare program, a liberal Democratic member of the Ways and Means Committee, Frank Karsten of Missouri, talked about Mills, who for several years had helped to keep the bill in Committee:

> Stalemates have to await the arrival of a peacemaker. So it has been in this case. The distinguished chairman of the Committee on Ways and Means, the gentleman from Arkansas, has been the peacemaker. He has brought together the divergent viewpoints of the present as well as the past, and the bill before us is a tribute to his ingenuity, skill, and dedication to a task which seemed almost insurmountable.[23]

Other Committee members, many of whom had long supported the King-Anderson medicare bill, were no less effusive in their praise of the compromise bill (H.R. 6675) that the Chairman, assisted by Byrnes, had worked out in the Committee. Eugene Keogh of Brook-

[23] *Congressional Record*, April 7, 1965 (daily edition), p. 6979.

lyn spoke about the "towering figure of the greatest legislative master of them all." [24] Jonathan Bingham of the Bronx apologized on the House floor for the unkind things he had said during the fall campaign about the Chairman's handling of medicare.[25] When Mills finished his opening speech on the bill an unusually crowded House gave him a standing ovation, and Byrnes was one of the first on his feet.

Making the usual allowances for the hyperbole of debate in the House, it is nonetheless impressive that when Mills brought medicare to the floor he was instantly transformed from villain to hero. The 1964 presidential election, which brought 295 Democrats to the House and led to the defeat of two conservative Republican members of Ways and Means, settled the question of whether or not medicare would pass. (For insurance, the Committee ratio, with Mills's approval, was changed from 15–10 Democratic to 17–8.) But this massive majority — the largest afforded either party since 1936 — only assured that some administration-approved program would be reported by Ways and Means and passed into law. The full-scale benefits package of H.R. 6675 was the result not of an electoral or presidential mandate but of the legislative process. And, curiously enough, the impetus for the new program came initially from the Republican side of the Committee: John Byrnes and William Quealy, the minority counsel of Ways and Means.

Assisted by Quealy, Byrnes devised a medicare plan for the elderly patterned after the high option program available to federal employees. Actuarial data showed that the Byrnes bill, which contained a much larger benefits package than H.R. 1 (King-Anderson), offered to those over 65 years of age health protection much closer to their needs than the more limited administration bill. The Republican bill was simple, but ingenious: an optional plan, funded by a small monthly payment from each enrollee together with federal funds taken out of general revenues, included a benefits package so attractive to the elderly in terms of cost to them that practically everyone would participate (HEW estimated 90 to 95 per cent would participate). In voluntary form, the Byrnes bill was in its attractiveness as compulsory as the administration's social security approach. In one stroke the Byrnes bill answered several objections to King-Anderson: (1) it was, in theory, a voluntary program; (2) a generous benefits

24 *Ibid.*, p. 6951.
25 *Ibid.*, April 8, 1965, p. 7168.

package highlighted, and resolved, the problem of limited care provided in H.R. 1; (3) it was actuarially sound and did not endanger the social security system as did, some argued, medicare.

Ways and Means, rejecting a move by some Republicans for more public hearings on medicare, began executive session hearings on January 27, 1965. In the following weeks the Committee ironed out many questions regarding the King-Anderson program; they had never discussed — until the Byrnes bill came up — the possibility of doing much beyond H.R. 1. On March 1 when the discussion of H.R. 1 was completed, Mills asked Curtis to explain to the Committee an alternative bill introduced by him and A. Sydney Herlong (D., Fla.) that was dubbed "eldercare" and supported by the American Medical Association. After Curtis, assisted by Wilbur Cohen, Assistant Secretary of Health, Education and Welfare, was through, the Byrnes bill was next on the agenda.

Byrnes and Cohen spent the morning of March 2 explaining the Byrnes bill. It elicited a good deal of interest from Mills who, at first, seemed highly attracted by the bill's liberal benefits but skeptical about financing it out of general revenue rather than the payroll tax. Byrnes admitted that tying the plan to a payroll tax would put some controls on the size of the program but he argued that partial funding from the participants would remedy that. The key to the greater benefits package of the Byrnes bill was that the money received from the participants would be supplemented by general revenue funds, thereby enabling the participants to buy a subsidized insurance policy at a cost far below existing private insurance plans. Such a liberal program could not be financed under the payroll tax alone.

Mills — and others — put Byrnes through a lengthy interrogation on his bill and the longer it went on the better the plan appeared. HEW was put in the incongruous position of raising philosophical objections to the Byrnes bill, including the argument that H.R. 1, by covering only hospitalization costs, left an area of health care costs open for private insurance companies to insure. Byrnes replied that by preempting the field of coverage, his bill was a better deal for the elderly than H.R. 1. Cohen summed up the policy question at stake: did the Committee want the federal government to help the elderly meet the cost of hospitalization, which accounted for the greatest difference between health costs of the elderly and younger persons, or did the Committee want to insure other benefits as well?

The Committee's answer came that afternoon. The Byrnes proposal was irresistible, and shortly into the afternoon session Mills suggested that the Committee draft a compromise "medi-elder-Byrnes" bill, to which Byrnes replied that he preferred the term "better care." The Chairman proposed that hospital benefits be financed from payroll taxes, as in H.R. 1, and that they add contributions from participants and from general revenues, as in the Byrnes plan. Mills argued that H.R. 1 simply did not go far enough in meeting the health care costs of the elderly and that adoption of part of the Byrnes bill would protect the Committee from the inevitable demands that would flow from dissatisfaction with H.R. 1. Once Mills did this the issue, except for specifics, was settled. A few weeks later the House passed medicare, now known as the Mills bill, not King-Anderson. Byrnes, although the Committee accepted the essence of his bill, could not accept H.R. 6675 because it contained H.R. 1 with its payroll tax feature. Enough Democrats in the House, however, defeated the Republican recommittal motion easily (191–236) and H.R. 6675 was then passed 313–115.

MILLS: INFLUENCE AND EXCHANGE

Influence, not power, is the concept to use in thinking about the leadership of such individuals as Chairman Mills. Power means many things to many people but intuitively it conjures up the notion that A, who "has" power, can through the expression of his will activate obligations on the part of B that stimulate B to do something he would not otherwise do.[26] Despite the general agreement that power is a relational or transactional concept of some presumed utility for describing and analyzing political relations, the tendency is still to speak of power as a commodity that some persons have and others do not. Influence is another relational concept, which for shorthand purposes is spoken of in commodity terms when, in fact, it refers to relationships among people. When the term "influence" is used in connection with Mills, it means a relationship between him and the other members of the Committee, not something he has and they do not.

Influence is a better concept to use in analyzing Mills than power not because it has fewer theoretical problems, nor is it easier to devise

[26] This intuitive definition of power is, of course, taken from the definitions of Parsons, Dahl, and Catlin. See Talcott Parsons, "On the Concept of Influence," *Public Option Quarterly*, XXVII (Spring, 1963), 37–62; Robert A. Dahl, "The Concept of Power," *Behavioral Science*, II (July, 1957), 201–15; G. E. G. Catlin, *The Science and Method of Politics* (New York: Alfred A. Knopf, 1927), pp. 222–23.

an operational definition of influence and measure it than power, but
because the theoretical and empirical meaning of influence is much
closer to the kind of relationship between Mills and the Committee
than the meaning usually given to power. Influence, as Parsons points
out, may be distinguished from power because influence is, in essence,
a means of *persuasion* that involves giving reasons or justifications for
doing certain things and avoiding others, whereas power may be
taken to mean the communication of decisions that activate obligations.[27] Power has a much more direct connotation than influence.
When one thinks about power between A and B there is a tendency
to view the relationship as unidirectional, A → B; with influence, the
relationship is more apt to be seen as a mutual process of stimula-
tion, A ⟷ B. The essence of a consensus-seeking form of leadership,
the kind practiced by Mills, is mutual dependence, a relationship between Mills and the Committee that involves the flow of influence
from the Committee to Mills just as much as the flow from Mills to
the Committee.

Interestingly, two Committee members drew their own distinctions
between Mills's power and influence in interviews. Most Committee
members spoke in terms of power, but these two Democratic members
argued that Mills is best thought of in terms of influence, and it is
safe to assume that the rest of the Committee would agree with their
formulation of the distinction. The first, reacting as though using the
term "power" in connection with Mills was somehow unrealistic,
said:

> Power — you mean influence? In the sense of influence? I
> agree with that. He's considerate. He's as considerate of the
> most junior member as he is of the most senior. That's why
> he's "powerful." In the Committee, too, it all starts in the
> Committee. I don't think Mills is the wizard he's made out
> to be, it takes him time, he doesn't always see the full mean-
> ing of what you're doing. But he does, finally, through hard
> work.

The second member compared Mills, the influential Chairman, to
Carl Vinson, the powerful former chairman of Armed Services:

> I wouldn't use the term powerful, I'd say influential. There's
> a difference. I'll compare him with . . . Carl Vinson. Carl
> had power and he used it, he wasn't afraid to use it. Mills is

---

[27] Parsons, *ibid.*, p. 48.

different. He has influence. I don't mean influence in the sense you peddle influence. It isn't you do this for me or on a committee assignment. . . . It isn't this way with Mills. He can always bring you together. He has such great respect and influence.

Thus this conception of influence, drawn both from the conception of leadership and from the empirical findings of interviews with Committee members, leads to the interaction between Mills the leader and the twenty-four other Committee members. More precisely, we are led to questions about the kinds of exchanges that occur between Mills and his Committee colleagues — the rewards and costs that are involved in these transactions, what Mills does for the members and what they do for him, and, most specifically, the bases of his influence in the Committee.

Parsons, further elaborating the differences between influence and power in response to a critique by Coleman, insisted on the utility of the distinction, adding that influence is backed by arguments and giving or withholding of approval or disapproval. Power, on the other hand, is a way of activating obligations backed by the threat of negative sanctions.[28] This distinction is useful but still too nebulous to analyze the Ways and Means Committee. The difference between a negative sanction and withholding social approval, for example, is not too clear, and in any event it is possible to think of a more detailed typology of the bases of influence than Parsons's two-part breakdown. Focusing on, in Coleman's words, "the investments that a person makes in another which permits the other to have influence on him," [29] draws attention away from the influencer to the influenced, and with this focus five bases of Mills's influence will be discussed. These bases are adapted from French and Raven's useful classification of the bases of power:

1. *Expertise:*   Mills's knowledge of the subject matter.
2. *Legitimacy:* Mills's rights as the formal leader of the Committee.
3. *Rewards:*   what Mills can do for the members in a positive way.
4. *Reference:*   the identification of others with Mills.

[28] For Coleman's critique see James S. Coleman, "Comment on 'On the Concept of Influence,'" *Public Opinion Quarterly*, XXVII (Spring, 1963), pp. 63–82.
[29] *Ibid.*, p. 67.

5. *Sanctions:*   what Mills can do, in a negative way, to promote
                    compliance with his objectives.[30]

EXPERTISE. As befits a leader whose style is that of persuasion,
Mills, as seen by the members, has great expertise in the abstruse
areas considered by the Committee. When asked to explain Mills's
influence in the Committee the reason most often given was the
Chairman's knowledge of the subject matter, and next in importance
was his fairness. The evidence gathered from the members illustrates
perfectly Blau's comment that "A person whose demands on others are
fair and modest relative to the great contribution he makes to their
welfare . . . earns their approval." [31]

Mills has earned the approval of the Committee members on his
hard work and his mastery of the subjects coming before the Committee. Moreover, by becoming an expert Mills has reduced the cost
of Committee membership to others. Members who are unsure of the
answers to complex questions can rely on his judgment and expertise,
and those members who do not care to immerse themselves in technical complexities are confident that he knows what he is doing. By ac-
quiring some degree of expertise the Chairman has allowed other
members "to perform rewarding activities with less effort, less anxiety,
or in less time — in general, at lower cost." [32] And by lowering costs
to others Mills has raised his own influence.

A Republican Committee member articulated the theme that the
members feel secure with Mills because of his expertise: "His knowledge, the fact that he does his homework, is in the back of why they
feel safe, why he gives them security." Referring to the complexity

[30] John R. P. French, Jr., and Bertram Raven, "The Bases of Social Power,"
Group Dynamics, ed. Dorwin Cartwright and Alvin Zander (Evanston, Ill.: Row,
Peterson, 1960), pp. 612–21. These may not be the only bases of power which
can be distinguished but they are more inclusive than other typologies, such as
Weber's threefold classification of authority. For Weber's treatment of charis-
matic, rational-legal, and traditional authority see Max Weber, *The Theory of
Social and Economic Organization*, ed. Talcott Parsons, trans. A. M. Henderson
and Talcott Parsons (New York: Macmillan, Free Press, 1964), pp. 328–63. I
have substituted the term "sanctions" for Raven and French's "coercive" power
because of the connotation of the latter, and their third base of power, legitimacy,
is considerably different from the way it is used here. By "legitimate power" they
mean internalized values which dictate that someone has a right to influence
someone else. As used here, "legitimacy" refers more to the decisions Mills can
make because he is Chairman, and how these decisions affect his influence.

[31] Peter M. Blau, *Exchange and Power in Social Life* (New York: John Wiley,
1964), p. 201.

[32] Thibaut and Kelley, *op. cit.*, p. 109.

of the subject matter, he said, "They know he won't lead them into anything, and there's a lot of things to get into in these things." "He knows the bills thoroughly," a second Republican observed. Mills "knows what he's talking about," said another, and three of his colleagues agreed:

> Mills is preeminent. He's a real student. I don't know what the Democrats will do when he goes. He was the real leader before he became chairman because he studied so much. Leadership depends on hard work and knowledge.
>
> He knows the tax code inside and out and he knows what Ways and Means has done for the last twenty years. He can cite and does cite section after section of the code.
>
> He's so single minded, never goes out, no social life or cocktail parties. He's thoroughly absorbed, goes home and thinks about the legislation.

Democratic Committee members are equally impressed — if not more so — with the Chairman's ability. They see him as a man who has put years into the study of Ways and Means business ("work is his hobby"), knows more than they do ("takes the experts, the specialists who have spent 40 years in the subject, apart"), has great natural ability ("best mind on the Committee"), understands the material ("isn't anything in taxes he fails to understand or fails to relate to what has gone before and tie it into today"), and who, with all of this, is fair and considerate in his relations with them. A Democrat summed up the general opinion, "He's an astounding man." [33]

These odes to Mills's expertise and ability, qualified only by a few members who attributed Mills's influence more to hard work than to great native intelligence ("he's a plodder"), help to explain his great influence with the Committee members. Some see his expertise as of great value to them. "He sort of quarterbacks it and lets me off. Takes the burden off me." But just as important as the general benefits they derive from his knowledge is that he is inclined to use his knowledge not as a barrier to their policy objectives but as a guide to finding acceptable compromises. He is perceived as an expert who sometimes argues persuasively against proposals (e.g., the Griffiths motion to reduce auto excise taxes), but also as a pragmatist who more often

---

[33] Similar comments were received from staff members and executive branch specialists. The following is typical: "He has a memory like an elephant, never forgets a thing, and he can tell you more about the welfare administration than most people in this building."

hits upon, as one member put it, the "honorable agreement." When
he does this the members, more often than not, will settle for the
compromise he offers as the best they are likely to get.

LEGITIMACY. Committee chairmen are not ipso factor leaders in
Congress, but they can become leaders if they have certain kinds of
skills and certain kinds of followers. The men on Ways and Means
are oriented toward bargaining, accommodation, peaceful settlement
of disputes, and the subordination of specific policy objectives to the
maintenance of the power and prestige of their Committee. They
actively strive for legislation but operate on the principle that the
legislative process makes one fundamental demand, patience. What
does it take to exert influence in a decision-making system composed
of men who are, in theory, peers, and who must make important decisions while they are engaged in close, long-term relationships with
one another?

Seniority is one answer the members of Congress have given. Seniority is the norm that organizes the decision-making process, giving
the senior members the right to make certain decisions that structure
the legislative process. The list is familiar: control over the legislative
agenda; appointment of junior members to subcommittees; such organizational questions as whether to have subcommittees and how
many; management of the committee staff; the right of recognition
of members who desire to speak; and general leadership in the shep-
herding of bills through the House. But none of these rights guarantees influence to the senior leaders. They are resources to be used in
meeting the demands of the members or in reducing the cost of committee membership, and only if they are used in this way will there be
a relationship between seniority and influence.

Homans, in discussing the successful leader, illuminates the basic
qualification that must be placed on the formal prerogatives of senior
leaders in the House: "If his chief external job is to be successful, his
chief internal one is to be just. 'He's fair,' are the words in the
mouths of his followers from which all other praises spring." [34] The
successful committee chairman in the House is the just chairman in
the committee; justice meaning in this case distributive justice, a
favorable balance between rewards and costs (inducements and contributions) for the members resulting from the actions of the chairman.

[34] George C. Homans, *Social Behavior: Its Elementary Forms* (New York:
Harcourt, Brace & World, 1961), p. 295.

If the chairman so uses his prerogatives he enhances his influence with the members. If, however, the costs of the way he performs his leadership functions exceed the benefits to the members he may be able to implement his will for a time but his influence with the members will decrease, and if it decreases to a certain point the members, as they have done in some committees, may strip him of all but the gavel.

The argument applied to the Ways and Means Committee is, we may state baldly, that the rights granted to Mills because he is chairman are sources of influence because he exercises them in such a way that the members approve of his leadership. By so doing Mills is seen by the members as a chairman who makes important contributions to their welfare and, in Blau's words, "their common approval of his fairness, reinforced by their consensus concerning the respect his abilities deserve, generate group pressures that enforce compliance with his directives." [35]

"He has the ability and he's very fair," was one Republican's judgment on Mills, and no one interviewed for this study disagreed. Even the member who was highly critical of Mills said, "He is considerate of the fellow members; no one is more considerate. Don't get me wrong — I have to say his good points. He knows his stuff." A Democrat declared, "He is fair. He doesn't ride roughshod over anyone, although it has happened — it's been known to happen. But it's rare that he's roughshod." According to a Republican, "If I have an idea he's always ready to hear it out, to listen, and if he doesn't agree he says so and we go from there." This man compared Mills to another chairman:

> If Wilbur said what the hell there's fifteen votes why not vote it through, don't waste all this time, then of course it'd be different. Jere Cooper was this way. Hell, he'd get a social security bill one day and report it the next.

Another Republican noted that Mills does not have to call bills up if he does not want to and Republicans could do little to force him to act. "I think it's a tribute to him that he lets them be aired." He also related how one of his early experiences on the Committee bound him to Mills:

> Inside [Ways and Means] complete fairness so I feel attached to him. I remember when I was lowest man on the totem pole and I had some interrogation I wanted to do and there

[35] Blau, *op. cit.*, p. 202.

were a couple of secretaries there but it was late, 5:00 or 5:30. He said we'll come back in the morning the next day to hear Mr. ———, and they had to come back. I appreciate that.

"The Chairman," said a junior Democrat, "always allows everyone to get his questions in." If anything, Mills runs the Committee meetings so loosely that his patience with some members sometimes aggravates — while it impresses — others. A Democrat, for instance, said:

He'll listen forever. We have one member . . . who can never get enough information. I once said we'd need a building as large as the Rayburn Building to store all the information he wants. He's always asking for more information and Mills gets him more, more, more, more, more, and more. He's a fine chairman. I don't think you'll find anyone who wouldn't say that about him.

The man who said Mills never rides roughshod over anyone summed up: "The overriding thing is his patience. He just keeps going and going and going and he *outlasts* everyone else. This is the most important thing. He is fair."

From this perspective, the contribution of his legitimate prerogatives to Mills's influence is not that he has certain rights but that he uses them to win approval from the members. His staff is a good example. As one perceptive member said: "Sure, all the members have the staff but they are his men first — the Chairman's men. *And the reason they are is that he does the work.*" The staff gives Mills's needs precedence over other members', but it is available to the other members who mostly are quite satisfied with the staff. A few think the Committee could use more staff but there is no widespread demand for more and, if there were, the Chairman would probably be receptive to hiring more people. An expert staff in the hands of an inexpert chairman can be a liability instead of an asset, and the staff professionals are seen as the "Chairman's men" on Ways and Means not because Mills is chairman but because Mills is the kind of chairman he is. The other members do not begrudge him the staff because they know that he puts more into the Committee than they do and consequently has more need of the staff.

Another example is the Chairman's strategic decision not to use subcommittees for legislative purposes. Committee members prefer to work without subcommittees, and their absence makes for a highly centralized operation around Mills in the Committee. As a Democrat said, "This means that he is there with five or six members who would normally be a subcommittee and he is chairman of all the subcommittees." But the main significance of conducting the Committee's legislative business in plenary session is that although it makes for high centralization the members do not mind. With Mills as the center the members prefer to conduct the Committee's legislative business in plenary session to the normal subcommittee arrangement. No doubt they realize that this style of operations increases the opportunities for the Chairman to influence their decisions but the Chairman's influence is precisely what they like about the Committee. "If we had a new chairman we might have subcommittees," a Democrat commented, "someone who wanted to delegate. But as long as Mills wants all the responsibility we're willing to let him have it. We don't have white hats as I told you. A lot of the bills are tough." A second Democrat, when it was suggested that perhaps one reason Mills does not establish subcommittees is that it might lessen his control on the Committee, gave the revealing reply that, "No, Wilbur just isn't that kind of person. He's too big for that. I think the reason is just because it'd be hard to get the members interested enough to attend." And a senior Democrat said that if he were chairman he would *have* to have subcommittees because he could not be as central a figure in the Committee as Mills: "I'd have to have two or three members around me. I don't have the ability or the interest to do it like Mills. I might need two or three subcommittees." For this man, were he to become chairman, the establishment of subcommittees would be a sign of weakness and the need for decentralization, not a decision by which he could enhance his own influence. To save some influence he would have to use his authority to share the potential for influence with others. For Mills, the authority of the chairmanship is used to centralize the resources of influence in the Committee, and no one seems to mind.

In considering legitimacy as a base of influence for the Chairman, it is important to remember that many of the mundane functions of the Chairman which may increase his ability to persuade the members on certain questions fall within what Barnard calls the "zone of indifference." [36] For a member like Curtis the zone was very narrow,

---

[36] Chester I. Barnard, *The Functions of the Executive* (Cambridge, Massachusetts: Harvard University Press, 1956), pp. 167–70.

and he constantly supervised Mills to make sure that the Committee, by his standards, was well run, an oversight function that on occasion irritated the Chairman. For other members, however, the zone of indifference is comparatively large and may include everything but how to cast votes in the final stages of the Committee process. On many questions the members are content to rely on Mills. Ranking the tedious Committee meetings low on their list of priorities, these members open up a wide area in which Mills can make decisions in a relatively unrestrained way. Mills, characteristically, has a good feel for the boundaries of his autonomous zone and when he receives requests from members which fall within it, such as having someone in particular testify before the Committee, he accedes and thus ensures the continuation of his general control. It is likely that such decisions as allowing executive department representatives to participate in the executive sessions of the Committee affect the decisions of the Committee in ways desired by Mills, but few members care deeply about such matters. For the most part, the members are willing to let Mills run the Committee because he consults them on many questions of procedure and he runs the Committee, with or without consultations, to their satisfaction. By so doing, Mills maximizes the potential influence of his formal powers while minimizing the complaints that are sometimes heard about other committee chairmen in the House. Thus he is considered by most members as "the best damn chairman in the House, best I've ever seen in all my years in the legislature."

REWARDS. If it takes money to make money the same is true for influence in Congress. Those in Congress who lead, who are powerful, or who are influential operate on the same principles. They use their resources to induce others to make investments in them to help them realize their objectives. But to induce others to help them involves a cost — called "credits" on the Hill — and the trick is to build a large enough supply of credits so that other members will reciprocate when needed. This game is far more complex than banking, the exchanges more diversified than money, but the ultimate principle is the same: the leader is superior to but dependent upon the follower, and if something goes wrong the leader, having risked more, loses more than the follower.

There are, however, crucial differences between banking and the congressional game of influence. In banking, the depositor and the banker, presumably, have the same interest: to make money. In Congress not only is there a multitude of interests but many members lack shared interests with other members, and in many cases the interests are in conflict. To bring unity out of this diversity is the leader's problem, and most leaders unify in the only way possible: bargaining.

Bargaining, regardless of what form it takes (logrolling, side payments, splitting the difference), is peculiarly suited to a decision-making system in which every man has some influence, no man or group has undivided control over important resources of influence, and in which men who are in a formal sense equals must bring a common interest out of a diversity and conflict of interests. Such a system is built for bargaining, as those who built it — with their concern over factions — no doubt realized. And such a system, if it is to function smoothly, requires agreement on one fundamental norm: the duty to reciprocate assistance or rewards received from others.

Political scientists and others have given inelegant names to most of the subtle exchanges that take place in Congress: logrolling, quid pro quo, and back-scratching. Normally there is little need for the members to spell out what is expected when one gives or receives assistance. Most of the bargaining in Congress is implicit.

To become an influential leader in such a system requires more than seniority, which confers some special advantages; influence in Congress is earned, not bestowed. Those men whose influence transcends their own vote have made use of whatever limited formal advantages they are given plus the vital factor of their skill at exchanging benefits with their colleagues. No one, neither the Speaker nor the most influential committee chairman, commands; he negotiates.

Compared with leaders of many organizations, committee chairmen have few material incentives or rewards with which to negotiate.[37] A committee member's salary, for example, is not dependent upon how well he performs in the committee, his attendance record at committee meetings, nor the number of hours he spends each week on committee business. Nor does the chairman have control over such other common rewards as stock options, insurance plans, and paid vacations. He may, of course, allocate committee funds so some members can travel to boring conferences in exciting places but the Ways and Means Committee Chairman is notoriously frugal on such matters. How, then, does Mills, by using the limited rewards

[37] See Barnard's discussion of incentives, *ibid.*, pp. 139–49.

and favors at his disposal, induce the members to make contributions to the Committee's work and to his own objectives? [38]

Before discussing Mills's use of rewards it should be noted that by constantly guarding the Committee's reputation in the House Mills in effect is protecting one of the most significant rewards the members have. Like leaders of all groups, the Chairman symbolizes the organization to others, which is particularly important in the House where the tendency is strong for committees to be equated with and judged in terms of the chairman.[39] If the Ways and Means Committee ranks high in the House it is partly because of Mills and his leadership.

Because most members are attracted to the Committee by its status in the House it is important that the Chairman sustains — and contributes to — this status.

To some, decision-making through bargaining and exchange of favors has pejorative connotations. It contrasts with making decisions according to a normative "rational" model: Step 1: problem; Step 2: weigh pros and cons of alternatives; Step 3: study merits; Step 4: make decision. Congressmen are as sensitive to the pejorative aspects of exchange as other decision-makers; indeed, given the persistence of the rumor that legislatures are bastions of logrolling, congressmen are probably more likely than others to deny or discount the importance of the exchanges that occur. This makes gathering of evidence on exchange in Congress difficult. Bargaining is an intensely personal relationship among the members, about which they are reluctant to talk to outsiders.

It is true nonetheless that bargains, implicit or explicit, are made in Congress, and that exchanges of rewards and favors are inevitably associated with the decision-making process.

But to go beyond the assertion that men such as Mills use rewards and favors to build good relationships with other members, though necessary, is not easy. With the difficulties clearly in mind, it was decided to attack the problem frontally by asking the members of the Committee how they stood with Mills on the exchange of rewards

[38] Parsons uses the term sanction to include rewards and punishments. Talcott Parsons and Edward A. Shils, eds., *Toward a General Theory of Action* (New York: Harper Torchbooks, 1962), p. 191. Rewards and sanctions are distinguished here because the former increase the attractiveness of the giver, while the latter decrease his attractiveness. On this point see French and Raven, *op. cit.*, p. 615.

[39] On the importance of this function in a very different setting see William Foote White, "Corner Boys: A Study in Clique Behavior," *American Journal of Sociology*, XLVI (March, 1941), 661.

and favors. It was clear that Mills was the source of at least some rewards for the members, in addition to the rewarding aspects of his leadership previously discussed, and it was felt that Mills probably did more for the members than he requested. If true, this is another reason why the members are inclined to respond favorably to his leads and is one reason for his influence.

Accordingly, ten Democratic and eight Republican Committee members were asked the following question:

> In the normal course of passing legislation Mills has the opportunity of doing a number of things for the members. He also calls on members to do things for him occasionally. In your relations with Mills how do you stand: would you say you have done more for him, he has done more for you, or are you about even?

Because no political scientist had ever reported the results on such a question, it was not known what to expect. The results, despite the good reasons for going after such information in a more subtle way, were better than expected. The question had the merit of posing the issue starkly and forcing the members to confront it explicitly, perhaps for the first time. The results, in Table 4.2, are deemed of sufficient validity and interest to warrant reporting here. Most members were aware that I had done a good deal of research on the Committee and rapport had been established with most, and so although a few appeared to be taken aback no one seemed to take offense at the question. Most of the members replied that in their opinion Mills has done more for them than they have for him, a close second was the response that it does not work that way in the Committee, four members felt they are about even with the Chairman, and only one man felt the balance favored Mills. As we shall see, this man's reply was one of the most interesting received.

TABLE 4.2
MEMBERS' ESTIMATES OF THEIR BARGAINING
POSITION WITH THE CHAIRMAN

Responses	Democrats	Republicans
1. Mills has done more for me.	2	5
2. It doesn't work that way.	4	2
3. We are about even.	3	1
4. I've done more for him.	1	0

Unexpectedly, the Republican members of the Committee feel more in Mills's debt than the Democrats, which supports the common Republican observation that Mills tends to take the Committee Democrats for granted while he pays relatively more attention to the minority members. More than half the Republicans who were asked the question and fully half of the ten Republicans on the Committee said that Mills has done more for them. Only two of the ten Democrats replied in kind.

Two Republicans who said Mills has done *much* more for them than they have reciprocated revealed how they felt about Mills in the process, and why they are likely to be influenced by him on some questions. The first Republican stressed Mills's loyalty to the members of the Committee, regardless of party affiliation. "If I want a letter any time for my campaign, support for reelection, he'll give it. A picture with him — anytime. He's loyal with his members and I appreciate this." He also discounted his ability to repay the Chairman: "He's a hundred thousand watts and I can't light that candle." When asked if he ever used a letter from Mills in his campaign he said no, but that he has used a picture of himself with the Chairman. Moreover, he thinks the picture has helped him:

> I think it helps you that the Chairman hasn't put you in the isolation box. I'd love to have him come out to my district and give a speech. Not an endorsement, just a speech. I'd love to show him to my businessmen. Why, he'd draw a crowd twice as big as I do. I think he's the top fiscal brain in the country.

Mills has visited the second Republican's district to make a speech. Some local people contacted the Committee member about inviting Mills; he approached Mills impersonally, telling the Chairman that he knew how busy he was and would understand if he could not take time to make the trip, but that these people did want him to come, so, if possible, it would be a nice thing to do for them. Mills made the request very personal by asking the man, "Do *you* want me to do it?" The member, a bit reluctantly, said yes. Mills did him the favor.

They both know that repayment of the favor will not involve defecting from the Republican side on a major party issue. It may not involve anything specific at all for, as the member said, "Wilbur Mills is not the kind to ask you on specifics." It is important to understand that the second step in the exchange is implicit, vague, and if Mills ever directly asks the man for assistance on something neither one will have to recall the Chairman's trip. The trip did lay the foundation for future exchanges and, because Mills did the first favor, its value may never be completely exhausted.

Similar favors were mentioned by other Republicans but more revealing than a catalog of the little rewards Mills gives the Republicans is that the two Republicans who said it does not work that way in Ways and Means meant that their relationship with Mills is based more firmly than an emphasis on reciprocation of benefits would allow. Both men admitted that they have received kindnesses from the Chairman but that they play a minor part in their relationship. A senior Republican had difficulty answering the question:

> It's a good question but I don't know. . . . I never think in terms of due bills and maybe this is more applicable to the fellows farther down the table. When you get to the top you want to avoid due bills. I don't think anyone keeps a ledger. I certainly wouldn't want to get into a position of owing the Chairman something for what he's done because I'd never know what it would be I'd have to pay off on. We cooperate but it's not on that basis. . . . What most of the fellows want he can't give them, they're so big, so I don't know how much of this there is, actually.

His junior colleague also discounted the importance of favors in accounting for Mills's influence. He argued that if Mills can convince him, fine, but if he cannot he will not follow the Chairman.

> Doesn't operate that way. I suppose it's an unwritten rule. . . . You see in the press about member's bills but it's not as easy as the Chairman saying Jim's a nice fellow let's give him this. It takes unanimous consent, one objection is usually enough, and for most of them the departments are agreed. They have to be good little bills. I suppose Mills by objecting has control over all of them. I can honestly say Wilbur Mills has never asked me for a vote on anything. It doesn't operate that way. If he can convince me, fine, but I haven't seen much of the other generally. I'm a representative of my people and he's a representative of his, and we look at the merits.

The Republican members revealed the final subtlety that Mills is so cooperative and helpful with the members that they impose their own limits on what they ask of him. The Chairman's willingness to do favors for them is its own control on what they request. "In fact," said one Republican, "he's so cooperative and agreeable that you, I do at any rate, hold off on taking advantage, don't want to ask too much. If it's something big but not quite right yet I'll hold back; something small, I'll go to him and he'll say remind me to bring that up." Like others, this man has received praise from Mills which he has used in his campaign for reelection.

Democratic responses to the reward question, as indicated, discounted the importance of favors more than the Republicans. Two Democrats, however, did say that Mills has given them more than he has received. One cited three bills that were passed with Mills's help and, he felt, because of Mills's help. The other said, "He's never refused me on anything — any reasonable request I've had — *and I've never asked for anything unreasonable.*" He feels he has repaid Mills by, among other things, speaking for Committee bills on the floor where his reputation as a conservative Democrat might help get some southern votes, but in the light of the Chairman's own influence among the southerners he feels that his efforts may be a little redundant.

It is important that although the Democrats are less apt to say that Mills has done more for them, they feel that he has done much for them; and if they ever need his help, he will very likely give it. Five of the seven Democrats whose answers fell in categories two and three made one or the other comment, or both. The other two claimed that in Ways and Means merit alone determined all the outcomes.

One member who denied the importance of the quid pro quo in Ways and Means stressed the importance of group identity in the Committee. "You have to understand that we are twenty-five men in very close relationship. We have rapport with each other. It isn't quid pro quo. We do things for each other but it's not on a quid pro quo basis." The predominant form of exchange in the Committee is implicit, but this does not mean that exchanges do not take place. Indeed, it might be argued that exchange probably always will be implicit in a cohesive group, and, when transactions are overt, the group is probably in the process of disintegrating. That Committee members help one another without signed contracts is evidence of a highly integrated group with exchanges occurring among the members.

Mills interacts with the members in such a way that they sometimes feel indebted to him without quite knowing why and without being conscious of what is exchanged between them. A Democrat who answered "about even" reflected:

> I've probably done things for him but I'm not aware of any. I'm not conscious of it. It's not a transferral of mortgages

with Mills. There are a lot of mortgages around here, all of a
sudden the paper is presented and the mortgage falls due.
But not with Mills. I suppose I've done things for him but I
can't remember any. That's the kind of man he is. No reasonable request of mine has been turned down.

His relationship with Mills is much more nebulous than one based
on an explicit series of exchanges, but, for this reason, he is probably
that much closer to the Chairman.

Yet the vagueness of the exchanges should not be overemphasized.
There was nothing unclear or imprecise in the statement of the
Democrat who said, "It's pretty much a one-way street. Me to Mills
rather than Mills to me." Most interesting — and this serves as a
warning against the proposition that an influential man is one who
makes debtors out of others through the skillful use of rewards — is
that this man, far from feeling that he had a claim on Mills, was, of
all the members interviewed, probably the most likely to be influenced by Mills. The symbolism he used to describe his situation was
extreme but revealing: "It's like being allowed to touch the hem of
the Lord's gown. That's how it was with me." He said:

> Mills is autocratic as hell, but he doesn't make you feel that
> he is. He'll give you just enough things, let you ask enough
> questions, so he'll have you. This is what he does: you have
> something you want, you bring it to him, you bring the peo-
> ple who are on your back to him, and after making you sweat
> he'll let it in. And then he has command of you from then
> on. I always thought of myself as one of his boys. He's aloof
> but he'll bring you in.

Asked by the member for support on a proposal, Mills, after an appropriate wait, gave his support, gained the man's backing, and, by not
alienating the member, kept his backing until it would be useful to
his own purposes. Mills probably never had to ask this member for
assistance; the member no doubt looked for ways of helping the
Chairman.

At one end of the continuum Mills may do no more for a member
than agree to spend a few minutes listening to someone who has
asked a member to set up a meeting with him. This costs Mills time,
if not agreement with the supplicant's proposals, but it allows the
member who acts as the middleman to impress those who have access
to him, and it makes him indebted to the Chairman. Mills listens
patiently to the interest group representative, who, informed before-

hand by the Committee member not to expect Mills to give any un-equivocal reaction, leaves content with having stated his case. To the uninitiated lobbyist this can be a disconcerting experience. One former lobbyist found Mills "always cooperative, courteous, but you could never get Wilbur Mills to take a stand. If you didn't know him well you could go out of his office thinking he agreed with you and then realize later that he didn't really say that after all." But, at the very least, the interested party has had a hearing and a memo to a client that begins, "Today I had a chat with Chairman Mills," is an accomplishment. At election time, when he is confronted by the congressman with "Remember that chat you had with Wilbur . . . ," he is likely to respond. In between these events, the chances are good that Mills has put his arm around the member's shoulder and without reference to past favors asked if he couldn't possibly see his way clear to doing this or that, thus closing the circle of exchanges that makes up a large part of congressional life.

At the other end of the continuum, Mills may commit himself to include some member's proposal in a Ways and Means bill and ex-pend a great deal of energy in getting it enacted into law. The mem-bers know that because of his influence in the Committee his backing or at least his benevolent neutrality are important for them to imple-ment their ideas. Mills rewards the members every time he actively supports and adopts one of their suggestions.

Selling ideas to Mills is one primary task of a member of Ways and Means, and the Chairman appears to buy enough of them to retain a temperately used veto power over other proposals. By respond-ing favorably to some requests and negatively to others, Mills illus-trates the paradox which requires him to nourish his influence by rewarding members with his support for their goals while he judiciously kills some proposals, thereby dramatizing the importance of getting his support. The members may need the Chairman's backing to get something through the Committee but Mills, if he is to continue this relationship, must give his backing to some of the members' de-mands and, by rewarding them, continue to keep them in his debt if not in absolute bondage.

The Chairman's reward power is not confined solely to assisting members in meeting the substantive demands of their constituents and friends. As the formal leader of the Committee he can make decisions that determine how the Committee functions, his legitimate power, but he can also use his formal powers as rewards for the members. Too much should not be made of the little favors the Chairman does for members, but they should not be dismissed as irrelevant. As a Democrat said, with some exaggeration, "Members have bills they want passed, members they want to get on committees, provisions they want enacted, hearings they went held — these are the little intangibles that make him powerful."

For example, he controls such procedural matters as hearings and witnesses. It is not accidental that members commonly have the opportunity to deliver a flowery introduction for a prominent constituent. And, should a member get into a tight spot with a witness, Mills will often help extricate him. In both of these ways Mills utilizes the public hearings to improve his relations with the members.

Mills also controls the terms of House floor debate on the Committee's bills. Committee members have first call on debate time although there is usually sufficient time for all members. Mills can shift the spotlight from himself by letting other members handle time on the floor while he does other things.[40] He may even let a member's name appear on the Committee report and permit him to floor manage a bill, as Keogh did on a bill he pushed for years, H.R. 10.[41]

Another tactic the Chairman uses on the floor is the public acknowledgment of the great contribution some members of the Committee have made to the legislation being considered. This inducement, which Mills dispenses on a bipartisan basis,[42] is so much a part of the floor ceremony by now that it is doubtful if anyone gives it a second thought, but it is precisely the commonness of the practice that tells much about how Mills operates. It is, simply, something one expects from him; however, the same expectation is not universally associated with committee chairmen.

A related example of the Chairman's reward power is that he will help the members defend their records on the Committee. A staff man's disparaging remarks about a member's attendance and participa-

---

[40] This happened to Dan Rostenkowski during the 1965 debate on excise taxes when he happened to be close to Mills when the Chairman wanted to leave the microphone. See *Congressional Record*, July 2, 1965 (daily edition), p. 11891. Rostenkowski was pleased.

[41] House, Committee on Ways and Means, *Contributions By Self-Employed Individuals to Pension Plans, etc.*, 89th Cong., 2d Sess., 1966, H. Rept. 1557 to accompany H.R. 10. *Congressional Record*, June 6, 1966 (daily edition), pp. 11672–82.

[42] In 1965 Mills lauded Joel Broyhill's contribution to the medicare bill. Broyhill, who was strongly criticized for leaving the District and Post Office committees for Ways and Means, might not have found it necessary to use Mills's statement in his campaign but he could have if he wanted to. *Congressional Record*, April 7, 1965 (daily edition), p. 6959.

tion in the Committee were once used by the member's opponent. Mills wrote a letter testifying to the attacked member's service on the Committee and thereby helped to blunt the force of the charge. By thus protecting the members from criticism he gains their favor (and, it might be noted, removes one more stimulus for them to attend the meetings).

Taken singly, none of these favors is of great consequence. The members are right: only those concerned have an interest in such little things as members' bills. But without exaggerating the importance of favors and rewards to Mills's influence in the Committee it can be said that many members benefit from their relationship with him, and that the members, especially Republicans, believe that they get more from Mills than they return. Mills does not have a large number of valuable rewards to offer the members in return for their help, but by making use of what he has he establishes positive relationships with most of the members. When he suggests a compromise in the Committee, when he requests some assistance in passing a bill in the House, when he needs a minor adjustment in the social security law to help a lady in Arkansas, when he wants a freshman from Arkansas appointed to the Appropriations Committee — all of which have happened — the response of the Committee is likely to be favorable because of all the favors Mills has done for them. For, as one member said regarding the committee assignment, once Mills let it be known he wanted it for his man "you might as well not even have had a vote, no one is going to vote against him on this kind of thing. *He doesn't ask that much. . . .*"

REFERENCE. Most Committee members, if not all, identify with Mills. The members feel a sense of oneness with him, they like being closely associated with him, they care about their relationship with him, and they are influenced by him. The Chairman, by treating the members with respect, by being fair, by being knowledgeable in the subject matter, and by being receptive to their demands and needs, has ingratiated himself with them. Consequently, when a member disagrees with Mills he does it in such a way that the disagreement does not strain their relationship and, if possible, he prefers to agree with the Chairman more often than not.

The reference factor appeared in the interviews in different ways. One member, a Republican recently appointed to the Committee, commented that Mills treats the members so well — unlike some chairmen he has heard about — that the members feel drawn to him even though they may oppose him on certain issues. In his own case, he mentioned that one reason he attends the lengthy Committee meetings is because of Mills: "I feel compelled to go because he's there and if he does it. . . ." He also observed that Democratic attendance is not too good, "But Mills is there, he's conscientious." A Democrat, when asked if anyone had given him any advice as a newcomer to the Committee, said yes, but perhaps more important, "Unconsciously you sit there, watch Mills, and you start following him — that's all." A few members were asked if they would tell a newcomer to the Committee to emulate anyone, and the answers were predictable:

> Mills. He's quite a guy and a new member should watch the Chairman closely and get to know him well.
>
> I'd tell them to emulate Byrnes and Curtis. They are real students and they have done their homework. Mills too. Wilbur is a real student. He's not arbitrary but he's got respect and he's effective.
>
> Mills. No one else.

Another member talked disparagingly about those members who take pains to get close to Mills; who praise him all the time; who want, in his imagery, to "get close to the throne." This man finds it "repulsive." But in 1967 when Mills received a lot of publicity about the tax surcharge issue, the member visited his district and received an unusual amount of attention because of his membership on Ways and Means. He returned and told the Chairman, "Wilbur, you've made a great man out of me." That this member cares about his relationship with Mills was manifest in a story he told about what happened after he put something in the *Congressional Record* critical of a bill the Committee had reported. Mills "called me to task on this and I learned a lesson early." He assured the Chairman the material was not meant as a personal criticism of him and that, on the contrary, he had always tried to be one of Mills's "biggest public supporters." A similar thing happened to a second member who, informed by a staff man that Mills thought something he had said was critical of the way the Committee was run, informed the go-between that the statement in question was directed at the administration, not at the Chairman. It is not known if the word ever got back to Mills but the incident does show that this member, like his chastised colleague, is sensitive to his relationship with the Chairman.

This evidence indicates that Mills has great influence with the

Committee members. The members themselves see him as a master at influencing them and others. But Mills is not a master puppeteer. He deals with men who have all kinds of interests and are subjected to all sorts of competing demands and it sometimes happens that these demands pull them in ways contrary to the Chairman's direction. To a large extent, his influence lies in his skill at aligning his demands on the members with the other demands made upon them. In this process, his aforementioned proclivity to compromise, to bring opposing sides together, and to negotiate settlements of disputes is of prime significance.

Although nonconformity with Mills's decisions may turn out to be a necessity, once one has been drawn close to Mills it is an unpleasant necessity; if at all possible, the member is apt to agree with Mills and to behave in ways approved by Mills. This intricate process reaches its height when the member relieves his inner tension by explaining to Mills why he cannot go along with him and the Chairman, who probably has enough votes anyway, casually dismisses the incident as of no importance to their future, and firmly rooted, relations. By so doing the Chairman maintains — indeed adds to — his base of influence with the members.

SANCTIONS. "You talk about a chairman who uses his power ruthlessly, you're not talking about Wilbur Mills." This fact, commented on by a Democrat, is abundantly clear: the influence of Mills in the legislative process is not based on the sanctions that he, as the Committee Chairman, could use. Sanctions are defined as actions designed to bring about results through nonphysical coercion or force and hence, in contrast to rewards, generate negative affect on the part of other members of a group.[43]

The mark of Mills's leadership is that in doing the job as he defines it he relies on rewards, favors, expertise, persuasion, negotiation, and bargaining, not on coercing the members by using the sanctions that are available to him.

Unlike some committee chairmen, such as Graham Barden of North Carolina who chaired the Education and Labor Committee for eight years, Mills has not used his authority as chairman in such a way as to provoke extreme hostility — mixed with grudging respect — from the members. Mills's objective has been to get legislation out of his Committee with enough support behind it to pass in the House.

[43] See French and Raven's treatment of coercive power, *op. cit.*, pp. 614–15.

Barden's objective was to kill and, failing that, delay as long as possible federal aid to education, and his behavior as chairman reflected his perception of the Education and Labor Committee's job.[44]

With fundamentally different objectives Mills and Barden typify fundamentally different styles of leadership in the House. To marshall a majority Mills allows members and witnesses to speak at length; to prevent a majority from coalescing Barden permitted and encouraged the filibuster. To mark up legislation Mills holds the Committee to a stiff regimen; to thwart legislation Barden called meetings irregularly and established ad hoc subcommittees which he controlled. To proceed with speed Mills actively seeks a quorum; to procrastinate Barden banged the gavel and adjourned when a quorum was not immediately present. To ease the burdens of formulating legislation Mills surrounds the Committee with expert help; to heighten these burdens Barden kept the staff weak. To promote a workmanlike atmosphere in the Committee Mills seeks consensus; to promote confusion Barden sowed dissensus. To pass the bill Mills carefully maps the House terrain; to defeat the bill Barden allocated disproportionate time to opponents and once, near the end of the proceedings, threw the House into confusion by resigning as floor manager.

The intent of these comparisons between two chairmen is not to make one look good and the other bad but rather to highlight the kinds of sanctions Mills could use if he wanted. Given Barden's goals, the internal composition of the Education and Labor Committee, and the controversial nature of the subject matter his strategy is quite understandable; with different goals, a different parliamentary situation, and different tasks so too is Mills's.

At one time or another Mills has used many of the tactics employed by Barden, but with basically different objectives. Extended public hearings have delayed legislation, while Mills has quietly sought a reconciliation of demands with the objective of passing some form of the legislation. Confronted by resistance to a compromise on federal unemployment compensation standards in 1966 he, on at least one occasion and to the chagrin of no one, adjourned the Committee for lack of a quorum with twelve members present whereas, if time were of the essence, the thirteenth member probably could have been found. Like Barden, Mills has relied on Republicans to defeat certain

---

[44] The comments on Barden are based on Fenno's analysis of him: Richard F. Fenno, Jr., "The House of Representatives and Federal Aid to Education," *New Perspectives on the House of Representatives*, eds. Robert L. Peabody and Nelson W. Polsby (Chicago: Rand McNally & Co., 1963), pp. 209–12.

measures over the protest of a majority of Democrats on the Committee (e.g., medicare), but he has not done this so often that the members criticize him for being a Republican in Democratic disguise, as
they did with Barden. And, perhaps of greatest significance, Mills has
never brought his opposition to the House floor and attempted to defeat the bill by parliamentary legerdemain; as a matter of fact, bills
he opposes do not come to the House floor.

The contrast between Barden and Mills is stark even when, objectively, their tactics seem the same. For Barden, federal aid to education was an issue on which he was willing to sink, and go down with,
the ship; for Mills, there has never been a no-holds-barred issue on
which he has risked everything. The only bill before the Ways and
Means Committee that bears a strong resemblance to federal aid to
education is medicare and even here Mills, characteristically, had informed Speaker McCormack and through him the White House that
given enough time he would be able to work something out.[45]

Thus Mills, in seeking a consensus, relies on four of the five bases
of influence with which we began: expertise, legitimacy, rewards, and
reference. In the Committee's deliberations he will, if possible, stay in
the background by letting the active members, with some coaxing,
hit upon the compromise through their own effort. But because the
Quaker-like sense of the meeting may evade them, he will often articulate the compromise, and when he does the Committee has made a
"decision," always tentative depending upon further developments.
The low amount of negative affect expressed toward the Chairman
indicates that his style of leadership is approved of by the members,
and their agreement on the way he influences them through four of
the five bases of influence helps explain why, when he intervenes in
the discussion, his suggestions often constitute a Committee decision.

MILLS: THE SWING VOTE

When Mills persuades the members of the Committee to make certain decisions it may be on the basis of his expertise, or his influence
may be based on the way he has handled interpersonal relations in
the Committee, or it may be because the members are indifferent on
the outcomes. But then again it may be none of these. It may be a
simple matter of arithmetical influence: he has the votes. The Chairman's influence in the Committee is on some issues closely related to

[45] Theodore C. Sorensen, *Kennedy* (New York: Harper & Row, 1965), p. 343.

his position as the crucial swing vote between the coalitions that appear most often on Ways and Means issues. If the parties split cleanly Mills and the fourteen Democrats beat the Republicans 15–10. If an issue divides the Committee along liberal-conservative lines Mills and twelve Democrats can beat the Republicans and two conservative Democrats 13–12; or, in some cases, Mills and two conservative Democrats plus the Republicans can defeat the twelve Democrats 13–12. Mills, as a moderate, straddles the coalitions in Ways and Means and, because he does, he is rarely on the losing side. In recent years two conservative Democrats close to Mills, A. Sydney Herlong of Florida and John Watts of Kentucky, played leading roles in the coalition makeup of the Committee. Even if the other Democrats on the Committee banded together into a twelve-vote bloc, they still lost 13–12 without the Chairman, Herlong, and Watts. With the Chairman, the twelve Democrats won by the same margin. The pivot was the Chairman.

Evidence for the nature of coalitions in the Committee comes both from interviews and Committee votes. Because most issues are resolved without votes (a "consensus" is reached), partly because the shape of the blocs is relatively easy to predict, there are not many recorded votes to consider. But a few have been collected and they substantiate, with exceptions, the results of the interviews.

An HEW official sees Mills this way: "If he took an all-out Democratic or administration line he could steamroller it through, but he's more conservative than the administration, he doesn't do this." One of his HEW colleagues sees the importance of Mills's coalition position to his influence in the Committee even more clearly:

> It's not only that he's prestigeful, it's not only that he's chairman. It's that Mills stands at the center of the Committee and when he accepts something it doesn't get enacted just because he says "poof," but because he's at the center. He's generally more moderate than the Republicans and he's more conservative than the Democrats, so the Republicans know they can get just about what he accepts and same with the Democrats. If you sell Mills you've got it is both true and a truism. It's not just his personality, it's the nature of things in that Committee.

Liberal Committee Democrats are a potentially sizable bloc of votes but, with one or two exceptions, they are unlikely to split off into a discordant minority and attempt to reverse Committee decisions on the House floor. They are aware of the political realities in the Committee but given the style of Mills's leadership they are not closed off from influence in the Committee, which is one more reason they do not usually attempt to overturn the Chairman on the floor. One liberal Democrat, a typical non-crusader with a 100 per cent rating by the Americans for Democratic Action, understands the Chairman's "problem" in these terms: "Two or three of us on the Committee don't always get everything to our liking — liberals — but we understand his problem. I think the worst thing in the world for him would be to get defeated on a proposition on the floor. We understand his situation so it doesn't cause any problems — we can't win, we know it." He explained that if the Committee reported a bill by one vote the bill would have trouble passing the House so, although the Committee liberals may not be fully satisfied with the Mills consensus, they support it anyway. He illustrated his approach to liberal questions by a story about Aime Forand's unsuccessful efforts to get medicare reported by the Committee. According to this Democrat, Forand got so upset with Mills that he planned to force the issue to a vote in the Committee even though the Forand bill did not have a chance. This man, no less ardent in his desire for medicare than Forand, felt that Forand was unwise to press so hard for a lost cause.

Another liberal Democrat confirmed the futility of having votes in the Committee because of Mills's strategic position, but another liberal Democrat, who sees Ways and Means as "two-thirds conservative, probably always will be," feels that despite their minority status liberals can affect the legislation under a chairman like Mills:

> We liberals, though a small band, have an impact. I remember when aid to dependent children came up and they were going to cut it off at five children. I told them they had just declared war, it was an act of war in my district, and if they wanted a revolution they'd go ahead with it. I got so mad I walked out — but Mills said, "Oh come on back, let's talk about it" — that's what he says. I killed that proposal. . . . I was ready to take it to the floor, and they knew I would too, the bastards. They changed it.

With the presence of some conservative Democrats on the Committee and with the possibility of a stray Republican vote or two, poaching by Mills and Byrnes is a familiar part of the coalition-building process in Ways and Means. Both party groups have defectors except on the most basic issues (e.g., debt bills, reporting medicare, major revenue bills). On other issues the Republicans can lure some Democratic votes, and Mills can lure some Republicans. A Democrat said "The Republicans can reach right across and get Herlong and Watts anytime they want them. Mills is a swinger." It is not that easy for the Republicans (or for Mills), and the two Democrats most likely to defect often stay with Mills, but the minority is aware of their potential. A Republican told how it works:

> It's not the sort of thing you do formally. You don't sit down with them and say if we do this . . . it's not any kind of logrolling operation. But yes we have done this. You anticipate, sometimes you get it from how the hearings are going, and we may leave something out in hope of getting some of them. I thought we had Sydney [Herlong] on that provision you remember that tied the tax cut to some sort of expenditure control — he had introduced it. I talked with Sydney about it but Mills got to him and talked him out of it — even made a speech on the floor. Mills can do this sort of thing.

Forty recorded votes in the Committee have been collected since Mills became chairman in 1958,[46] and the results confirm the dominant position of the Chairman in the Committee. These votes are not comprehensive because more were taken than were reported. It must be noted, too, that many important issues never come to a vote in the Committee. For example, in 1964 Cecil King did not force medicare to a vote because he knew it would lose.

Of the forty votes, the Chairman has been on the losing side only seven times: a 1959 bill dealing with interest rates, a 1961 bill regarding tax treatment of the self-employed, a 1962 vote on unemployment insurance, two votes during the consideration of the tax reduction bill in 1963, a social security vote in 1964, and a 1966 vote providing federal standards for unemployment compensation programs. According to available data, therefore, Mills's reputation as a winner is deserved.

It is impossible to know if Mills could have won the seven votes he lost in the Committee had he made an all-out effort, but regardless of

---

[46] The forty votes include those reported in the *Congressional Record, CQ,* an unpublished doctoral dissertation on the 1964 Revenue Act by Everett Cataldo (Ohio State University, 1965), the public press, and, in some cases, by private sources.

the circumstances surrounding these votes he was on the losing side. He can be and has been beaten in the Committee, more often than in the House.

The 1963, 1964, and 1966 votes he lost are particularly important. In 1963 the administration, as part of its tax cut and tax reform proposal, suggested that Congress repeal the 4 per cent stock dividend credit and $100 exclusion. Under existing law, long subject to criticism by tax reformers, a person with dividend income from domestic corporations could exclude from his income the first $50 of dividends received and take a 4 per cent credit against dividend income over $50. This provision, worth $460 million a year in tax revenue, was put to a vote in the Committee, and the administration lost. By an 11–14 vote, with four Democrats joining the ten Republicans — and with Mills on the minority side both times — the Committee rejected outright repeal and a compromise plan to repeal the credit but keep the exclusion. Then, by a 13–12 vote, with only Herlong and Watts voting with the Republicans, Ways and Means adopted a compromise that repealed the 4 per cent credit but doubled the $50 exclusion. Evidently Mills could not persuade enough Democrats to move very far toward the administration proposal, but he could get twelve of them part of the way.

The next year Mills was on the losing side of a vote that some people believed would have killed medicare under social security. Mills, Herlong, and Watts joined the Republicans on a motion to increase social security benefits by 6 per cent, thereby raising social security taxes so high that it would have been difficult to fund medicare without an unacceptable increase in the tax. The Republican plan lost on a 12–12 vote when, with one Democrat absent, Bruce Alger voted with the pro-administration majority because he could not vote for such an increase in benefits. Were it not for this anomaly, Mills's side would have won.

Another defeat for Mills came in 1966 on the extremely controversial issue of the establishment of federal standards for minimum state payments for unemployment compensation. Backed by organized labor, a plan acceptable to the administration was defeated in the Committee when five Democrats, four of them conservatives, voted with the Committee's eight Republicans (the ratio had been changed in 1965) to kill the plan 13–11. One Democrat was absent but Mills could hold only ten of his party colleagues on this issue. Thus, even with a 17–8 majority in 1966, it was possible for the Chairman to lose on a key vote. After the vote the Committee proceeded to write a bill that could pass the House but, as Mills accurately predicted, "won't please either the White House or organized labor." [47]

If Mills is on the losing side it is most often because enough Democrats have defected to the Republicans to decide the issue. Five of his seven losses fall in this category. On the two remaining losses Mills did not take enough Democrats with him to win on one vote (1964 social security) and on the other he was well in the minority with four Republicans. Available data, therefore, indicate that for the Ways and Means Committee the primary job of the Chairman on votes is to contain Democratic defections, not take Democrats with him to defeat the Democratic majority through a bipartisan coalition. Mills's ability to defeat the Democrats by voting with the Republicans has deterred pressing issues to vote. Such a coalition kept the vital question of medicare in the Committee for several years.

This analysis of voting in the Committee treats Mills as a swing vote, but vote patterns alone do not show a causal relationship between the way he votes and the votes of the other members. His votes are treated as of special significance to the Committee because of the findings reported in the first two parts of this study, plus the perceptions of many observers that he does in fact stand at the center of coalitions in the Committee. From the mere fact that two Democrats voted "present" on the Republican amendment in 1963 to cut taxes only if the budget was no more than $98 billion in FY 1965, and the debt no more than $303 billion, for example, we cannot conclude that Mills influenced them. It is obvious that such a conclusion cannot be inferred from the vote despite the additional fact that this key amendment lost by only one vote (11–12). But everything that is known about the inner workings of the Committee suggests this conclusion and, in the absence of contrary evidence, the leap from the votes to Mills's influence does not appear to be unwarranted. Many other influences are at work in these votes but the Chairman is most certainly one of the most significant factors.

CONCLUSION

An intensive look has been taken at the Chairman of Ways and Means because, in the eyes of the members and those associated with the Committee, he is the dominant figure around whom much of the

[47] Quoted in "Jobless Aid Plan Facing Reversal," *The New York Times*, May 13, 1966, p. 21.

Committee's life revolves. Contrary to the impression one sometimes receives from newspaper stories about the "all-powerful" Chairman Mills, he is perhaps as responsive to the Committee as the Committee is to him. He no doubt has great influence with the members, but it is earned by the way he approaches his job and develops its potential. Ways and Means is highly centralized under Mills but the Committee's policy decisions emerge from an exhaustive — and collegial — process. The decisions of the Committee are shaped and articulated by Mills, but his word comes close to being law in the Committee because he has listened to others, particularly to the ranking Republican, John Byrnes. The fact that Mills legitimates Committee decisions in no way lessens his leadership of the Committee, but it is a particular kind of leadership and very likely to be effective given the nature of the group he leads.

Mills's influence in the Committee is also attributable to his pivotal position in the blocs that form on policy questions in the Committee. The Chairman, known as a leader who keeps his position if he has one to himself, has good reason to be cautious on the controversies surrounding Ways and Means. By letting others commit themselves first he follows a winning strategy that has paid rich dividends: he rarely loses. And because he leads the members as he does he sometimes can persuade enough of them to help him win by voting present, by voting with him, or by not voting at all.

CHAPTER FIVE

The Committee and the House

We don't move out very far ahead of the House.
Ways and Means Democrat

If Chairman Mills's idea of going on the offensive is to lean forward
in his foxhole, there is a sound reason behind it. Majorities are built
in the House, not elected to it, therefore House politics is coalition
politics. Neither party contingent is cohesively arrayed against the
other on many of the most controversial issues in the House, and the
possibility always exists that such issues will be decided by coalitions
of like-minded representatives, regardless of party considerations. To
see southern Democrats walk down the aisle with Republicans on
teller votes while the Democratic leaders watch nearby is to observe
an essential feature of the contemporary House in action.

Our purpose in this chapter is to investigate the relationship between the Ways and Means Committee and its parent chamber, the
House. Historically, of course, students of Congress have accepted
Wilson's dictum that the key decisions in Congress are made in the
committees with little control by the parent chamber. Some years
after Wilson's *Congressional Government* Bryce's observation was
easily accepted that "the House has become not so much a legislative assembly as a huge panel from which committees are selected." [1]
And one of the most perspicacious congressional observers wrote a
few years ago that "Congress is a collection of committees that come
together in a Chamber periodically to approve one another's actions." [2]

The emphasis on committee autonomy overlooks the fact that Wil-

[1] James Bryce, *The American Commonwealth*, rev. ed. (New York: Macmillan,
1911), Vol. I, p. 161.
[2] Clem Miller, *Member of the House*, ed. John W. Baker (New York: Charles
Scribner's Sons, 1962), p. 110.

son himself said that not all the committees were equally autonomous of the House. Two sentences before his famous comment that
"Congress in session is Congress on public exhibition, whilst Congress in its committee-rooms is Congress at work," he made the crucial but forgotten qualification that, "The House never accepts the
proposals of the Committee of Ways and Means, or of the Committee on Appropriations, without due deliberation; but it allows almost
all of its other Standing Committees virtually to legislate for it." [3]

Taking Wilson's qualification seriously, we will explore in this
chapter the patterns of interaction between the Ways and Means
Committee and the House since 1933. Of particular interest is the
level of party voting on Ways and Means bills in the 1930's, during
World War II, in the postwar Truman period, under Eisenhower in
the 1950's, and in the 1960's when the Democrats once again controlled Congress and the presidency. Partisanship varies greatly from
period to period, and the high internal integration of the Committee
that has been dominant in the 1960's has not always been characteristic of Ways and Means. Longitudinal differences in party voting and
integration are explained in terms of: (1) general societal conditions
within which the Committee and the House function; (2) the structure of coalitions in the House, with special reference to changes in
the strength of the two major parties and the emergence in the late
1930's of the conservative coalition; and (3) which party controls
Congress and the presidency. (For an explanation of which bills are
considered major legislation see Appendix B.)

In Part II, based mainly on data relating to the Committee in the
1960's, the Committee's independence of and dependence on the
House is studied. Chairman Mills emerges as the main link between
the Committee and other members of the House; he acts as the
conduit for House influence on the content of Committee legislation.
The closed rule is examined both as a source of independence for the
Committee and as a privilege granted to Ways and Means because
the Committee does its job in accordance with House expectations
centering around the demands of the interest groups that are affected
by Committee legislation. The policy consequences of the closed rule
and its effects on the Committee's relations with interest groups are
discussed.

In Part III we will focus more directly on three major elements in-

[3] Woodrow Wilson, *Congressional Government* (Cleveland: World Publishing,
Meridian Books, 1956), pp. 68–69.

volved in passing Ways and Means bills in the House: (1) the substance of Committee output, which tends to be an amalgam of provisions desired by liberals and conservatives but with relatively greater emphasis on the conservative side; (2) the activities of the Chairman who, as a southern Democrat, helps shape the content of Committee bills so that liberal demands and conservative demands are reconciled, and who then plays the central role in getting the Committee's decisions passed by the House; and (3) the importance of party considerations, and the role of party leaders, in helping the Committee majority pass its bills on the floor.

Throughout this chapter, the term "House demands" refers both to widespread attitudes in the House such as support or opposition to medicare and to such very specific attitudes as the demand that the Committee give interest groups a fair chance to express themselves on legislation considered by the Committee. The usual variety of opinions in the House tends to make the concept of House demands somewhat nebulous. By and large, "House demands" here refer to attitudes and opinions held by enough congressmen to become relevant inputs to Committee decision-making. In one case this may mean general antipathy toward increasing taxes; in another case it may mean the demands of a bloc of members for import controls on foreign-produced meat. Whether House demands become relevant to the Committee is both a Committee decision and a function of the voting power behind the demands. In general, the Committee has been more responsive to conservative rather than liberal demands because since the 1930's the conservatives have been more potent in votes in the Committee and in the House.

Two additional problematic terms are "conservative" and "liberal." Not every issue considered by the Ways and Means Committee falls in either one category or the other. Nor is there a perfect association between the members' positions on issues and their general tendency to take a liberal or conservative line on diverse policies. But the issues decided by Ways and Means can be described realistically in terms of liberalism or conservatism. Generally speaking, liberals on Ways and Means issues support the reciprocal trade program and the devolution of authority for trade decisions to the president; they support greater expansion in social security benefits and coverage than conservatives; and they are more willing to support fiscal policies designed to regulate the economy than are conservatives. If a tax question is related to government spending, a liberal is less inclined to support expenditure cuts than a conservative, and if the question of tax reforms comes up a liberal is more likely to see why certain reforms should be made than to accentuate the reasons for not acting. Obviously the diversity of policy covered by the Committee leaves much room for individual members to be conservative on some issues and liberal on others; these terms here describe general orientations toward questions handled by the Committee. The terms conservative and liberal, though notoriously vague, do describe general tendencies among members of the Committee and the House as a whole on Ways and Means issues.

I. MAJORITIES: 1933–1968

GENERAL SETTING. When the Ways and Means Committee reports a bill to the House and calls it up on the floor for passage, the bill's supporters must know if the majority formed in the Committee will be strong enough to pass the bill substantially unchanged on the floor. The Committee, of course, may report a bill that is bound to be amended on the floor or that has a slim chance of passing, but the normal objective is to pass the measure intact.[4] If there is a conspicuous incongruity between the Committee majority and the political alignments in the House, the bill may have to be amended on the floor to attract enough votes to pass it; in rare cases, the bill may be defeated outright. The immediate political task of the Committee is to construct a bill and a coalition to prevent floor amendments and ensure passage of the legislation.

Since 1933 the responsibility for enacting legislation has, in all but four years, fallen on the Democratic party. The House Democratic party — like its Republican counterpart — is composed of many diverse elements but has two major blocs: conservatives, mostly from

---

[4] The 1967 poverty bill is a good example of an alternative strategy. In 1967 the House went on an economy drive and there were grave doubts about the continuation of the poverty program. Republicans wanted to restructure the program by transferring OEO activities to other government agencies, and conservatives in general wanted to cut the program's authorization. Since cuts were inevitable, the problem facing the administration and House Democratic leaders was how to keep the program together with enough money to weather the economy wave. The Education and Labor Committee Democrats adopted the Green amendment to draw southern Democratic cooperation (by giving local authorities more control over Community Action Programs) but did not cut OEO's request for funds. Enough southern Democrats absented themselves from teller votes or voted with the leadership to defeat Republican amendments dismantling OEO, and the spending cut — the lesser of two evils for OEO supporters — was adopted on the floor.

the South, and liberals. A majority coalition can be built in three general ways: (1) the Democrats win if they do whatever is needed for a majority Democratic coalition regardless of how the Republicans vote; (2) the Democrats win if issues do not split the parties along party lines, i.e., if wide bipartisan agreement is attained; and (3) the Democrats win if enough Republicans cross over to offset Democratic defections, which are more likely among the southerners.

Which strategy is followed and the success of alternative strategies are obviously affected by the voting base of each of the elements in the House. If, for example, the Democrats have an overwhelming majority of the House, the potential voting power of the Republicans and southern Democrats is much less than under a closely balanced situation. With a large working majority the Democrats can win with or without the Republicans and southerners. Under these circumstances high partisan voting might be expected in the House; and, if the conservative coalition should appear, it would be relatively impotent. Changes in presidential programs should also be less because the premium placed on southern Democratic and Republican votes is less. As the party balance narrows, however, the importance of southern Democratic votes rises, intraparty bargaining may become more salient; either partisanship or bipartisanship may be high depending on the kinds of bargains that are made. Intraparty bargaining leads to high partisan voting; biparty bargaining to bipartisan voting.

These propositions are not startling, but they are important in understanding how decisions are made in the House and why bargaining and compromise are common features of the legislative process. Figure 5.1 shows the variety of situations that have existed in the House since 1933. Observers of the 89th Congress (1964–65) were struck by the relative ease with which the Democratic party enacted controversial and long-postponed legislation (e.g., medicare) when, after the 1964 election, two hundred and ninety-five Democrats organized the House. The 89th Congress was the nadir of the contemporary conservative coalition, but it is interesting that in his first three congresses Franklin Roosevelt had larger Democratic majorities three times running: 313, 322, and 333. If one hundred and forty Republicans posed little problem for the Democrats in the 89th Congress, even with the southern Democrats, the 75th Congress (1937–1938), when there were eighty-nine Republicans and the conservative coalition was still in the embryo stage, should have provided an even greater working majority for the Democrats.

FIGURE 5.1
PARTY CONTROL OF
HOUSE OF REPRESENTATIVES, 1933–1968

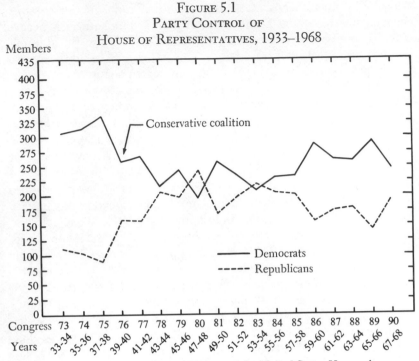

Source: George B. Galloway, *History of the United States House of Representatives*, H. Doc. No. 250, 89th Cong., 1st Sess., p. 218.

Southern Democrats are essential parts of the coalition-making process in the House, so it is necessary to know how their potential power has fluctuated since 1933. Using *Congressional Quarterly*'s definition of the South (eleven Confederate states plus Oklahoma and Kentucky), Figure 5.2 shows that although the number of seats held by southern Democrats has remained constant since 1933, with a drop beginning in 1963, the number of non-southern Democrats has oscillated wildly in response to electoral shifts. From a high of over 200 from 1935 to 1938 to a low of 72 in the 1947–48 period, with significant gains and losses in almost every congress, the non-southern Democrats — never constituting an absolute majority of the House — have alternated in strength while the southerners have remained at about the same level.[5] This helps explain why southern

[5] Actually, if independent "liberals" are added to the non-southern Democrats in the first three Roosevelt congresses there was, in effect, a liberal majority in the House.

FIGURE 5.2
SOUTHERN AND NON–SOUTHERN DEMOCRATS
IN THE HOUSE, 1933–1968

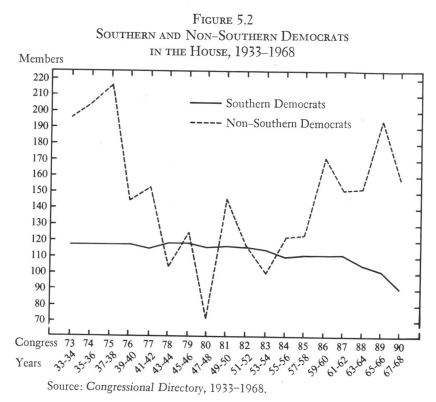

Source: *Congressional Directory, 1933–1968.*

Democrats occupy seniority positions in the House but it also means that once the conservative coalition began functioning in the late 1930's the southern half of the coalition always included a large part of the Democratic party in the House. In only one Congress (the 90th) have southern Democrats numbered less than one hundred of all the Democrats in the House.

Assume that the non-southern Democrats are in perfect harmony, and the problem confronting them on a bill is how to get enough votes for a majority. Figure 5.3 shows the severity of the problem. Except for the first three Roosevelt congresses, the 86th Congress (1959–60), and the 89th Congress, the non-southern Democrats have needed sixty or more Republican or southern Democratic votes for an absolute majority of the House. Of course, an absolute majority is rarely needed but the non-southern Democrats are as or more subject to absenteeism as other blocs, and though neither the Republicans nor the southerners are perfectly cohesive it is rare for all the rest of

FIGURE 5.3
NUMBER OF VOTES NEEDED BY
NON–SOUTHERN DEMOCRATS FOR ABSOLUTE
MAJORITY OF THE HOUSE, 1933–1968

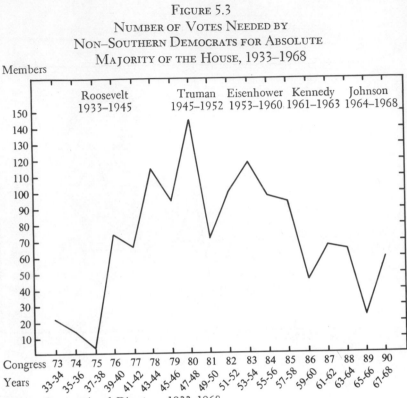

Source: *Congressional Directory*, 1933–1968.

the Democrats to vote alike. Since 1939 the potential for a powerful Republican–southern Democratic coalition has existed in the House requiring the Democratic party to draw enough southern or Republican votes or both to defeat the coalition or win with the coalition over a dissident liberal minority.

A rough picture of the coalitions that have appeared on Ways and Means bills since 1933 is presented in Table 5.1. Using the Rice Index of Party Likeness (IPL) on two hundred and forty-eight roll call votes from 1933 to 1965, it is apparent that the incidence of partisan voting on Ways and Means bills varies widely from period to period.[6]

[6] The IPL measures the difference between Republican and Democratic voting. It is computed by subtracting the percentage of yes votes of one group from the percentage of yes votes of the second group, and subtracting the remainder from 100. See Stuart A. Rice, *Quantitative Methods in Politics* (New York: Alfred A. Knopf, 1928), pp. 209–11.

TABLE 5.1

INDEX OF PARTY LIKENESS, WAYS AND MEANS AND THE HOUSE,
ALL ROLL CALL VOTES, 1933–1964 [a]

Roll calls in:	I		II		III	
	25% or less Committee	House	75% or more Committee	House	26%–74% Committee	House
1933–1939 (n = 65)[b]	43	38	29	26	28	35
1940–1946 (n = 29)[b]	31	31	45	41	24	28
1947–1952 (n = 45)	47	40	13	27	40	33
1953–1960 (n = 64)	16	16	41	59	44	25
1961–1964 (n = 45)	47	47	18	22	36	31

[a] On 59 of the 248 votes the Committee and the House fell in different categories. Because figures are rounded, they do not add up to 100 per cent in all cases. Pairs are included in calculating the IPL.

[b] Roll call votes on conference reports excluded.

Three of the five periods stand out for a high degree of partisan voting: 1933–39, 1947–52, and 1961–64. In the 1930's the Committee and the House voted along party lines (defined arbitrarily as an IPL score of 25 per cent or below) on 43 per cent and 38 per cent of the roll calls, respectively. In 1961–64, 47 per cent of the roll calls went along party lines for both the Committee and the House. Partisan coalitions in the Committee and the House were also common in the postwar years from 1947 to 1952. During World War II and the Eisenhower years Committee bills were more likely to elicit bipartisan and mixed voting than party-line voting, as expected during a national emergency and divided government.

Table 5.1 also shows that after the war, party division within the Committee occurred on more votes than in the House as a whole (column II), and that the vote in the House was more likely to be mixed than in the Committee (column III). From 1933 to 1947 the Committee was bipartisan and mixed on more votes than the House, though the differences are small.

These findings about House-Committee relations show that partisanship on Committee bills was high during the New Deal, low during World War II, high in the postwar years, low during the Eisenhower years, and high during the Kennedy-Johnson years. In addition, if the IPL for the Committee is compared to the House, the Committee index on the two hundred and forty-eight votes is lower than the House in 65 per cent of the cases, higher in 31 per cent of the cases, and the same in 5 per cent. Therefore the party differences

within the Committee are sharper than they are in the House, which
is expected from the earlier discussion of recruitment to the Committee. Generally the Committee split is reflected in the House vote,
though this is not true in every case.

Out of two hundred and forty-eight roll call votes since 1933, the
Committee coalition has won 93 per cent. Only eighteen votes have
gone against the Committee, as shown in Table 5.2, and only three
defeats were inflicted by the conservative coalition. Thus the rare
times when the Committee loses a roll call vote in the House are not
attributable to the conservative coalition.

In fact, the Committee coalition and the conservative coalition
when it appears are more often in harmony than in conflict, which
reveals much about the kinds of decisions reached in the Committee.
Table 5.3 shows that the conservative coalition has appeared on 22 of
the 248 roll calls, and has prevailed in the House on all but 2 of the
22. Thus it is much more common for the Committee coalition to be
assisted by the conservative coalition than defeated by it; it is the
liberal minority in the Committee and the House that loses when the
conservative coalition appears.

The most common reason behind a losing coalition on a Committee bill is that the bill does not divide the parties sharply enough. On
only two of the eighteen losses was the House highly partisan, on five
the vote in the parties was similar, and on eleven losses the House
vote was mixed. Thus mixed voting, not conservative coalition voting
in a strict sense, accounts for the bulk of Committee defeats.

These findings underline the importance of the recruitment process
to Ways and Means. The presence of conservative southern Democrats on the Committee, in the light of the political balance that
typically exists in the House, is functional for the passage of Committee bills. If the Committee splits along party lines this means that
liberal Democrats and conservative Democrats have reached agreement in the Committee, and this agreement may then be passed by
the House by a party-line vote.

That Ways and Means bills are not defeated by the conservative
coalition does not mean the coalition is irrelevant to the Committee.
Indeed, it suggests that the Committee, with southern Democrats
always represented on it, shapes many bills along conservative lines
and thereby prevents the coalition's appearance. Liberal Democrats
in the House rarely have enough votes to pose a serious threat to
Committee bills, but conservatives do. Hence decision-making in
Ways and Means has traditionally been oriented along conservative

TABLE 5.2

ROLL CALL VOTES LOST BY THE WAYS AND MEANS COMMITTEE, 1933–1964

Year	Bill and issue	House vote (yea–nay)	Committee vote (yea–nay)	Committee IPL (percentage)	House IPL (percentage)	Conservative coalition			
						Yes	No	Win	Lose
1. 1935	H.R. 3896. Patman amendment to Bonus bill.	202–191	7–16	59	64		x		
2. 1935	H.R. 3896. Vinson substitute amendment.	204–207	14–9	70	58		x		
3. 1938	H.R. 9682. McCormack amendment.	234–153	10–13	29	52		x		
4. 1938	H.R. 9682. Thompson amendment.	201–181	8–12	20	39		x		
5. 1941	H.R. 5417. Buck amendment to Revenue bill.	242–160	10–15	100	75		x		
6. 1943	H.R. 2218. Carlson recommittal motion.	248–168	9–16	10	23		x		
7. 1943	H.R. 2570. Robertson-Forand substitute.	230–180	11–13	13	28		x		
8. 1944	H.R. 2539. Pass tax bill.	126–168	13–4	85	100		x		
9. 1950	H. Res. 842. Excise tax bill conference.	105–226	12–10	44	83	x			x
10. 1951	H.R. 1612. Simpson peril-point amendment.	225–168	10–13	0	23		x		
11. 1951	H.R. 4473. Tax bill conference report.	157–204	11–9	40	53		x		
12. 1952	H.R. 7800. Pass social security bill.	151–141	13–7	30	67		x		
13. 1953	H.R. 5894. Recommit trade bill.	242–161	12–12	56	78	x			x
14. 1955	H. Res. 142. Closed rule on trade bill.	178–207	16–7	40	83		x		
15. 1956	H.R. 12227. Wool tariff bill (⅔ needed).	216–123	17–3	88	71		x		
16. 1958	H.R. 12065. Amend unemployment bill.	223–165	10–13	7	39		x		
17. 1959	H.R. 3151. Withhold city taxes (⅔ needed).	251–133	19–3	85	67	x			x
18. 1964	H.R. 8864. Implement coffee agreement. Conference.	183–194	17–7	40	40		x		

TABLE 5.3

ROLL CALL VOTES ON WHICH THE CONSERVATIVE COALITION HAS
APPEARED, WAYS AND MEANS BILLS, 1933–1964 [a]

| | | | Conservative coalition | |
Year		Bill	Win	Lose
1.	1935	H.R. 9100. Guffey Coal Bill.		x
2.	1944	H.R. 2539. Pass tax bill.	x	
3.	1944	H.R. 5564. Insurance contribution tax bill.	x	
4.	1945	H.R. 3633. War reconversion bill.	x	
5.	1945	H.R. 3633. Passage.	x	
6.	1947	H.R. 3950. Pass tax reduction bill.	x	
7.	1947	H.R. 3950. Override Truman veto.	x	
8.	1948	H.R. 4790. Pass tax reduction bill.	x	
9.	1948	H.J. Res. 296. Maintain status quo on social security.	x	
10.	1948	H. Res. 510. Accept Senate amendments to H.R. 4790.	x	
11.	1948	H.R. 4790. Override Truman veto.	x	
12.	1948	H.R. 5052. Override Truman veto.	x	
13.	1948	H.J. Res. 296. Override Truman veto.	x	
14.	1950	H.R. 6000. Social security bill.	x	
15.	1952	H.R. 7800. Pass social security bill.	x	
16.	1953	H.R. 5173. Recommit social security bill.	x	
17.	1954	H.R. 9709. Recommit unemployment bill.	x	
18.	1954	H.R. 9666. Pass trade bill.	x	
19.	1958	H.R. 12065. Herlong amendment.	x	
20.	1960	H.R. 5. Foreign investment bill.		x
21.	1960	H.R. 12381. Closed rule debt-tax bill.	x	
22.	1964	H.R. 1839. Conference report beef imports.	x	

[a] "South" defined here as the eleven former Confederate states.

lines, and if the Republicans are not satisfied with the result, the
Democratic majority usually is. The roll data suggest that this is
usually sufficient.

MAJORITIES: 1933–39. In the 1930's the Democratic majorities
were so large that the majority party had little need of and hardly
any use for Republican votes. The period was unique.

Under the circumstances, the main problem facing the Democrats
was to keep enough of their members together to decide outcomes,
and the obvious way for this to be done was through intraparty bargaining. High partisanship, therefore, could be expected. But what
was not expected was that the Ways and Means Committee throughout much of this period was more a bipartisan committee in composi-

tion than in operation. Partisan disagreements over policy were accompanied by virtually complete disintegration of the Committee. On many of the major bills in the 1930's the Democratic members of the Committee marked up the legislation, made the bargains, and reported the results to the House with no more than perfunctory recognition that Republican members of the Committee existed.

This observation, of course, requires a distinction between partisanship and integration. High party conflict over issues may lower the integration of committees but, as is apparent with the contemporary Ways and Means Committee, this need not always be true. Integration refers to a sufficient imbalance on the side of rewards compared to costs so that the members of a group — regardless of internal differences — are motivated to do whatever is necessary to protect the power and prestige of the group. A concomitant of integration is a sense of unity that transcends party lines and limits the style, if not the content, of party conflict. In this sense the Committee under Mills has been highly partisan on many issues, but highly integrated as well. In the 1930's the dominant characteristic of the Committee was partisan conflict and disintegration.

In the first Roosevelt Congress, the 73rd (1933–34), Democrats outnumbered Republicans 313–117, but it took about a year for partisanship to become the dominant factor on Ways and Means bills. Politics as usual was suspended in 1933 as a result of the economic emergency, and not until the following year did party lines begin to break cleanly, a pattern that was to be repeated on major bills until 1939. When the Committee reported its first bill in 1933, a tax measure allowing the manufacture and sale of beer, a Committee member set the tone, "Mr. Speaker, this is the third time within a week that a great majority of the Republican side of the House will support President Roosevelt in his request for important legislation looking toward the balancing of the National Budget. It is by far the finest demonstration of nonpartisan politics that has been presented during my more than twenty years' service." [7]

The thrust toward bipartisanship was still going strong two months later when the House took up the National Industrial Recovery Act (NIRA). The Committee's senior Republican, Allen T. Treadway of Massachusetts, was willing to try anything for economic recovery: "A balloon has been sent up which may or may not aid industry and return people to work. We have tried various expediencies without suc-

[7] *Congressional Record*, March 14, 1933, p. 376.

cess. Here is a new lotion. Try it. Try anything." [8] The act was reported by Ways and Means without a dissenting vote, a Republican
noted, and in "the consideration of the measure itself partisanship
was laid aside and every member thereof was animated by but one
purpose — to give to the President every possible cooperation in his
program. . . ." [9] On final passage, only one Ways and Means member voted nay. Of six substantive roll call votes on Ways and Means
bills in 1933, only one was party-line for the Committee and the
House.

Harmony in 1933, however, was not the start of an era of good feeling. Giving Roosevelt every possible cooperation in his program died
in 1934 and was not reborn until another national emergency, World
War II, once again united the parties.

The year 1934 began on a peaceful note. During floor debate on a
liquor tax bill Committee Republican James A. Frear took time to
praise the administration of the Committee under Chairman Robert
L. ("Muley") Doughton of North Carolina. Frear claimed that there
were no serious controversies in the Committee or in the tax subcommittee headed by Samuel B. Hill of Washington. "We recognize," Frear said, "those in control of the committee, the majority,
could put through any piece of legislation desired. But they have
been very fair. I speak as an individual, and I want to thank the
gentleman from North Carolina and the gentleman from Washington for the consideration they have both given us." [10]

The Democrats might have refrained from simply voting this bill
out of the Committee without regard to the Republican position, but
party differences appeared when Treadway revealed that the minority
refused to vote on the question of how high the tax on distilled spirits
ought to be. They took the position — and voted "present" twice —
that not enough evidence had been presented on which to base a fair
opinion, and laid responsibility for the tax on the majority.[11] Moreover, the Committee Republicans offered a motion to recommit
(kill) the bill, which split the Committee along party lines. On final
passage, however, only five members of the House — none of them
members of the Committee — opposed the bill.

[8] *Ibid.*, May 25, 1933, p. 4331. For an analysis of minority party strategies see
Charles O. Jones, "The Minority Party and Policy-Making in the House of Representatives," *American Political Science Review*, LXII (June, 1968), 481–93.

[9] *Congressional Record*, May 25, 1933, p. 4227.

[10] *Congressional Record*, January 4, 1934, p. 103.

[11] *Ibid.*, p. 131.

After the liquor tax bill, Ways and Means came together in a bipartisan coalition behind a revenue raising and reform bill. The Republicans lined up solidly behind a motion to recommit the bill to lower the first class postage rate from $.03 to $.02, but when this failed the tax bill passed the House with no Committee member opposing.[12] At the appearance of the next major bill reported by the Committee, the Reciprocal Trade Act, party lines hardened in the Committee and did not soften until the emergence of a strong conservative coalition in 1939.

During the mark-up of the trade bill the Committee met at least the minimum standard of bipartisanship, i.e., the Democrats let the Republicans participate in the discussions. But on the substantive issues involved there was no common ground. Nor was this unexpected. "There is no economic subject," a Ways and Means Republican said, "upon which there exists greater differences in opinion than on the tariff. Indeed, it is the main line of cleavage between the two major political parties, so it was inevitable that the majority and minority reports submitted with the measure now under consideration should reflect the attitude of the two groups." [13]

With such an issue, and with enough Democratic votes to obviate any need for bipartisan bargaining, the substance of the bill was wholly determined by the majority party. One Republican member of the Committee told his colleagues that he would not join them in a minority report if certain amendments were adopted, but when these changes were defeated by party-line votes he joined the opponents.[14] The result was a straight party-line split on the bill.

Party conflicts over issues, however, were not the only kind of conflict to appear in 1934. The Committee also had open conflict over such procedural questions as whether to hold public hearings. There was some grumbling over the speed with which the trade bill went through the Committee, but two months later the Committee split apart completely on a major silver bill. The Republicans complained — on the floor of the House — that the majority was in such a hurry to pass the bill that they would not even hold open hearings on the matter. Doughton denied the Republican charge but the Committee was disintegrating.[15] By 1935 the cooperative spirit of 1933 and the national crisis no longer permeated Ways and Means; on most major

[12] *Ibid.*, February 16, 1934, p. 2657 ff.
[13] *Ibid.*, March 24, 1934, p. 5343.
[14] *Ibid.*, March 27, 1934, pp. 5522, 5527.
[15] *Ibid.*, May 30, 1934, pp. 10,002–006; 10,020–21.

issues the Committee was in effect a committee of the Democratic majority. Party government, of a sort, came to the House. As Frear had recognized at the start of 1934 the Democrats could put through almost anything they desired; in 1935 and subsequent years they did almost that.

"We do not want their advice, because we know they are going to stick a knife in our Democratic backs every time they can on everything we propose." [16] This was not a member of the Education and Labor Committee speaking in the heat of a bruising fight over federal aid to education or the poverty program. The speaker was, rather, a Democratic member of Ways and Means in 1938 defending the practice of writing Ways and Means bills in Democratic caucuses without the Republicans present. He articulated an attitude and a practice that made the Committee in the 1930's basically different from the Committee of the 1960's.

The 322–103 Democratic majority in the House after the off-year 1934 election was even larger than it had been in the 73rd Congress, and the party ratio on Ways and Means was changed accordingly, from 15–10 to 18–7. An eleven-vote margin inside the Committee and two hundred and nineteen votes in the House created less of a stimulus for bipartisan coalition-building than before, and it is hardly surprising that the Republicans in the House felt slighted.

They felt more than slighted; they were enraged. Ways and Means reported five major bills to the House in the 74th Congress and on four of the five the Republicans claimed — and the Democrats acknowledged — that the majority developed the bills in caucus and presented the results to the minority, for their information, not for approval.

No bill captured the high ideological overtones of the New Deal better than the so-called soak-the-rich tax bill of 1935. As a partial response to the popular "share the wealth" battlecry of Huey Long, Roosevelt proposed steps to increase taxes on upper income taxpayers, and the Ways and Means Committee hastened to respond to his requests. In fact, in some ways the Committee went further in increasing taxes on the wealthy than the president had recommended.

The Committee Democrats did not stop to consider the predictable Republican response. "We knew from the very beginning," a leading Ways and Means Democrat told the House, "that they were

[16] *Ibid.*, March 4, 1938, p. 2868.

opposed to the legislation. We knew that the bill that was written would have to be written by the Democratic members of the committee, and we did the job." [17] The product of the Democrats' labor was, to Treadway, a "monstrosity" which would only pass the House "under the crack of the whip of the White House." [18] The Republicans also claimed that without inordinate party pressure there would have been enough Democratic votes in the Committee to join the minority in rejecting important parts of the bill. With such pressure, they dolefully concluded, "Representative government ceases to exist. . . ." [19] Interparty relations were so strained on this bill that Chairman Doughton observed that if a Republican member attended Ways and Means sessions as regularly as the Democrats he would know how hard the Committee worked. The Republican answered Doughton that his attendance was good, he never missed an important vote, and, anyway, the Democrats locked the Republicans out.[20] After three dozen amendments and a recommittal motion by Treadway were turned back, the Democrats passed the bill 282–95.

The winning vote was 267–93 on the revenue bill the following year. At first the Democrats established a bipartisan subcommittee to study the Revenue Bill of 1936 but, according to Doughton, it became clear that the Republicans wanted no bill so the Ways and Means Democrats wrote one without them.[21] This time Treadway inveighed against the Committee not only for ignoring the Republicans and doing a bad job, but for actually intimidating the witnesses who appeared to testify on the proposal:

> In the Ways and Means Committee room they went snooping around, instructing their clerks to find out the salaries being paid to men appearing before the committee. This is a fine way to treat people appearing, and it is a splendid way to induce witnesses not to appear. If this sort of procedure keeps up, the only way we will ever get any witnesses will be by subpena [sic]; they will not come voluntarily if this is the way they are to be treated by what is supposed to be one of the leading committees. Humph! [Laughter].[22]

[17] *Ibid.*, August 1, 1935, p. 12299.
[18] *Ibid.*, pp. 12304–05.
[19] *Ibid.*, p. 12306.
[20] *Ibid.*, p. 12312.
[21] *Ibid.*, April 23, 1936, p. 5979.
[22] *Ibid.*, p. 5991.

One Ways and Means Democrat who opposed the bill on the floor revealed that when he asked Doughton for time to speak he was told to get it from the Republicans. Treadway obliged.[23]

Two other bills were handled without the Republicans in 1935. During the mark-up of S.J. Res. 113 (to extend Title I of NIRA for one year) the Republicans "applied for admission" to the Committee room and were barred because the Democrats were having a caucus.[24] Similar Democratic caucuses were held on the Guffey coal bill.

The Guffey coal bill illustrates precisely how independent of the Republicans the Democrats were in this period. Five Ways and Means Democrats opposed the bill and even John McCormack spoke against it on the floor. By getting two Democrats to vote "present" the bill was reported from the Committee and, after several floor amendments were adopted, passed the House over the opposition of the conservative coalition, 194–168. A major controversial bill, in other words, could be passed despite Republican opposition and a large number of southern Democratic defections.[25]

By 1937 despair had replaced anger among the Republicans. On the first bill brought to the floor Treadway said, "Why should we even take the time to read the bill? There is no use reading it. We know how the majority is going to vote." [26] The 1936 Roosevelt landslide brought 333 Democrats and 89 Republicans in the House in 1937. Small wonder the Republicans lost their fight.

Yet there was relative calm inside the Committee throughout 1937. No new major bills were considered and the only piece of legislation of major consequence to come from the Committee was a three-year extension of the Trade Act. The Committee and the House split along party lines on this question, almost routinely, but the bitter recriminations of 1935–36 were missing. In the absence of major administration proposals to resolve there were no major conflicts. The first session of the 75th Congress was the quietest in a long time.

The second session, except for one major bill, appeared devoid of significant conflict. Actually the developments surrounding the Revenue Act of 1938 marked the end of an era in party politics for the Committee. It was the last time for many years that the Democrats worked completely without the Republicans and it was the first time that a fatal split occurred within the Democratic coalition. Surpris-

---

[23] *Ibid.*, April 24, 1936, pp. 6084–85.
[24] *Ibid.*, June 7, 1935, p. 8881.
[25] *Ibid.*, August 16–18, 1935, p. 13437 ff.
[26] *Ibid.*, March 9, 1937, p. 2063.

ingly, the split was occasioned not by one of the southern Democrats on Ways and Means but by John McCormack, an unlikely candidate for leader of a bipartisan coalition against the administration.

At issue was the taxation of undistributed corporate profits, which was cherished by Roosevelt "as one of the main weapons against economic royalists. . . ." [27] Ways and Means, as before, divided into two camps after the Republicans proved intransigent on the bill. "It happened," said Treadway, "that we occasionally stumbled into the committee room and found our Democratic colleagues hard at work." [28] According to Dan Reed of New York, fourth-ranking Republican on the Committee, Treadway "made it a practice every morning to rap upon the door of the committee room, only to find it locked and to hear the buzz of voices in heated argument within. . . . In due time, of course, we were invited in, when their will power had been bent to that of the Executive." [29] Even when notified of Committee meetings, the Republican members, in the words of another Republican, did not attend because they "did not want to waste our time sitting there watching the Members of the majority driving another peg into the coffin of American industry." [30]

But this was, by now, standard procedure on controversial bills. Of far greater significance, the Democratic members of the Committee failed to construct a solid majority party coalition behind the bill in the Committee and to drive it through the House untouched by amendments. This was new.

It was also curious. McCormack's objection to the bill was that one section of it would tax small companies — newspapers, textiles, etc. — not large monopolies, and though he said he would vote for the measure even if it contained this section he felt it should be stricken from the bill.[31] A few days later, after Doughton noted that two Democrats had voted with the seven Republicans against reporting the bill (16–9), McCormack felt compelled to defend his love of party and his long record of party regularity. He hurled the charge back at Doughton saying that the Chairman's party record, if anyone's, was suspect.[32]

[27] James T. Patterson, *Congressional Conservatism and the New Deal* (Lexington: University of Kentucky Press, 1967), pp. 229–30.
[28] *Congressional Record*, March 3, 1938, p. 2772.
[29] *Ibid.*, p. 2787.
[30] *Ibid.*, pp. 2787–88.
[31] *Ibid.*, March 4, 1938, pp. 2855–57.
[32] *Ibid.*, March 9, 1938, p. 3136.

The Democrats were no longer united. McCormack's amendment to strike the section was adopted on the floor by a 180–124 teller vote. Because amendments passed in the Committee of the Whole can be subject to a roll call vote after the House completes action on all amendments, the McCormack amendment could have been defeated after the teller vote. But, in fact, it was sustained on a 234–153 roll call. Four Ways and Means Democrats were joined by six of the seven Committee Republicans (one did not vote) plus two hundred and twenty-four other House members in what was, according to Treasury Secretary Henry Morgenthau, "the worst slap the President had had to take during his entire administration." [33]

The slap stung because it was inflicted by a previously united and virtually omnipotent Democratic majority in the House. It was the first self-defeating break in the Democratic ranks and a portent of things to come. True, the coalition was not spearheaded by disaffected southern Democrats. McCormack was the leader and none of his three followers on Ways and Means was a southerner. But the break was a signal that the days of tight Democratic majorities were numbered; it also signaled that henceforth controversies had to be reconciled in the Committee. The days of easy majorities on almost any given issue were over.[34]

In his annual review of the past congressional session, the ranking Republican on Ways and Means, Allen Treadway, observed in 1939 that "looking back over the past session of Congress it becomes apparent that sanity in government is on the way back and that the Congress is gradually reasserting its legislative authority." [35] Why the change? He gave two reasons: (1) the skillful leadership of the newly elected Minority Leader, Joseph W. Martin; and (2) the 1938 election. "By increasing the Republican membership in the House from 89 to 169," he said, "they [the electorate] made it possible for the minority, with the assistance of a small group of Democratic Mem-

[33] Quoted in Patterson, *op. cit.*, p. 231. For the executive branch view of this issue see John Morton Blum, *From the Morgenthau Diaries* (Boston: Houghton Mifflin, 1959), Vol. I, pp. 439–51.

[34] Many minor bills in this period were handled by the Committee in a bipartisan way. There was even one major one, the 1935 Social Security Act. This was a partisan bill in the sense that the parties divided on it but Ways and Means marked it up with the Republicans present and participating in the discussions. Of all the bills in the 1930's the handling of social security most nearly resembles current Committee practice: no subcommittees, deep party differences on basic questions, but restrained partisanship while the bill was before the Committee.

[35] *Congressional Record* (*Appendix*), August 5, 1939, p. 4069.

bers who put country above party, to muster sufficient strength to check New Deal waste and extravagance, to remove some of the impediments which the present administration has placed in the way of recovery, and to take definite steps toward the restoration of representative government." [36]

One may completely discount the partisan rhetoric in this statement, and wonder if a minority party joined in a voting coalition by a minority of the majority party really heralded the return of representative government, but it is indisputable that Treadway identified two aspects of the 76th Congress that make it the forerunner of the modern Congress. In all Congresses since the 76th the party balance has given at a minimum the minority party the base for building a strong coalition, and, in conjunction with like-minded Democrats, the wherewithal to make their votes important.

Joe Martin's contribution to the conservative coalition was in erecting a bridge between himself as Minority Leader and such disaffected Democrats as Eugene Cox of Georgia and Howard Smith of Virginia. He also persuaded the Republicans to tone down their anti-Democratic outbursts that drove conservative Democrats back to their party. He and his Republican followers let conservative Democrats carry the brunt of the attack on some New Deal legislation and, after temperate cheers from the sidelines, joined the Democrats when the roll was called. The strategy was simple, but it worked.[37] And it worked because in 1939 there were 169 Republicans in the House whereas in 1937 there had been 89. As one writer estimates, only fifty Democratic defections were needed to defeat the administration.[38]

Not enough evidence has been gathered to support a direct causal relationship between the party balance in the House, the subsequent development of the conservative coalition, and the changes within the Ways and Means Committee, but the changes in the Committee are most striking indeed. From a partisan, fractious, and discordant organization Ways and Means was suddenly transformed into a bipartisan, orderly, and harmonious group in 1939, and this pattern of internal decision-making was not to change until the Republicans gained control of the House in 1947. The war obviously had much to do with the internal transformation of the Committee but the change

[36] *Ibid.*
[37] Patterson, *op. cit.*, pp. 306–08. For Martin's own account see Joe Martin (as told to Robert J. Donovan), *My First Fifty Years in Politics* (New York: McGraw-Hill, 1960), pp. 84–85.
[38] Patterson, *op. cit.*, p. 290.

antedated the national crisis, it coincided with the new political structure of the House in 1939, and, it appears, might have been attributable to the new political realities in the House.[39]

Ways and Means reported two major bills in 1939: the Social Security Amendments of 1939 and the Revenue Act of 1939. The Committee did not reach perfect agreement on either of them but, compared with previous years, the level of agreement was noteworthy.

Doughton opened debate on the Social Security Amendments: "This is the first bill of this magnitude and importance, and of such controversial a nature, to be free from any evidence whatever, the least trace, of partisanship, as far as our deliberations were concerned during the consideration and preparation of the bill in executive session." [40] A supplemental report was filed by the Republican members of the Committee but it was not in opposition to the bill. In fact, Treadway spoke *for* the bill on the floor and Dan Reed, who also backed the bill, observed that it was a much better measure than the one he had opposed in 1935.[41]

The policy consequences of the new relationship between Democrats and Republicans on the Committee were significant. Two major bones of contention between the parties over social security — Democratic insistence upon the accumulation of a $47 billion reserve fund for old-age insurance and Republican insistence in 1935 on increasing the federal contribution for old-age pensions — were both resolved. The $47 billion reserve fund was dropped and the federal contribution increased. An amendment offered by Committee Republican Thomas Jenkins of Ohio in 1935 regarding aid to the blind, and rejected by the Democrats, was offered again by Jenkins in 1939 and this time he offered it as a Committee amendment. Not only was it unusual for a Republican to offer a Committee amendment but

---

[39] It may be more than a coincidence, and it is fascinating, that the conservative coalition in the House did not develop until the party structure in the House made it possible for such a coalition to have an effect. In the 1930's the House, in sharp contrast with later years, was more liberal and less of a problem for the administration than the Senate. Signs of a conservative coalition began to appear in the House as early as 1937, particularly in the House Rules Committee, but not until 1939 did an effective full-fledged coalition emerge. Its emergence was no doubt assisted by growing disenchantment with Roosevelt, the half-hearted effort to purge some Democrats in 1938, the Court-packing plan of 1937, and the election in 1939 of Joe Martin as the Minority Leader. But the fact that in 1937 there were 333 Democrats in the House compared to 262 two years later should not be overlooked. For a recent study of the coalition see Patterson, *op. cit.*

[40] *Congressional Record*, June 6, 1939, p. 6689.

[41] *Ibid.*, June 9, 1939, p. 6891.

Jenkins and the Republicans received a special tribute from McCormack: "The statement of the gentleman from Ohio indicates the very fine spirit that existed among the entire membership of the Committee on Ways and Means, without regard to party affiliation, during the entire consideration of this bill, which extended over several months." [42] In his year-end report Treadway could claim that the Republicans had had a marked effect on the social security program, that the increased money for vocational rehabilitation was the result of Reed's efforts in the Committee, and that "Social security is not a partisan question." [43] For it had not been.

With a solid bipartisan majority behind the Committee bill, thirty-nine floor amendments were easily defeated. Toward the end of the floor action Treadway praised Doughton for the way he ran the Committee, his love of harmony, his nonpartisanship, and his courtesy toward the Republicans. Doughton reciprocated with an equally saccharine tribute to Treadway and the Committee's minority. A Republican newcomer to the Committee then offered a pro forma motion to recommit that lost by voice vote, and the bill was passed 364–2.

One bill does not, of course, mean that the Committee underwent a basic change in 1939. The 1935 social security bill had, after all, been handled in a bipartisan way with the Republicans claiming credit for some of its provisions even though they offered major amendments on the floor of the House. But another major bill in 1939 — the Revenue Act — was developed in the Committee and presented to the House in the same way as the social security bill, i.e., with strikingly less partisan acrimony than had been true of prior revenue bills. Together these two bills ushered in a period of relative harmony for the Committee.

Treadway's opening speech on the Revenue Act of 1939 was notable in that the standard denunciation of the Democrats was absent. Not that he failed to criticize the New Deal, which, he claimed, made the removal of tax inequities necessary, but he was restrained in his remarks. He said that he did not want to attack the bill severely — he made only two suggestions for change — and, when a Republican broke in with some caustic remarks about how badly the Democrats treat the Republicans, Treadway, in keeping with Martin's strategy, poured oil on the water by, mirabile dictu, defending the

[42] *Ibid.*, June 10, 1939, p. 6960.
[43] *Ibid.* (Appendix), August 5, 1939, p. 4071.

Democrats. He declared that the privilege of the majority party is to bring bills to the floor under closed rules prohibiting amendments (he himself had been a vocal critic of closed rules in earlier years), and, anyway, the Democrats had not been all that bad because the 1935 Social Security Act and the present bill both had open rules.[44]

Despite this outbreak of peace in the Committee, important if not fratricidal differences between the parties remained on specific issues. Treadway noted with satisfaction that after rejecting a Republican proposal on the carryover of business losses by a 15–10 party-line vote the Democrats reversed themselves and adopted the minority amendment. He lauded the Democrats for letting the controversial undistributed-profits tax expire (Secretary Morgenthau had sold expiration to Roosevelt with great difficulty), but he argued that excise taxes should not be extended and that the bill's relief provision for business should take effect in 1939 rather than 1940. He offered amendments to implement these proposals and, when the amendments were turned down, he offered a substantive motion to recommit that lost on a party-line vote, 150–205. Once the Republicans lost on these questions, however, the basic appeal of the bill to both parties was reflected in the 357–1 vote by which it passed the House.

MAJORITIES: 1940–1946. From 1940 to 1946 World War II was of vital importance to politics in the House. The Democrats gained five seats in the 1940 election, which were hardly enough to give them policy control of the House, and in the two remaining World War II congresses the Democratic majority was a good deal slimmer than it was in 1939, 222–209 and 243–190 respectively. There were, then, two reasons for bipartisan policy-making: (1) the war; and (2) the Democrats did not have a large enough majority to be immune from defeat by a conservative coalition. In addition, the war effort precluded serious consideration of the social and economic questions most likely to divide the parties. Social welfare legislation and tax reform were not, of course, prominent issues in the war years.

Party differences over Ways and Means issues, though attenuated during World War II, were not, as Table 5.4 records, completely absent. There was a strong tendency for the Committee to be united on the floor but on five of the twenty bills presented in Table 5.4 the Committee split along party lines, and on four of the twenty Committee voting was mixed. Bills in each of the three categories reveal

[44] *Congressional Record*, June 19, 1939, pp. 7467–78.

TABLE 5.4

INDEX OF PARTY LIKENESS, WAYS AND MEANS COMMITTEE VOTING, 1940–1946 [a]

Bipartisan majority (IPL 75% and above)			Partisan majority (IPL 25% and below)			Mixed majority (IPL 26–74%)		
Year	Bill	Committee IPL (percentage)	Year	Bill	Committee IPL (percentage)	Year	Bill	Committee IPL (percentage)
1940	H.R. 10039. Revenue Act.	100	1940	H.J. Res. 407. Trade Act Extension	0	1943	H.R. 1780. Debt Limit-Salary Bill.	50
1941	H.R. 5417. Revenue Act.	100	1941	S.J. Res. 43. Coffee Agreement.	0	1943	H.J. Res. 111. Trade Act Extension.	47
1942	H.R. 6691. Debt Limit.	100	1943	H.R. 2218. Income Tax Collection. Recommittal motion.	10	1944	H.R. 5564. Social Security.	43
1942	H.R. 6682. Coconut Oil Tax Bill.	100	1943	H.R. 2570. Income Tax Collection: Carlson amendment.	10	1945	H.R. 3633. Reconversion Bill.	67
1942	H.R. 7378. Revenue Act.	100		Robertson-Forand substitute.	0			
1943	H.J. Res. 171. Feed Grain Duty.	78	1945	H.R. 3240. Recommit Trade Act Extension.	13			
1944	H.R. 4646. Income Tax Bill.	100			7			
1944	H.R. 2539. Revenue Code Amendment Bill.	85						
1945	H.R. 2404. Debt Limit.	100						
1945	H.R. 4309. Revenue Act.	100						
1945	H.R. 3395. Renegotiation Act.	100						

a Votes on rules and conference reports excluded. When two or more votes were taken on one bill all the votes had to fall in the same category. H.R. 2570 in 1943 is the only exception to this rule. The Committee split along party lines on two votes but had a 33 per cent IPL on final passage.

some of the subtleties involved in House-Committee relations during World War II.

BIPARTISAN COALITIONS. When a bill is reported by Ways and Means with little or no party conflict not only have the two party contingents on the Committee been satisfied but so too have elements within each of the parties. The term "bipartisan" committee means that a coalition agreement has been reached between at least three distinct groups: conservative Democrats, liberal Democrats, and Republicans. On Ways and Means, liberal Republicans have been scarce so the normal bipartisan coalition is tripartite in composition.

Such bills normally have no difficulty passing the House. Table 5.5 shows that bipartisan agreement in the Committee is followed by bipartisan agreement in the House and, except for one bill in 1944, by easy passage.

Three of the eleven bipartisan bills illustrate some of the complexities that are involved even when bills are free of party differences. H.R. 5417, the Revenue Act of 1941, was developed in the Committee in a bipartisan way but on one part of the bill a significant minority of the Committee dissented, took their dissent to the floor, and beat the Committee coalition on a roll call vote. In the case of H.R. 7378, the Revenue Act of 1942, the Committee members similarly took pride in their ability to subdue partisanship in the course

TABLE 5.5
INDEX OF PARTY LIKENESS, WAYS AND MEANS AND THE
HOUSE, BIPARTISAN BILLS, 1940–1946

Year	Bill	Committee IPL (%)	House IPL (%)	House vote (yea-nay)
1940	H.R. 10039. Revenue Act.	100	97	396–6
1941	H.R. 5417. Revenue Act.	100	75	242–160
1942	H.R. 6691. Debt Limit.	100	100	367–0
1942	H.R. 6682. Coconut Oil Tax Bill.	100	98	185–74
1942	H.R. 7378. Revenue Act.	100	99	395–2
1943	H.J. Res. 171. Feed Grain Duty.	78	70	255–55
1944	H.R. 4646. Income Tax Bill.	100	100	358–0
1944	H.R. 2539. Revenue Code Amendment Bill.	85	100	126–168
1945	H.R. 2404. Debt Limit.	100	98	356–4
1945	H.R. 4309. Revenue Act.	100	98	343–10
1945	H.R. 3395. Renegotiation Act.	100	99	302–1

of their deliberations but during the weekend preceding final action the Committee, by a split vote, co-opted a Republican recommittal motion in order to pave the way for passage. And on the third bill, H.R. 2539 in 1944, the bipartisan Committee coalition was defeated on the floor by the conservative coalition.

The only significant controversy over the 1941 Revenue Act that was not resolved in the Committee was a provision requiring husbands and wives to file joint tax returns. The Rules Committee reported a modified closed rule allowing a vote on an amendment to strike the section. Frank Buck, sixth-ranking Committee Democrat from California (a community-property state), offered the amendment to strike mandatory joint returns, explaining that the only reason he got a chance to offer such an amendment was because the Committee was badly divided on the question.[45] Buck's amendment was adopted on tellers 197–139. Chairman Doughton later forced a roll call on the amendment and it was sustained 242–160. Ways and Means split with nine of its fifteen Democrats opposing the amendment and six of ten Republicans opposing. Split this closely, the Committee majority took a gamble bringing the provision to the floor, and they lost. With this question settled, a pro forma motion to recommit was rejected by voice vote and the bill was passed 370–29.[46]

As the war intensified so did the need for revenue. In 1942 Ways and Means brought a major revenue-raising bill to the floor after scaling down by a substantial amount the tax increase proposed by the administration. It appears that the first settlement reached by the Committee did not raise corporate taxes enough to satisfy some members of the House, and the Committee, in effect, purchased a closed rule from the Rules Committee by agreeing to increase the taxes on corporations by $750 million.[47] Because the Committee bill was already short of the Treasury request a closed rule was necessary to prevent amendments that would increase the run on the Treasury.

In vivid contrast to the revenue bills of the 1930's, the Committee presented this bill to the House as the product of the finest possible bipartisan effort. Doughton and Treadway exchanged toasts on the

[45] *Congressional Record*, August 4, 1941, p. 6704 ff.

[46] The IPL for the House on the Buck amendment was 75 per cent. The party groups on the Committee split in the same proportions so the IPL for the Committee was 100 per cent.

[47] See the remarks by Rules Committee Chairman Adolph Sabath, *Congressional Record*, July 16, 1942, p. 6252.

floor, and the latter noted that although there were many differences of opinion in the Committee none of them, as he recalled, involved a party-line vote.[48] The Committee's third-ranking Democrat, Jere Cooper of Tennessee, observed that Ways and Means was so nonpartisan on this bill that the Democrats sat where the Republicans usually sat.[49]

Bipartisanship might have been the rule in the Committee but not everyone was happy with the result. Specifically, a Republican member of Ways and Means, Harold Knutson, opposed the bill and planned to offer a substantive recommittal motion to lower the corporate surtax rate and increase the excess profits tax. The second part of his proposal — increasing the excess profits tax — was minor and noncontroversial, but the corporate tax was a different matter. For some reason, a majority of the Committee decided to accept Knutson's amendments and offer them on behalf of the Committee. Several members of the Committee opposed this last-minute switch and, though Doughton and others had the votes in Ways and Means, the House defeated the Committee amendment on corporate taxes by a 160–180 teller vote. Increasing the excess profits tax from 87½ per cent to 90 per cent passed with no trouble. The House then approved the bill 395–2.

If the Committee overestimated the adjustments it had to make to pass the 1942 Revenue Act (or could make and pass the bill), it underestimated the opposition to H.R. 2539 in 1944. H.R. 2539 was a relatively minor bill dealing with the tax treatment of distilled spirits, but some economy-minded members objected to it on the ground that it would lead to the hiring of five hundred more federal inspectors. Fourteen Ways and Means members were recorded for the bill on the roll call and only five opposed it, but the bipartisan minority in the Committee was joined by the conservative coalition on the floor. The bill lost 126–168.

With these three exceptions, the remaining bipartisan bills passed the House rather routinely. As a matter of fact, the Committee was even more bipartisan in the war years than is indicated by the ten bills which passed by large majorities. If bills on which there were no roll call votes are included in the analysis, as they should be, the degree of bipartisanship is most impressive. The House passed a billion dollar tax bill in 1940, a major excess profits tax bill in 1941, a bill in 1944 raising the debt limit by $30 billion, and an important social

[48] Ibid., pp. 6262, 6265.
[49] Ibid., p. 6265.

security bill in 1946 — all by voice vote — as well as a $2 billion tax bill in 1943 by a nonrecord division vote 200–27. The war years were a unique period in the Committee's life.

DEMOCRATIC (PARTISAN) MAJORITIES. On five bills during the war the Committee, as Table 5.6 shows, broke along party lines, and on two votes the Committee majority was defeated on the floor.

The original income tax law of 1913 was passed so late in the year that taxpayers were allowed to pay taxes on their 1913 income in 1914, which meant that tax payments were always a year behind. In 1943 the Committee decided to try to correct the anomaly.

Everyone was for making taxpayers current but how this could be done was tricky. The Republicans adopted a proposal to abate 1942 taxes and simply make tax payments current on 1943 income, with no loss of revenue. This plan — known as the Ruml Plan after its originator, Beardsley Ruml — was rejected by the Democrats on the grounds that ultimately it allowed taxpayers to pay one year's taxes on two years' income (a boon of particular importance to the wealthy). But the Democrats found it extremely hard to frame an acceptable alternative.

When the first Democratic plan reached the floor in March 1943, the House preferred the Ruml plan to the cumbersome Democratic bill. Frank Carlson of Kansas offered the Ruml plan as an amendment and the House approved it on tellers, 199–188. The Democrats had enough votes to reverse this defeat on a roll call (198–215, as

TABLE 5.6
INDEX OF PARTY LIKENESS, WAYS AND MEANS AND THE
HOUSE, PARTISAN BILLS, 1940–1946

Year	Bill	Committee IPL (%)	House IPL (%)	House vote (yea-nay)
1940	H.J. Res. 407. Trade Act Extension.	0	9	163–222
1941	S.J. Res. 43. Coffee agreement.	0	7	178–115
1943	H.R. 2218. Income tax collection:			
	Carlson Amendment.	10	21	198–215
	Carlson recommittal motion.	10	23	248–168
1943	H.R. 2570. Income Tax Collection:			
	Carlson Amendment.	0	14	202–206
	Robertson-Forand substitute.	13	28	230–180
1945	H.R. 3240. Recommit Trade Act Extension.	7	10	181–212

TABLE 5.7
INDEX OF PARTY LIKENESS, WAYS AND MEANS AND THE
HOUSE, MIXED BILLS, 1940–1946

Year	Bill	Committee IPL (%)	House IPL (%)	House vote (yea-nay)
1943	H.R. 1780. Debt Limit-Salary Bill.	50	47	268–129
1943	H.J. Res. 111. Trade Act Extension.	47	74	343–65
1944	H.R. 5564. Social Security.	43	59	262–73
1945	H.R. 3633. Reconversion Bill.	67	57	246–91

shown in Table 5.6), but when Carlson moved to recommit the bill the House concurred by an 80-vote margin, 248–168. Ways and Means divided as it had before (only one member, a Republican, crossed party lines) but the Republicans, aided by more than forty Democrats, had enough votes to send the bill back to the Committee. On this issue the Democrats could beat the Republicans and the Republicans could beat the Democrats. Both lost.

When the same problem came up again in May, a third alternative — neither the Committee bill nor the Republican plan — was passed. All three plans now involved the forgiveness of some 1942 taxes. The Committee bill forgave about $4.6 billion in taxes, the Carlson-Ruml plan about $8.5 billion, and the third alternative, known as the Forand-Robertson plan after its two Ways and Means sponsors, about $7.6 billion. The Committee Democrats, joined by most House Democrats and a handful of Republicans, had enough votes to defeat the Carlson-Ruml plan again, this time on a 202–206 roll call after the plan had passed on tellers 197–166. A Republican then moved to recommit the bill and adopt the Robertson-Forand plan. This motion carried 230–180 and the Ways and Means bill was thereby defeated on the floor.[50] The conservative coalition appeared on neither of the bills; the Republicans and a few Democrats had enough votes by themselves to force changes in the Committee bill.

OTHER COALITIONS. What happens when the Committee comes to the House neither united nor divided along party lines? Table 5.7 shows four bills that fit this description. Significantly, the conservative coalition appeared on two of them, with a near miss on a third.

[50] For the debate on these bills see the *Congressional Record*, March 25, 1943, p. 2487 ff.; and May 3, 1943, p. 3835 ff.

Controversy over H.R. 1780, a bill raising the debt limit to $210 billion, centered around a rider added in the Committee that changed President Roosevelt's wartime attempt to limit business salary increases. Congress had rejected the president's request for salary controls but, ignoring the opposition, Roosevelt issued an executive order in open defiance of the legislature. Five Ways and Means Democrats joined the ten Republicans in negating the executive order. When the House voted on the bill the fourteen Committee Democrats who voted split in half but all the Committee Republicans, nearly all the House Republicans, and a near majority of southern Democrats were enough to pass it, 268–129.[51]

Two months after the bipartisan coalition reversed Roosevelt an unprecedented vote occurred in the House: the Trade Act, always a close party fight, passed 343–65. But this did not signal a basic shift of Republicans away from opposition to the reciprocal trade program. The trade bill passed only after Ways and Means was defeated by an amendment to extend the Act for two years instead of three. A Committee Democrat, Milton West of Texas, broke with his Democratic colleagues and helped beat them on the floor. West, who was concerned about increasing imports (cattle, in particular), offered three other protectionist-oriented amendments but Doughton and others were able to defeat them. On passage, all the Ways and Means Democrats except West supported the bill; the ten Republicans divided with four voting yea and six nay.[52]

In 1943, therefore, the majority coalition in the Committee was overturned three times in the House: twice on tax payments and once on the Trade Act. Although none of these votes involved the conservative coalition they did reflect the second great constraint on Committee majority-building — the party balance in the House. Only thirteen votes separated Democrats and Republicans in the House in 1943 and, as a result, the only way to guarantee Committee victory on the floor was with bipartisan unity. If a minority of Democrats sided with the Republicans the Committee majority was in trouble; on the Trade Act a single Ways and Means Democrat defected and the Committee lost a key vote.

Yet a Committee minority as such did not pose a serious threat in the House. Since the 1940's the nature of the minority has been the crucial factor. It has been much more important for the Committee

---

[51] *Ibid.*, March 11, 1943, p. 1871 ff.
[52] *Ibid.*, May 10–12, 1943, p. 4151 ff.

to guard against the development of a conservative minority than a liberal one.

The division within the Committee on two bills, the 1944 social security bill and the 1945 reconversion bill, was along liberal-conservative lines. In both cases the conservative majority on the Committee was joined by the conservative coalition on the floor to pass the legislation over liberal protests. On the 1944 social security bill the liberals objected to freezing the social security tax on the grounds that an increase was needed to keep the fund sound and pay for increased benefits, but the conservative coalition passed the bill with ease, 262–73. On this vote a majority of the Ways and Means Democrats actually opposed the bill, but six Democrats and all eight of the Committee Republicans who voted favored passage. Among Democrats, only the South cast a majority of its votes for the bill, but coupled with Republican votes this was more than enough.[53]

The liberals claimed that the 1945 reconversion bill gave a tax break to corporations that had made excess profits (railroads, in particular). Four Ways and Means Democrats voted against the bill but again the conservative coalition prevailed, 246–91. A majority of southern Democrats and Republicans passed the bill as it came from Ways and Means.[54]

No bill exposed the weakness of the liberals in this period better than a major bill on which no roll call vote was taken. S. 2051, passed first by the Senate in 1944 and known as the George bill after Senator Walter George, was intended to deal with anticipated postwar unemployment. Liberal Democrats on Ways and Means, such as John Dingell of Michigan, attacked S. 2051 as too conservative when it passed the Senate and even more odious after Ways and Means "emasculated" it.[55]

Dingell offered a substitute bill that had the support of organized labor, but his appeal to provide money for increased unemployment compensation benefits and other liberal-backed measures had no chance in the House. Despite the dissenting views of four Committee Democrats on S. 2051, the bill passed the House by voice vote. Aime Forand of Rhode Island, a leader of the liberal band on Ways and Means, could not even get enough members of the House to force a roll call vote on the bill. On some issues in the 1940's it was the lib-

53 *Ibid.*, December 5, 1944, p. 8840 ff.
54 *Ibid.*, July 6, 1945, p. 7303 ff.
55 *Ibid.*, August 29, 1944, p. 7373.

eral Democrats, not the Republicans, who were locked out of influence in the Committee.[56]

MAJORITIES: 1947–1952. The Republican-controlled 80th Congress
— immortalized by Harry Truman in American political folklore as
the "do-nothing 80th Congress" — opened in January 1947 with two
hundred and forty-six Republicans anxious, in fact, to do three
things: cut taxes, cut spending, and cut the war-inflated national
debt. Paramount was a tax cut: "20 percent across the board" had
been a popular campaign slogan the year before.

The Democrats, led by President Truman, espoused all three goals
but perceived an inflationary tax cut as inimical to both a balanced
budget and payment on the debt. With clear-cut, well-publicized,
and firm differences in the way the parties ranked the priorities (or,
perhaps, defined the connection among them) a collision was inevitable. It came and Truman lost, but not without a fight.[57]

The first act of the Republican Ways and Means Committee was
not to cut taxes but to report a bill extending existing excise tax rates
for an indefinite period. General tax reduction was pending and
both parties agreed on the need to retain the revenue raised from the
excises, especially, the Republicans claimed, because Truman's budget
was so large. In the midst of unanimity on this bill, however, there
was a hint of the conflicts that would later permeate the Committee's
relations with the president and affect the internal workings of the
Committee. Aime Forand, ninth-ranking Democrat on Ways and
Means, referred to "star-chamber sessions" that the Republican members of the Committee were holding on the question of extending
the reciprocal trade program. Forand complained about the Republican caucus and warned Chairman Harold Knutson (Minn.) not to
continue meeting without the Democrats "because if he does I stand
here and tell him very frankly that I will simply pull out the record
of the old Smoot-Hawley tariff bill and recite the history of how the
Republicans at that time kicked the Democrats out, brought in
lobbyists, sat them in the place of the Democrats, and permitted log
rolling to the point where these lobbyists practically wrote that tariff
bill." [58] Forand's rhetoric, stimulated by the Republican caucus,

[56] Committee liberals in the 1940's were much more likely to attempt to
change Ways and Means bills than liberals in the 1960's.
[57] Many of the events discussed in this section are also treated in A. E. Holmans, *United States Fiscal Policy: 1945–1959* (London: Oxford University Press,
1961), Chaps. 5, 6, 9.
[58] *Congressional Record*, January 29, 1947, pp. 682–83.

merely indicated what was to come during one of the most partisan
and conflict-ridden periods in the Committee's history.

Knutson's famed 20 per cent campaign pledge, opposed by Democrats and liberal Republicans for giving too much tax relief to the
rich and too little to the poor, was never offered to the House. Instead, the Ways and Means Committee called up H.R. 1 on March
26. Bitterly opposed by the Truman administration and by the Ways
and Means Democrats, H.R. 1 reduced tax rates by 30 per cent in the
lowest income brackets (taxable income up to $1,000), 20 per cent
for those with taxable income between $1,000 and $302,000, and 10.5
per cent for those with taxable incomes above $302,000. Such progres-
sivity was hardly adequate to save H.R. 1 from the label of a rich
man's tax bill but it did give the lower brackets more relief than the
original 20 per cent plan.

The Republicans used a battery of arguments in support of H.R. 1.
Tax rates, they felt, were too high and H.R. 1 gave equitable relief to
all taxpayers.[59] Moreover, economic progress would be stimulated by
increasing the amount of money in private hands and, as a result, federal revenues would increase, thereby creating funds that could be
applied to the national debt. In support of the argument that a tax
cut, by promoting economic expansion, would result in more, not less,
federal revenue (an argument later used in 1963 by the Democrats on
behalf of tax reduction), Knutson cited the example of the 1920's
when the Republicans cut taxes and revenues increased, the example
of New York State which cut taxes and prospered, and Australia's
similar experience.

Democrats, on the other hand, argued that H.R. 1 would aggra-
vate the inflationary pressures in the economy, that there was no
shortage of investment funds, that in prosperous times a budget sur-
plus (possible if tax rates were not cut) should be used to pay the
national debt, and that H.R. 1 was unjust because it gave disproportionate relief to higher income people. For the Democrats a balanced
budget came first, payment on the debt second, and tax reduction
third. "Only when the budget has been balanced," Doughton told
the House, "and a substantial amount set aside for debt retirement,
should we consider tax reduction." [60] The Republicans saw tax re-

[59] See Knutson's opening statement, *Congressional Record*, March 26, 1947,
pp. 2637–42.

[60] *Ibid.*, p. 2646. On this issue, Democrats such as Judge Smith were in the
mainstream of the party.

duction as a means to the other two objectives, especially since they planned to curtail federal spending anyway.

To the Republicans H.R. 1 represented the fulfillment of a campaign promise, repudiation of the fiscal policy of Roosevelt and Truman that had involved high tax rates, and a start back to the proved fiscal policy of Andrew Mellon.

Associated with the conflict between the congressional Republicans and the president, and perhaps caused by it, was a dramatic change in the nature of the Ways and Means Committee. With a pressing goal of tax reduction, Chairman Knutson and the Republican members of the Committee (with five new members as a result of the election) did not waste much time getting H.R. 1 through the Committee, and a howl of protest went up from the Democrats.

Doughton complained about the partisan way the bill had been rushed through the Committee without sufficient study, fair hearings, or the usual nonpartisan consideration by all the members. "During the years when I was chairman of the Committee on Ways and Means," he argued, "every effort was made to keep politics out of tax legislation. Revenue bills were drafted with the fullest cooperation with minority Members, and very rarely, if ever, was a tax problem decided along party lines." Now, with the Republicans in control, he continued, the Democrats were left out of the decision-making process. "This departure from precedent was carried even further by the majority membership of the Committee in setting aside only two days for public hearings, and in hand-picking the only two witnesses permitted to testify, other than Treasury officials." Doughton, ignoring the 1930's, lamented the Republican action: "It is because I see this splendid spirit of nonpartisan cooperation in the Committee on Ways and Means being destroyed that I feel it necessary to advise the House that H.R. 1 has not received the customary, careful, nonpartisan consideration, and should not be hastily passed." [61] *The Washington Post*, which also saw a need for debt reduction, supported the Democratic charges against the "steam-roller tactics" and "indecent haste" with which H.R. 1 was "rushed" through Ways and Means.[62]

As the debate continued, John Dingell prophesied: "What, in good conscience then, can we say about H.R. 1: Here is a $4,000,000,000 swindle which will prove to be a scaffold built by you Republicans

[61] *Ibid.*, pp. 2642–43.
[62] *Ibid.*, p. 2673.

which will be used by the irate electorate to hang you, come next election day." [63] Aime Forand felt aggrieved: "I was precluded from expressing freely my thoughts and my opinions. That was not the only instance where we had to face that type of boss rule [from Knutson]. Read the hearings, read the reports of the newspapers during the consideration of this bill, particularly during the two days of hearings." [64] And eighth-ranking Democrat Walter Lynch (N.Y.) said: "The tax-reduction plan embodied in this bill was conceived in political expediency, nurtured by political demagoguery, and delivered to you today in political desperation." [65]

After Doughton's motion to recommit failed by a vote of 172 yeas to 237 nays (only four Democrats voted against the motion, two Republicans voted for it), H.R. 1 passed the House. It passed the Senate in somewhat altered form but Truman vetoed it for the previously mentioned reasons.

The Republicans were down but not out. Shortly after Truman's veto they called up H.R. 3950, which was identical to the vetoed version of H.R. 1 except it went into effect in 1948, not 1947. The arguments were the same as those used on H.R. 1.[66]

This time the Democrats had a substantive motion to recommit (as opposed to the motion on H.R. 1 that would have postponed the tax cut until it had been studied more and until the appropriation bills had been passed). It would have reduced taxes by increasing the exemption from $500 to $600 and given a greater percentage of the tax cut to lower income people. The Democratic motion, offered by Forand, was defeated by over one hundred votes, 151 yeas to 261 nays. Democratic party lines were slightly less solid on this vote than they were on H.R. 1 (twenty-nine voted against Forand's motion) but again the Republicans lost only two members. The bill passed by an overwhelming 302–112 vote.

Truman, finding the final version of H.R. 3950 unsound fiscally, unfair, and alien to his objective of making payments on the national debt, vetoed it. But the House, with three Ways and Means Democrats joining the conservative coalition, voted to override the veto 299 yeas to 108 nays (the attempt to override the veto of H.R. 1 had failed earlier 268 yeas to 137 nays). The entire issue was postponed until 1948, however, when the Senate refused to override the veto.

[63] *Ibid.*, p. 2660.
[64] *Ibid.*, p. 2739.
[65] *Ibid.*, p. 2678.
[66] For the floor action on H.R. 3950 see *ibid.*, pp. 8436–68.

Conflict between Congress and the president over fiscal policy broke out again in 1948 when the Republicans, their persistence undoubtedly fed by the successful vote overriding Truman's veto, passed H.R. 4790, another version of tax reduction shaped to appeal to a large majority of Congress. H.R. 4790, through a number of changes, gave more of a tax cut — but not enough to satisfy its liberal critics — to lower income brackets. "The bill was a political Christmas tree with something for everybody," Holmans writes, "containing elements of each of the forms of tax reduction that had been canvassed during the previous year." [67]

President Truman proposed an alternative that was embodied in a bill introduced by Dingell. The Dingell bill would have taken over ten million people off the tax rolls (compared to the six million plus of H.R. 4790), given a $40 tax credit to every taxpayer and his dependents, and, to recoup some of the lost revenue, increased taxes on corporate profits.[68]

The Republican bill, now presented as a tax reduction and tax equalization bill, passed by a wide margin (297–120) after a motion to recommit offered by Minority Leader Sam Rayburn was defeated 159 yeas to 258 nays (twenty-two Democrats and no Republicans broke party lines).

Presented with another tax reduction bill that did not meet his standards, Truman used the veto again. This time both the House and the Senate overrode the President and H.R. 4790 became law.

Tax policy was the major battleground between the Ways and Means Committee and President Truman during the 80th Congress, but the Republicans also reported and passed a major trade bill that departed radically from the one proposed by the administration and supported by House Democrats. The president signed it most reluctantly rather than lose his authority to enter into new trade agreements.

The Gearhart bill (H.R. 6556), named after Bertrand Gearhart of California who chaired the Ways and Means trade subcommittee, was considered by the House on May 26, 1948. In place of President Truman's request for a three-year extension of the Trade Agreements Act, H.R. 6556 provided a one-year extension. Moreover, the bill contained several features opposed by the administration and the House Democrats.

[67] Holmans, *op. cit.*, p. 86.
[68] *Congressional Record*, January 29, 1948, pp. 706–07.

Eschewing the outright repeal of the Trade Agreements Act and refusing to get into the question of what the tariff on particular commodities ought to be, the Republicans centered their criticism on the administration of the program. They sought to correct several of its (to them) poorer features, such as the Committee on Reciprocity Information (CRI) that had been established by executive order to hold hearings on contemplated trade agreements. In Gearhart's view the "Committee on Reciprocity Information is a nonscientific, nontechnical, nonexpert body composed of representatives of various executive agencies of the Government." [69] He referred to the CRI as a "Punch and Judy show" that had little or no impact on the kind of trade agreements negotiated with other countries.[70]

To correct this "pious fraud" H.R. 6556 gave CRI's functions to the Tariff Commission, described by Gearhart as "an impartial, nonpartisan, independent, scientific, technical organization of experts. . . ."[71]

Having upgraded the Tariff Commission, the Republicans went further by giving it the responsibility to determine the point at which a reduction or an increase in the tariff on goods would injure the domestic economy or impair the national defense. If the president wished to set a tariff rate above or below the limits recommended by the Tariff Commission, he could. But it would be up to Congress to determine, within sixty days, who was right — and, possibly, veto the presidential decision.

The Democrats who supported Truman's three-year extension request vigorously attacked the Republican bill as a return to the high tariff days of Smoot-Hawley (passed in 1930, the Smoot-Hawley tariff was the highest in history). Doughton led the attack: "The present law is such an improvement over the old log-rolling, back-slapping, monopoly-breeding, enemy-making method of dealing with the tariff. The one-year extension would be nullified by red tape which would make it impossible to negotiate any new agreements within that limit. The majority apparently desire to kill the program without assuming responsibility for its death." [72] He warned of the return to the "swarms of the tariff lobbies of 1930" and, in similar language, Dingell predicted the same outcome. "The instant result," said Dingell, "would be a swarm of special-interest lobbyists descend-

[69] *Congressional Record*, May 26, 1948, p. 6500.
[70] *Ibid.*
[71] *Ibid.*
[72] *Ibid.*, p. 6505.

ing on Congress and an avalanche of demands that the agreement be turned down. The old logrolling and tariff bickering would move back into the capitol." [73] These predictions did not frighten one Ways and Means Republican, Thomas Jenkins, who welcomed the return of congressional activity in trade matters: "So I repeat that the present legislation which we are now considering will do away with this autocratic assumption of power by the Executive and will bring back to Congress some of the rights which the Constitution reposed in it." [74]

Doughton moved to recommit H.R. 6556 and to substitute a straight three-year extension of the Act. His motion was voted down with only six Democrats and seventeen Republicans breaking party lines. The Gearhart bill then passed on a party-line vote, 234–119. The protectionist gains in 1948, which were far from what might have been expected from the Republican rhetoric on the virtues of protectionism, were short-lived. The next year the Democrats controlled Congress and reversed the Republican changes in the program.

Party conflict over major policy and signs of disintegration in the Committee were common throughout the postwar period, not just in the 80th Congress. Forty-seven percent of all the roll call votes taken from 1947 to 1952 evidenced a high degree of party difference in the Committee, which was true of 40 per cent of the votes in the House. With the Democrats in control of the House after the 1948 election the Committee and the House split along party lines on key votes on the following major bills:

	Committee IPL (%)	House IPL (%)
1. 1949 Social Security bill	0	19
2. 1949 Trade Act extension	0	9
3. 1950 Excise tax bill	0	7
4. 1950 Excess profits tax bill	0	8
5. 1951 Revenue bill	20	9
6. 1951 Trade Act extension	0	23

[73] *Ibid.*, pp. 6504, 6517.
[74] *Ibid.*, p. 6519. The classic study of Smoot-Hawley and the activity of interest groups is, of course, E. E. Schattschneider, *Politics, Pressures and the Tariff* (Englewood Cliffs, N.J.: Prentice-Hall, 1935). For a study of Truman's role in the above events see Kenneth W. Street, "Harry S. Truman: His Role as Legislative Leader, 1945–1948" (Ph.D. Dissertation, University of Texas, 1963).

Disputes over various policy proposals presented to the Committee were often attended by Republican charges of Democratic foul play. In 1949 the Democratic majority, said Republicans on the House floor, stacked the hearings on the Trade Act extension bill. The next year the Democrats rejected minority requests to call certain witnesses on the major excess profits tax bill, met in secret sessions without the Republicans, and, after what the minority felt was hasty consideration, reported a "bad" bill. Much the same was true the following years, according to Republicans, on the Revenue Act of 1951 and on the 1952 Social Security Amendments.[75] A number of bills in this period were handled in the mode of decision-making followed by the Committee in the 1930's. Many if not all the major pieces of legislation reported before the Eisenhower administration were clear-cut party fights in which the Ways and Means Democrats developed the bill on their own with little apparent concern for the Republican position. Ways and Means in this period, as in the 1930's, was a fundamentally different kind of body from that described by contemporary Committee members.

Unlike the 1930's, however, the postwar years were marked by the frequent appearance and invariable success of the conservative coalition. Ten of the conservative coalition's twenty-two appearances on Ways and Means bills came in the 1947–1952 period, and eight of these ten were, not surprisingly, in the 80th Congress. Most significant, the Committee majority was out of step with the coalition on only one of the ten votes, and on this one the Committee majority lost.

The conservative coalition in the House, joined by a number of southern Democratic members of the Committee, defeated the majority of Democrats on eight of the ten roll calls. On the two remaining conservative coalition victories no Committee Democrats voted with the coalition, but even so the coalition won. Thus the conservative coalition usually formed inside both the Committee and the House, but if it did not form in the Committee it could still win on the House floor. Democratic majorities in the 81st and 82nd Congresses were not large enough to defeat the coalition easily, and in the 80th Congress the coalition decided many of the crucial Ways and Means issues, including the 1947–1948 battle over tax reduction.

---

[75] For evidence on these bills see, in the order they appear above, *Congressional Record*, February 8–9, 1949, p. 984 ff.; December 4, 1950, p. 16082 ff.; June 21, 1951, p. 6894 ff.; May 19, 1952, p. 5470 ff.

It is difficult to know if a partisan strategy was deliberately followed by the Democrats in this period in order to pass legislation by forestalling the conservative coalition, but giving short shrift to the Republicans exacerbated the natural partisan tendencies on Committee bills and guaranteed some party-line votes on the floor. This strategy, designed for success, was not without some policy cost. As Doughton said during his remarks on the 1949 Social Security bill,

> Although H.R. 6000 does not go so far in certain respects as some members of the committee desired, other members felt that some parts of the bill go too far. In my opinion, the lengthy deliberations and discussions have resulted in a bill that is free from extremes either way. And that is the legislative road I have always considered it wisest to follow.[76]

Not all the Democrats found Doughton's road agreeable.

Minority reports signed by Republican members of the Committee commonly were filed on the major bills in this period (eight were filed from 1949 to 1952), as were Democratic minority reports in the 80th Congress (seven were filed), but in 1951 three Committee Democrats, all liberals, dissented on a tax bill. Dingell, Forand, and Herman Eberharter of Pennsylvania felt too many decisions were contrary to the liberals. They took their position to the floor and, predictably, lost.

Eberharter argued that the bill opened up a "monstrous loophole" favoring the wealthy in the estate tax law.[77] The bill, debated under a closed rule, was supported by the other twenty-two members of the Committee, however, and under these circumstances the liberal objections probably were made more for the record than with any hope of success. The bill passed by voice vote. This single incident is not much evidence that Committee decisions tended to fall on the conservative side, but Democratic opposition came from the liberals, not from the conservatives. In most cases the liberals, if dissatisfied, kept their feelings hidden, which under the circumstances was probably realistic.

Some liberal Democratic members of the Committee prevailed over the Committee majority on the floor on two votes in this period. Both were conference reports on tax bills and as such were not as clearly Ways and Means bills as when the House votes for the bill in the first instance. But a majority of the Committee voted contrary

[76] *Ibid.*, October 4, 1949, pp. 13820–21.
[77] *Ibid.*, May 7, 1951, p. 5003.

to the House and liberals composed the winning Committee minority.

The first atypical victory came on a 1950 vote to direct House conferees to press for an excess profits tax in conference with the Senate. Doughton, three other Committee Democrats, and eight Republicans lost the vote when nine Ways and Means Democrats were joined against the Committee majority by two hundred and seventeen House members. Eberharter spoke for the Ways and Means Democrats and, after winning the vote on the right to offer amendments to the resolution sending the bill to conference, he lost an amendment to incorporate an excess profits tax in the bill. Mills made a point of order against this amendment, the point was sustained by the chair, and a compromise amendment offered by Eberharter passed 331–2. The compromise directed Ways and Means to report to the House on the matter before the close of the 81st Congress.[78] Of the 226 votes to amend the resolution southern Democrats made up the only regional majority opposing Eberharter, but the Republicans split badly and the conservative coalition did not appear.

The second Committee defeat was in 1951 when the House rejected a conference report on the Revenue Act of 1951 by a 157–204 vote. Two liberal Democratic members of Ways and Means, Eberharter and Forand, voted with seven of the ten Committee Republicans against nine Committee Democrats and two Republicans. The House also split and the liberal Democrats, in conjunction with the Republicans, won the unusual vote. The bulk of the Democratic votes against the conference report came from the Northeast, the bulk of the Democratic votes for the report from the South. Northeastern Democrats and the Republicans, therefore, defeated the majority of Democrats and a minority of Republicans. Republican objections to the conference were based on fiscal grounds but Eberharter — and probably other Democrats — felt that the House bill had been "butchered" in the Senate. And, as he put it,

> I do not object to butchering quite so much if everybody gets a fair cut of the hog. But when a favored few get all the ham and pork chops, and the rest of the people get just plain old sow belly, at least the people are entitled to know what they are swallowing.[79]

His objection, to be precise, was that too much of the tax relief

[78] *Ibid.*, September 14, 1950, pp. 14832–49.
[79] *Ibid.*, October 16, 1951, pp. 13270–82.

granted in the Senate and accepted by the House conferees went to upper income taxpayers.

Thus liberal Democrats on Ways and Means occasionally could win votes in the House with the rare confluence of interests between them and the Republicans. More likely was agreement between Republicans and conservative Democrats. That this agreement was not reached very often on roll call votes is shown in the incidence of partisan votes on which the Democrats, regardless of internal differences, could reach agreement on the necessity to vote against the Republicans.

Two more roll call votes were lost by the Ways and Means majority in this period, both in the 82nd Congress after the 1950 off-year elections reduced the Democratic majority from 263 to 234. With nearly two hundred Republicans in the 82nd Congress the Democratic party had to be almost perfectly cohesive to defeat the Republicans on party-line issues. On H.R. 1612 in 1951, the Trade Agreements Extension Act, the Democrats were not cohesive enough to defeat a Republican amendment dealing with peril-points in tariff negotiations. In 1952 the Committee majority was defeated by the conservative coalition on a social security bill.

The peril-point amendment, which required the president to explain to Congress the reasons why a tariff was cut below the peril-point set by the Tariff Commission, was a partisan issue in the House but carried on a 225–168 roll call vote. Ways and Means split along party lines but the solid Republican minority plus a number of Democrats — most of whom were southerners — passed the amendment. With this amendment ratified by the vote, and with other amendments accepted by voice vote, H.R. 1612 then passed the House without a record vote.[80]

In 1953, H.R. 7800 shows how the House may override its committees. This bill was called up under suspension of the rules procedure and was defeated when it failed to receive the required two-thirds majority.

The Republican attack on H.R. 7800, led by Dan Reed, the Committee's ranking Republican, and generated by the American Medical Association, centered around certain features of the bill that granted powers to the Federal Security Agency headed by Oscar Ewing. The Republicans and the AMA charged that these powers opened the door to socialized medicine. Specifically, the Agency was authorized

[80] *Ibid.*, February 7, 1951, pp. 1080–81.

to name the doctors who would examine people wishing to qualify
for disability assistance. After H.R. 7800 was turned down by the
conservative coalition, the Ways and Means Committee met and
decided to offer an amendment to still the doctors' fears. Wilbur Mills
explained:

> The doctors raised objection to one section in particular on
> page 16 of the bill, section 220, which provided for an ex-
> amination of disabled individuals. They raised objection to
> the fact that Mr. Ewing, as Administrator of this program,
> would have authority to select doctors; that he could pay these
> doctors for examining the applicants; that he could pay mile-
> age fees, and so on, of the applicants in going to and from the
> doctor. Now that language of the bill has been stricken.[81]

MAJORITIES: 1953–1960. Of the five periods here, the Ways and
Means Committee and the House were least likely to divide into partisan coalitions during the Eisenhower years. Only 16 per cent of the
roll call votes — compared to 47 per cent in the postwar period —
were marked by high party differences in Committee voting from
1953 to 1960. Over 80 per cent of the Ways and Means roll calls
were nonpartisan and mixed, and the House percentages were about
the same. Compared to the 1930's and the Truman years, the Committee in the 1950's was remarkably free of party voting.

Yet the Committee was anything but free of conflict over policy.
The most notable feature of the Eisenhower period was that Republican Committee members were caught between their traditional
stands on Ways and Means issues and the uncomfortable necessity
of supporting their party's president, the first Republican president
since Hoover, on requests that resembled what they had been fighting for twenty years. Several never made the transition and became
more of a problem for the administration than the Democrats.

President Eisenhower's first two years with the Ways and Means
Committee were, despite Republican control of Congress, almost a
repeat of Truman's 1947–1948 experience. The Eisenhower administration, like its Democratic predecessor, clashed over tax and trade
policy with the Republicans who controlled the Committee. When
the Committee moved to cut taxes and change existing trade policy
Eisenhower faced the same — if somewhat more embarrassing —
problem as Truman. Unlike Truman, however, Eisenhower won —
mostly.

[81] *Ibid.*, June 16, 1952, p. 7292.

In domestic affairs Daniel A. Reed, the new Ways and Means Committee chairman and an ardent fiscal conservative, caused Eisenhower so much trouble that a standard administration joke was to compare Reed with one of Eisenhower's main foreign policy problems, Syngman Rhee, and to refer to them jointly as Syngman Reed.[82] H.R. 1, reported by Ways and Means early in 1953, partly caused the joke.

H.R. 1 provided that income tax rates, scheduled to drop on January 1, 1954, would go down six months ahead of schedule. An 11 per cent increase in the personal income tax rate had been voted in 1951 to finance the Korean War. The president, however, did not share Reed's enthusiasm for an early tax cut — at least not until cuts could be made in federal spending. For Eisenhower a balanced budget took precedence over tax reduction; for the Republican majority of the Ways and Means Committee a tax cut was an immediate objective, just as it had been in 1947.[83]

II.R. 1 never got out of the Rules Committee. The Republican Speaker, Joe Martin, torn between his friendship for Reed and the need to support the newly elected president, stranded the bill in the Rules Committee (which, incidentally, acted in this case as a reliable arm of the party leadership).[84] Reed's hopes for a tax cut in 1953 did not prevail.

In addition to using the Rules Committee to thwart the objectives of the Ways and Means Committee, the House Republican leadership relied on Rules to force a bill out of the Committee that the administration felt was essential to its fiscal program. The bill, an excess profits tax measure, became a cause célèbre in the House and, over the booming protests of Reed, came to the floor for a vote.[85]

The excess profits tax bill was scheduled to be considered on June 29, 1953, but before the showdown could take place Majority Leader Halleck said that he had received assurances from enough members of the Committee that an excess profits tax bill would be reported,

[82] Robert J. Donovan, *Eisenhower: The Inside Story* (New York: Harper & Brothers, 1956), p. 61.

[83] *Ibid.*, pp. 59–61, 353. See Eisenhower's own account in Dwight D. Eisenhower, *Mandate for Change: 1953–1956* (Garden City: Doubleday, 1963), pp. 201–03.

[84] Joe Martin, *My First Fifty Years in Politics* (New York: McGraw-Hill Book Co., 1960), pp. 230–31. For a character sketch of Reed and a report on his position in this conflict see John D. Morris, "The Ways and Means of Dan Reed," *The New York Times Magazine*, July 5, 1953, p. 9 ff.

[85] For this bill see *Congressional Record*, June 29, 1953, pp. 7575–81; July 10, 1953, p. 8481 ff.

whereupon he announced, after extracting explicit commitments from several Committee members on the floor, that the unusual procedure of bypassing Ways and Means would not be necessary. Reed, who apparently felt able to beat the Republican leaders, railed against their usurpation of the rights of his Committee as well as their sudden capitulation on the issue. "This threat of usurpation," he argued, "ought to be settled now once and for always so that ambitious men seeking power [i.e., his party's leaders] will never again try to usurp the constitutional prerogatives of our committee or of any other committee of this great legislative body." [86] Challenging Halleck and others to "stand up like men," Reed declared that the majority of the Committee really opposed the excess profits tax, that constitutional procedures could have been followed to get the bill out of the Committee if it had enough support, and that he had never said "I would not compromise — although it becomes somewhat difficult to maintain an open mind when the Committee on Rules sees fit to point a gun at my head." [87] One of Reed's supporters, Noah Mason of Illinois (whose favorite line was, "My name is Noah and I prophesy . . ."), revealed what happened inside the Committee:

> Mr. Speaker, the chairman of the Ways and Means Committee polled the 15 Republican members of his committee on the extension of the excess-profits tax early in the session and found they stood 12 to 3 against extension. Weeks later, the Speaker polled the 15 members and found that they stood 10 to 5 against extension. Now the leaders claim they have assurance that the 15 members now stand 10 to 5 for extension. What has happened to change a 10-to-5 majority against extension to a 10-to-5 majority for extension? Of course, we know that party pressure or party discipline has been applied.[88]

Without intense party pressure the excess profits tax bill would not have been reported by the Committee. Even with such pressure, one Ways and Means Democrat noted:

> Out of the 25 votes in the committee, the vote was 16 to 9 for reporting the bill favorably. The proportions as regards Democrats and Republicans are as follows: We, Democrats, out of 10 votes delivered 7 for the proposal, and the Repub-

[86] *Ibid.*, p. 7576.
[87] *Ibid.*, p. 7577.
[88] *Ibid.*, p. 7580.

licans produced only 9 out of 15. I want to remind the
Republicans as I did my good friend, the gentleman from Indiana [Mr. Halleck] the distinguished majority leader of the
House that we Democrats, having helped them out, as we
have in many instances in this season, do not like to be kicked
in the teeth for helping the President out of a bad situation.[89]

No amount of party pressure and nothing Eisenhower could do
could make Dan Reed and a handful of Republican members of
Ways and Means budge from their opposition to the excess profits
tax. One such Republican warned:

> Can they count upon reelection on the ethereal popularity
> of President Eisenhower in the face of specific material prom-
> ises broken. If I know anything about the average American
> voter, the answer is "No." By their records they will be
> judged, not by ethereal popularity of someone in the White
> House.[90]

On the motion to recommit the bill four Ways and Means Republicans voted against Eisenhower (Reed, Mason, Jenkins, and Thomas
B. Curtis), and on final passage two more joined the holdouts
(Byrnes and Utt). Committee Democrats split in half on the recommittal motion, five for, five against, but seven of them voted for the
bill on final passage. Reed, adamant to the end, got his time to speak
against the bill from the Democrats.

Trade policy was another problem facing the Republican administration. Speaker Martin indicated its magnitude by estimating that
when Eisenhower took office about two-thirds of the House Republicans opposed the reciprocal trade program and said that he himself
was not too keen on it.[91]

[89] *Ibid.*, p. 8495.
[90] *Ibid.*, p. 8496. Noah Mason was typical of the Republican who found the
Eisenhower administration as objectionable as the Democratic administrations.
On a latter occasion he declared his independence from Eisenhower: "Would
any of you farmers in this audience, would any of you people who run an industrial plant hire the best doctor in Washington to go out and run your farm or
to run your industry? Why, of course not. . . . When we hire the greatest military expert in the world, of course we trust him in military affairs. . . . But on
this matter of dealing with foreign nations and trade restrictions, that is a different question. . . . For that reason, I say I trust the President of the United
States in military matters but not in these other matters, in which he never has
had 1 minute of actual experience in handling, and, as a result, he must depend
upon outside advice." *Congressional Record*, February 18, 1955, p. 1769.
[91] Martin, *op. cit.*, p. 229.

If the House Republicans were generally disaffected with United States trade policy, the heart of the opposition was located in the Ways and Means Committee. Both Reed and Richard Simpson (Pa.), the third-ranking Republican on the Committee who also chaired the Republican Campaign Committee, told the authors of one study that as boys "their fathers had told them that the crucial differences between the parties was that the Republicans believe in protection." "Such were the men on whom Eisenhower had to lean to enact his legislative program."[92] Such were the men who gave Eisenhower more trouble on trade than the Democrats.

One of the first acts of the new administration was a request that the Trade Agreements Act be extended without change. The Act was extended in 1953, but only for one year and only after the House Republicans were persuaded to modify their push for major changes in the program.

H.R. 5495 was passed by the House in mid-June with strong bipartisan support after the Democrats failed to strike out one of its key protectionist-sponsored features. The bill extended the Act for one year, added a seventh member to the Tariff Commission (presumably a protectionist), reduced from one year to nine months the period within which the Commission had to make its report on escape clause appeals, and established a Commission on Foreign Economic Policy to study the trade program.

Reed opened debate and backed H.R. 5495 as an interim measure, noting that a seven-man Tariff Commission would prevent tie votes on peril-point cases.[93] Jere Cooper (Tenn.), the ranking Democrat on Ways and Means and a liberal on trade matters, opened debate for the Democrats. He too supported the bill but opposed increasing the size of the Tariff Commission.[94] Jenkins, who wanted immediate protection for American industry, and Mason, who explained that he had voted against every trade extension bill since 1937 and saw no reason to change on H.R. 5495,[95] represented a third position.

The Democratic motion to recommit contained instructions to kill the increase in the Tariff Commission but it was defeated 185–215.[96]

---

[92] Raymond A. Bauer, Ithiel deSola Pool, and Lewis Anthony Dexter, *American Business and Public Policy* (New York: Atherton Press, 1963), p. 30. Chapters 2, 3, and 4 of this book give a longer account of the issues treated here.

[93] *Congressional Record*, June 15, 1953, p. 6528.

[94] *Ibid.*, p. 6531.

[95] *Ibid.*, pp. 6533, 6555.

[96] For a study of these events see Murray Clark Havens, "Congress and the Tariff, 1945–56" (Ph.D. Dissertation, Johns Hopkins University, 1958).

Fourteen of the fifteen Committee Republicans voted against recommittal (one did not vote but was paired nay), and all ten Democrats voted for it. The bill then passed 363–34 with three Republican members of Ways and Means voting nay (Jenkins, Mason, and Utt) and the ten Democrats voting yea.

Extension of the Act for one year while the whole question was studied was a victory of sorts for the Eisenhower administration as well as for the protectionist Republicans. The following month, July, the protectionist majority in the Committee laid down a direct challenge to the administration in the form of H.R. 5894, the so-called Simpson bill, which President Eisenhower, trapped by a question at a press conference from a reporter who had been primed by the opponents of the bill, was forced to oppose.[97]

Member after member extolled the virtues of H.R. 5894 with the common theme that it would help the depressed sectors of American industry: coal, lead, zinc, wool, tile, glassware, watches, pottery, and the like. Such famous protectionists as Simpson, Reed, Cleveland Bailey of West Virginia, and members from the mining states of Colorado, Idaho, and Kentucky found the bill to their liking.

Unfortunately for the protectionists, and in no way deterring them, the State Department, President Eisenhower, and the leadership of both parties in the House did not agree.

Cooper led off the opposition to the Simpson bill by arguing it was opposed by six different government departments and by Eisenhower who had asked only for a one-year extension of the Act.[98]

The Simpson bill fractured the Ways and Means Committee. Majority Leader Charles Halleck spoke on behalf of a motion to strike the enacting clause to be offered by Thomas B. Curtis, thirteenth-ranking Republican on Ways and Means, and Simpson (who had helped Curtis get on the Committee without checking his views on trade) spoke against Curtis's motion. The motion passed on tellers 175–119 and Curtis then offered a motion to recommit H.R. 5894. The bill was recommitted, 242 yeas to 161 nays. Ten Committee Republicans voted against recommittal, five voted for it. Seven of the Committee's Democrats voted for recommittal, two voted nay, and one did not vote. The Republican leadership voted against the majority of the Committee's Republicans. The administration won a victory almost in spite of itself.

[97] Bauer, Pool, and Dexter, *op. cit.*, p. 32.
[98] *Congressional Record*, July 23, 1953, p. 9658.

Another one-year extension of the Act in 1954 was passed before Eisenhower, after the Democrats won control of Congress, could get a three-year extension and be free of protectionist efforts to change the nature of the program. Reed supported the one-year extension as a stopgap measure pending a full review of the program by the Ways and Means Committee. He argued that the Committee was too busy to take up the trade question and that the Act should be extended because allowing it to expire would afford protection to no one and, possibly, damage the United States trade position.[99] With the administration and the protectionist-minded Republicans unable to resolve their differences, a one-year truce seemed to be the best way out for all concerned.

After the Democrats won control of Congress in 1954, revenue bills, as in the earlier years, were more likely to divide Ways and Means and the House along partisan lines than social security bills or debt bills. Trade bills, once the classic party issue, were also less partisan in the 1950's than in prior years.[100] Table 5.8 presents data on the major tax, social security, and debt bills voted on during the Eisenhower years. Except for revenue bills, party differences were not very prominent after the 83rd Congress on the major legislation reported by the Committee.

Those party differences that did occur were important. On one occasion the Democratic majority was victorious, and on the second they were defeated by the conservative coalition.

Jere Cooper, Chairman of Ways and Means, and Dan Reed had introduced identical bills in 1955 for a routine extension of the temporary corporate and excise tax rates. Before the bill was passed, however, Speaker Rayburn and some of the Committee's Democrats (Reed said eight) decided to add a provision giving a $20 tax credit to every taxpayer and his dependents. Known as the "Mills amendment," the $20 credit was rushed through the Committee as part of the noncontroversial bill despite the opposition of the Republicans and leading newspapers (*The Washington Post* accused Ways and Means of "capricious irresponsibility"; *The New York Times* thought the action just plain "irresponsible" and a "100 per cent political deal"). The tax credit, opposed, of course, by the Eisenhower administration, was a result of the meeting between the Democratic leadership and

99 *Ibid.*, June 11, 1954, pp. 8077–78.

100 For an analysis of the shifting patterns on reciprocal trade see Richard A. Watson, "The Tariff Revolution: A Study of Shifting Party Attitudes," *Journal of Politics*, XVIII (November, 1956), 678–701.

TABLE 5.8

INDEX OF PARTY LIKENESS, MAJOR BILLS, 1953–1960 [a]

REVENUE BILLS

Year	Bill	House IPL (%)	Committee IPL (%)
1953	H.R. 5898	57	77
1954	H.R. 8224	1	0
1954	H.R. 8300	11	0
1955	H.R. 4259	10	7
1956	H.R. 9166	99	90
1959	H.R. 9035	4	7

SOCIAL SECURITY BILLS

Year	Bill	House IPL (%)	Committee IPL (%)
1953	H.R. 5173	57	50
1954	H.R. 9366	98	86
1954	H.R. 9709	50	40
1955	H.R. 7225	92	67
1958	H.R. 12065	39	13
1958	H.R. 13549	99	88
1960	H.R. 12580	99	78

DEBT LIMIT BILLS

Year	Bill	House IPL (%)	Committee IPL (%)
1953	H.R. 6672	12	33
1955	H.R. 6992	85	88
1958	H.R. 9955	80	87
1958	H.R. 13580	86	89
1959	H.R. 7749	94	70
1960	H.R. 12381	96	80

[a] Votes on conference reports and rules are excluded. When more than one roll call occurred on a bill the vote with the lowest IPL score was selected for presentation.

the Committee Democrats, and Rayburn even took the floor to speak against Reed's motion to strike it from the bill. It passed the House in a classic example of the influence party leaders can have on the Committee. All but one Ways and Means Democrat supported the credit on the floor and, although the Democrats had a rather slim 234–201 majority in the House, enough southern Democrats voted with their party to pass it. The credit was rejected in the Senate and never became law.[101]

Party lines held firm within the Committee on a 1958 unemployment compensation measure, but one Committee member, A. Sydney Herlong (D., Fla.), took his opposition to the House floor and the resulting conservative coalition defeated the Committee majority. The bill, H.R. 12065, was one of the first bills reported by the Committee under Chairman Mills and, after the Committee failed to secure complete southern support from its members, the House extracted the controversial section.

Title I provided sixteen weeks of unemployment benefits for those who had exhausted their funds under existing programs, and Title II provided benefits to those working in positions not covered by the unemployment compensation program and hence not qualified for any assistance.[102]

Title II, opposed by the Eisenhower administration, was more controversial. Judge Smith called it "pure unadulterated, undisguised, unabridged, and unabashed socialism," noting that the only people who would not get the "unearned dole" were students who had never worked and members of the "Amalgamated and United Order of Hobos." [103] The Committee's ranking Republican, Reed, charged in his initial press release on the bill that "the Democrat Party has placed itself in orbit in the miasma of panicky political irresponsibility. The apogee and the perigee of the Democrat orbit have not yet been determined but the proposal is expected to exceed the wildest dreams ever visualized by either the New Deal or Fair Deal social planners of the Roosevelt-Truman era." [104] Republican leader Joseph Martin of Massachusetts soberly stressed the President's opposition to H.R. 12065 and predicted that Eisenhower would sign the substitute

[101] *Congressional Record*, February 24, 1955, pp. 2031–181.
[102] *Ibid.*, April 30, 1958, pp. 7747–911.
[103] *Ibid.*, p. 7747. Smith also argued that Ways and Means was so badly split, with fifteen of the twenty-five members signing supplemental, differing, or minority views, that only ten members could be said to support the bill as is.
[104] *Ibid.*, p. 7766.

plan to be offered by the Committee's eleventh ranking Democrat, Herlong.[105] Herlong's substitute amendment provided for an extension of benefits different from Title I of the Committee bill, but more important it omitted Title II. Nine Ways and Means Republicans voted for Herlong's amendment (the tenth was paired for it), one Democrat voted for it (Herlong), thirteen Democrats voted nay, and one Democrat was paired for it (Burr Harrison of Virginia). The amendment carried 223–165 and the bill was then passed 372–17. H.R. 12065 was the Committee's first and last flirtation with direct payments to unemployed workers who had paid nothing into the unemployment compensation fund, a plan perceived as so radical that Charles Halleck argued that it was not even suggested during the depths of the depression in the early 1930's.[106] The Herlong amendment is a perfect example of what may happen if the southern Democratic members of the Committee are not placated before the bill is brought up in the House.

Two more cases of the House controlling the activities and decisions of Ways and Means during the Eisenhower period have been uncovered. In one, the House Republican Conference in effect instructed the Committee Republicans to co-opt a proposed Democratic motion to recommit; the second involved a quid pro quo between Ways and Means and the Rules Committee over a closed rule.

Disagreement over a 1954 bill extending excise taxes centered around the question of a termination date. By a straight 15–10 party vote the Republicans rejected a Democratic amendment extending the taxes for one year only. Then an unusual thing happened. The Republican Conference instructed the Ways and Means Republicans to set an expiration date, the Committee met, and a date was set. As the Committee's ranking Democrat, Jere Cooper, told the House, "So the caucus had to recommit the bill for them in order to get it in shape so that they could bring it in here and prevent the adoption of our motion to recommit." [107] Aime Forand had even more fun twitting another Committee member, Thomas Jenkins: "I am tickled to death that most of us intend to vote for the bill after what you fellows did this morning. You had to eat crow, just remember; remember that." Jenkins, nonplussed, replied, "Remember, if we did, that was our own crow." [108]

[105] *Ibid.*, p. 7907.
[106] *Ibid.*, p. 7749.
[107] *Ibid.*, March 10, 1954, p. 3013.
[108] *Ibid.*, p. 3016.

In 1958 Ways and Means brought tax bill H.R. 8381 to the floor and offered several amendments to it before final passage. During the floor debate on the closed rule, Representative Ray Madden (D., Ind.) explained that in 1957 the Rules Committee granted a rule that would have permitted an amendment to strike section 56 but because the Committee agreed to offer such an amendment the rule was fully closed.[109] (Section 56 dealt with thc tax trcatmcnt of the proceeds of life insurance for estate tax purposes.) Mills explained that he and others reached the conclusion that section 56 was not an adequate solution to a complex and controversial problem, and "the committee therefore thought it advisable to eliminate the section at this time so as to afford the Treasury and the staff an opportunity to further study the matter with the idea of finding a better solution." [110] With section 56 eliminated, H.R. 8381 passed by voice vote.

Both cases illustrate how the House, on occasion, may determine what one of its most influential committees reports to the floor, and both raise warnings about unqualified generalizations concerning committee autonomy.

In addition to the 1953 Simpson trade bill and the 1958 unemployment compensation bill, the Ways and Means Committee majority lost roll call votes three times in the 1953–1960 period. One loss came on a closed rule but was reversed by a second vote shortly after the defeat, and the two other Committee defeats were on bills requiring a two-thirds majority under suspension of the rules. In both cases a majority of the House — but not a two-thirds majority — voted with the Committee. Although neither bill was a major piece of legislation they are interesting because, on one, the House opponents criticized the Committee for not holding hearings so all the interested parties could express themselves, and on the second bill the floor manager was Wilbur Mills.

Representatives of domestic woolgrowers, the felt industry, and paper manufacturers opposed and helped defeat a bill reported unanimously by Ways and Means in 1956. The bill would have suspended the duty on certain imported coarse wool and hair used in the manufacture of carpets but it was defeated when spokesmen for these industries argued on the House floor that at the very least Ways and Means should hold hearings. Not even protectionists Reed and Simpson, who swore that the bill would not injure domestic industries,

---

[109] *Ibid.*, January 28, 1958, p. 1205.
[110] *Ibid.*, p. 1221.

could save the measure, and one Committee member who listened to the floor complaints declared his intention to change his vote and oppose the bill on the grounds that hearings were needed. The Committee voted 17–3 to support the bill, but the 216–123 House vote was short of the required two-thirds. Thus the House members interested in the question found in the lack of hearings an effective argument against passing the bill — a minor incident which shows that in the face of uncertainty House members prefer caution to taking the chance of injuring concerned publics.[111]

Suspension of the rules procedure has two advantages: it eliminates the necessity of going through the Rules Committee to get a rule for a bill; and no floor amendments are in order, i.e., the bill is voted up or down as reported from the committees. Its one great disadvantage is that a House minority can win the vote. In 1959 this happened again to Ways and Means when a majority outvoted the minority 251–133 but lost. The bill in question would have allowed the federal government to withhold city taxes from the paychecks of federal employees, a proposal which was anathema to New Jersey congressmen whose constituents worked in Philadelphia. Mills called the bill up under suspension of the rules because opposition was localized and seemingly weak, but one hundred and thirty-three negative votes were enough to kill the bill. In 1960 the measure came up again under an open rule and with the late William J. Green of Philadelphia as floor manager. Green won this time on a 221–160 roll call with nineteen of his twenty-two voting colleagues on Ways and Means supporting him.[112]

Conservative voting power in the House and liberal weakness were manifest throughout the Eisenhower years. The Herlong amendment was a dramatic example of what could happen if the Committee majority was on the wrong side of the coalition, but there were others. In 1953 Dan Reed and the House Republicans allowed Forand to offer floor amendments to an unemployment compensation bill, but the amendments, opposed by the vast majority of the Committee, were easily defeated by the conservative coalition. The 93–292 roll call vote on Forand's recommittal motion split the Committee Democrats in half with the following four members backing Forand: Dingell, Eberharter, Cecil King of Los Angeles, and Tom O'Brien of Chicago. The following year Forand's attempt to liberalize another

---

[111] *Ibid.*, July 23, 1956, pp. 14113–118.
[112] *Ibid.*, February 17, 1960 (daily edition), pp. 2541–57.

unemployment compensation bill failed by a 110–241 vote and, in the same year, the conservative coalition passed a trade bill over the objections of some liberals.[113] Committee liberals could take credit for liberalizing portions of some bills, as Forand did on the major 1954 social security bill,[114] but by and large the settlements in the Committee did not go as far as some liberals desired. A liberal Democratic minority filed five minority reports in the 1955–1960 period but their voting strength in Ways and Means was manifested in 1960 when the Forand medicare bill was defeated 8–17. Indeed, the true test of the conservative coalition's voting strength in the Eisenhower years was that medicare never came out of the Committee and, if it had been reported, it would have been rejected in the House by a wide margin. Incrementally the liberals had an effect on legislation, but the votes for major policy changes were absent. For such programs as medicare, an electoral realignment of the House was required, which did not occur until the 1964 Johnson-Goldwater election.[115]

MAJORITIES: 1961–1968. Party differences over basic policy questions returned in force to the Ways and Means Committee in 1961. As in previous years, the Committee and the House tended to split along party lines more often on revenue bills than on social security legislation, but the Kennedy-Johnson years were also marked by the evolution of debt bills from a relatively nonpartisan issue in the 1950's to a highly partisan issue in the 1960's. Through 1964, 47 per cent of the roll call votes taken on Committee bills showed high party conflict in the Committee and in the House. This compares with 16 per cent in the Eisenhower years; it is very similar to voting in the postwar years; and it is slightly higher than the party differences recorded during the New Deal. In a sense, Ways and Means returned to normal under a Democratic president and Democratic Congress: high party conflict.

Many factors are involved in the striking shift from the relative calm of the 1950's to the conflict of the 1960's, but high on the list is the fact that Ways and Means became the focal point of several major initiatives of the new Democratic administration. President Kennedy, unlike President Eisenhower, proposed legislation that in-

113 For these bills see the following votes in the *Congressional Record*: July 8, 1953, pp. 8240–41; July 8, 1954, pp. 10093–94; and July 30, 1954, p. 12810.
114 *Ibid.*, June 1, 1954, p. 7448.
115 In all, the conservative coalition appeared on six votes in the 1953–1960 period. It lost one of the six, H.R. 5 in 1960, by four votes.

evitably aroused sharp differences between Democrats and Republicans. In the 1950's Ways and Means faced relatively few innovating proposals from the administration. In the 1960's the Committee had to deal with two highly controversial tax reduction proposals, a major new step in handling tariff negotiations with other countries, persistent and serious efforts by the administration to enact medicare, a series of proposals to raise the debt ceiling, and, as a consequence of increased spending and the Viet Nam war, the tax increase bill in 1967 that dominated much of the 90th Congress.

In the 1960's, however, one thing remained the same in the House: except for the 89th Congress, the conservative coalition was always a basic problem that had to be dealt with. In the 1961–1968 years Ways and Means lost only two roll call votes, which indicates that the Committee dealt with it successfully.

Except for social security bills, as shown in Table 5.9, the Committee and the House tended to vote along strict party lines in 1961–1964. The Democratic majority coalition in the Committee was followed by winning Democratic coalitions on the floor. From 1962 to 1969 the conservative coalition appeared on only three roll call votes on Committee bills, passing one (a conference report on meat imports), losing one (medicare in 1965), and winning the third (a 1968 vote to cut spending by only $4 billion compared to $6 billion).

Despite the reappearance of party differences on roll call votes Committee integration was high. As late as 1955 some members of Ways and Means strongly criticized the Committee's handling of legislation. Curtis, for example, had chastised the Democrats for rushing the Reciprocal Trade Act extension bill through the Committee and for absenteeism, saying that "it is no executive session writing up the bill if you have to spend your efforts trying to persuade 13 proxies instead of 13 colleagues present and paying attention to the language of the bill." [116] Dan Reed deplored the handling of the $20 tax credit in 1955, saying that such practices endangered the prestige of the Committee.[117] And in the same year, John Dingell attacked the Committee Republicans for using "hypocritical and obstructionist" tactics to delay the social security bill.[118] Since 1955, and particularly since the beginning of Mills's chairmanship in 1958, such attacks have been rare. In the 1960's, except for frequent criticisms from

[116] *Ibid.*, February 18, 1955, p. 1744.
[117] *Ibid.*, February 25, 1955, p. 2162.
[118] *Ibid.*, July 18, 1955, p. 10774.

TABLE 5.9
INDEX OF PARTY LIKENESS, MAJOR BILLS, 1961–1964 [a]

REVENUE BILLS		House IPL (%)	Com- mittee IPL (%)
Year	Bill		
1961	H.R. 7446	22	0
1962	H.R. 10650	11	0
1963	H.R. 6755	48	40
1963	H.R. 8363	11	0
1964	H.R. 11376	11	0
1964	H.R. 8000	9	28

SOCIAL SECURITY BILLS		House IPL (%)	Com- mittee IPL (%)
Year	Bill		
1961	H.R. 6027	90	60
1961	H.R. 4806	85	67
1962	H.R. 10606	16	0
1964	H.R. 11865	98	90

DEBT LIMIT BILLS		House IPL (%)	Com- mittee IPL (%)
Year	Bill		
1961	H.R. 7677	44	50
1962	H.R. 10050	58	50
1962	H.R. 11990	14	11
1963	H.R. 6009	12	0
1963	H.R. 7824	19	10
1963	H.R. 8969	14	0
1964	H.R. 11375	14	0

[a] Votes on conference reports and rules are excluded. When more than one roll call occurred on a bill the vote with the lowest IPL score was selected for presentation.

Curtis over Committee procedure, Republicans and Democrats on Ways and Means have generally disagreed on specific policies but co-operated to write the legislation with few public complaints. The general approach since 1958, and particularly since Mills and Byrnes have been the senior leaders, was expressed well by Byrnes in 1967.

> I think those of us on the minority, the Republicans in dealing with the chairman, I know I've tried to . . . find ways that we both could work together to . . . get a solution, get the job done. . . . In many cases there's no disagreement between either the Democrats or the Republicans that a problem exists, the . . . conflict may be on how do you approach the problem. . . . So both he and I, I think, have taken the attitude that our principal function as a member of the Congress should be to get the job done. . . . And if we differ philosophically, well sure, there's going to be a cleavage, but let's at least put our objective, have as our target the solution of it rather than a conflict and developing an issue for some election purposes or otherwise.[119]

The position of the liberals on the Committee, though strident complaints about Committee decisions are rare, remained about the same in the 1960's — except for the 89th Congress — as it had been in earlier periods. The decision-making process in Ways and Means allows every member an opportunity to affect policy but the composition of the Committee, and of the House which it represents, puts constraints on the kinds of programs that come out of Ways and Means. On some issues, such as medicare, the balance in the Committee was tilted in a negative direction for several years. On other issues, such as unemployment compensation, the Committee has been willing to extend benefit payments but, as the Herlong amendment in 1958 showed, the Committee could go only so far in a liberal direction. And on such issues as the highly controversial public welfare amendments of 1967, which were designed to reduce the increasing number of welfare recipients, the conservative majority on the Committee had the upper hand. The best the liberals could do on the welfare issue in 1967 was temper the Committee's decisions, not stop them. A Committee liberal explained why the welfare restrictions never even came to a vote in the Committee: the liberals only had about five votes. The bill, a blend of improvements in the social

---

[119] "Interview with Congressman John W. Byrnes," for "Operation Government," Westinghouse Broadcasting Company, October 17, 1967, pp. 10–11.

security programs and one or two controversial sections, passed the House 415–3.[120]

SUMMARY. The pattern of party voting on Ways and Means bills and the degree of Committee integration have varied widely since the Roosevelt years. None of the five periods discussed above is "pure," that is, in any period deviant cases may be found. For example, although the dominant characteristic of the 1930's and postwar years is that of a highly partisan Committee with relatively low integration, exceptions may be found. The same is true of the three other periods.

But despite the qualifications that must be made and the imperfections in the data collected, some consistency appears in the way the Committee and the House have acted on important issues at different points in time. Generally speaking, the following conclusions are true for Ways and Means and the House:

ISSUES

1. Revenue bills elicit greater party differences than either trade or social security bills.

2. Trade has evolved from a highly partisan issue to a mixed issue.[121]

3. Debt legislation, once a minor issue for the Committee, has become a highly partisan issue in the 1960's.

EXTRA-CONGRESSIONAL EFFECTS ON ISSUES

1. Party differences are lower in times of national emergency than in "normal" times.

2. Divided government with a Republican Congress leads to high party differences.

3. Divided government with a Democratic Congress leads to low party differences.

CONGRESSIONAL ELECTORAL EFFECTS ON ISSUES

1. The nature of coalitions in the House affects the decisions that are made in the Committee.

2. The existence of an actual or potential conservative coalition in the House requires decisions to be acceptable to the conservative majority, whether or not party differences preclude the appearance of the conservative coalition.

---

[120] *Congressional Record*, August 17, 1967 (daily edition), pp. 10663–743.
[121] See Watson, *op. cit.* and Bauer, Pool, and Dexter, *op. cit.*

3. Liberals do less well than conservatives in the Committee and in the House not because the rules of the game are against them but because they have been a minority in most of the Congresses since 1933.

4. High party differences are to the advantage of liberals because only if partisanship is high are they part of the majority.

5. Electoral results dictate that whether partisanship is high or low the bargains that are made in the legislative process will be more acceptable to conservatives than to liberals.

EFFECTS OF COALITIONS ON INTEGRATION

1. As one party approaches or attains a working majority in the House, party differences go up and Committee integration goes down.

2. High partisanship need not always lead to low integration if the rewards and costs of Committee membership are not affected to the extent that the rewards of membership outweigh the costs.

In terms of the autonomy of the Ways and Means Committee, Committee decisions are highly dependent upon the political structure of the House. Ways and Means does its job successfully if the low number of defeats on the floor is a fair measure of success, but the Committee has not always brought its decisions in line with what a voting majority of the House will accept. Moreover, cases have been cited in which the Committee majority has been far out of line with the House majority and, when this happens, the House majority has, in effect, compelled the Committee to change its position or be overturned on the floor. What is most impressive about House-Committee relations is not the autonomy of the Committee from the House but the sensitivity of Ways and Means to widely held sentiments in the House.

II. HOUSE-COMMITTEE RELATIONS: DEPENDENCE AND INDEPENDENCE

Except for the testimony that Ways and Means receives from congressmen at Committee hearings, letters from members, signatures on discharge petitions, and public statements, the Committee determines what will be acceptable to the House in informal ways. No one, least of all the Committee under Mills, takes the House lightly, and much of what takes place within the Committee is dictated by how Mills and other members calculate the House is likely to respond. House demands and expectations are largely self-imposed by the members of the Committee in that their experience has taught them what is likely to be popular in the House and what will be inadmissible. Many times the Committee simply "knows" the limits beyond which it cannot go; no canvass of House opinion is needed. When "soundings" are taken the sample is likely to be small but representative of the blocs that compose the House, and the final assessment is likely to be remarkably accurate. The intuition of people like Mills, honed by years of trying to predict what the House will take or reject, checked against the results of soundings, and tested by every final vote, is a major conduit of House influence on the decisions of its committees. A string of victories for the Ways and Means Committee may be as much a testimonial to its ability to read the House as it is evidence for the lack of House influence on the Committee.

Committee members revealed in interviews that they are well aware of the need to take into consideration what their non-Committee colleagues think about various issues. Responsibility for gauging the reaction of the House to Committee bills falls most heavily on Mills.

Twenty-five members of the Committee were asked about House influence on Committee decisions. Three members said the House has little or no influence over what the Committee does, but all the rest recognize that the House has at least some influence on their decisions, and most of them feel that the House has a good deal of influence. Twenty-one members mentioned Mills in connection with this question. The typical opinion is that the views of their House colleagues are channeled to the Committee through Mills and, in this way, are reflected in legislation. Mills has the primary responsibility for passing the bills reported by the Committee and he meets this responsibility by: sensing what kind of bill can pass the House; determining what kinds of changes should be made in the bill to ease its passage; and actively building a majority for the bill after it is reported by the Committee.

Finding or building a majority for an important bill takes time, caution, and contacts. A Democratic party leader who, when asked if the prime responsibility for passing Ways and Means bills falls on the Committee or the party leadership, replied "Mills," and commented:

> Mills is conservative, careful, and cautious. He always takes three times longer bringing a bill out than we think he should. Nothing ever comes out of that Committee on time. He's cautious and he won't risk losing the bill on the floor.

Very careful about this and this takes time. But in this time
he's always working, counting noses. And by the time he's
done, although it takes a while, it's ready to go.

Mills's time-consuming caution was a common theme throughout the
interviews. "Some say he takes too long and is indecisive," said a
Treasury Department official. "Perhaps he is," he continued, "but
he has to get the votes." "Mills keeps his ear close to the ground," said
a Republican, and a Committee colleague concurred: "What the
House will accept is taken into account by Mills and does affect what
we send them. Mills does not like to lose on the floor and he never
has yet. One reason he doesn't is because he takes soundings and
checks on what the members will accept."

Other evidence supports interview responses that the Committee,
through Mills, keeps the lines of communication open to the House
and that potentially strong demands, as perceived by the members of
Ways and Means, find their way into bills. An example of the House
influencing the Committee is the 1965 administration proposal intended to help alleviate the United States balance of payments problem by reducing the dollar amount of goods American tourists could
bring back with them from abroad without paying a duty. With a
lower limit on duty-free goods tourists would be induced to spend less
in foreign countries, thereby helping to curb the gold drain.

In May 1965, the Johnson administration proposed that the duty-
free limit of $100 be reduced to $50, and that the base price used in
determining this amount be changed from the wholesale value of
the goods to the fair retail value (a higher amount that would of
course further reduce the amount of money spent abroad by tourists). This proposal met strong opposition early in the executive session of Ways and Means from both sides of the table. Democratic
members from states that have many people travelling to Canada
and Mexico were especially upset over the idea. Before the issue was
resolved, the Committee first rejected the administration's plan, then
reversed itself after the administration applied some pressure, and
finally, after Mills canvassed sentiment in the House (and Senate),
reversed itself again to avoid defeat on the floor.

The administration's initial defeat came on May 10 when the Committee adopted an amendment offered by John Byrnes to keep the
$100 limit but to change the base from the wholesale price to retail
value. Byrnes's amendment, which was opposed by Mills as well as by
Treasury, carried by a voice vote with several Democratic members

of the Committee supporting it. The Committee discussed the bill
a little more after the vote but Mills, seeing that a quorum was not
present, abruptly adjourned the meeting. (An unusual move — the
Committee often sits without a quorum.)

The Committee met again the next day, May 11, and this time
Treasury had its first team in the room: Secretary Henry Fowler and
Under Secretary Joseph Barr. Fowler argued that the Byrnes amendment would have a bad psychological effect on foreign nations because it would look like the administration wanted a tough bill to
help the payments problem but Congress had refused.

Eugene Keogh, who had voted for Byrnes's amendment, moved to
reconsider the vote and, by voice vote, the prior decision was "recon-
sidered." Byrnes moved an amendment providing for a $100 limit in
place of the administration's $50 limit that was rejected by a straight
party-line vote, 7–16. Another amendment by Byrnes was defeated
by another party-line vote, 8–17, and the Committee, having undone
what it did the day before, reported the $50 fair retail value bill.[122]

However, the reaction of the aberrant Democrats, who had been
persuaded to get back into line with the administration, tipped Mills
off to the potential House reaction to the bill. He checked in the
House, took soundings in the Senate where he found similar opposition to the $50 limit, and on June 7 Ways and Means met again to
consider the matter. Mills, who felt that the bill might be defeated
on the floor, proposed a compromise that set a permanent level of
$100 fair retail value which passed unanimously. The next day the
amended bill passed the House by voice vote. Three weeks later the
Senate, by a 61–31 vote, turned down the $50 limit and the figure
originally suggested by Byrnes, $100 fair retail value, became law.

Among many other examples of Committee sensitivity to general
House sentiment, two recent cases are of special importance. One
reason why medicare took so long to be reported to the House, and why
the Committee did not act favorably in 1967 on the president's request for a 10 per cent tax surcharge, was that both proposals were
short of votes in the House.

Medicare, of course, was "bottled up" in the Ways and Means
Committee for several years, but one primary reason the Committee
never reported it was that the bill would not have passed the House.
As late as the year before medicare became law, one of its supporters

122 An accurate story is contained in "House Panel Votes Cut in Duty-Free
Limit On U.S. Tourists' Goods to $50 Retail Value," *The Wall Street Journal*,
May 12, 1965, p. 3.

in the House, William Fitz Ryan (D., N.Y.), noted that the petition to discharge Ways and Means of the bill and bring it to the floor for a vote had only thirty-two of the two hundred and eighteen needed signatures.[123] More than thirty-two members of the House supported medicare, of course, but either they did not feel strongly enough on the issue to overcome their natural antipathy to using an unusual method of forcing a vote on a bill or, more likely, they realized that a majority of the House opposed the measure. According to one of the key HEW officials involved in medicare Mills also realized this, as did HEW:

> The Ways and Means Committee wants consensus. They don't want to bring out a bill thirteen to twelve. They will work it around until they have consensus — they would like to have about twenty-three to two. That was one of our troubles on Medicare in sixty-one, sixty-two, sixty-three, and sixty-four. Mills wouldn't vote for it until he got a consensus in the committee and until he had neutralized the opposition. Wilbur would have made the thirteenth vote, but he wouldn't bring out a bill that way. He would say, "It just doesn't make sense." I remember once when Cecil King and I went to see him to try to get him to vote for medicare. He said, "You don't have the votes on the floor." And he was right — we didn't. That was 1964.

Whatever the substantive arguments against medicare, there was a strong political argument against reporting the bill: lack of votes.

Committee sensitivity to the House and a strong aversion to risking defeat on the floor also explains why Ways and Means, despite an unusually vigorous effort by party leaders, the administration, and professional economists, shelved the tax surcharge proposals by a 20–5 vote in 1967. No whip poll was needed to know that the surcharge was in trouble with House Republicans and southern Democrats demanding spending cuts as a prerequisite for the tax increase, other members demanding that the money be raised by tax reforms instead of a tax rise, and anti-war Democrats attacking the surcharge as a tax to finance an unjust war. One Democratic member of the Committee said that even if the Committee reported the surcharge it would not receive one hundred votes, and, he felt, "There's no sense bringing a bill to the floor if you're going to get your brains bashed in." At the time, this was probably an accurate summary of the Committee posi-

[123] *Congressional Record*, July 29, 1964, p. 17292.

tion and the voting line-up in the House. And one was not separate from the other.

It is a mistake to see only the autonomy and independence of Ways and Means as it interacts with the House. But it is equally dubious to overreact to the traditional emphasis on committee power and overlook the ways in which the Ways and Means Committee takes the lead in forming opinions in the House, in determining what policy choices to present to the House, and in creating a majority behind its bills. One key decision the Committee and its leaders have is whether to lead and shape House opinion or follow existing opinion. Again, medicare and the surcharge illustrate the complex interdependence between the Committee and the House.

In one sense, the Committee majority in 1964 did nothing more than follow the majority view in the House, which was against the King-Anderson bill. This was, perhaps, more a case of agreement between the Committee and the House than of the Committee following the House. But, in another sense, the Committee did bottle up medicare — if it is up to the Committee to find solutions to conflicting demands. By remaining passive, or by holding hearings without reaching a compromise, the Committee did more than agree with the House majority. It insured that no bill would be forthcoming in 1964; if Ways and Means could not settle on a compromise program the House surely could not. In this sense, the Committee was influential in the decision, and the Chairman, who proposed no solutions though he might have been looking for one, was more than a passive register of the majority view in the Committee and in the House. He was the key to the whole problem.

The nature of the relationship between the House and the Committee on medicare in 1964 was expressed well by one of the Democratic party leaders. The leadership was stymied and could not force the bill out of the Committee in his judgment because, for those members who were not irrevocably committed for or against King-Anderson, the support of the Committee and of Mills was indispensable to getting their votes for the bill. Medicare, a highly controversial issue with a well-financed and intense lobby unalterably opposed to it, required the prestige of the Committee and of the Chairman to pass. Without this as an umbrella, the members who were willing to support the program only if they had Mills and the Committee behind them remained negative votes. According to this Democrat, "Mills is conservative and if he's for it the members can feel safer voting for it. It's the same in my case. I could use the fact that he supported it to justify my vote. I didn't have to use it in my case but it's better to have him with you." Mills, in other words, was the key to medicare because his support was crucial for the swing votes in the House. When the HEW official and others tried to get Mills's support for medicare they were acknowledging his central position between two blocs (which checked each other); this gave disproportionate importance to a relatively small number of votes that many people felt would be affected by the Chairman's position. The facts of the matter went far beyond agreement between the Committee majority and the House majority. The House vote could be used by the Committee to justify inaction on the legislation; but by the same token the House majority was susceptible to leadership from the Committee, which in 1964 and earlier was not forthcoming. In this case it was the Committee's decision to lead or not to lead; and, in essence, the decision was the Chairman's.

All of this was changed by the election of 295 Democrats to the House. Precisely how large the three blocs of votes were on medicare will never be known, and it might have been possible for Mills, had he been of a mind, to defeat the King-Anderson bill on the floor even though there were enough votes to report it from the Committee with or without his support. But this is a moot question. The Committee, at Mills's behest, made the seemingly incongruous decision to report a bill much more liberal and costly than the one it had rejected for many years. In fact, the decision was by no means incongruous given the new liberal majority in the House plus the tactical shift by the AMA, which in early 1965 declared that King-Anderson was so limited in its benefits that the elderly could not fail to be disappointed. These new developments probably did not require the Committee to go beyond King-Anderson to enact a medicare bill, but they were good reasons for going beyond the administration request and they acted as conditions, if not causes, of the Committee action. In this way the interaction between the Committee, the House, the administration, and the chief interest group concerned with the legislation led to the Mills medicare bill, with an assist from Byrnes and the Republicans who devised the first compromise bill with any chance of being accepted by the main antagonists in the stalemate.

The tax surcharge offers another lesson in Committee dependence-independence. One member of Ways and Means, who supported the surcharge and had supported medicare for years, drew a parallel between the two issues with which other Committee members would probably agree. According to this member, the House has a great deal of influence on what the Committee does, and Mills will not bring a bill to the floor unless it will pass. "I think this is true on the tax bill and I think it was true of social security. I think if a majority of the House would vote for the tax bill you'd have a tax bill, and if a majority would have voted for medicare, same thing." He felt, in other words, that the Committee could do very little in the face of strong House opposition to these measures; the Committee faced almost certain defeat if the bills were reported.

But he also recognized that the situation as he described it put the Committee in a quandary and raised questions about its reported power in the House: "Of course, some people say we are the Ways and Means Committee and we should be the leaders and bring it out for a vote. I don't know. I don't think there's much sense in getting beaten on the floor." He emphasized how closely the Committee listens to the House and how the Committee must try to draft a bill that will pass. For this man, a good bill that cannot pass the House is a contradiction in terms, as it no doubt is for most Committee members.

At the center of the quandary was Mills. Mills and the Committee, by rejecting quick action on the surcharge, were demonstrating their power to withstand enormous pressure from the White House and its affiliates. The surcharge issue was a clear case of Committee power in the House. From another perspective, however, the Committee's decision to postpone action on the surcharge in late 1967 was a clear case of Committee impotence. All the Committee action showed, from the view of party leaders, was that the Committee simply was reflecting the majority sentiment in the House. Under these conditions, the leadership could do nothing. As one party leader put it, "We didn't try to go around the Chairman because we couldn't have gotten the votes. He's in control and the Committee took the popular House stand. There is some question about whether we *should* do this but we couldn't and so we didn't try." Mills, in particular, was seen as a leader who did not lead. Where you stood, in this case, depended upon where you sat.

But Mills and the Committee did more on the surcharge issue than merely reflect House opposition to the measure. They agreed on a compromise that could pass the House, did pass, and became law in 1968. The issue that the Committee and the president could not resolve in 1967 was how much federal spending would be cut, the conservative sine qua non for the surcharge.

Conservatives in the House wanted heavy spending cuts; liberals, and the White House, realized that some cuts were necessary to get the surcharge but wanted to keep the cut as low as possible. In April 1968, the Senate, not waiting for the House to act first, adopted an amendment that called for a 10 per cent surcharge and a $6 billion reduction in FY 1969 spending. In May, the Ways and Means Committee Democrats rejected a Republican motion to accept the $6 billion reduction and instructed its conferees to work out a $10 billion tax increase either through the surcharge or by increasing tax rates, and to accept a spending cut of at least $4 billion. This motion, offered by Herlong, was acceptable to liberal and conservative Democrats on the Committee, and was supported by four of the Committee's ten Republicans as well. Two liberal Democrats on the Committee abstained.

It appeared, therefore, that the Committee and the House would accept something less than the $6 billion cut made by the Senate and opposed by the president. House conferees, however, agreed to the $6 billion figure and brought the matter back to the House for a vote. What happened in the conference committee is not known but subsequent events in the House showed that there was more support for a conservative compromise than for a liberal compromise. A liberal Democratic member of Ways and Means, James A. Burke, offered a motion to instruct the House conferees to hold out for a $4 billion reduction but his motion was easily defeated by the conservative coalition, 137–259.[124] Three weeks later the $6 billion cut passed the House 257–162.

The tax surcharge issue shows that the Committee is sensitive to broad sentiments in the House, but it is also true that unless the Committee had acted first on the surcharge the House, regardless of what the Senate did, probably would not have resolved the conflict by forcing the issue to a close. In the House, southern Democrats could not agree with liberal Democrats, and without a conservative coalition in the Committee a successful conservative coalition in the House was most unlikely. Mills, as before, was the key to the issue because he was central to building a majority. It is possible that the majority would have evolved without Committee action and without frequent consultations between Mills and the Republicans, but this is not what happened. Once the Committee acted the deadlock was broken.

Why is the Ways and Means Committee sensitive — "as sensitive

---

[124] *Congressional Quarterly Weekly Report*, June 7, 1968, p. 1417.

as an adolescent girl," according to one HEW man — to the feelings of the House? The explanation lies in how the Committee members see their job and in the relationship between this perception and the satisfactions that they derive from being members of Ways and Means. Members are attracted to the Committee because of its unusual amount of power and prestige in the House, and its power and prestige are two of the most important inducements the members derive from the Committee. To protect this power and prestige, the members must guard against ignominious defeats in the House, the embarrassment of having their bills rejected as unacceptable by their colleagues, and the upsetting awareness that after months of labor on a bill they have not met the most basic qualification of a good bill, that it stand up well in the House. Committee members — led by the Chairman — take pride in their Committee's reputation for doing quality work in a technical sense and, in a political sense, for working out a compromise that a majority of the House can support.

The closed rule combines all of these elements. On most major bills reported by the Committee the House gives up its right of amendment and agrees to debate them under a closed rule. That is, the House limits its power to accepting or rejecting the bill in toto with no intervening amendments unless they are first approved by the Committee. In a few cases, a modified closed rule permits some kind of amendment but normally the rule is closed completely. Of the ninety-six bills debated under a rule from 1947 to 1966, only sixteen have been open rules, eight have been modified closed rules, and seventy-two have been fully closed.[125]

The arguments usually given in favor of a closed rule may be divided into three separate but related classes. First, Ways and Means bills are seen as so complex by the proponents of closed rules that they cannot be reasonably considered on the floor or open to amendments from anyone who might want something different from that reported by a majority of the Committee. Second, tax, trade, and social welfare bills are so susceptible to the demands of interest groups that the members feel it is better to avoid temptation by precluding all amendments than face the nightmarish necessity of voting against a popular proposal because the Treasury Department could not afford to lose the revenue.

[125] Data compiled from an examination of all 697 bills considered by the House during this period. It appears that Ways and Means is by far the biggest consumer of closed rules. See James A. Robinson, *The House Rules Committee* (Indianapolis: Bobbs-Merrill, 1963), pp. 43–46.

TABLE 5.10

BILLS AMENDED OR DEFEATED AND TYPE OF RULE, 1947–1965

Type of rule	Amended	Defeated
Closed (N = 72)	0	0
Modified closed (N = 8)	1	1
Open (N = 16)	6	1

SOURCE: Ways and Means *Calendar*, 1947–1965; relevant volumes of *Congressional Record*.

A third reason for closed rules, rarely articulated on the floor, is that Ways and Means bills are likely to be major administration measures, and it is much easier to pass them intact if the party leaders can concentrate on the final votes without having to worry about defeating objectionable amendments. The closed rule prevents the opponents of a bill from whittling away at it through amendments and gives them only two chances to alter or defeat it: a motion to recommit, which may amend the bill by containing substantive instructions; and the vote on final passage. Since 1947, as Table 5.10 shows, the Committee has been most successful when operating under a closed rule, next most successful under a modified close rule (the one bill defeated under this type of rule was the protectionist tariff bill in 1953 opposed by the Republican leadership and Eisenhower), and least successful under open rules.

Closed rules on complex tax bills have been well established for many years. Speaking in favor of a closed rule for a 1947 tax bill, for example, Leo Allen (R., Ill.) inaccurately said, "To the new Members today I would explain that since I have been in Congress, almost 15 years, every tax bill has come before the House under a closed rule." [126] In justification of the rule another member argued that "the reason for requesting such rule [*sic*] and the justification of the gentleman's committee for always granting such rules has been that the bills are of such technical nature that they could hardly be well considered in any other manner." [127] Interviews conducted almost twenty years after these quotes were made show that the complexity argument is still viable. "Most of our stuff, because it's so intricate, gets a closed rule," a Republican Committee member said. "You just can't open a tax bill on the floor. The House knows we won't pull any fast ones." Revenue legislation, the consensus seems to be, just cannot be written on the House floor.

[126] *Congressional Record*, March 26, 1947, p. 2627.
[127] *Ibid.*, p. 2628.

The mere adoption of closed rules indicates that the House is willing to rely on the Committee's judgment in countless decisions, but more direct evidence also supports this observation. William Avery (R., Kan.), for example, told the House in 1963, "Mr. Speaker, I am always a little reluctant to take the floor under a rule when we have a bill from the Ways and Means Committee. I always get a feeling of an inferiority complex. Mr. Speaker, we look to the members of the Ways and Means Committee as being experts in the field of public finance." [128] William J. Randall (D., Mo.) commented on a 1964 social security bill:

> It is my opinion far too many people underestimate the importance of the careful scrutiny this committee gives to the countless provisions of social security legislation. What would seem to be a minor change in an obscure subsection of the Social Security Act actually results in large and beneficial changes in the day-to-day lives of millions of our deserving elderly citizens covered by the act. On the other hand, just a small error in drafting these changes could adversely affect the lives of these senior citizens. It is comforting to know that Mr. Mills' committee is not in the habit of making mistakes.[129]

In selling a closed rule to the House on a 1949 social security bill, Rules Committee Chairman Sabath took the competence of Ways and Means as his theme:

> Mr. Speaker, lest I forget, I wish to state that I am indeed proud of my Democratic colleagues, Chairman Doughton of the Ways and Means Committee, Mr. Cooper, Judge Mills, and Mr. Camp, because never before have I witnessed such an able presentation by a committee on behalf of a rule. Nearly every provision in the bill was thoroughly and intelligently explained. Every query propounded to these gentlemen was answered most satisfactorily — and there were many. . . . The Ways and Means Committee devoted nearly 6 months of tireless effort, toil, study, and consideration to the bill, hearing over 250 witnesses both for and against. The bill was reported by the Ways and Means Committee by a vote of 22 to 3. I as well as the majority of the Committee on Rules believed that such effort, study, and consideration, placed the Ways and Means Committee in the best position

[128] *Ibid.*, May 15, 1963, p. 8559.
[129] *Ibid.*, July 29, 1964, p. 17292.

to determine the type of rule that would be required. . . . Is any nonmember of the Ways and Means Committee so conceited and vain to believe that he would be in a better position, without having the advantage of 6 months of hearings and deliberations, to improve the bill? Surely, I doubt whether this is possible.[130]

In 1947, Robert L. ("Muley") Doughton complained about Republican partisanship on a major tax bill in Ways and Means, and also summed up the rationale behind closed rules:

Historically, it has become the custom of the House to entrust the drafting of tax bills to the committee on the theory that revenue legislation is too complex to be satisfactorily amended and perfected on the floor of the House, and because it was known that tax bills were reported only after the fullest, fairest, and politically impartial consideration by the members of the committee. Consequently, the practice of considering tax bills under a closed rule has developed.[131]

Doughton's complaint about the Republican deviation from these norms did not prevent the adoption of the closed rule, which he supported, but it does reveal the existence of the norms and the kind of behavior expected of the Committee in return for the closed rule.

The second argument on behalf of closed rules is the pragmatic realization that trade bills, tax bills, and social security bills, if subject to unrestrained floor proceedings, might be so riddled with amendments that United States fiscal, welfare, and foreign trade policy would be damaged. The closed rule acts as a shield for Ways and Means bills against hundreds of interest group demands that would be articulated if not fulfilled if the bill appeared naked on the floor. Interest group pressure is channeled into the committee stage of the legislative process, freeing House members to complain about their inability to offer amendments while they probably breathe a sigh of relief that they do not have to face certain kinds of choices.

The Ways and Means Committee and the House often find it necessary to make widely unpopular decisions on fiscal matters. For example, excise taxes, disliked by everyone, are an important source of government revenue that can be withdrawn only under certain conditions (decrease in the government's need for revenue, influx of money from alternative sources, and so on). In the 80th Congress,

[130] *Ibid.*, October 4, 1949, p. 13809.
[131] *Ibid.*, March 26, 1947, p. 2642.

the Republicans, with great reluctance, had to ask for an extension of excise taxes even though their campaign slogan in 1946 had been a tax cut (achieved on general taxes). Confronted by the argument that at least the excise tax on electric light bulbs should be removed because no one could seriously claim that bulbs are not a necessity, Committee Chairman Knutson argued that absolutely no amendments could be made in the bill without setting off an avalanche of equally enticing, but impractical, demands. As he said, "I would be glad to, but if we open up this Pandora's Box on the floor of the House we may not know where we will stop." [132] Told that the danger was slight because only amendments approved by the Committee can be offered, Knutson replied, "The gentleman must not forget that there are 25 members on the committee and each one might wish to offer a different amendment." [133] Even if the number and scope of amendments could be restrained, a modified closed rule would force the Committee to deny some members' requests; it is, therefore, easier to deny all requests.

Two years later Sabath, no lover of closed rules, defended one on a social security bill:

> For years tariff and other complicated revenue bills emanating from the Ways and Means Committee always were considered by the House under a closed rule. During the hearings before my committee it was contended that some members have amendments that they would like to offer and under a closed rule they would be precluded. As a matter of fact my colleague from Illinois (Mr. Mason) said he would personally like to offer some 40 or 50 amendments to this bill. Now then if only one-tenth of the members offered one-tenth of the amendments that the gentleman from Illinois (Mr. Mason) would like to offer, we would have over 220 amendments, and if on the average, each amendment offered had two members making 5-minute speeches for and against — that being 20 minutes on each amendment — almost 4,400 minutes or months of time would be consumed thereon.[134]

Sabath's somewhat exaggerated contention approaches the sublime but it exemplifies the feeling that any amendment, regardless of merit, might destroy the bill.

Predictions of disaster under an open rule frequently accompany

132 *Ibid.*, January 29, 1947, p. 672.
133 *Ibid.*, p. 673.
134 *Ibid.*, October 4, 1949, p. 13809.

the argument for the closed rule. Most interesting in this regard is that the argument is based on examples of the House debating a Ways and Means bill under an open rule and reaping the inevitable result: chaos. Note the common theme in the following evidence:

> *1948 Revenue Act:* I served for many years on the Rules Committee under the leadership of the distinguished gentleman from Illinois (Mr. Sabath) . . . and when the gentleman from Massachusetts (Mr. McCormack) was the majority leader. I believed at that time, and had the courage to come onto the floor and say so and vote with the gentleman from Massachusetts and the gentleman from Illinois in granting a closed rule exactly like this on every tax bill but one, and at that time we let down the bars. I insisted, with others, and we had an open rule; and after 7 days' debate in the House, the House adjourned, and the Ways and Means Committee came before the Rules Committee and we who had voted for an open rule under Democratic leadership's insistence and crack of the whip, admitted we were wrong, and we voted a closed rule.[135] (Earl C. Michener, R., Mich.)

> *1951 Revenue Act:* Mr. Speaker, for 10 years I served on the Ways and Means Committee before being elected majority leader in 1940. With one exception, I have no recollection of any tax bill that came out of the committee . . . that was not considered by the House under a closed rule. The exception was in 1930, when the tax bill was considered under an open rule, and what happened on the floor on that occasion caused the responsible members of both parties to recognize the practical situation that existed and the difficulty of writing a tax bill on the floor. You will remember that a very important part of that bill was stricken out, carrying with it some few billions of dollars, and members of the Committee on Ways and Means were meeting unofficially, picking out this tax, that tax, or the other tax, and coming into the House and proposing it.[136] (John Mc-Cormack, D., Mass.)

> *1962 Revenue Act:* I think we should adopt the closed rule, which has been the policy of this Congress as long as I can remember. Now, I remember the first term of Congress when I came here. We Democrats had won control of the

---

[135] *Ibid.*, January 29, 1948, p. 690.
[136] *Ibid.*, June 20, 1951, p. 6838.

House after a great many years of Republican control. We
were all fired up and pepped up to change things around.
I remember that in my first session here the late Charles
Crisp of Georgia, who was chairman of the Ways and
Means Committee, was going to have things democratic, and
we all wanted to have things democratic. He brought in a
tax bill with an open rule. It was a sales tax bill. We scram-
bled around here for about a week or 10 days with that bill
and things got into such a state of confusion that nobody
knew what he was doing and it went back to the committee.
I think nobody regrets more than I do having to bring in a
closed rule here. I do a lot of fussing about it, but when the
chips are down I think the only feasible and practical way
we can operate is under a closed rule.[137] (Howard W. Smith,
D., Va.)

1963 Revenue Act: I think the gentleman will discover, if
he looks back over the history of the House of Representatives, that there was a time a number of years ago when a
bill, not a revenue bill but a tariff bill, came to the floor under an open rule. There were so many amendments, good or
bad, offered by so many members that finally, after 2 weeks
of futile debate, the committee rose and went to the Committee on Rules and asked for a rule which would allow the
Committee of the Whole to take a bill proposed by the Committee on Ways and Means, or reject it, giving to the minority the right to offer one motion to recommit which could
be even a substitute. This was a practical experience which
convinced a great many members that the only way in which
you could effectively handle a revenue bill or a tariff bill was
in this fashion.[138] (Richard W. Bolling, D., Mo.)

The practice of having closed rules on major tax bills, for these
reasons, has never been seriously endangered since the 1930's. On
major tariff and social security bills, however, the use of the closed
rule has evolved during the past twenty years until it now embraces
these bills as strongly as it does tax bills.

In 1948 John McCormack vigorously objected to the Republican
request for a closed rule on the 1948 extension of the reciprocal trade
program. McCormack, who along with the Truman administration
opposed the Republican bill, pointed out that heretofore every simi-

[137] *Ibid.*, March 28, 1962, p. 5300.
[138] *Ibid.*, September 24, 1963, p. 17900.

lar extension bill had been considered without a closed rule.[139] Jere Cooper of Tennessee, a high-ranking Democrat on Ways and Means, agreed with McCormack. Cooper argued that although he, as the designated parliamentarian of Ways and Means, had made several points of order against amendments to previous trade extension bills, the bills were always considered under open rules and the general rules of the House. Referring to the closed rule applied to the 1930 Smoot-Hawley tariff bill, Cooper accused the Republicans of repeating the same mistake and warned them that they would regret it.[140] The Republicans extended the same justification for closed rules on tax bills to trade bills and argued that they were only expediting the business of the House. Over Democratic protests, the trade bill was given a closed rule, the first such case since Smoot-Hawley.

With the Democrats in charge of the House in 1949, the trade extension bill came up again and was considered on the floor under an open rule. No protectionist floor amendments were adopted so the open rule worked well for the Democrats. In 1951, however, the Democrats, consistent with their 1948 position, again brought the trade bill to the floor under an open rule and the result was a debacle. Several protectionist amendments were adopted on the floor; this was the last time a major trade bill was debated under an open rule.

Social security bills have gone through a similar development. The late Clarence Brown (R., Ohio) opposed a 1949 closed rule on a social security bill by tracing the history of open rules:

> Mr. Speaker, the original Social Security Act which was passed in 1935 was considered under an open rule. Oh, that was a great legislative body back in 1935; you could trust the members of the House of that day to use good judgment in passing upon an important bill. And then in 1939 when the legislation was amended it was considered under an open rule. The House of that day was also a great legislative body, with men of responsibility and judgment. You could trust them to legislate. Then in 1946 again the Social Security Act was amended under an open rule — by another great legislature. The men and women of the House in 1946 could be trusted to work their will. . . . But not in this Congress.[141]

Majority Leader McCormack defended the closed rule by pointing to

[139] *Ibid.*, May 26, 1948, p. 6494.
[140] *Ibid.*, p. 6495.
[141] *Ibid.*, October 4, 1949, p. 13810.

a 1948 social security bill that the Republicans first planned to call up under a closed rule but later used suspension of the rules procedure (under which no amendments are possible). A member of Ways and Means, Thomas Jenkins (R., Ohio), rebutted McCormack: "The Committee on Ways and Means has never, so far as I know, asked for a closed rule unless it was practically a unanimous matter or unless it was a tax matter or a tariff matter. This is not a tax matter or a tariff matter . . . it is a social security matter." [142] The House voted for a closed rule in 1949; it has been used commonly for social security bills ever since. By 1963, with the possibility of medicare being added on the floor, even such a dedicated opponent of closed rules as Clarence Brown was willing to allow one on a noncontroversial social security bill because he felt (perhaps due to medicare) that it was unwise to open the Social Security Act to amendment.[143]

Committee members expressed the same reasons for the closed rule as found in the floor debates. Except for Curtis, the Committee members support the closed rule because it is impossible to write Ways and Means legislation on the House floor, it is essential to prevent unrestrained and irresponsible logrolling, and because it can always be rejected by the House. Committee members have good reason to slough off the opposition to closed rules as inconsequential: no request for a closed rule has ever been rejected on the floor. Moreover, only one closed rule has come close to death (one vote) although several have been subjected to roll call votes.[144]

Ostensibly, the closed rule is a procedural question, but it has crucial substantive implications as evidenced by requests of Republican members of Ways and Means for modified closed rules that would permit them to offer alternatives to what is contained in the bill reported by a majority of the Committee. This request signals a little noted and subtle strategic difference between a motion to recommit with instructions and a proposed amendment: the former is more likely to be seen as a Republican move and hence is less effective in getting Democratic votes than a simple amendment.

The difference between these tactics became manifest during the

142 *Ibid.*, p. 13811.
143 *Ibid.*, April 29, 1963, p. 7226.
144 The one close call came in 1955 on a trade bill. The previous question on the closed rule was voted down but Brown's motion to make the rule open was then defeated 191–193 and the closed rule adopted 193–192. The Committee's ranking Republican, Dan Reed, opposed the bill but did not vote against the rule because Chairman Cooper had helped him when Reed was chairman in the previous Congress. *Congressional Record*, February 17, 1955, pp. 1671–84.

1965 Rules Committee's hearings on the Ways and Means request for a closed rule on medicare. The ranking Committee Republican, John Byrnes, asked the Rules Committee for a modified closed rule so an alternative plan supported by him and the Republicans could be voted on as a substitute amendment, not as part of a Republican motion to recommit. He contended that a recommittal motion is more likely to be perceived as a party issue than is an amendment; it was obviously to his advantage to downplay partisanship as much as possible in order to get Democratic votes. Hence, closed rules work to the advantage of the majority; modified closed rules and open rules help the minority.

Representative Byrnes, who often accompanies Mills to the Rules Committee to support Mills's requests, was probably not surprised on this occasion when Rules — more under the control of Democratic leaders than ever — acceded to Mills's request and denied his own.

Two more examples of the policy questions involved with the closed rule concern bills considered in 1967: the 1967 debt bill first defeated then passed by the House, and the 1967 Social Security Amendments that contained extremely controversial amendments to the public welfare law.

On June 6, 1967, Mills and Byrnes appeared before the Rules Committee to request a closed rule on H.R. 10328, which raised the debt limit to $365 billion.[145] The Republicans on Ways and Means opposed this figure as too high but Byrnes supported Mills's request for a closed rule nonetheless. Rules Committee Chairman William Colmer (D., Miss.) agreed with Byrnes that a lower debt ceiling was desirable and asked why Byrnes did not support an open rule. Colmer, like Byrnes, thought the $365 billion limit was too high but unlike Byrnes he desired an open rule to permit amendments to lower it. Byrnes replied that to force the administration to review its fiscal policy a straight recommittal motion was preferable to adopting a lower ceiling, which is what he planned to offer in the House at the end of debate. Colmer, who traditionally opposes closed rules as a matter of principle, said that he realized the closed rule "is something of a sacred thing to the Ways and Means Committee" but that, addressing himself to Byrnes, "I think you're cutting your own throat." Byrnes, who on some occasions has requested modified closed rules, replied: "I have to support my chairman on some things, Mr. Chairman." Rules granted the closed rule, as usual.

[145] Rules Committee meetings are open to the public but no transcript is kept of what goes on. The events recorded here are based on personal observation.

At the time, it appeared as though the Republicans were throwing away conservative Democratic support by offering a straight recommittal motion. Debt bills are usually hard votes for the Democratic leadership and, in the absence of an open rule, it seemed that the bill's chances were improved. Perhaps they were. But not even Colmer's vote for the bill — his first positive vote ever because of the war in Viet Nam — could save the measure. Byrnes's recommittal motion was defeated by voice vote but the bill was then defeated 197–210, an outcome that caught nearly everyone — including Byrnes — by surprise. The closed rule had passed by a 291–99 vote, which was still not enough to save the bill.[146] A slightly changed bill passed the House later in the month.

As the 1967 debt bill illustrates, the closed rule is a factor in passing Ways and Means bills, although in this case not even the closed rule was sufficient for victory. The relationship between the closed rule and policy outcomes also is illustrated by the 1967 bill expanding social security benefits and tightening up on public welfare. The welfare amendments passed the House without a separate vote because of the closed rule.

Mills and Byrnes appeared before the Rules Committee on August 15, 1967, to request the usual closed rule on H.R. 12080, the Social Security Amendments of 1967. In his opening remarks, Mills stressed the amount of work the Committee put in on H.R. 12080, mentioning that they spent sixty-four executive sessions marking it up. He also observed that the bill was a complex measure over two hundred pages long and said: "It is a Committee bill. Mr. Byrnes has joined me in the introduction of it indicating that it is *completely* a Committee bill." Thus Mills set forth three arguments for granting the closed rule: (1) Ways and Means did a good job on the bill; (2) the bill is very complex and technical; and (3) the Committee is bipartisan.

---

[146] *Ibid.*, June 7, 1967 (daily edition), pp. H 6778–814. This vote was, of course, a defeat for Mills, the first since the 1964 conference report on coffee imports. Mills, according to the conventional wisdom on the Hill, never brings a bill up without the votes. After this loss, some observers felt that he expected the bill to be defeated but decided to teach the administration a lesson on what could happen if they were not more sensitive to congressional fiscal views. It is true that, unlike previous bills, the Committee did not reduce the administration request for an increased debt ceiling, but up until the vote the whip counts showed that the bill would probably pass by a small margin. Whether or not Mills expected to lose the vote — and the evidence available to me leads me to doubt it — the fact remains that he lost and there is no evidence that he planned the defeat.

H. Allen Smith (R., Calif.), the ranking Republican on Rules, asked why a modified closed rule would not be acceptable to Ways and Means. Smith wondered why a few members who wanted to offer amendments should not be allowed to, and Mills answered by referring to the limitless amendments that would come under an open rule: "You want to get away from here by Labor Day?" Smith replied that one member wrote the Rules Committee regarding a simple amendment he wanted to offer but Mills refuted the idea that on a social security bill an amendment could be simple. According to Mills, the bill was an intricate whole and one amendment would affect other parts of the bill and perhaps require the restructuring of the entire complicated package. This argument, coupled with Mills's observations that no one could claim their suggestions were not considered by the Committee because the Committee had done a "good" job on the bill and that twenty-four members of the Committee supported the bill, seemed to satisfy Smith. After the exchange a Republican member of Rules observed to a colleague: "When you get somebody up here with a bill like this you just have to rely on these guys. Jesus, this is pretty deep snow." His colleague nodded, apparently impressed with the complexity of the bill.

Nor was Mills impressed when Smith observed that the Ways and Means Committee could risk a modified closed rule because if the Committee opposed the floor amendments the House would surely follow the Committee's lead. For Ways and Means, a fully closed rule — supported by Byrnes — was necessary, and Rules granted the rule.

"Back to Barbarism" was the title of a *Washington Post* editorial on the public welfare amendments passed as part of H.R. 12080.[147] HEW Secretary John Gardner launched a belated but lively attack on the amendments shortly before the House passed the bill. But by the time the opposition was felt the bill had received a closed rule from the Rules Committee and there was not enough time to mobilize an effort to change the controversial sections even if some changes might have been possible. *The Washington Post* and others railed against the closed rule but, despite some last-minute criticism from a small number of liberal Democrats, the closed rule was adopted on a division vote, 120–7. The rule was adopted by a division vote instead of a roll call because its opponents realized that the closed rule was impregnable. When no one forced a roll call on the rule,

---

[147] August 18, 1967, p. A20.

several liberals who had hopelessly opposed the rule expressed relief.
One liberal summed up the general feeling:

> Yesterday I was of the belief that title II should be subject
> to an open rule, but my position did not prevail in the Rules
> Committee. A closed rule was reported. But after consider-
> ing it during the course of the night, in my opinion there
> are so many inequities in title II of the bill in regard to
> needy children, Medicaid, and a half dozen other provisions
> in the bill, I do not think we honestly could write this bill
> on the floor of the House.[148]

The position that the bill presents so many problems that the House
cannot open up the measure to amendments is understandable in the
light of the aforementioned reasons behind the closed rule.

To get a closed rule and to pass important legislation the Ways and
Means Committee must produce, as Mills has said, a widely acceptable bill. An occasional defeat, of course, does no permanent damage
to the Committee's reputation in the House. It is doubtful if the
1967 debt bill defeat had much effect on the Committee's reputation
in the House, particularly since substantially the same bill was later
passed after more careful preparation of the head count. Yet, whatever the causes behind a Committee defeat — carelessness, shrewd mis-
calculations, or bad luck — the infrequency of defeats shows that the
Committee normally prepares a bill that at least a majority of the
House supports.

One element in a widely acceptable bill that takes on unusual
significance under the closed rule is that individuals and groups who
are affected by the legislation considered by the Committee have
their views heard and, to some degree, heeded by the Committee.

As seen, the 1956 wool-duty bill had trouble in the House because
the Committee did not hold "good" hearings. The House expects
that the Committee will, at a minimum, give interested parties a fair
chance to state their case on legislative proposals.[149] What is less
clear is how much beyond access must be given to those affected by
Committee bills to pass the bills in the House under a closed rule.

If there is a point at which group disenchantment with Committee

---

148 *Congressional Record*, August 16, 1967 (daily edition), p. H 10610.
149 E.g., *ibid.*, May 28, 1948, p. 6079; February 8, 1949, p. 984; July 13,
1953, p. 8665. A related House expectation is that committees will protect the
House members from "sleepers." See former Representative Jerry Voorhis, *Confessions of a Congressman* (Garden City: Doubleday, 1947), p. 8.

bills may endanger passage in the House, the Committee appears to have as much difficulty determining what that point is as the outsider. Characteristically, the Committee responds favorably to external demands rather than run the risk of an irate group successfully appealing to the House for floor changes in Committee decisions. The search for a consensus in the Committee, the bargains and compromises that typify Committee decision-making, and the Committee's sensitivity to the House mean that the Committee, by reconciling the demands of its members as well as the demands of other House members, is at the same time reconciling the demands of those outside Congress who have a stake in Ways and Means decisions and access to Ways and Means decision-makers. The formal title of House members is not "Congressman" but "Representative," and in Ways and Means the representation of hundreds of groups and individuals is part of the everyday job of the members.

PRESSURE: A DIGRESSION. The onus for dealing with group and individual demands is placed on the Committee by the closed rule. Among the questions this raises is the extent to which Committee members feel pressure from those who are concerned with Committee decisions. Traditionally, of course, political scientists and others have identified interest groups as pressure groups and, although group theorists such as Truman have been well aware of the independence of legislators,[150] the tendency has been to assume that political decision-makers are under almost constant pressure from interested parties. The authors of a 1963 study of foreign trade, for example, "started with the notion that public officials would see themselves as under almost constant pressure from those who have a stake in the decisions they make." [151] On the contrary, they found that congressmen and others tended to equate pressure with threats or illegitimate forms of pursuing an interest, and denied that they were subject to this kind of pressure very often.[152]

---

[150] David B. Truman, *The Governmental Process* (New York: Alfred A. Knopf, pp. 332–33.
[151] Bauer, Pool, and Dexter, *op. cit.*, p. 433.
[152] *Ibid.*, pp. 434–35. In a separate study Dexter reported that on the trade issue "pressure is how you see it." " 'Pressure' and 'pressure politics' are regarded by most 'sophisticated' people today as 'explaining' a great deal that happens. But it was frequently impossible to find any admission of or apparently any awareness of 'pressure.' " See Lewis Anthony Dexter, "The Representative and His District," *New Perspectives on the House of Representatives*, ed. Robert L. Peabody and Nelson W. Polsby (Chicago: Rand McNally, 1963), p. 24.

Ways and Means, with the closed rule and heavy involvement with pressure groups, provides a good laboratory for analyzing the perceptions of pressure groups held by members of Congress. As in Bauer, Pool, and Dexter, the word "pressure" was used deliberately in interviews to see how the Committee members would respond.

Some responses were very similar to those collected by Bauer, Pool, and Dexter, but in general the results do *not* confirm their emphasis on the high degree to which congressmen fail to perceive pressure as pressure.

Some members of the Committee stress their independence from pressure and some members discount the degree of pressure felt in conducting Ways and Means business. One member said, "I don't know what the word 'pressure' means. No one has ever tried to pressure me if by pressure you mean some kind of threat. I've never been pressured, no president has ever tried to pressure me." A second Democrat said, "I find interest groups helpful. They are practical men. I don't feel any pressure from the pressure groups. I've had them all in here — labor, business." Another member, who noted which interests each member promotes, declared:

> Hell, I don't represent any interests. Look at my district, Who in their right mind could be for free trade with chemicals, zinc, and lead, electrical, and others in their district? Well, they have learned that I'm not their stooge. I've told them all to go to hell, in effect, at one time or another. They *ask* me my opinion. I have good personal relations with the top executives of ———— but I've told them that I'm here to study the issues and make up my own mind. I'll listen but they know better than to try to pressure me. One of them got mad and didn't contribute very much to my campaign one year but I never even knew it until later.

A colleague also stressed his immunity from pressure: "I'm 62 with only a few more years up here, I'm not rich but I've got no money worries, who's going to pressure me? No one dominates me. I'm not dominated by anyone back home, anyone here, or by presidents who sometimes try." One member said that he would rather risk defeat than vote contrary to his beliefs: "Oh, I'll listen when they come in but they don't have too much influence. I make up my own mind and I wouldn't vote for anything just to get reelected. It doesn't matter to me that much."

The low esteem in which pressure groups and lobbyists are held in American politics, the value assigned to the independent, Burkean legislator in Western political culture, and the pejorative connotation of the word "pressure" obviously load any question to congressmen about pressure. They tend to respond defensively. But the answers to a loaded question are useful (e.g., attention may be directed to the way legislators discount interest group demands), although they should be handled with care. Legislators themselves deny the existence of — *and then complain about* — the pressure they receive from pressure groups.

Consider this comment: "I never get pressured by lobbyists. The most pressure I ever got was when we considered taxation of savings and loan associations. I got up to 2,000 letters a day on that one. . . ." One man who said that he has had labor and business groups in his office but does not feel any pressure continued: "The labor people have put the heat on because of medicare but they have told me they would rather have my clear 'no' than vacillation." The man who was never pressured by threats remarked during the 1965 executive session on excise taxes that the tax on fishing equipment could not be lifted because in 1954 the Committee had the sportsmen on its neck before the bill reached the House floor (the money from this tax is used to restock fishing streams).

Two members did not go on the defensive when asked about interest groups. Regarding excise taxes one said, "Oh, oh yes. All they did was traipse through my office." He did not find this unpleasant but another spoke in a somewhat different tone:

> Well, I underwent a baptism of fire last year with the tax bill. There were just so many groups, each of them wanted something. The pension plan provision, which the Committee changed from the Treasury's proposal, led to a lot of mail, especially from Sears Roebuck. I've got a lot of Sears Roebuck employees in my district and I'd see my congressman too if such a plan was important to me.

Then, in a statement which fits perfectly with one of Bauer, Pool, and Dexter's main observations, he said, "It's only pressure if you regard it as pressure."

Some members of the Ways and Means Committee, in sum, are aware that they are under pressure to do things for interest groups even though the pressure may not be in the form of a threat of reprisal. "The only pressure I've felt for a long time is from the doctors on medicare. I guess once you are here long enough the lobbyists get to know your position and don't bother to try to change you." One member reacted as if "lobbyist" were a dirty word and assured me that he has very little to do with them. He said Drew Pearson once wrote that he was controlled by a group in his district, and others have claimed that he is controlled by an oil company, but both charges are false. After noting that he has little to do with the oil company he went on to say that some of its officers are friends, he has social relations with them, but they never discuss "business." He concluded that he does feel pressure from groups but he resists it.

Another member, who does not find interest groups of much use, acknowledged that he feels pressure from lobbies but he went to great lengths to convince me that he is not disposed to favor any particular group. One of the saddest things, he feels, is for a member of the Committee to become the captive of special groups.

Twenty members of the Committee were asked directly if they ever had felt any pressure from the groups interested in Ways and Means business. The question was: "Have you ever felt any pressure from the interest groups that are concerned with what Ways and Means does?" Contrary to what might be expected from using the word "pressure," and contrary to what was expected from the findings of Bauer, Pool, and Dexter, more members replied affirmatively, as Table 5.11 shows, than negatively. Eleven members, just over half of those asked, did say that they have felt pressure from interest groups while on the Committee. Nine members denied that they felt any pressure or so discounted the pressure that their answers amounted to a denial. Only one member translated "pressure" into threats and most did not hesitate to say that they are under some pressure on the Committee.

These findings, though at odds with what appears to be part of the general interpretation of Bauer, Pool, and Dexter (who present no numerical distribution of their findings), support their emphasis on the relative freedom of congressmen from pressure. Though Commit-

TABLE 5.11
WAYS AND MEANS MEMBERS' RESPONSES TO
PRESSURE GROUP QUESTION

Have you ever felt any pressure?	Yes	No
Democrats	7	5
Republicans	4	4
Total	11	9

tee members do see pressure as pressure they have great latitude in how they respond to it, and for many of them, pressure on Ways and Means simply goes with the job. Referring to newspaper advertisements opposing the administration's 1968 travel tax, a Republican Committee member saw this as pressure but said, "You see it, you feel it, but what the hell." He explained that you deal with it. A Democratic colleague said this about the intense pressure on him: "Oh yeah! All the time! I guess with pressure you have to learn to let it hit you like water running off the back of a duck. Otherwise you'd be a nervous wreck." Though some members are probably more immune from pressure than others (one man feels "they pester the hell out of you") none of them found the pressure terribly onerous. In fact, as one member indicated, it can even be fun: "You pull this string and people come down from New York, you pull another string and you get these people coming in, and it's a lot of fun to watch them squirm." [153]

PASSING COMMITTEE BILLS

Southerners have never opposed me on a tax bill.
Wilbur D. Mills [154]

By the time the Ways and Means Committee is finished marking up a bill enough conflicting demands have been met so that, although not everyone wins or is satisfied, the Committee majority does not lose on the floor. The ultimate forms of House control remain just that, ultimate. No doubt the closed rule gives the Committee floor advantages that other committees would like to have, but far from destroying House influence on the Committee the closed rule depends for its existence on such influence. Ways and Means anticipates what other members of the House will support, compromises more demands than it categorically rejects, and, by being predisposed to act favorably to what House members and others desire, prevents effective demands for an open rule.

In part, the closed rule and the necessity of getting a majority of

[153] The responses in Table 5.11 do not vary depending on the seniority of the members except that senior Republicans were more likely to feel pressure than junior Republicans. Nor does there appear to be any pattern in the responses depending upon the nature of constituencies or regions.

[154] Quoted in David J. Stern, "Congress, Politics, and Taxes: A Case Study of the Revenue Act of 1962" (Ph.D. Dissertation, Claremont Graduate School, 1965), p. 262.

the House explain why a medicare bill when it leaves Ways and Means bears some resemblance to the original administration bill, some resemblance to the plan devised by the Republican members of the Committee, and even some resemblance to the alternative proposed by the American Medical Association. From what is known about the Committee it is easy to believe Mills when he said of the 1962 Trade Expansion Act, "Every member of the committee on the Republican side as well as on the Democratic side can point to some provision in this bill that he or she desired to have written into it." [155]

The first stop for a major bill is, of course, the Rules Committee. The Rules Committee presentation, which usually consists more of Ways and Means justifying the bill than a discussion of the rule, is in effect a test run before subsequent action on the floor. Mills tests his mastery of the bill in the Rules Committee by explaining the substance of the bill and by responding to questions, just as he will do later in the well of the House; he can smooth off any rough edges before meeting the ultimate test. Occasionally, one last bargain may be made as the result of the Rules Committee's reaction to the bill, as a Republican reports:

> A few years ago Wilbur went to the Rules Committee to get a rule on a bill and I asked Judge Smith to grant a rule that allowed me to offer an amendment. Well, Mills withdrew the bill and he and I got together and put my amendment in the bill! I never knew why Judge Smith did this, I guess he was trying to get Mills in line or something. . . . This is a good example of how Mills operates — he'll hold bills up to be sure they'll pass.[156]

Normally, however, the Rules Committee grants the Committee's request for a closed rule, although it may from time to time hold up the rule until the Committee complies with some request or other.[157]

In passing its bills in the House the Committee majority — whether

---

[155] *Congressional Record*, June 28, 1962, p. 11991.

[156] Because the Rules Committee hearing is a substantive test it is to be expected that when Rules presents the resolution which will govern debate its members discuss the merits and demerits of bills. Floor debate begins, therefore, with the Rules Committee telling the House what it has learned about the bill and setting the outline for the ensuing debate. What transpires in the Rules Committee may also give party leaders one more clue as to whether or not the bill is ready for House action, as evidenced by the practice of the Democratic Whip Office regularly sending a staff man to monitor Rules meetings.

[157] Stern, *op. cit.*, pp. 227–29.

the majority includes all the Committee members or just the Democrats — has a number of important assets, including the bill itself. In most cases the Committee product, although more reflective of the voting power of conservatives in the Committee and in the House than liberals, contains elements attractive to both groups. A second asset is Mills, a southern Democrat who maintains good relations with the southerners on the Committee and in the House, but who uses his southern ties to guide major administration proposals through the House. A third asset is the Democratic party loyalty on major Democratic administration measures, supplemented by the fact that the Committee Democrats are leaders in their delegations and regions who have control over such rewards as committee assignments, and reinforced by the party leadership, which works hand in hand with the Committee at the floor stage. On major bills the Committee is assisted by the legislative aides of the president and, at times, by the president himself. All these — plus the support of interest groups which have a stake in passing the bill in question — give the Committee majority a powerful combination of factors working against the Committee minority and whatever support it can marshall.

COMMITTEE OUTPUT. Important exceptions may be made to almost any generalization about the Ways and Means Committee, particularly its policy decisions. Nonetheless, the Committee majority is more likely to come down on the conservative side of policy issues than on the liberal side. The decisions of the Committee are seen, by liberals, as conservative decisions. Conservatives, of course, may see Committee decisions differently but the research conducted to date has turned up more evidence for liberal discontent with Committee decisions than conservative malcontent. As a Democratic party leader responded to a question about whether House members think Ways and Means does a good job:

> I don't know what you mean by good. I think they feel Ways and Means is more conservative than the whole House and that they sometimes come out with things because of this. They have no problem with the mechanics of what Ways and Means does but the policy — that's another matter. It's more conservative.

The 1966 unemployment compensation bill is a case in point. This bill came up to the Committee containing a proposal to establish federal standards for state unemployment compensation programs — a proposal eagerly sought by organized labor — and the Committee rejected the proposal in toto. The bill reported by the Committee was supported by liberals and conservatives. For the former the bill contained numerous liberalizations in the unemployment compensation program, including extension of coverage to about three and one-half million workers; for the latter it struck out federal standards. Behind the 374–10 roll call by which the Committee bill passed the House, however, was a good deal more support from conservatives than from liberals, although the latter did not mount an attack on the measure. It is significant that although the Republican Policy Committee and all the Ways and Means Republicans except one were enthusiastic on the bill, only one Committee Democrat besides Mills, Frank Karsten, supported the bill in the debate, and Karsten decried the loss of federal standards.[158]

Most bills are — like the 1966 unemployment compensation bill — a composite of elements with appeal for both liberals and conservatives. When the Committee liberalized public welfare in 1962 it rejected at the same time a proposal to prevent states from requiring more than a year's residence to receive welfare payments. When the Committee made major liberalizations in social security benefits in 1967 it also tightened up on public welfare. When the Committee finally supported a tax surcharge in 1968 it also approved a cut in expenditures too deep for liberals to accept. When the Committee, after months of deliberation, reported an $11 billion tax cut in 1963 it rejected changes in the revenue law supported by liberals. Ways and Means bills invariably have contained a mixture of provisions that reveal the policy inclinations of the major blocs composing the House.

The exact combination of provisions in any given bill is hard to predict, but if the Republicans oppose the final version — as they do on many of the major bills considered by the Committee — passage of the legislation requires the Committee Democrats to accept, with or without enthusiasm, proposals designed to hold the Democratic party together on the key roll call votes. To do this means holding the southerners, and for this task Mills is well suited.

MILLS. In 1963, speaking on a debt bill, Representative William Avery explained why he could not go along with Chairman Mills

[158] *Congressional Record*, June 22, 1966 (daily edition), pp. 13273–304.

even though, in his opinion, the Chairman is certainly not a liberal: "If the administration had not continued to send up these requests to spend in this fashion, I think in good conscience I might still be able to go along with the gentleman from Arkansas [Mr. Mills], who certainly is not a liberal." [159] Avery's perception of Mills is important in understanding why the House rarely rejects a Ways and Means bill. Not only have the contents of Committee bills been shaped to pass but the Chairman, even though he may not get Republican votes on every bill, has close ties to both Republicans and southern Democrats. He plays an important role, therefore, in generating the conservative coalition to support Committee positions (e.g., the surcharge-expenditure issue of 1968) and in blocking the conservative coalition by retaining enough southern Democratic votes in the House to pass partisan bills (e.g., 1963 Revenue Act). To some extent, Mills's pivotal position in the Committee is duplicated in the House.

"We work hours, days, weeks, and months on this stuff," a Democratic Committee member said, "we weigh and balance and chart and graph and it is damn hard work. But you have to have balance on these bills. We put it together, balance, balance, balance." This man was speaking of substantive balance — fiscal balance — but political balance also is involved in the passage of Ways and Means bills. One early interviewee made two comments that are basic to analyzing House-Committee relations. He observed: "Mills is powerful even with the southerners who are most likely to vote against us," and said, "We can win with just the Democratic votes on the floor, and we get them." Another Democrat noted when asked to explain Mills's power in the House: "With our southern friends — he consults with them and they respect him."

In this connection, Mills's rapport with southern Democrats is complemented by southern Democrats on Ways and Means who, if they support the Committee bill (as they usually do), help the Chairman pass the legislation in the House. Such southerners as Herlong, Watts, and Phil Landrum (D., Ga.) all have assisted the Chairman on bills. Herlong's identity as the most conservative Democrat on the Committee was particularly valuable to Mills. Speaking for the Committee version of a debt bill in 1963, for example, Herlong helped defeat a Republican recommittal motion that naturally appealed to conservatives, after identifying himself in these terms: "I

[159] *Ibid.*, May 15, 1963, p. 8559.

do not think I am going to shock anyone here when I make the statement that I am a conservative. This is the political philosophy to which I subscribe, and one of which I am not ashamed." [160]

It is, of course, impossible to know how many votes are affected by getting the Committee's conservative Democrats to support the bills on the floor, but Herlong frequently speaks for the Committee on debt bills, the Chairman on one occasion (it was reported) delayed floor action on a debt bill because Herlong was out of town, the conservative coalition has been notably absent on most of the major bills reported by the Committee, and it certainly does not hurt to have popular conservatives such as Herlong back the Democratic position in the House. In 1963 when the Committee Democrats faced a popular Republican recommittal motion linking the tax cut to expenditure cuts Herlong went before the Boll Weevils and argued against the Republican plan. These efforts probably help to explain why leading Boll Weevils such as Omar Burleson of Texas have spoken for the Committee position on such key bills as the 1963 tax cut and the close 1967 fight over the debt bill.[161] In mid-1968 Herlong resigned from the Committee and was replaced by Burleson, who was thereby assured of a senior position on the Committee in the next Congress when the Democrats expected at least three vacancies. It is hard to believe that the events linking Herlong, Mills, and Burleson are unrelated to Burleson's election to the Committee or to the Committee's success on the floor.

PARTY. The Revenue Act of 1962, the 1962 Trade Expansion Act, the Revenue Act of 1963, Medicare in 1965, and debt bills every year were major administration bills that called forth from House Democrats whatever feelings of party identification exist. Party feeling, as a recent study argues, is prevalent in the House even though it may not

[160] *Ibid.*, May 15, 1963 (daily edition), p. 8085. For additional evidence on Herlong's activities on behalf of the Committee bill see the following issues of the *Congressional Record:* June 18, 1964 (daily edition), p. 13859; September 25, 1963, pp. 18089–91. For an example of Landrum's efforts see June 21, 1967 (daily edition), p. H 7622.

[161] For Burleson's activities see *Congressional Record*, September 25, 1963, p. 18105; June 21, 1967 (daily edition), p. H 7610. Mills has also gone before the Boll Weevils and state delegations to defend Committee bills, plus devising such stratagems as the "Mills Preamble" (of fiscal responsibility) which was added to the 1963 tax reduction bill to help conservatives vote for the measure.

have been an overriding factor for many Democrats on major bills.[162]
Its existence provided a base for passing Ways and Means bills in the
House.

The role of the Democratic party leadership in helping Ways and
Means pass its bills — and this is the proper way to phrase the leaders' job — depends almost entirely upon the nature of the voting line
up in the House, which in turn depends on the nature of the majority
formed in the Committee. If, despite the dilution that occurs on
Ways and Means bills, the Republicans still do not support the legislation as reported, the Democratic leadership may have to secure
enough votes behind the Committee majority by intensive persuasion
on man-by-man head counts. The Chairman, primarily, and then the
Committee carry the primary burden for passing Committee bills, but
the party leaders are involved on controversial bills and provide important ancillary assistance to Mills.

A key problem at the floor stage of the legislative process is knowing how much effort has to be expended to pass bills and, perhaps, to
defeat Republican recommittal motions. Mills and the party leaders
canvass the members to make this judgment. Sometimes such key
group spokesmen as Judge Smith or Carl Vinson when they led the
southern bloc, or leaders of the Democratic Study Group, or large
state delegations provide enough information. If such information is
mixed, or if some normally dependable members change their usual
positions, or if the bill obviously will not pass easily, polls are made
by Mills, by the Democratic Whip, and by executive branch–White
House lobbyists.

Information on how the Democrats in the House will vote comes
together in leadership meetings attended by Mills, the Democratic
leadership, executive branch–White House lobbyists, and at times by
important individual congressmen such as Armed Services Chairman
L. Mendell Rivers during the February 1967 meeting on the debt
bill, or Appropriations Chairman George Mahon during the June
1967 meeting on the same issue. Responses collected by Mills, the
results of the Whip poll conducted by House Democratic Whip Hale
Boggs and his assistants, plus the executive branch counts are pooled
and compared. Calls are made to individual House members who
are not "right" on the vote and, at times, Speaker McCormack and

---

[162] Randall B. Ripley, *Party Leaders in the House of Representatives* (Washington, D.C.: Brookings Institution, 1967), chap. 6.

Mills get on the phone together with a wavering member. The results of all this activity decide when the bill will be scheduled and what, if anything, needs to be done to insure a positive outcome.[163]

In addition to polling the Democratic members of the House to find out how they feel on Ways and Means bills, party leaders help Mills pass the bill in other ways. In the May 1963 debt limit fight, for example, the House Whip's office arranged for two Democrats to attend the session in wheel chairs and it distributed information on what defeat of the bill would mean to the country and to Democrats generally. To pass the 1963 tax bill, the Whip's office distributed a letter in support of the bill signed by Mills, Speaker McCormack, Majority Leader Carl Albert, and Boggs. On the 1962 tax bill, one wavering member was escorted into the Speaker's office to speak to President Kennedy over the phone. Mills asked that poll results be transmitted to him ahead of time so a bill could be delayed if defeat appeared imminent, and he has held a number of "pocket votes" (i.e., members who will vote with the leadership if they are needed) gathered by himself and the party leaders.[164] In most cases personal appeal by party leaders is the major tactic used to get votes, but occasionally a member may negotiate more specifically; one bargained for the continuation of two military bases in his district during the June 1967 debt bill contest. But such hard bargaining is more usually the job of White House lobbyists than the House Democratic leadership.

If the backing of the president, party leaders, and Mills is not enough, the Committee also derives strength from the fact that the Democrats constitute the Committee on Committees. Mills has used the Democratic members as an informal whip system of his own, notably on the 1963 tax reduction bill, but more important most of them are recognized leaders of their zones who do not have to be told by Mills what to do on behalf of the bill. Inclined toward party

---

[163] Since 1962, the first year for which records are available, whip polls have been taken on the following Committee bills: 1962: Final passage of the 1962 Revenue Act; final passage on debt bill; recommittal motion on Trade Expansion Act. 1963: Final passage on debt bill; final passage of second debt bill; recommittal motion on 1963 Revenue Act; final passage of third debt bill. 1964: Final passage of debt bill; recommittal motion on excise tax bill. 1965: Recommittal motion on medicare; final passage of coffee agreement. Data kindly made available by Randall B. Ripley of the Brookings Institution. For a general description of the whip system see his, "The Party Whip Organizations in the United States House of Representatives," *American Political Science Review*, LVIII (September, 1964), 561–76.

[164] *Ibid.*, pp. 570–74.

regularity, and naturally concerned that their bills pass the House, they help Mills almost as a matter of course. One Democrat revealed that, at Mills's request, he took a secret poll of his delegation on medicare long before the bill came out of the Committee. Another Democrat who defined part of his job in terms of getting his delegation behind Ways and Means' bills called attention to his ultimate weapon, "If I can support it in Committee and on the floor then they can support it too. . . . Well, I suppose if it were [a senior member] I couldn't do very much, but if it were some new member who didn't have a prime committee yet I could do something." Another Democrat, who was upset with some members for voting against the Committee on the first debt bill in June 1967, was even more explicit about what he planned to do:

> That cost us a lot of prestige, sure it did, and you wait until they want committees. I'm going to read the log: "Oh, he wants to go from Post Office to Foreign Affairs. Let's see how he voted. Against us. Well fellows, where the hell was he when *we* needed him?" And let them see what they get. You wait.

CONCLUSION

A look at the nature of party alignments on Ways and Means legislation since 1933 reveals wide variability in the degree of party conflict over issues that come under the Committee's jurisdiction. The highly variable nature of party conflict has been explained by the relative strength of the two parties in the House, the role of the conservative coalition in the House after 1939, and partisan control of the presidency and Congress. Issues of taxation have historically been more partisan than social security legislation, debt legislation has moved from a relatively nonpartisan issue to become a basic source of conflict between the parties, while the issue of reciprocal trade has undergone an opposite development.

Two constants throughout this period are the Committee's success in passing its bills in the House with little or no substantive changes on the House floor, and, second, the conservative direction of the Committee's policy decisions. Since the 1930's many policy changes have been made in the fields considered by Ways and Means, but they have been made slowly and incrementally. In the area of foreign trade only one piece of legislation since the 1934 Reciprocal Trade Act, the Trade Expansion Act of 1962, was a major new step for the Committee and even the 1962 Act was more a new step in an old direction than a basic break with past legislation. In social security legislation the 1935 Social Security Act was liberalized and added to after World War II, but it took twenty years for medicare to be enacted and, though the 1965 Act was more liberal than the administration expected, it was still a much smaller step than the postwar plans to provide medical care for persons of all ages. In the area of fiscal policy serious attempts to use the revenue laws to direct the economy were not made until the 1960's, and all attempts to enact major changes or reforms in the Code failed before 1969.

Ways and Means has been successful in the House because its conservative policy recommendations have been consistent with the voting composition of the House. There has not been a liberal majority in the House since the 1930's, with the exception of the 89th Congress, and new policy changes have as a consequence been slow in coming and temperate in content. The 1958 bill to extend unemployment compensation benefits to persons who did not qualify under existing law was a rare case in which the Committe majority went farther in a liberal direction than the House majority warranted, and the Committee proposal was rejected on the floor.

Ways and Means, in its relations with the House, seems to be much more dependent upon the sentiment of House majorities on basic issues than independent of its parent chamber. On basic policy questions the major job of the Committee majority is determining what can pass the House, and in making this determination the Committee, through the Chairman, is responsive to the wishes of House members.

On many questions of detail the Committee is free to do whatever it pleases but on matters that concern large numbers of congressmen and interested parties the Committee serves its interest by listening well to the views of others. The Committee is more inclined to heed conservative rather than liberal views. On this point a senior Republican member of the Committee expressed the Committee's independence-dependence problem and, significantly, cited two examples of liberal demands the Committee resists:

> Something that looks good in a constituent letter may not look good after you have gone into all the aspects and seen all the interwoven features of the thing. Take the elimination of the retirement test for social security. Some would like to turn the program into an annuity program. They look and see $20 billion in the fund and say, "Well, why can't you

do it?" Well, goddamn it they don't see what this would mean. So we have to resist these kinds of things, they don't know what's involved. Take the exemption. Suppose you raise it to a thousand dollars — you may not ever be able to do anything else. We have to explore all of this and we can't let them have everything they want. It's more the temper, you talk around and get a general feeling, Mills does this. It's true we don't operate in a vacuum, as I say, but House influence is more a matter of temper than individual items.

Committee sensitivity to broad questions relating to what can or cannot pass the House is, however, only part of the House-Committee relationship. Of equal significance is the Committee's decision to determine what does pass the House by taking the lead on such bills as the 1963 tax reduction, forming a majority in the Committee that, with the assistance of party leaders, can attract a majority in the House, and in the process making bargains and compromises that transform executive branch proposals into passable legislation. In most cases this means conservative bargains and compromises, such as the $6 billion expenditure reduction price tag of the 10 per cent surcharge in 1968, but liberal demands do place some effective constraints on the conservatism of the Committee's decisions. And as all the House participants know, there is always the Senate.

CHAPTER SIX

The Committee and the Senate

*I guess you could say they act as an Appellate
Court but, like most courts of appeal, Senate Finance is wrong most of the time.*

Ways and Means Democrat

When the final name is heard on a roll call vote in the House one
phase of the legislative process has ended, and another begins. Legislative decision-making, as Bauer, Pool, and Dexter have stressed,[1]
progresses from one stage to another through the postponement of
final, irrevocable decisions. What is done in the House committees
may be undone on the floor, what is done in the House may be undone in the Senate, and what is done in both chambers may be undone in the conference committee.

Despite the many barriers to legislation, including the internal
structure of the House that makes hurdling the barriers a real test of
political skill, the House somehow resolves enough conflicts to make
the final tentative decision expressed in its votes on bills. The act of
passing a bill in the House is a temporary respite from the chore of
building a majority consensus behind some plan of action, not the
final word of the House on what should or should not be done with
any given problem. It is a rare House coalition that will brook no
change in the agreement holding it together; indeed, sometimes the
very fact that the House has formed a majority behind a measure is
due to the understanding that changes in the bill may be made in the
Senate.

In this chapter the primary concern is with the pattern of relation-

---

[1] Raymond A. Bauer, Ithiel deSola Pool, and Lewis A. Dexter, *American
Business and Public Policy* (New York: Atherton Press, 1963), pp. 426–27.

ships that have existed between the House and Senate on revenue matters during the past two decades. No attempt is made to chronicle the Ways and Means Committee's interaction with the Senate in this period; rather, the emphasis is on the politics of this interaction. The process and the policy outcomes of House-Senate relations in the areas of taxation, social security, and trade will be analyzed. Who gets what from the House differs from who gets what from the Senate, and the present task is to explain why this is so.

The first part of this task is the description and analysis of how the members of the House Ways and Means Committee perceive the "other body." In general, Ways and Means members do not like what they see in the Senate. The House, under Article I, section 7 of the Constitution, has special prerogatives in the area of revenue legislation, but the Senate has earned the condemnation of Committee members for the way it makes major changes in their bills. Differences over policy, therefore, are at the base of the negative image of the Senate but, it is suggested, this image may also be explained by general differences in status between Senators and House members. The suggested explanation for why Ways and Means members are critical of the Senate is that when two institutions are equal in theory but there are important status differences between individual members, the members of the lower status body will compensate by comparing themselves favorably to members of the higher status body.

In the legislative process all roads lead to the conference committee. Conference committee decisions on major tax, social security, and trade bills have been examined to answer the question of which house has over the years come closest to passing the bills that become law, which is the obvious question to ask about conference committees. The answer depends both on the kinds of policy questions involved and on the nature of interest group support for the House or Senate bill.

In this chapter an analysis is also made of conservative influence in the decisions made by the conferees of the Senate Finance Committee and Ways and Means, and of the role of the staff of the Joint Committee on Internal Revenue Taxation in these decisions. Special attention is given to the issue of tax reform in this chapter because of its unusual importance in understanding the relationship between Ways and Means and the Senate. The issue of tax reform, like no other issue, sheds light on the peculiar nature and importance of conference committees in the legislative process.

WAYS AND MEANS-SENATE RELATIONS

Consonant with general House attitudes toward the Senate, members of the Ways and Means Committee, when asked about the Senate, gave critical, if not disparaging, replies. Their general perception is that Ways and Means does most of the work on the legislation and the Senators irresponsibly amend it in response to their own wishes or, more likely, the wishes of interest groups and executive department officials who are dissatisfied with the decisions reached by Ways and Means.

Ways and Means members see themselves as responsible legislators who — in the midst of strong demands for tax cuts, liberalization of social security benefits, and protection against imported goods — act responsibly by refusing to give in to these demands at the expense of sound fiscal policy, actuarial balance in the social security trust funds, and good trade relations with other countries. To Committee members, the Senate is characterized by irresponsible logrolling and by capitulation to politically popular but unwarranted demands; by the kind of decision-making, in short, that one could expect in the House without the closed rule. The members feel that the House, having held the line against certain decisions, jettisons the irresponsible Senate amendments in conference and thereby restores fiscal integrity to the House-passed bill.

Insight into House perceptions of the Senate was obtained, unexpectedly, when the members of Ways and Means discussed the closed rule. Several Democratic and Republican members of Ways and Means cited the Senate's lack of restraint on Committee bills as a good argument for protecting against amendments in the House. These members feel that it would be disastrous if both the House and Senate opened Ways and Means bills to floor amendments. The closed rule ensures against attractive but unfeasible Senate amendments just as it ensures against unrestrained logrolling in the House. In this sense, the closed rule is erected in the House as a barrier to Senate amendments just as it bars House amendments.

The members of the Committee defend the closed rule against House opponents who argue that the House is every bit as competent as the Senate to consider Ways and Means bills without a closed rule. This argument, designed to appeal to the institutional pride of House members, is frequently heard in the House. But it is possible to turn the equality argument around and use it to support the closed rule. As a Democrat who reverses the argument said:

> Bill Colmer, you know, has never supported the closed rule. He says we are as smart as the Senate. I tell Bill, "Yes, we are as smart as the Senate and that's why we need the closed rule!" The Senate is the best argument for the closed rule. They put all those screwball things on there. We can't be screwballs or where would we be?

A colleague, who at one time did not support the closed rule but after a short time on the Committee came to see its "wisdom," made the same argument using medicare as an example. "Look at the silliness of the Senate. Medicare: five hundred and eight amendments, eight were left in. Silly bastards, no restraint, just irresponsible. Someone has to be responsible, they don't care." Another member said that if the House operated under an open rule, "Why, it'd be the same as it is in the Senate. They don't have any responsibility over there." A fourth Democrat described the House considering a Ways and Means bill under an open rule in these terms, "Everybody and his brother would have axes to grind. It's bad enough over in the Senate." Finally, another Democrat argued that the Senate simply does not know what it is doing when it amends Committee bills:

> With all due respect to the Senate, they don't know what the hell they're doing over there. They're so damn irresponsible you can get unanimous consent to an amendment that costs a *billion* dollars! And the Senate is supposed to be a safety check on the House. We really act as the stabling influence, the balance. Social security — they put over five hundred amendments on over there, and five hundred came out in conference. They don't know what they're doing. Some staff man writes up the section, they take it. Why, they can't stand up to Wilbur Mills. He knows every line.

Republican members of the Ways and Means Committee, though they disagree with the Democrats on major policy matters, agree that the House has to protect itself with the closed rule against the same tendencies that go unrestrained in the Senate. "It's for a discipline reason that we have the closed rule," a Republican said. "There's enough demagogic appeals in the Senate." Comparing the House and the Senate, a second Republican observed:

> What the hell, you can't have both engaging in demagoguery or lord knows what you'd have. The Senators, Jesus

> Christ! They put this in, take that out, spend three days —
> and we've spent months on the bill. Someone has to be re-
> sponsible, and it's up to us with the closed rule.

One Republican castigated the Senate:

> They use it for ballyhoo back home. They know it'll never
> survive but they decorate it up and we, the House conferees,
> have to take the blame for being against "Widow Jones."
> I don't like that. I think you ought to come out like a man
> and state your position.

Such attitudes help explain why in 1967 Chairman Mills defended
the closed rule before the Rules Committee by alluding to what the
Senate, without the closed rule, would do on the Social Security
Amendments bill. From past experience, no one had to be told in
detail that the Senate would probably make liberalizing amendments
that could not be reasonably supported through the payroll tax. The
closed rule, in this case as in others, was granted partly because of
House expectations concerning Senate action on Committee legislation.

These perceptions of the Senate may be explained in terms of what
the Senate does to carefully drafted Ways and Means bills, but the
unfavorable House image of the Senate is probably rooted more in
the status differences between the two bodies than in policy differences. In theory, the House and Senate are coequal legislative bodies
but Senators enjoy much more prestige than the average House
member — even more than the average member of Ways and Means.
Today, the House is used as a launching pad to the Senate but no
Senator, willingly, has moved from the Senate to the House, as some
did early in the nineteenth century. Like other members of the
House, the members of the Ways and Means Committee naturally
tend to compare their Committee favorably to what the Senate Finance Committee does in the same policy areas, but no amount of
caustic criticism of the "show horses" in the Senate compared to the
"work horses" in the House can hide that the group equality of the
two bodies is not matched by equality in prestige.

SENATE AUTONOMY. House members probably would not be so
highly critical of Senate handling of Ways and Means bills if the
Senate took a strict constructionist approach to Article I, section 7,
of the Constitution. Although the Senate may not originate revenue
bills in a formal sense, it has made ample use of its power to "propose

or concur with Amendments as on other Bills." The Senate has, in fact, lived up to the warning of James Madison who said, "The Senate may actually couch extraneous matter under that name (amendment)." [2]

In recent years, the most vivid examples of senatorial autonomy of the House, upon which the previous mentioned House criticisms of the Senate are based, have occurred on the Senate floor, not in the Senate Finance Committee. But whether the Finance Committee changes the essence of Ways and Means bills or such changes occur on the Senate floor is of little importance to the restraining power of the Constitution: as a constraint on Senate behavior in the face of a Senate majority, Article I, section 7, might as well never have been written. This does not mean that the Senate is superior to the House or that the Senate is an equal partner in the making of revenue policy, but an important part of Senate behavior on Ways and Means bills is its freedom to respond to House bills any way it sees fit. As such, Senate autonomy of the House in revenue matters is an important part of the legislative process that warrants some attention before asking which body is generally most influential in making tax, trade, and social security policy.

H.R. 1839 in 1964 reveals precisely how far the Senate may go in "amending" Ways and Means bills. In the case of H.R. 1839, the Senate version of the bill resembled the House bill only in that the number of the bill remained the same.

The bill, providing for the free importation of wild animals and wild birds for exhibition in the United States, was passed in 1963 by voice vote in the House. In 1964, the Senate attached a rider imposing import quotas on certain meat and meat products, a measure desired by the United States cattle industry. The Finance Committee and the Senate not only imposed the meat quotas on H.R. 1839, a step favored by many Senators, including Majority Leader Mike Mansfield from meat-producing Montana, but the Senate even struck the House bill's enacting clause. The original sponsor of the wild animals bill, Charles M. Teague (R., Calif.), sketched the legislative history of H.R. 1839 humorously, but accurately:

> Mr. Speaker, a few days ago, I stood here in the well of the House and pleaded with my colleagues to be sure that they referred to H.R. 1839 as the Teague bill.

[2] Quoted in George H. Haynes, *The Senate of the United States* (Boston: Houghton Mifflin, 1938), Vol. I, p. 430.

This was because I was proud to have been the father of such a clean, beautiful little fellow as 1839. Every one of you helped me in his delivery because he emerged from this body by unanimous vote. He was prepared to do great things for boa constrictors and gorrillas and their owners.

But in the course of events, my little baby was sent to the Senate pediatric hospital. IIe was horribly neglected there for a year and a half. During all of those months he was kept in dank closets and pigeonholes.

Then, recently, some of the eminent surgeons in the Senate hospital, headed by Drs. Mansfield and Keating, I believe, decided to perform major surgery on poor little 1839.

The operation was a great success by the standards which prevail in the Senate hospital. My little fellow was completely gutted. All that remained of him was the identification number on his poor little wrist. He no longer even bore my name. His little shell, however, had been stuffed by the surgeons in the Senate hospital with all sorts of things entirely foreign to 1839, his heritage and ancestry.

This new creature was sent back to the House not bearing the slightest resemblance to the splendid little fellow who left here three years ago. . . .[3]

Teague's parody on the Senate delighted his House listeners but, on the serious side, the Senate amendments to H.R. 1839 posed a direct challenge to the House's authority to originate all bills relating to revenue. Ways and Means had held one executive session on the meat import question but had not reported the bill. With the second session of the 88th Congress drawing to a close, the Senate decided not to wait for the Ways and Means Committee to act.

Dozens of House members had introduced bills similar to the Senate amendment so the possibility of the House rejecting H.R. 1839 and sending it back to the Senate because of the meat amendment was slim. William Colmer, for example, explained that although he always opposed ungermane Senate amendments and had tried to get the House rules changed to prevent the Senate from doing what it did on this occasion, his desire to get some relief for the cattle industry was so strong that he voted to accept the amendment in the Rules Committee. "You see," he told the House, "some of us wanted to use this procedure ourselves this time, I being among

[3] *Congressional Record*, August 18, 1964 (daily edition), p. 19499.

them. It all depends on whose ox is being gored, you understand, but the practice is still bad." [4]

Because of the strong pressure on the House to accept the amendment (prodded by lobbyists for the cattle industry), Chairman Mills had to work hard to get the House, and the cattlemen, to allow a conference committee on the bill. He succeeded by promising that a conference report on the bill would be submitted to the House for final judgment; i.e., he would not let the issue die in conference. Mills bound himself, in other words, to let the House vote on some form of the Senate-sponsored amendment: "I am only saying this after very careful consultation with others who will be conferees. I do not mean to say that I can handle them, but together I believe we can assure the Members of the House that there will be a conference report." [5] With this ironclad commitment from Mills, and with the acquiescence of the livestock lobby, the House sent the bill to a conference with the Senate. A week later Mills called up a compromise version of H.R. 1839 that, to the complete satisfaction of no one, restored part of the wild animal section and altered several parts of the Senate amendments. It passed and was signed into law.

The legislative history of H.R. 1839 shows that under certain conditions the House is unwilling to let constitutional niceties stand in the way of the resolution of pressing political demands. In this case, form mattered less than substance. A protest was lodged by Ways and Means Committee member Thomas B. Curtis, but he stood virtually alone in the face of the fait accompli presented to the House:

> I wish to discuss procedures a bit. People seem concerned about the Constitution of the United States only when it pertains to something which is of concern to them. In the Constitution it is provided that tax measures — and this is a tax measure, having to do with tariffs — shall originate only in the House of Representatives. This is why I have been fighting the nongermane amendments which are tacked on to our tax bills when they come back from the other body.
>
> This has gone to the extreme that the other body knocked everything out of the tax bill of the House except the num-

[4] *Ibid.*, August 11, 1964 (daily edition), p. 18312.
[5] *Ibid.*, pp. 18312–13.

ber. I raised this question in conference. After knocking
out everything but the number, can Members so violate
the Constitution as to bring this matter back with nothing
but a bill originating in the other body. It is no amendment
to a House tax bill.[6]

Ways and Means did, of course, preserve some semblance of its
prerogatives, but the stimulus behind H.R. 1839 clearly came more
from the Senate than the House. Curtis's argument, perhaps sound
constitutionally, was politically weak, and no one but him seemed too
disturbed over the Senate action — least of all the members with
cattle in their districts and cattlemen in their offices.

"Once you open Pandora's box, church is out," is how a Republican Senator characterized what occurred in 1964 when the Senate
went on an excise tax cutting spree and demonstrated again its freedom from House constraints on revenue measures. When the Senate
was through with H.R. 11376, which as it passed the House provided
for a simple extension of excise tax rates on certain commodities,
over $500 million in excise taxes were repealed in what *The Washing-
ton Post* critically branded as a "tax cutting romp." [7]

Contrary to the recommendations of the Senate Finance Committee, excise tax after excise tax was removed or reduced on the Senate
floor until Senator Lausche, in speaking on behalf of his amendment,
argued that "if we are going to be foolish, if folly is to dominate us,
let us go the whole way." [8] Senator Russell Long of Louisiana, in the
midst of chaos, attempted to put the lid back on the Internal
Revenue Code, with mixed success:

> Today I have witnessed a situation in which a responsible
> committee of the Senate did the best it could to do a re-
> sponsible job for the Senate. It did the best it could to rec-
> ognize all the political factors with which we must contend.
> Yet I have seen the Senate repeatedly, on vote after vote,
> vote down one of its most responsible committees. In some
> respects I almost hope that the pending amendment will be
> agreed to, because the author offered the amendment with
> the explanation that it was completely irresponsible and
> that it made no sense whatsoever. It was completely politi-
> cally motivated, and it would be a disgrace to the Senate
> to agree to it. But it was offered on the basis and on the

[6] *Ibid.*, August 18, 1964, p. 20119.
[7] *The Washington Post*, "Excise Tax Mischief," June 30, 1964, p. A16.
[8] *Congressional Record*, June 25, 1964 (daily edition), p. 14648.

theory that other Senators, similarly motivated, had offered amendments which would remove excise taxes from
other items.[9]

The Lausche amendment was defeated but the Senate was not
through. Senator Smathers of Florida, on behalf of Hartke of Indiana
who was out of town, offered an amendment removing the tax on
musical instruments. In response, Senator Long said, "The Senate
committee at one time agreed to the amendment, and then reversed
its action because we did not want to have happen what has happened on the floor today. We did not want to open the floodgates." [10]
Now, with the gates down, Long told the Senate that he had "promised the Senator from Indiana that if we took such action, in adopting the kind of amendments that we have adopted today, I would try
to have his amendment adopted. I am happy to support it on that
basis." [11] Hartke's amendment passed by voice vote and, after another
amendment was adopted, the Senate went on to other business, leaving a $500 million hole in the Treasury Department.

To no one's surprise the House conferees, or more precisely the
House Democrats led by Mills, refused to budge from the original
House version of the bill. When the bill passed the House the
Republicans had made a vain effort to cut some of the excises later
removed by the Senate, and Byrnes, perhaps with tongue in cheek,
told the House that he did not see why the Democratic conferees had
been so adamant: "It seems to me here, as in many other cases, we
should be willing to compromise at least a bit in order to maintain
proper comity and relationship with the other body." [12] In any event,
with an $11 billion tax cut already passed in 1964, with the Ways and
Means Committee holding hearings on excise taxes in anticipation of
reducing them in 1965, and with the administration's adverse response to the Senate free-for-all, H.R. 11376 became law in the same
form as the House-passed bill.

With no closed rule on the Senate floor, the Senate in 1964 was
completely free to cut excise taxes and thus exemplified what may
happen to Ways and Means bills in the Senate. The Senate rarely
strikes the enacting clause of the House bill but it commonly adds
amendments and riders to measures originating in the House. By so

---

[9] *Ibid.*, p. 14649.
[10] *Ibid.*, p. 14651.
[11] *Ibid.*
[12] *Ibid.*, June 30, 1964 (daily edition), p. 14955.

doing the Senate has initiated such important proposals as the 1966 plan providing federal financing of presidential elections, the 1964 medicare plan that passed the Senate only to die in conference, the $6 billion expenditure cut–10 per cent tax surcharge package in 1968, tax credits for parents of college students in 1967, and a host of lesser provisions sought by lobbyists for a wide variety of interests. Senate changes in House revenue bills are not, of course, a new phenomenon in Congress, but in recent years the Senate increasingly has tended to let the conference committee worry about the fiscal consequences of the amendments. In both 1966 and 1967 the Senate, late in the session, packed House bills with so many amendments that the bills became known as "Christmas tree" bills, and in March 1968 the Senate went on the offensive again with a bill known as the "Easter egg basket act of 1968." [13]

In some cases of Senate largesse no one seriously expects the amendments to become law. The Senate (as Mills had predicted) gaily expanded social security benefits in 1967, for example, without providing the necessary increases in the social security tax to finance the increases, and the following report from Senator Russell Long on what happened in conference with the House was expected:

> They let us know as soon as we met with them that our bill was actuarially unsound. That is understandable, since we added $1½ billion of extra benefits to the committee bill after it reached the floor of the Senate without providing a single dollar of new tax to pay for them. . . .
> The House conferees were arguing from strength. They argued with a single voice. They were united to a man; and the theme of their opposition was that if it costs money, they cannot accept it, on the theory that the money is not there with which to pay for it.[14]

But not all Senate changes suffer the fate of the 1967 social security amendments or of medicare in 1964. Senate amendments have resulted in laws that have, on a secondary level, opened the way for the establishment of the New Orleans Saints professional football team

[13] For these bills see Robert C. Albright, " 'Yule Tree' Bill Voted by Senate, Laden with Tax Goodies for All," *The Washington Post*, October 14, 1966, p. A4; *Congressional Record*, December 12, 1967 (daily edition), pp. H 16729–32; Frank Porter, "Senate Sets Quotas for All Textiles," *The Washington Post*, March 28, 1968, p. A1.

[14] *Congressional Record*, December 13, 1967 (daily edition), p. S 18608.

(a joint project of Russell Long and Hale Boggs of New Orleans),[15] saved American Motors $22 million in taxes to help the company out of its financial difficulties,[16] and extended depletion allowances,[17] to name just a few. At a more general level, the Senate has initiated revenue legislation on such majoi issues as the tax surcharge in 1968. Under certain conditions the House has willingly overlooked the fact that the Senate has, in fact if not in form, initiated revenue legislation.

The 1968 surcharge issue brought the question of Article I, section 7 before the House in no uncertain terms. In the debate the House proponents of the Senate plan, led by Mills, spelled out the broad guidelines that govern Senate amendments.

After several months of deadlock between the House and the Johnson administration over how much spending should be cut and taxes raised, the Senate voted for an amendment that provided for a 10 per cent surcharge and a $6 billion reduction in spending. House and Senate conferees, after long negotiations, finally adopted the Senate plan, and on June 20, 1968, the House conferees brought the measure up in the House.

Individual members of the House had many reasons for opposition to the Senate amendments, but the key vote in the House came on a motion by Representative H. R. Gross (R., Iowa) to return the bill to the Senate as a violation of the Constitution. Gross, citing numerous precedents for rejecting the conference report, argued that the House had not acted on the question and, consequently, the Senate had exceeded its authority to amend revenue bills.[18]

The substantive issues involved were clear: if the Gross resolution passed the House, weeks of effort would have been wasted, the House would have to pass separate legislation on a sensitive topic, and further delay could adversely affect the economy. On the other hand, the Gross resolution provided an opportunity for those who opposed the conference action to reject it by arguing that the Senate action was unconstitutional.

[15] *Ibid.*, October 20, 1966 (daily edition), p. 27076.
[16] *Ibid.*, December 12, 1967 (daily edition), p. H 16729.
[17] Although the 27.5 per cent oil depletion allowance is the best known, a large number of minerals receive depletion allowances, at various rates. Thus an effort to reduce the oil depletion allowance activates opposition from producers of other items who have an economic stake in the principles underlying depletion if not in the rate granted to oil.
[18] *Ibid.*, June 20, 1968 (daily edition), p. H 5231.

In reply to Gross, Mills argued — as he had on previous occasions [19] — that the Senate action did not infringe on the prerogatives of the House because the Senate has wide authority to make amendments as long as the bills are passed first by the House. He said:

> If this bill before us had been a measure originating in the Senate and had borne a Senate number, there would have been no question about it having contravened the provision of the Constitution we have been talking about. This would have been true because it would have been a bill involving revenue which did not originate in the House of Representatives, as the Constitution requires.[20]

Mills's argument saddened at least one member of Ways and Means, Curtis, who noted that the Chairman's position permitted the Senate to do anything it pleased as long as it retained the House number on bills.[21] The issues went far beyond maintaining the House prerogatives in revenue legislation, but to the extent that this was part of the issue the House clearly took a minimal position regarding Senate amendments. The vote was, after all, merely recognition of the actual relationship between the two bodies on revenue questions that had existed for many years.[22]

From this evidence Article I, section 7, of the Constitution might be seen as having no important effects on the legislative process involving revenue bills. Such is not the case. The right of the House to originate revenue legislation can be and has been important as a strategic factor in House-Senate deliberations. The constitutional provision has been employed to block Senate amendments to House bills, though with little success, but it is important in the timing that can affect the substance of legislation.

In September 1965, Senator Long raised a point of order against an amendment to the Railroad Retirement Act that would have raised the taxable wage base from $450 to $550 a month.[23] He argued that it was a tax amendment to a nonrevenue bill and, as such, was

[19] *Ibid.*, October 10, 1962, p. 23043.
[20] *Ibid.*, June 20, 1968 (daily edition), p. H 5232.
[21] *Ibid.*
[22] For an earlier example of the scope of Senate amendments see the study of the 1950 excess profits tax bill in Stephen K. Bailey and Howard D. Samuel, *Congress at Work* (New York: Henry Holt & Co., 1952), pp. 338–56. For related material see Edmund B. Brownell, "E P T — The Politics of a Tax" (Ph.D. Dissertation, University of Michigan, 1956).
[23] *Congressional Record*, September 1, 1965 (daily edition), pp. 21761–67.

unconstitutional. Long restated the constitutional prohibition against Senate origination of revenue bills, said that he could not remember when the Senate ever attempted to originate such a bill, and concluded that the unconstitutional amendment would transform a non-revenue House bill into a revenue bill in clear violation of the senatorial oath to uphold the Constitution. In rebuttal to Senator Morse's contention that the amendment was permissible because it was incidental to the primary, nonrevenue purpose of the bill, Long said:

> If the Senator from Oregon is right in what he says, the Finance Committee would have had a right to originate the social security bill and the medicare bill. The Senate Finance Committee agreed so strongly to the contrary that our chairman and the committee declined to hold hearings on that bill until the House acted and sent the Senate a bill. . . .
>
> When revenues are to be raised, those measures should originate in the House. The Senate Committee on Finance sometimes has to wait 3 months for the House to send to the Senate revenue bills so the Senate may act on them. Religiously and respectfully, the Finance Committee respects the House of Representatives in respect to the Constitution. . . .[24]

The Senate did not support Long's point of order and the amendment passed, but the incident reveals: (1) Senator Long's commitment (on this occasion) to the maintenance of the House's right to originate revenue bills (a cynic could argue that Long's position was due to his opposition to the substance of the proposal and not to a concern for procedure — a tenuous supposition because he voted for the bill after his point of order failed); (2) the potential strategic value of Article I, section 7 — the point of order lost by just three votes, 41–44; and (3) the standing decision of the Finance Committee, as illustrated by medicare, to await House action in all but the most unusual cases, i.e., situations in which House action is problematical and Senate pressure, or pressure on the Senate, is irresistible.

Timing may be an important strategic factor in the legislative process involving revenue bills. Virginia's Harry F. Byrd, who was chairman of the Senate Finance Committee from 1955 until his retirement in 1965, never encroached upon the House's right to give first consideration to all revenue bills. "You know the old man is a

[24] *Ibid.*, p. 21765.

stickler for proper procedure," a Republican Senator commented. "He won't begin a bill unless it's sent over by Ways and Means. He's a stickler on this." Then he added: "Of course, one of the reasons is that he's opposed to doing anything anyway." Byrd, in other words, found Article I, section 7, useful in delaying legislation for which he had little sympathy. By synchronizing the activity of the Finance Committee with the pace (usually slow) of the House, he could control the timing of the legislative process. Majority Leader Mansfield once was rebuffed when he tried to get the Finance Committee to act before the House on a bill.

Timing has also been important, on occasion, to House influence on policy. As the deadline approached for extending unemployment compensation benefits during the 1959 recession, for example, Senate liberals who were dissatisfied with the limited nature of the conference report agreement ran into the argument that the report had to be accepted as written or the entire bill might have been lost. With only a few days in which to complete action, Senator Byrd argued that 400,000 people would be denied benefits if the Senate insisted on a more liberal bill. Byrd said, "Any member of the Senate who has any doubts about the seriousness of the situation should communicate with the House leadership. If they will do that, they will be advised as to whether it is possible to get the bill through a conference committee at this late hour." [25] Despite Byrd's warning, which was backed up by Mansfield who checked with Speaker Rayburn, the Senate adopted a liberalizing amendment offered by Eugene McCarthy. A conference committee was hastily assembled the same day, the House conferees stood firm against the Senate amendment, and the Senate adopted the report later in the day. Those desiring a more liberal bill made their record on the Senate floor and, confronted by a deadline, the Senate accepted the House position by voice vote. The policy result was that those workers who might have qualified for unemployment benefits under the McCarthy amendment were still unqualified.

Excise taxes, imposed as a temporary source of revenue during World War II and the Korean war, have been extended yearly because the revenue that they accumulated was needed. The 1964 tax-cutting movement in the Senate came to nought partly because unless the rates were extended by June 30, the federal government would start losing revenue. Senate conferees receded on the Senate

[25] *Ibid.*, March 25, 1959, p. 5218.

cuts in the conference committee, as everyone expected, but one of the leaders behind the Senate amendments, John Pastore, protested that the House had put the Senate at a disadvantage by sending the tax extension bill to them near the June 30 deadline. Pastore remarked:

> There is a circumstance about these measures that irks the Senator from Rhode Island, and I think that irks every Senator, including the members of the Finance Committee. It is that these measures that have a deadline of midnight June 30 should come tardily from the House to the Senate. This measure was passed by the House on June 17. And I would suppose that it came to the Senate immediately thereafter.
>
> The time stricture puts the Senate in a straightjacket. There seems to be little that we can do about it. I know that the House Ways and Means Committee is a rather busy committee. They have a lot of work to do. I can understand that they cannot come around to these measures as quickly as they would like. But I hope in the Congress we are not working ourselves into an operating procedure where the House holds up these measures and when it sends them over to us we are then placed in the position where under the pressure of deadlines we cannot make a free choice of what we think is right as against what we think is wrong.[26]

INTEREST AGGREGATION. It appears that more interests are aggregated in the Senate than House. From past experience, the members of Ways and Means have learned to expect the Senate to add amendments to House bills. Commenting on an excise tax reduction bill that did not reduce revenue by more than the House bill, a Committee member said, "This is not the usual procedure. Usually we hold the line and they have a picnic." The normal situation as seen from the House was summed up by Mills, "As is nearly always the case, the Senate added a good many amendments to the bill passed by the House." [27]

To an undetermined extent, the Ways and Means Committee anticipates Senate action on its bills and shapes the legislation accordingly. In 1965, for example, Ways and Means heard the argument that if the Committee did not reduce excise taxes far enough

[26] *Ibid.*, June 30, 1964, p. 15444.
[27] *Ibid.*, October 20, 1966 (daily edition), p. 27075.

the Senate no doubt would make the cuts. The Committee made the
cuts. In interviews, one member observed that the Committee sometimes drafts a bill with an eye toward likely Senate action, and then,
he feels, Ways and Means wins in conference. Another member said
that Mills "will say, 'Maybe we can live with 10 per cent but if we
send it over there they'll make it 15 and we'll have to live with 12. So
let's make it 8.' You say O.K. and go along."

Although Ways and Means anticipates and takes into account
some Senate action, the Committee still leaves many questions for
the Senate to decide. The Senate Finance Committee and the Senate
consider the objections to House bills as well as new proposals not
presented on the House side. Senate Finance Committee Chairman
Eugene Millikin, for example, clearly stated the Senate job in 1954:
"In our deliberations, care was given toward meeting the objections
of the witnesses to the House version of the bill. Suggestions not submitted to the Ways and Means Committee were also considered, and
the Senate Finance Committee amendments contain many of these
suggestions." [28] House complaints about the Senate bear witness to
the independence of Senate action on Ways and Means matters.

To the interest groups and lobbyists who are concerned with questions falling within the jurisdiction of Ways and Means, the Senate
provides an opportunity not only to appeal House decisions but, with
the House floor roped off by the closed rule, to add new and sometimes nongermane provisions to House-numbered bills. The American Motors amendment in 1967 is a good example, when one member
of the Committee (Curtis) protested:

> I was pleased that the chairman of the committee men-
> tioned the name of the only company that is benefited in
> amendment No. 4 that we accepted, one of the nongermane
> amendments — the American Motors Co. I think I am prob-
> ably sympathetic to their problem. But when I find that the
> American Motors Co. lobbyists go over to the other body
> and get in touch with some Senators to introduce their legis-
> lation, which is contrary to the Constitution, I ask, Why do
> they not come over to the House side? I did not know about
> the American Motors matter until about two weeks ago,
> when one of the lobbyists came in to talk to me about it.
> I said to him then, "Why do you not follow orderly proce-
> dure? If there is nothing wrong with this." — And I do not

[28] *Ibid.*, June 28, 1954, p. 8993.

believe there is; do not misunderstand me, I do not think there is anything wrong with this, other than the fact that this is bad procedure — this kind of procedure does breed corruption. Believe me, I think it is very important that the Congress of the United States starts exercising some self-discipline and understanding. It is this kind of improper procedure that tends to cause the people to lose confidence in what we are doing here in the Congress.[29]

Curtis also observed that it is not only bad procedure for the House to permit lobbyists to score gains on the Senate side but the House members lose an opportunity to gain political credits of their own:

I can talk a little bit politically, if Members want me to. This renders the House a weaker body. This is one reason our colleagues in the other body can get certain things from people back in their communities that House Members cannot. If the people in American Motors know that this body is no place to go, but they should go to the other body to introduce revenue measures, knowing also they are going to bypass public hearings and a full discussion by the Ways and Means Committee, as I say, we, in effect, weaken ourselves. I want to see this House strengthened, and it badly needs strengthening.[30]

The Senate proved useful in 1960 to wool producers who were leery of permanently suspending the duty on certain kinds of imported wool,[31] to life insurance companies who received a $50 million improvement in a tax bill the year before,[32] and in 1965 to persons interested in the tariff treatment of wild rice, rubber footwear, particle-board, automatic bowling pinsetters, picker sticks, imported aluminum, and the like.[33] In the case of the tariff bill, the Ways and Means Committee adopted guidelines limiting tariff changes to corrections of errors or unintended consequences of existing law, and in the conference committee the substantive Senate amendments were (for the most part) subjected to the House guidelines and discarded.

No systematic attempt has been made to compare interest aggregation in the Finance Committee to the Senate floor, but the Finance

[29] *Ibid.*, December 12, 1967 (daily edition), p. H 16730.
[30] *Ibid.*, p. H 16731.
[31] *Ibid.*, June 17, 1960, p. 13076. The wool growers later dropped their opposition.
[32] *Ibid.*, June 10, 1959, p. 10411.
[33] *Ibid.*, September 16, 1965, pp. 24057–58.

Committee is no more respectful of the House bill than the Senate.
After redoing the 1962 Revenue Act, for example, the Finance Committee spent the last two days considering "bobtail" amendments
offered by various Senators. As one Finance Committee member said,
"The ship was leaving port and everyone wanted to get his cargo
aboard." [34] Among the last-minute amendments were: (1) the deduction by farmers of expenses for clearing land; (2) deduction of charitable contributions not covered under existing law; (3) taxation of
small business corporations under certain conditions; (4) taxation of
a two-man partnership upon the death of one of the partners; (5)
exemption of the pension plan trust of Local Union No. 435 of the
International Hod Carriers' Building & Common Laborers Union of
America; and (6) treatment of losses incurred in 1953 and 1954 by a
street railway company in converting from streetcars to buses.[35]

On some Ways and Means bills Schattschneider's comment about
the Smoot-Hawley tariff — "the minutiae of the bill carry its meaning" [36] — is applicable. And, what is more, not all the minutiae added
by the Senate is generated by the Senate. Ways and Means members,
despite their generally critical attitude toward the lack of restraint
in the Senate, sometimes find the openness of the Senate helpful in
pushing their bills. H.R. 7502, a member's bill sponsored by Al Ullman (D., Ore.) providing special income tax treatment for certain
losses attributable to major disasters, was amended so much by the
Senate that a staff member of Ways and Means jokingly referred to
it as the "Technical Amendments Act of 1965," and conveyed the
feeling that "pork" would be a more appropriate term than "technical." A second staff member quoted Mills as laughing about Ullman's
minor bill as the "Revenue Act of 1965." In one day, the Senate Finance Committee tacked on, according to a press release, eleven separate amendments, including one to eliminate the $10,000 ceiling on
authorizations for the Joint Committee on the Reduction of Non-
essential Federal Expenditures.

Some Committee members rushed to get a friendly Senator to offer
their bills as amendments to H.R. 7502. "It reminds me of a candy

[34] Quoted in David J. Stern, "Congress, Politics, and Taxes: A Case Study of
the Revenue Act of 1962" (Ph.D. Dissertation, Claremont Graduate School,
1965), p. 354.
[35] *Ibid.*
[36] E. E. Schattschneider, *Politics, Pressures and the Tariff* (Hamden, Conn.:
Archon Books, 1963), p. 9.

store that's burning down," said a staff man. "All the little kids are running over to the Senate to get the candy while the door's open." Asked who is likely to succeed in getting the Finance Committee to include a bill he said, "Anybody who doesn't score in this type of a fiasco is a real fink!"

This time, however, the Senate rolled one log too many. An amendment sponsored by Senator Dirksen on behalf of the Tennessee Gas Transmission Company created so much opposition within the Finance Committee and received so much unfavorable publicity that Finance was forced into a public hearing on it. H.R. 7502, a delicately constructed omnibus bill, tumbled down in the Senate under the weight of this one amendment.[37]

That the Senate is, in practice, probably more receptive to interest groups and lobbyists than the Ways and Means Committee and the House is evidenced by the 1967–1968 move to enact import quotas for major segments of American businesses. In late 1967, Senators Dirksen and Russell Long, with support from dozens of Senators, sought a way to attach import quotas to a veto-proof House bill. The 1967 Social Security Amendments appeared at first to be a likely vehicle for the protectionist amendments, but after a good deal of consideration Long and his supporters decided to postpone action until the following year. "The thing about riders," Long said, "is that you don't want to have one bigger than the horse." [38]

Public hearings on the import quota bills introduced in the Senate were held by the Finance Committee in October 1967; five months later the first tangible result of the quota drive, the adoption on the Senate floor of quotas for textiles, was made.[39] The Senate initiative was nullified in conference with the House, despite the fact that Chairman Mills had formally lessened his commitment to free trade by introducing import quota bills, but the important point about the quota question was that the Senate had acted before the House. The same factors leading to the demand for quota legislation in the Sen-

---

[37] For additional examples of House bills being incorporated into Senate bills see the *Congressional Record*, August 31, 1960, pp. 18751–52; September 21, 1962, p. 20245; October 20, 1966, pp. 27074, 27090. For the Tennessee Gas Transmission Co. amendment see "Dirksen-Long Tax Measure is Withdrawn," *The Washington Post*, September 10, 1965, p. A2.

[38] "Social Security Rider on Trade Trips in Senate," *The Washington Evening Star*, October 16, 1967, p. A2.

[39] Frank Porter, "Senate Sets Quotas for All Textiles," *The Washington Post*, March 28, 1968, p. A1.

ate were at work in the House (both bodies may take restrictive action in the future), but Ways and Means did no more than hold public hearings on the issue in 1967–1968, far less than the Senate.

Why are more interests aggregated in the Senate than in the House? One reason has to do with general differences between the House and Senate.[40] Power resources are more evenly distributed in the Senate, the rules in the Senate are more flexible, and the impulse toward personal comity with one's peers is stronger in the Senate than in the House.[41] All three factors make the Senate more likely to proceed on the basis of mutual noninterference in the interests of one's colleagues, which is supported by the realization that in many cases logroll amendments will be "taken to conference" and dropped.

In addition, the job of the Senate is to consider the interests of those who do not get what they want from the House. Senators, as a Senate conferee once reminded the Ways and Means conferees, have to get elected too, and there is small percentage in ratifying House decisions at the expense of the groups and lobbyists who want to change those decisions.

The nature of the Ways and Means Committee's subject matter should not be overlooked. Tax reductions, social security increases, and trade protection are extremely sensitive matters that are contained in the House through the closed rule. Business interests are particularly enmeshed in tax and trade questions, and social security expansions are popular for broad electoral appeal. Against these attractive objectives must be balanced fiscal and economic conditions that limit the size of tax cuts, the actuarial status of the social security system that constrains the degree of liberalization that can be made, and the foreign policy implications of restrictions on imported goods. The House finds it much easier to let these factors affect its decisions with the closed rule than the Senate does without a similar procedural safeguard

Finally, a Senator has more interests to represent than a member of the House. The larger representational unit of a Senator may make him freer of some state interests than a Representative whose district is confined to a dominant interest or two, but members of the Senate generally are in contact with and receptive to a wider variety of inter-

---

[40] For a discussion see Lewis A. Froman, Jr., *The Congressional Process* (Boston: Little, Brown, 1967), pp. 5–15.
[41] *Ibid.*, p. 7.

ests than individual House members. Dirksen of Illinois may have led the campaign for steel quotas while Percy of Illinois opposed them, but Senators are more likely to have more provisions to promote on individual items in an omnibus revenue bill than the average House member.

CONFERENCE COMMITTEE DECISIONS

Which body wins in the conference committee? If members of the Ways and Means Committee are asked who wins in conference the typical response — given by seventeen of twenty-one members of the Committee — is the House. In essence, Ways and Means members view the Senate in these terms:

> They simply take the things of our bills which will get a lot of publicity, play them up, then recede to the House position. Sure they riddle our bills. It takes a lot of guts to come out with some of the things we do. Withholding on interest a couple of years ago, for example. You'd think that six-year terms would give them more guts but it doesn't.

Ways and Means does the bulk of the work, one member feels, then the Senate loads the bills with amendments, and it is up to the conferees to "weed out all those crumby amendments." "All the Senators are interested in is getting their amendments into these tax bills, when we come to conference," a Republican conferee stated. "They make no bones about it," he continued, "they're very open. They'll sit down for God's sake and say, 'Now let's see, whose amendment was this? Oh yes, it's ———— and I told him I would support it. We are going to stand firm on that.'" Spoken seriously, this comment was punctuated with an incredulous chuckle at the gay attitude of the Senators toward substantive amendments.

Interview data show that senatorial perceptions of what the Senate can do to revenue bills match Senate performance. One member of Finance claimed that the Senate feels no compunctions about changing Ways and Means bills even though it may not initiate them:

> We don't pay any attention to what the Ways and Means Committee is doing, other than reading it in the paper. It's a totally separate process. In a way we are unique because we are the only committee that cannot act before the House does. This is by constitutional provision. . . . But once the bill gets over here we feel no restraint on changing it. By

this I mean that there's no feeling that just because the
Ways and Means Committee has written a provision this
way we should keep it the same. Not at all.

From the behavior of the Senate, it is reasonable to infer that this
Senator's approach to Ways and Means bills is probably reflective of
the general opinion of the Senate.

But the perceptions of what happens in conference are by no
means completely uniform. One Senator, for example, said that the
Senate does some fairly important things but concluded, "I'd say
Ways and Means. If you are talking about overall policy, tax philosophy, innovations, then Ways and Means has the most influence." Another Senator, a Democrat, feels that the Senate does "very well in
conference. In fact we do better than the House. Yes we do." Most
Ways and Means members are quite content with the performance of
the House conferees but one member talked about what he called the
"capitulation" of the House to the Senate in recent years, citing the
1964 revenue bill as an example. A Treasury Department official
feels that, "In the conference committee I'd say the House gets more
of its positions adopted than the Senate. The House does better."
But a former staff member of Ways and Means made the point:

> Actually the House position isn't upheld very good in con-
> ference. The members may say it is but it's really not. Look
> at all the junk the Senate tacks on. They put a lot of junk
> in the bills then they retreat — but hell, by doing this they
> start out with a lot of junk and by retreating still retain a
> lot. For example, on this taxation of overseas income. The
> Senate wanted $50,000, the House $30,000, so the Senate
> asked for $70,000 and they settled for $50,000. That hap-
> pens all the time.

In the words of one student of taxes, "An observer would find it difficult to say which body over the years has had the greater influence on
official tax policy." [42]

Disparate answers to a difficult question as vague as "who wins in
the legislative process?" are hardly surprising; everything depends on
how the respondents rank the stakes. A House member incensed at

---

[42] Roy Blough, *The Federal Taxing Process* (New York: Prentice-Hall, 1952),
p. 62. For general treatments of conference committees see Gilbert Y. Steiner,
The Congressional Conference Committee (Urbana: University of Illinois Press,
1951); and Ada C. McCown, *The Congressional Conference Committee* (New
York: Columbia University Press, 1927).

the cashiering of one of his amendments in conference might well reply that the Senate has the upper hand. With the strong tendency toward institutional patriotism in both chambers the members are somewhat reluctant to admit that the other house beats them in conference, even if they really feel this way. A third factor is the timing of the question: the same question asked at different times (e.g., after the 1964 conference deadlock on medicare) is likely to get different responses from the same people depending upon current events.

The most important reason behind the contradictory responses to the "who wins?" question that reveals the most about the nature of congressional politics is that in many cases no unambiguous answers are possible because the process is not a zero sum situation. The overriding ethic of the conference committee is one of bargaining, give-and-take, compromise, swapping, horse-trading, conciliation, and malleability by all concerned. Firm positions are always taken, and always changed. Deadlocks rarely occur to the degree that the bill is killed. Someone gives a little, perhaps after an impressive walkout, in return for a little; compromise is the cardinal rule of conference committees. Small wonder that each side claims victory; because almost everyone does win — something, somehow, sometime.[43]

---

[43] Notice, for example, how Mills and Long, by using different figures and slightly different language, presented the conference report on the 1965 excise tax reduction bill to their respective chambers. "*Mr. Mills.* Mr. Speaker, preliminary to an actual discussion of what is contained in the conference report, permit me to take time to call attention to the fact that we are presenting a conference report on the Excise Tax Reduction Act of 1965 today, exactly 30 days following the receipt of the request for such action by the Congress from the President of the United States. Mr. Speaker, I mention this only to point out that when the Congress desires to act expeditiously with respect to matters of this sort, it seems clear that the Congress can so act. I do not recall, I must admit, however, that since I have been chairman of the Committee on Ways and Means at least, that we have acted quite this expeditiously with respect to all and sundry tax proposals that have been submitted to us; but, at least, it seems that the Congress has improved insofar as this particular bill is indicative. Now, Mr. Speaker, there are about five principal matters which I believe deserve attention at this point with respect to the conference report. I will, of course, before concluding include a more detailed explanation of all substantive changes. As the bill passed the House the Members will recall that it involved a loss of revenue of approximately $2.169 billion for the fiscal year 1966. Under the conference version now before us, the corresponding figure is $2.189 billion. However, it is estimated, in fiscal 1966 the figure, after 'feedback,' will be approximately $1.8 billion." *Congressional Record*, June 17, 1965, p. 13960. "*Mr. Long of Louisiana.* Mr. President, I have the honor to bring before the Senate the conference report on H. R. 8371, the Excise Tax Reduction Act of 1965. This is the bill that only the day before yesterday was passed by the Senate. I think you can see from this that the conferees acted with expedition. In fact I might take

Keeping in mind these qualifications on the way in which the participants see House-Senate relations and the fact that much depends on the seriousness with which individual legislators pursue their objectives, we will now analyze the pattern of congressional decision-making on Ways and Means bills since World War II. For this purpose, Committee legislation will be divided into major bills raising or lowering revenue, social security legislation, and trade legislation. In this way it will be possible to see how bicameral relations vary depending on the policy questions at stake, any variations over time will be captured, and the question of which body wins in conference may be put into the context of the diversity of policy handled by Ways and Means.

TAX LEGISLATION. The Senate Finance Committee and the Senate make major changes in major House tax bills, most commonly involving excise and corporate tax rate extensions. As one would expect, there is a tendency for these changes to lighten the tax burden passed by the House.

Table 6.1 presents the revenue estimates on seventeen bills that, as passed by the House, either raised taxes or extended existing taxes. In four cases the Senate made no changes involving revenue but in eight of the remaining thirteen cases the Senate amended the bill in a revenue-losing direction. Moreover, special circumstances surround the five deviant bills. In the case of H.R. 4090 in 1957 the Senate extended excise and corporation taxes for fifteen months instead of twelve months as in the House bill, and so did not really raise taxes

---

time to point out that the whole handling of this bill, I believe, sets some kind of a record for quick action. It was exactly 1 month ago today, on May 17, that the President first sent to Congress his recommendations for excise tax reductions. This is an indication of the speed with which Congress can act on tax legislation when there is a need to do so. All of us were aware of the fact that any delay in action on our part might affect the economy through the delay of purchases of the taxed articles by consumers. In my view, this demonstrates, and demonstrates quite clearly, that when there is general agreement in Congress that a tax reduction is needed, this action can be taken — in the regular legislative manner in a very short period of time. The bill, as agreed to by the conferees, does not depart to any appreciable extent from the bill as passed by the Senate the day before yesterday. This is indicated by the fact that the bill as initially passed by the Senate would, over a 4-year period, have reduced excise tax collections by $4,658 million. The bill, as agreed to by the conferees, is a reduction of $4,676 million which constitutes a difference of only $18 million from the bill passed by the Senate 2 days ago." *Congressional Record*, June 17, 1965, p. 14070.

Table 6.1
Major Revenue-Raising Bills, 1947–1966 [a]
(millions)

Bill	Year	House	Finance Committee	Senate floor	Final
1. H.R. 1030	1947	1,130	1,130	1,078	1,085
2. H.R. 8920	1950	−157	4,516	4,523	4,601
3. H.R. 9827	1950	3,000	3,200	3,200	3,300
4. H.R. 4473	1951	6,828	5,219	5,156	5,438
5. H.R. 5898	1953	800	800	800	800
6. H.R. 4259	1955	737	·2,830	2,830	2,830
7. H.R. 9166	1956	3,186	3,186	3,186	3,186
8. H.R. 4090	1957	2,975	3,700	3,700	3,700
9. H.R. 12695	1958	2,504	2,504	1,829	2,067
10. H.R. 7523	1959	2,033	1,845	1,828	2,033
11. H.R. 4245	1959	558	500	500	508
12. H.R. 12381	1960	3,948	3,196	4,578	3,998
13. H.R. 7446	1961	3,659	3,659	3,659	3,659
14. H.R. 11879	1962	2,745	2,673	2,673	2,705
15. H.R. 6755	1963	2,791	2,791	2,791	2,791
16. H.R. 11376	1964	1,900	1,641	1,375	1,900
17. H.R. 12752	1966	4,965	5,000	4,155	4,905

Source: Appropriate House and Senate reports, Treasury Department files, the *Congressional Record*, and *Congressional Quarterly Almanac*, 1947–1966.
[a] Major bills defined as bills involving at least $500 million.

despite the fact that the Senate bill was worth $700 million more to Treasury than the House bill. Two of the five atypical bills occurred in 1950 and are explainable as revenue increases needed to finance the Korean War. The fourth bill involved the $20 tax credit in 1955 which the House Democrats passed but which was rejected in the Senate. The fifth bill, which will be discussed later, broke several rules. The Senate Finance Committee adopted revenue-losing amendments to H.R. 12381 in 1960, and not only were these amendments rejected on the Senate floor but three revenue-gaining amendments offered by three liberal tax reformers were passed (only one of three amendments survived the conference). With these five exceptions, major bills raising or maintaining taxes have been reduced somewhat in the Senate.

A corollary hypothesis is that the Senate, in response to demands to lower taxes, would amend tax reduction bills to reduce revenue more than the House bill. Testing this hypothesis is difficult because only seven major revenue-losing bills have been discovered, but if the overall revenue estimates are used four of the seven do *not* conform to expectations.

Table 6.2 reports the data on these seven bills. Two of the four involved the 1947–1948 tax reduction controversy between Congress and President Truman. The Senate was willing to reduce taxes contrary to the administration's wishes but, probably for fiscal reasons, the Senate was not willing to lower taxes as far as the House.

TABLE 6.2
MAJOR REVENUE-REDUCING BILLS, 1947–1966
(millions)

Bill	Year	House	Finance Committee	Senate floor	Final
1. H.R. 1	1947	3,994	3,211	3,211	3,227
2. H.R. 4790	1948	6,658	4,773	4,773+[a]	4,773+
3. H.R. 8224	1954	912	958	1,019	999
4. H.R. 8300	1954	1,370	1,477	1,316	1,363
5. H.R. 10650[b]	1962	285	555	555	550
6. H.R. 8363	1964	11,475	11,660	11,960	11,545
7. H.R. 8371	1965	4,908	4,658	4,658[c]	4,676

[a] One floor amendment was adopted but its effect on revenue was negligible.
[b] Treasury estimates are different from estimates of the staff of the Joint Committee on Internal Revenue Taxation. JCIRT estimates are used here.
[c] Several floor amendments adopted but negligible revenue effect.

A more recent case of the Senate bill cutting taxes less than the House bill is H.R. 8371 in 1965. This measure, the Excise Tax Reduction Act of 1965, lost less revenue in the Senate because of the decision to retain 1 per cent of the automobile excise tax for use in disposing of junk cars. Ways and Means removed the automobile tax completely. The conference retained the Senate amendment.

The fourth bill that reduced taxes less in the Senate version than that passed by the House is H.R. 8300, the Revenue Act of 1954, which is of special interest because it suggests that in some cases the general impact of bills on the Treasury may hide important decisions made by the Senate.

Table 6.3 reveals that H.R. 8300 as passed by the Senate involved less revenue loss than the House bill, but that the Senate did cut certain taxes by more than the House. Specifically, the Senate bill involved the loss of $628 million from corporate sources compared to $592 million under the House bill. The Senate bill generally cost the Treasury less than the House bill because, as amended on the Senate floor, the Senate bill lowered taxes on individuals by $100 million less than the House version. The largest item involved the highly controversial dividend credit and exclusion that the Senate all but

TABLE 6.3
COMPARISON OF REVENUE LOSS UNDER HOUSE AND SENATE VERSIONS OF 1954 REVENUE ACT (millions, FY 1955)

	House bill	SFC bill	Senate bill	Conference
Corporations:				
Natural resources:				
Depletion	27	34	34	34
Iron ore	0	10	10	0
Foreign income:				
Branch profits	95	0	0	0
Differential	55	0	0	0
Denial of differential	+5	0	0	0
Tax credit	2	2	2	2
Depreciation:				
Declining balance	300	300	300	300
Construction	0	32	32	0
Restrictions	0	+9	+9	+9
Net operating loss:				
Extend carryback	90	90	90	90
Adjustments	10	30	30	30
Deny dividend credit	+27	0	0	0
Remove 2% surtax	0	35	35	35
Tax on earnings	0	10	10	10
Partnerships	0	50	50	0
Continue capital gain	0	+9	+9	+9
Accounting provisions	45	47	47	47
Distilled spirits	0	6	6	6
Total	592	628	628	536
Individuals:				
Head of family	50	0	0	11
Dividends:				
Exclusion	45 ⎫240	243	46 ⎫46	46
Credit	195 ⎭		0 ⎭	158
Annuities	10	10	10	10
Dependents	75	75	75	75
Other dependents	10	10	10	10
Child care	40	130	130	130
Medical expense	80	80	80	80
Retirement income	125	141	141	141
Trust exemption	3	3	3	3
Premium test	25	25	25	25
Charitable contribution	25	25	25	25
Partnerships	0	20	20	20
Installment interest	10	0	0	10
Grain facilities	0	0	36	0
Soil and water	10	10	10	10
Depreciation	75	77	77	73
Total	778	849	688	827

SOURCE: *Congressional Record*, 1954, pp. 8994, 12426.

knocked out on the floor but was restored in modified form in the conference.

Even though the summary form of a Senate tax reduction bill loses less revenue than a House bill, the Senate, depending on what cuts are involved, may be more responsive to those seeking lower taxes than the House. While the Senate dropped the dividend credit in 1954, it gave slightly more tax relief to corporations than the House, and it reduced several taxes on individuals by more than the House, although the amounts involved were relatively small.

Three of the seven major tax reduction bills do follow the expected pattern. One, the Revenue Act of 1964, is a particularly important example of the Senate increasing House tax reductions and decreasing House tax increases. As Table 6.4 reports, the Senate Finance Com-

TABLE 6.4

COMPARISON OF 1964 REVENUE ACT AS PASSED BY HOUSE AND REPORTED BY THE SENATE FINANCE COMMITTEE

(millions, 1965)

Provisions	Ways and Means bill	Senate Finance bill
Revenue raising:		
1. Group term insurance	5	less than 2.5
2. Bank loan insurance	5	5
3. Sick pay exclusion	110	110
4. Deduction of personal taxes	520	190
5. Casualty loss deduction	50	50
6. Aggregation of mineral properties	40	40
7. Personal holding companies	15	15
8. Repeal of dividend credit and increase exclusion	300	300
9. Multiple corporation penalty tax	35	30
Total	1,080	740
Revenue reducing:		
10. Medical expense deduction	10	10
11. Child care allowance	5	20
12. Moving expenses	60	105
13. Income averaging	40	40
14. Minimum standard deduction	320	320
15. Repeal 2% tax on consolidated returns	50	50
Total	485	545
Capital gains	+170	+120
Investment credit	−195	−205

SOURCE: Joint Committee on Internal Revenue Taxation.

mittee modified the revenue-raising provisions of H.R. 8363 by over $300 million and expanded the House bill's revenue-reducing provisions by $60 million. In addition, the Finance Committee added five revenue-losing amendments to the House bill of $35 million, and the Senate added amendments on the floor that raised the revenue loss by another $300 million. The 1964 Revenue Act shows that there is more than gross figures indicate to the hypothesis that the likely Senate response to revenue-cutting proposals is to cut more than the House.[44] In all, eleven of the twenty major revenue bills since 1947 that were changed by the Senate were changed in the expected direction; nine were not.

If there is more variability in the nature of decisions made by the Senate on revenue bills than originally expected, there is little variability in which chamber comes closest to writing the bill that becomes law. Contrary to the perceptions of contemporary Ways and Means members, the data show that as measured by the impact on federal revenue the Senate bill is closer to the final bill than the House bill. This is true, moreover, for bills raising (or maintaining) taxes and for tax reduction measures. Of the thirteen revenue-raising bills changed by the Senate, the final version was closer to the Senate version nine times; of the seven tax-cutting bills, the final version was closer to the Senate bill five times. Thus, in fourteen of twenty major bills in which the House and Senate versions differed, the Senate versions were closer to the end product of the congressional process than the House bills.

This finding resembles Fenno's observation that the Senate wins more often than the House on appropriations bills, and the finding here is subject to the same crucial qualifications.[45] Most important, Senate dominance in the conference committee on Ways and Means bills is not the same as Senate dominance in the policy-making process generally.[46] In most cases, the amount of revenue involved in the Senate bill compared to the House bill is scaled down toward the House figure in the conference committee, as shown in Table 6.5, even though the final amount is usually closer to the Senate figure. In the great majority of cases the final decision, compared to the total

[44] It should be remembered that we are dealing here with major bills. If the hundreds of minor tax bills and provisions are taken into account the evidence supporting the hypothesis is much stronger.

[45] Richard F. Fenno, Jr., *The Power of the Purse* (Boston: Little, Brown, 1966), p. 663.

[46] *Ibid.*, pp. 662–63.

TABLE 6.5
REVENUE EFFECTS OF HOUSE AND SENATE
REVENUE BILLS, 1947–1966

Bill	Year	Difference between House-Senate bills (millions)	Difference between House bill and final bill (millions)
Revenue raising (maintaining) bills:			
1. H.R. 1030	1947	52	45
2. H.R. 8920	1950	4,680	4,758
3. H.R. 9827	1950	200	300
4. H.R. 4473	1951	1,672	1,390
5. H.R. 4259	1955	2,093	2,093
6. H.R. 4090	1957	725	725
7. H.R. 12695	1958	675	437
8. H.R. 7523	1959	205	0
9. H.R. 4245	1959	58	50
10. H.R. 12381	1960	630	50
11. H.R. 11879	1962	72	40
12. H.R. 11376	1964	525	0
13. H.R. 12752	1966	810	60
Revenue reducing bills:			
1. H.R. 1	1947	783	767
2. H.R. 4790	1948	1,885	1,885
3. H.R. 8224	1954	107	87
4. H.R. 8300	1954	54	7
5. H.R. 10650	1962	270	265
6. H.R. 8363	1964	485	70
7. H.R. 8371	1965	250	232

amount of money involved in these bills, does not seem to be too far from the House bill. Senate changes are usually incremental, but there have been important exceptions to this rule since 1947.

When all these qualifications are made, the fact remains that when the differences between House and Senate revenue bills are considered, the Senate does better than the House. Why?

A possible explanation is that which Fenno gives for the appropriations process. Following logically from his system-subsystem framework, Fenno speculates that the Senate wins because:

> The Senate is stronger in conference because the Senate Committee and its conferees draw more directly and more completely upon the support of their parent chamber than do the House Committee and its conferees. . . .
>
> When the Senate conferees go to the conference room, they not only represent the Senate — they are the Senate.

The position they defend will have been worked out with a maximum of participation by Senate members and will enjoy a maximum of support in that body.[47]

The explanation here for Ways and Means is somewhat different from Fenno's, but equally speculative. The reason the Senate does better in cases of conflict with the Ways and Means Committee is because politically Senate decisions are more in line with the demands of interest groups, lobbyists, and constituents than House decisions. Ways and Means decisions, made under the closed rule, tend to be less popular with relevant publics than Senate decisions. Some Ways and Means decisions suppose that the Senate will respond favorably to extra-congressional demands, but the job of Ways and Means, as the members see it, is to balance the fiscal realities with the plethora of demands for tax reductions or special provisions. This sometimes means denying popular demands, rejecting demands. made by those who are attuned to the tax-making process, leaving such matters to the Senate, or postponing such matters to members' bill time. The items in dispute between the House and Senate, therefore, tend to have strong interest group-lobbyist support or wide appeal to the electorate, and it is almost inevitable that some will survive the conference committee. If this line of reasoning is correct, the surprising thing about congressional tax decisions is not that the Senate does well vis-à-vis the House but that not more revenue is lost in the final decisions of the two bodies.[48]

SOCIAL SECURITY LEGISLATION. Since the end of World War II, Congress has passed nine major social security bills. A tenth bill, H.R. 11865 in 1964, died in conference when the House conferees refused to accept a Senate-passed medicare plan, and the Senate conferees refused to allow the existing program to be liberalized at the possible exclusion of medicare.

Social security legislation is both similar to and different from tax legislation. The similarity is that the Senate is more liberal than the

[47] *Ibid.*, pp. 668–69 (italics his).

[48] The delicate balance of most revenue bills is illustrated well by the 1950 excess profits tax bill. As passed by the Senate this bill raised more money than the House bill but the impact of the major revenue-producing change in the Senate was offset by six major revenue-losing changes and a number of similar miscellaneous changes. The total effect was a revenue gain but the sting of the bill was lessened by the Finance Committee. What is more, eleven floor amendments were adopted in the Senate for which no revenue estimates are available. It is safe to assume that these amendments did not raise anyone's taxes.

House in extending popular benefits to social security beneficiaries; the difference is that in the social security field the House is the dominant decision-making body with far less qualification than in revenue legislation.

Table 6.6 presents data on ten bills considered from 1950 to 1967. In seven of the ten bills the Senate liberalized the benefits package passed by the House, one bill passed the Senate with the same level of benefits, and in two cases the Senate bill was less costly than the House measure. In addition, the bill reported by the Finance Committee has tended to be liberalized on the Senate floor whereas House bills have been handled under closed rules.

TABLE 6.6

LEVEL-COST [a] OF SOCIAL SECURITY BILLS, 1950–1967

(PERCENTAGES)

Bill	Year	House	Finance Committee	Senate	Final
1. H.R. 6000	1950	6.25	6.10	6.00	6.05
2. H.R. 7800	1952	5.85	6.00	6.00[b]	5.85
3. H.R. 9366	1954	7.34	7.65	7.65[b]	7.50
4. H.R. 7225	1956	8.39	7.50	7.96	7.85
5. H.R. 13549	1958	8.76	8.76	8.76	8.76
6. H.R. 12580	1960	8.97	9.18	9.18[b]	8.98
7. H.R. 6027	1961	9.33	9.33	9.33[b]	9.35
8. H.R. 11865	1964	9.61	9.63	10.82	Died
9. H.R. 6675	1965	9.44	9.64	9.73	9.49
10. H.R. 12080	1967	9.70	9.95	10.27	9.72

SOURCE: Actuarial studies by Robert J. Myers, Chief Actuary, Social Security Administration. Data on House and Senate Finance Committee bills taken from the appropriate committee reports.

[a] Level-cost is a better measure than dollar amounts of payments because it relates future disbursements to future taxable payrolls over the period covered by the cost estimate. It is therefore expressed as a percentage of taxable payroll and it makes the House and Senate bills comparable by controlling for the fact that Senate bills may provide more payments in one year but no more over the long run.

[b] Amended on Senate floor but amendments had a relatively minor effect on cost.

Once again data are mixed; nevertheless there is a fairly clear tendency for the House to be dominant in social security policy, and, in general, the House's dominance has meant a more conservative program than the one supported by the Senate. Of the nine social security bills passed in this period, the Senate simply accepted the House version on one, four more were reconciled in conference closer to the House bill than the Senate, differences between the two bodies were almost nonexistent on one bill (H.R. 6027 in 1961), and in three cases the Senate version was closer to the final bill than the House version. The dominance of the House has been most pronounced on the six bills considered in the 1958–1967 period.

In general, the House has been stronger than the Senate in the social security field because of the self-financing nature of the social security program. Liberalization of benefits must be accompanied by increases in the social security tax or the wage base upon which the tax is levied or both. The House has been insistent on protecting the actuarial soundness of the program and in expanding benefits slowly to keep the tax burden of the program within limits. Few people are opposed to expanding benefits and the Senate has been inclined to take major steps forward in recent years with apparently less concern for keeping the tax low than the House. In one case, the Senate added floor amendments without providing the necessary financing; when this happens, the conference usually will turn out a final bill more liberal than the House bill but less liberal than the one passed by the Senate. In two of the ten cases the House was more liberal than the Senate, but normally the House has been less willing than the Senate to expand the program in popular — but costly — ways.

Another reason why the House position prevails in social security conferences is that — unlike tax bills — Ways and Means decisions have strong support inside and outside Congress, though not so strong as the Senate's. Ways and Means, though less liberal than the Senate, has not been niggardly in expanding benefits. Even the 1967 bill, with the last-minute opposition to the public welfare section, sailed through the House with little significant opposition. The objectionable part was buried under a 12.5 per cent across-the-board increase in benefits, a liberalized retirement test, liberalization of benefits for the disabled, and other attractive provisions.

TRADE LEGISLATION. Measuring House, Senate, and conference committee decisions on tax and social security legislation in dollars and cents ignores the fact that not all of the important policy questions are reflected in the revenue figures. The basic question of financing medicare under social security, for example, was primarily latent after the Truman administration because a majority consensus for the program existed in neither the House nor the Senate. When, in 1964, the Senate finally acted on the question before the House was realigned by the election that year, the Ways and Means conferees stood firm against the Senate amendment and the entire bill went down to defeat. For decisions like this, actuarial cost estimates hardly give the whole story.

But measurement problems in the revenue decisions of the House and Senate are small compared to the subjective judgments that have to be made in the field of trade policy. Since Congress gave up its tariff-making functions in 1934 the policy questions facing the House and Senate have centered around the kinds of administrative constraints to be placed on the executive branch in negotiating trade agreements. These constraints are, of course, intended to affect the nature of the trade agreements made by the executive branch, but they have been indirect influences on trade policy, and some have been of more symbolic consequence than real. Only within this context, therefore, does it make sense to talk about the House or Senate as the most protectionist or least protectionist body, and given the kinds of questions at issue it requires some imagination to use the term protectionist for either one.[49] Peril points, escape clauses, congressional vetoes, packing the Tariff Commission — all opposed by the advocates of free trade, all sought by protectionists — cannot begin to compete as influences on policy with the symbolic heat surrounding the debate that accompanied them.

This does not mean that the policy conflict over reciprocal trade during the past twenty years lacked substance. But the substance was out-matched by the rhetoric, an observation that one might not be able to make were it not for the fact that only once since World War II has a protectionist majority in the House *coincided* with a protectionist majority in the Senate. Both bodies have been inclined to protectionism but at different times.

Protectionists have generally fared better in the Senate, and, of special concern here, the Senate has at times fared better than the House in conference. As a result, several bills passed by Congress have been more protectionist than those reported by Ways and Means.

The Reciprocal Trade Act came up for renewal for the first time since World War II in 1948, the second session of the Republican-controlled 80th Congress. As could be expected from historic Re-

---

[49] Because the conflict has been over how free the executive branch should be in negotiating trade agreements, and how long it should be given the authority first ceded in 1934, a more accurate term for the policy questions before Congress would be restrictionist, not protectionist. The latter term is used because it is traditional but it should be read as meaning the degree to which restrictions are placed on the autonomy of the executive branch to negotiate trade agreements.

publican antipathy toward the program, broken only in 1943 when a two-year extension was voted with unusual Republican support, the Ways and Means Committee reported a bill far from that proposed by the Truman administration. The House bill was tempered in the Senate and the Senate bill became law. As remarked at the time:

> The bill which passed the House limited the President's authority more severely than the Senate version, which became law.
>
> It (1) precluded action by the President until the Commission had reported; (2) set no time limit for action by the Commission; (3) gave Congress the right to disapprove, within a specified period, any agreement which exceeded the Commission's recommended limits; (4) allowed a tariff increase up to 50 percent of the rate existing June 12, 1934 (Smoot-Hawley rates).
>
> In the House, most long-time opponents of the reciprocal trade program fought for passage of the bill, while Democratic members who had supported the program since 1934 took the attitude of "better no renewal than this." Voting was along party lines.
>
> In the Senate, where the measure was modified considerably, and where the bipartisan foreign policy carried more weight, most Democrats voted for the bill.[50]

As enacted, the 1948 law extended the program for only one year but the congressional veto was replaced by a requirement that the president explain to Congress the reasons why he did not follow the peril-point findings of the Tariff Commission, and a time limit was placed on Tariff Commission deliberations. The proponents of the program were not overjoyed with the final bill but found it was considerably better than the House measure.

The 1948 Act was short-lived. In 1949, the Democrats again controlled Congress and repealed the 1948 amendments. A simple three-year extension of the Act was voted by the House and the Senate passed the House measure unchanged. In the Senate the Republicans, led by Eugene Millikin of Colorado, fought hard for the retention of the peril-point provision but they had as much success as their protectionist colleagues in the House. All protectionist amendments were rejected in the Senate and the House bill became law without a conference.

[50] *Congressional Quarterly Almanac*, 1948, p. 190.

Peril points and other protectionist amendments were written into the Act two years later when both the House and Senate, in a rare joint venture, adopted amendments opposed by the administration.[51] In 1951 there were only 234 Democrats in the House compared to 263 two years earlier when the peril-point amendment was stricken from the bill. On the key vote the Ways and Means Democrats were defeated on the floor when forty-two Democrats, about half of them from the South, left the party and voted with one hundred and eighty-three Republicans for the Simpson peril-point amendment. The administration, of course, had the opportunity to appeal the House decisions in the Senate but, as CQ reports,

> The Senate Finance Committee April 26 unanimously approved the bill (HR 1612) extending the Administration's reciprocal trade agreements program, after it had written into the legislation numerous changes and restrictions even more stringent than the provisions adopted in the House.[52]

Three minor floor amendments — all supported by protectionists — were adopted on the Senate floor, and the conference committee, with some minor changes, generally followed the Senate version of the bill.[53]

In 1953, as in 1948, the Senate was less protectionist than the Republican-controlled House. After a struggle, the Eisenhower administration was able to get a one-year extension of the Act through the House at some cost, i.e., the addition of one member (presumably a protectionist) to the Tariff Commission. The Senate Finance Committee was more amenable to the administration proposal than the House and dropped the addition from the bill. Most important, the Senate position prevailed in the conference committee.[54]

The next year Congress and the Eisenhower administration postponed resolution of the conflict by agreeing to a one-year extension of the Act, amid rumors that the House Republicans had an understanding with Eisenhower that no new agreements would be negotiated in the interim. Only minor changes in the House bill were made in the Senate (an effort by Senate Democrats to give Eisenhower new three-year authority was defeated) and, with no major differences to resolve, the House bill became law.

[51] For this bill see *ibid.*, 1951, pp. 214–19.
[52] *Ibid.*, p. 218.
[53] *Ibid.*, p. 219.
[54] For these events see *ibid.*, 1953, pp. 216–17.

Senate protectionism, vocal but ineffectual since 1951 when a protectionist House bill was made more so in the Senate, returned in 1955 and reappeared in 1958. In 1955 the Senate position prevailed in conference with the House; in 1958 the reverse was true.

The 1955 Trade Act extension "was so riddled by amendments in the Senate that some people felt it was no longer a free trade measure; a New Deal Congressman who voted for the Cooper Bill voted against acceptance of the Conference Report for the reason that the revised bill was so restrictive and protectionist." [55] Thomas A. Jenkins (R., Ohio), an avowed protectionist, lauded the conference report as being much better than the bill passed by the House, while in the Senate Paul Douglas and others denounced the final bill as an abandonment of free trade.[56] The bill, which Eisenhower called a victory but free traders such as Senator Gore called a defeat, extended the president's trade agreement authority for three years and gave him new tariff-cutting authority, but also contained a number of restrictive amendments: it allowed the use of escape clauses when imports contributed substantially to serious injury to domestic industry, expanded peril-point and escape clause authority, tightened the president's authority to suspend agreements with countries that discriminated against United States goods, and authorized the president to restrict imports that impaired the national security.[57]

Confronted yearly by competing trade demands, Congress has responded one way one time, and a different way another time. Consistency is not always one of the legislative virtues if it means that some groups consistently do poorly in the legislative process. Protectionists have had a hard time of it since 1934, but in 1958 they scored well in the House, better in the Senate, and — unlike three years earlier — the House bill was generally accepted in conference. *Congressional Quarterly* may have described something basic to the legislative process when it summed up the process that led to the 1958 Trade Act:

> The House approved HR 1259 June 11 after rejecting by substantial margins a move to substitute the text of a highly restrictive bill by Rep. Richard M. Simpson (R., Pa.) and a motion by Rep. Daniel A. Reed (R., N.Y.) to recommit

[55] Lewis A. Dexter, "What Do Congressmen Hear: The Mail," *Public Opinion Quarterly*, XX (Spring, 1956), 26.
[56] *Congressional Quarterly Almanac*, 1955, p. 299.
[57] *Ibid.*, p. 289.

without instructions. But the Senate Finance Committee proceeded to rewrite the House-approved bill, cutting the five-year extension period to three years, barring the carryover of unused tariff reduction authority from year to year, and replacing the veto provision in the House bill with one requiring the President to get the assent of Congress each time he disapproved a Tariff Commission recommendation in "escape clause" cases.

This latter provision, strongly opposed by the Administration, was eliminated on the Senate floor before HR 12591 was approved July 22 as a three-year extension. The conference version, endorsed by both chambers and the President, reflected a further shift in the direction of increased legislative restraint on Executive authority in the field of trade policy. At the same time, Public Law 686 preserved the essential ingredients of the President's power to pursue a principal American foreign policy goal — the progressive lowering and moderation of barriers to the free flow of international trade.[58]

Protectionist strength in Congress, possibly attributable to the 1958 recession and an increase in unemployment, was probably related to the Ways and Means decision to incorporate in its bill, for the first time, a major protectionist item allowing a congressional veto (by two-thirds vote of both houses) of a presidential decision rejecting escape clause recommendations of the Tariff Commission. Except for the rejection of the Finance Committee amendment requiring positive congressional approval of the president's decision not to follow the Tariff Commission's judgment in escape clause cases, the protectionists did well in the Senate. Their gains, however, were lost in the conference. The final bill satisfied neither the protectionists nor the liberal traders, but it did satisfy enough members of the House to be adopted by a 161–56 division vote and enough Senators to pass on a 72–18 roll call. CQ, quoting the leading free trade organization, summed up the bill: "Although the final version was closer to the House bill, a CNTP [Committee for a National Trade Policy] spokesman still called it 'the most highly protectionist measure ever passed by Congress in all the reciprocal trade renewals since 1934.' "[59]

Four years later Congress all but reversed the protectionism of the 1950's by passing the Trade Expansion Act of 1962. House and

[58] *Ibid.*, 1958, p. 166.
[59] *Ibid.*, p. 175.

Senate versions of this bill were so similar that the conference committee took only one day to reconcile differences. It is, therefore, difficult to say which body won more in conference but the final bill was, except for a few protectionist features added in the Senate, the same bill developed in the Ways and Means Committee. The Finance Committee was unusually receptive to the administration-approved House bill: "The basic authorities sought by the Administration emerged from the Committee intact. *This was a reversal of the Committee's role, in prior years, as the Congressional body that wrote the most 'protectionism' into trade bills.*" [60] A study of the two bills revealed no evidence to dispute the following summary of *CQ*:

> Conferees representing the Senate Finance Committee and House Ways and Means Committee resolved all House-Senate differences on the trade bill in a Sept. 26 meeting. Major actions taken by the conferees were to agree with the House in suspending most-favored-nation treatment to Poland and Yugoslavia, to return to the Administration and House language in dealing with the European Common Market, and to retain, in somewhat diluted form, most of the discretionary powers the Senate gave the President to retaliate against foreign import restrictions.[61]

The trade decisions of Congress since 1948 have been reviewed to see if any patterns exist in the decisions of the House and Senate and, if so, to explain them. Some regularity in the decisions made by the two legislative chambers was found, but not much. The striking thing about congressional trade decisions is their diversity — the way the policy outcomes of one body are balanced by the other and how the thrust of decisions one year is changed two or three years later. Moreover, if recent protectionist stirrings in Congress mean anything, the 1962 Trade Expansion Act, which appeared to take Congress further out of the picture than ever, may prove to be merely a phase in the process rather than a permanent policy fixture.

Other studies have attempted to explain the changing reaction of Congress to the trade program,[62] but the primary concern of this study is with whatever order is discernible in policy decisions where

---

[60] *Ibid.*, 1962, p. 280. (Italics added.)
[61] *Ibid.*, p. 284.
[62] Bauer, Pool, and Dexter, *op. cit.*

the House and Senate have formed almost every possible combination: House more/less protectionist than the Senate and the House wins/loses in conference, plus agreement between the two bodies with no changes made in the Senate.

Amidst the diversity, one fairly regular pattern emerges: the Senate is more protectionist than the House. Of the eight major trade bills since 1945 the Senate has passed essentially the same bill as the House three times: 1949, 1954, and 1962. In 1962 there were many, but for the most part minor, differences between the two bills; the one major difference, extending most-favored-nation treatment to Poland and Yugoslavia, was settled the House way by forbidding such action. On three of the five major bills left that were passed in different form by the House and Senate, the Senate bill was notably more protectionist than the House. The Acts of 1951, 1955, and 1958 were all more agreeable to protectionists as they left the Senate than as passed by the House. Two of the five Acts liberalized in the Senate were the 1948 and 1953 measures, products of the protectionist Republican majority on Ways and Means. The generalization that the Senate is more inclined toward protectionism than the House, though subject to serious qualification, takes on considerably more strength when the post-1962 protectionist moves, most of which originated in the Senate, are considered.

Available evidence shows that in four of the five cases the Senate version of the legislation was closer to the final bill than the House version. In 1948 the Senate prevailed on the central question of the congressional veto; in 1951 the protectionist House bill was made more protectionist in the Senate; in 1953 the Senate won on the question of expanding the Tariff Commission; and in 1956 several protectionist Senate amendments were written into the law. Only in 1958 when the House passed the most protectionist bill ever passed under Democratic control did the House bill clearly emerge from the conference committee in better shape than the Senate bill. In 1962, as noted previously, the House was also the dominant policy-maker, in part because the Senate voted few important changes in the House bill, and in part because these protectionist changes were overshadowed by the magnitude of the bill's liberal trade features.

Why is the Senate more protectionist than the House, and why does the Senate do better in conference than the House? The Senate is generally more responsive to the demands of interest groups, lobbyists, and constituents than the House. Group activity on behalf of free or unfettered reciprocal trade has generally been less intense than protectionist activity,[63] and the Senate — unless the House passes a protectionist bill — has acted in accordance with these demands. Interest groups, lobbyists, and protectionist constituency interests have been largely unsatisfied on the House side; appeals are then made to the Senate; and because the great bulk of the appeals are for more protection, not freer trade, the Senate decisions have normally been in the direction of protection. Congress, one study found, seems to receive more mail from protectionist businessmen than from liberal trade sources,[64] and if these interests are aggregated anywhere it is more likely to be in the Senate than in the House.

Despite the facts that in two cases the Senate was dominant in conference when it passed a less protectionist bill than the House and that in one case the House was dominant in conference even though the Senate bill was more protectionist than the House bill, there may still be, under certain conditions, a relationship between Senate protectionism and Senate dominance in conference. In 1958 the Ways and Means Committee prevailed over the Senate but the Senate might well have prevailed if the Committee had not passed a protectionist bill of its own. Three years earlier the Senate amended the House bill along protectionist lines; plausibly, the Senate amendments survived the conference because the House bill was not reflective of the intensity of protectionist demands. Indeed, on this occasion there was so much dissatisfaction with the Ways and Means bill that the closed rule was almost voted down. With protectionist demands at their peak and House demands for changes in the program so great that Speaker Rayburn had to make an unusual appeal to get the House to accept the closed rule,[65] it is not surprising that

[63] A content analysis of the public hearings before the Ways and Means Committee since 1934 shows that typically opponents of the Reciprocal Trade Act outnumber proponents. See James Walter Lindeen, "Interest Group Behavior Toward Reciprocal Trade Agreements Legislation in the House Committee on Ways and Means, 1934–1962," unpublished paper read at the 1968 Annual Meeting of the Midwest Political Science Association, Chicago, May, 1968.

[64] Bauer, Pool, and Dexter, *op. cit.*, pp. 209–13.

[65] Rayburn's plea was followed by the adoption of the closed rule by one vote. After the House had voted to consider an open rule he declared that "the House on this last vote has done a most unusual and under the circumstances a very dangerous thing. . . . Only once in the history of the House in 42 years in my memory has a bill of this kind and character been considered except under a closed rule. How long it is going to take, how far afield you will go, I do not know. . . . So as an old friend to all of you, as a lover of the House of Representatives and its procedures, I ask you to vote down this amendment offered by the gentleman from Ohio [Mr. Brown]." *Congressional Record*, February 17, 1955, p. 1678.

the Senate bill was accepted in conference. There was too much support for the Senate amendments inside and outside Congress for the
Ways and Means bill to be adopted without change.

It is not possible to go beyond these qualified generalizations about
the making of trade policy without imparting more order to the
process than there is. Ways and Means, with a consciously constructed Democratic majority in favor of the reciprocal trade program, is probably not as reflective of protectionist strength in the
House as the Finance Committee is in the Senate. Extra-congressional demands for protection are therefore more likely to be aggregated in the Senate, especially in light of the closed rule that makes
Ways and Means even less sensitive to protectionist demands than it
would normally be, given Democratic recruitment to the Committee.
To the extent that these factors influence outcomes they mean that
the Senate bill is more likely to reflect protectionist demands and
that some protectionism — though not much — will be written into
the law through the conduit of the Senate.

The symbolic nature of the issues involved in trade legislation must
be recognized.[66] The congressional conflict over trade policy takes
place within a consensus that Congress is not going to raise or lower
the tariff on anything. Trade politics falls in the regulatory policy
arena, to use Lowi's typology, not in the distributive or redistributive
arenas.[67] Because the issues are regulatory, the relationship between
any given issue and policy outcomes tends to be amorphous. The
great trade battles in Congress have an unreal air about them and
the policy consequences of having one side or the other win are by
no means clear, which might explain why Congress is less consistent
in the trade area than in taxes or social security legislation. Once the
basic question of who was to set tariff rates was answered, as many
observers have noted, whether the House or Senate was more receptive to procedural protection mattered little; therefore vigorous contests could be waged over the escape clause and peril points, only to
have President Eisenhower suggest the retention of both in his 1955
message. The nature of the stakes was fully revealed when in 1962
the major protectionist gain to date, the 1958 provision for a congressional veto of presidential escape clause decisions,[68] was made more

---

[66] For a general treatment see Murray Edelman, *The Symbolic Uses of Politics*
(Urbana: University of Illinois Press, 1964).

[67] Theodore J. Lowi, "American Business, Public Policy, Case-Studies, and
Public Policy," *World Politics*, XVII (July, 1964), 713.

[68] Mills refuted the protectionist charge that the congressional veto was a

protectionist by lowering the needed majority from two-thirds of both houses to a majority, and requiring at the same time approval of the motion by the Ways and Means and Finance Committees, a most unlikely possibility. Until the 1962 Act, Congress incrementally expanded the president's authority to reduce tariffs with one hand while it made protectionist gestures with the other. In 1962 the president was granted the largest tariff-reducing authority in history along with some unsought and largely meaningless authority to protect domestic producers.

SUMMARY: RECENT HOUSE DOMINANCE IN CONFERENCE. The Senate does better in conference than one might expect from interviews with the members of the Ways and Means Committee. The great majority of Ways and Means members feel that the House position will prevail on most of the important disagreements with the Senate. But policy outcomes over the past 20 years show that the House conferees have not always won the important disputes.

This finding does not mean that the contemporary Committee members are "wrong." Because they feel that they do most of the hard work on the legislation and that the Senate only loads their bills with easily removed "decorations," it is natural that they would see their bills emerging from the conference committee.

The interviews were conducted for this study when the House position on major legislation held up very well in conference. The Trade Expansion Act, the 1964 Revenue Act, the Excise Tax Reduction Act of 1965, Medicare, and the 1967 Social Security Amendments all were major pieces of legislation shaped largely in the House and when enacted into law were very similar to the House bills. On occasion, as Russell Long commented about medicare, the House conferees took a hard line on Senate amendments and word probably filtered back to Committee members: "Frankly, I have sometimes gained the impression in conference with some of the senior House Members that they would be opposed . . . to the great compromise, even, that brought this Union into being and created the United States Senate." [69]

In supporting their bill in conference the Ways and Means conferees have additional strength because their bill has been passed by

paper tiger, saying he had great confidence in the ability of Congress to employ the veto, but as of 1969 no use of the provision had ever been made. *Congressional Quarterly Almanac*, 1958, p. 174.
[69] *Ibid.*, 1965, p. 238.

the House without amendments. Chairman Mills on at least one occasion has assured the House members that if they refrained from amending the bill the Senate would not be allowed to succeed in passing popular tax cuts:

> There was, as I say, interest in the committee for giving consideration to a great number of these taxes, but the committee restrained itself on the specific assurance that if we would report this as a straight extension the administration would oppose moves to add any amendments that would reduce the revenues. Thus we were assured that the administration, certainly, will oppose amendments and I will assure the House, here and now, I will endeavor to maintain the House position, if I get into a conference, because I do not want the House to be put in a position of not being able to exercise its will with respect to some of these proposed reductions and then have to take something because it was put on somewhere else. I think our conference committee will certainly desire to protect the membership.[70]

As a Republican member of Ways and Means observed:

> For Wilbur Mills to maintain his image on what he sold the House, to be a big man over here, he has to send back what the House passed. He's sold the House so he can't go back on it in conference or in a couple of years he'll lose the confidence of the House, what he's built up. He's sold himself in the House over the years like no one else, and he's sold them on the legislation, and he has to stand by them.

Thus to some extent the closed rule both helps Ways and Means maintain its bill against Senate amendments and forces the Committee to place some limits on what it accepts in conference. For some House demands, the Senate may be held out as affording an opportunity to seek amendments not contained in the bill reported by Ways and Means,[71] but in many cases the House conferees hold firm

---

[70] *Congressional Record*, June 8, 1959, p. 10177.

[71] The following colloquy between Mills and Ohio Republican William Ayres over a tax problem facing the Akron, Canton and Youngstown Railroad is a good example: "*Mr. Ayres.* Even though they have sought relief in the courts, and the courts have ruled in their favor, they still will be forced to pay the $100,000 which it is estimated they would owe? *Mr. Mills.* They will be required to be treated as any other railroad will be treated under the provision if they elect to come in under section 1. *Mr. Ayres.* Under the provisions of that admendment, there is no way possible to exclude them? That would have to be done in the

against Senate action. If the House conferees want to be adamant it is probably useful to have members vocally opposing "nongermane" amendments, as Curtis did. One conferee, in fact, made this very point although he felt that Curtis's position had been a little too rigid:

> Well, I agree with Tommy that we have to keep a tight rein on them, we can't let them get out of control. But what the hell, the practicalities of the situation are that you have to make some *concessions to the system*. It's nice to have someone like Tommy around to keep a rein on them but I don't agree that every amendment has to be absolutely germane, like Tommy.

In explaining why the House or the Senate "wins" in conference, such matters as the extent to which a bill reflects the wishes of interest groups, lobbyists, and constituents are seen as more important than the technical expertise of one group of conferees as opposed to another. House conferees have usually spent more time studying the legislation and probably know the details better than the Senators who, after all, have more demands on their time than House members. But although technical ability and staff assistance enter into the decisions of conference committees [72] and may give the House some advantage, an understanding of the policies at stake does not necessarily require the ability to answer all the objections to those policies. If the House does better than the Senate in some cases, and

---

other body? *Mr. Mills.* It will have to be done in the other body, and while the gentleman is on his feet let me say that I hope the constituent to who he refers will take advantage of an opportunity of stating his case when the matter is taken up in the committee of another body. Frankly, I was not in a position to go along with the case they presented, but upon consideration by another body there is always the possibility, of course, that the other body might find itself amenable to going along. Whether it will, I do not know, of course. *Mr. Ayres.* I know the high esteem in which we hold the chairman of the Committee on Ways and Means. *Mr. Mills.* I thank the gentleman. *Mr. Ayres.* And I appreciate his comments here today and I want to make clear then that in your judgment it would be possible for the other body to give the Akron, Canton & Youngstown Railroad relief in this particular instance. *Mr. Mills.* I cannot go that far. I do not speak for the other body. I am suggesting that your constituents go to the committee in the other body and state your constituent's case to the other body so that it can be again considered over there in connection with this bill. *Mr. Ayres.* I thank the gentleman." *Ibid.*, January 28, 1958, pp. 1211–12.

[72] Russell Long has used the technical superiority of the House conferees to explain why some Senate provisions have been removed in conference. *Congressional Record*, April 20, 1966 (daily edition), p. 8240.

if the Senate does better than the House in other cases, the explanation probably lies more in the policy preferences of those involved in the legislation — including extra-congressional groups and individuals — than the substantive expertise or lack of it of the conferees.

CONSERVATIVE CONTROL OF THE CONFERENCE

After eighteen years in the Senate, the leading spokesman for tax reform, Paul Douglas, summed up his long fight for changes in the Internal Revenue Code: "I began my senatorial career in a quandary and when I left, the quandary was even bigger than when I started." [73] Douglas and his associates in the 1950's and 1960's made some progress reforming the Code, but, the former Illinois Democrat writes: "Despite all our efforts, the brutal fact must be admitted. We have largely failed." [74]

Few questions considered by the Ways and Means Committee are as difficult to treat objectively as the liberal efforts to reform the tax law. Simply using the term "reform" for the goals of the liberals connotes either a preference for their objectives or ignorance of the cliche that one man's tax reform is another man's equity. The complexity of this issue was manifest during a 1967 Rules Committee meeting when a Democratic member of Rules, in the course of imploring Chairman Mills to do something about tax reform, drew a distinction between "good" loopholes and "bad" loopholes. Mills promptly invited the member to testify before the Ways and Means Committee on good and bad loopholes. The incident reveals a fundamental ambivalence in the whole issue of tax reform that has contributed greatly to the maintenance of the status quo on major "loopholes" and, probably, to the slow but steady erosion of the tax base through the enactment of "special tax provisions." [75]

The issue of tax reform is raised here because the relationship between the two congressional tax committees has been of key importance in perpetuating the "conservative control" of tax policy. On these grounds, the conference committee warrants close attention and analysis.

Before turning to the conference committee it should be empha-

[73] Paul H. Douglas, "The Problem of Tax Loopholes: Or My 18 Years in a Quandary," *The American Scholar* (Winter, 1967–68), p. 38.

[74] *Ibid.*, 39.

[75] Stanley S. Surrey, "The Congress and the Tax Lobbyist — How Special Tax Provisions Get Enacted," *Harvard Law Review*, LXX (May, 1957), 1145–82.

sized that the policy stakes of the tax reform issue are very high, as shown by data gathered by Rep. Herbert Tenzer (D., N.Y.) and presented to the Ways and Means Committee in 1967:

1. In 1964, thirty-five individual tax returns were filed with adjusted gross incomes of $500,000 or more on which no federal income tax was paid.
2. Also in 1964, 24,084 individuals with adjusted gross incomes in excess of $10,000 paid no federal income tax.
3. The twenty-two largest oil companies in 1964 had a gross profit of $5,179,036,000 and paid $240,529,000 (or 4 per cent) in federal taxes.

Perhaps most interesting, one oil company in 1964 paid no taxes on a gross profit of more than $29 million and in fact received a credit of over $7 million.[76]

The recruitment criteria used for the Ways and Means Committee are likely to turn up pragmatic men, moderate in style, with a conspicuous absence of any tendency to launch a crusade against alleged tax inequities. The leading member who in personal philosophy and public statements most closely resembles the type of liberal reformer found on the Senate Finance Committee is Mills himself,[77] but in practice he has disappointed at least one of them: "Wilbur Mills has always been for reform right up to the opening day of Congress. . . . He pulled this three or four times until he found out he couldn't fool anyone anymore." This statement, whether an accurate assessment of Mills or not, indicates that until 1969 not much steam for tax reform came from the House.

Recruitment to the Senate Finance Committee complements that of Ways and Means. Extreme liberals have had a very hard time getting appointed to the Finance Committee, and, although the conservative hold on Finance has weakened, it has by no means been broken.

"I could have had the Capitol dome if I gave up my interest in getting on Finance," said a Senate Democratic liberal who made it to the Finance Committee after years of trying. "The lobbyists in Washington would have done anything to keep me off the Finance

[76] House, Committee on Ways and Means, "Hearings on the President's 1967 Tax Proposals," 90th Cong., 1st Sess., 1967, I, pp. 287–301.
[77] See Mills's plea for tax reform, "Are You a Pet or a Patsy," *Life*, November 23, 1959, p. 51 ff.

Committee. . . . And I've been driving them crazy ever since just to prove to them how right they were." To get on Finance he said, "You have to be approved by the oil interests,[78] the insurance interests." When asked if any other "interests" got involved he declared, "Yes, all the big interests." Another Senator had "tremendous trouble. I applied I don't know how many times and they kept moving people in front of me to keep me off. Oil interests primarily." "They also put the most pliant, the most compliant men on Finance," he continued, "men who are likely to bend, to be here, there, everywhere." Another Democrat said the Finance Committee "has never been known for an overabundance of flaming liberals. George, Millikin, Byrd, Malone, Frear, that sort of person." Asked what other than one's stand on the oil depletion allowance comes into play, he said, "Talk to Bill Proxmire. He tried like hell to get on but they forced Bill Fulbright to give up a committee he liked to go on a committee he didn't want to block Proxmire."

If the Democrats who control committee assignments prefer a Fulbright to a Proxmire their Republican counterparts are no less careful about who goes on the Finance Committee: conservatives who are not likely to upset the status quo on tax matters.

It's an "invisible, unspoken" thing one Republican Senator explained; "labels are always relative but by and large the Republican party is the conservative party . . . and I suppose that if the balance in the party shifted it would change on these two committees too." Said another:

> Let me give you an example. If Senator Javits, or a liberal Republican like him, wanted to go on the Finance Committee. . . . Well, let me give you a specific example from the other side. Senator Clark wants to get on the Finance Committee, and say Harry Byrd doesn't want a liberal like him to get on. Byrd goes to Fulbright and asks him to use

[78] Paul Douglas writes: "Indeed, I sometimes suspected that the major qualification for most aspirants for membership on the Finance Committee was a secret pledge or agreement to defend the depletion allowance against all attacks. I suspected, also, that campaign funds reinforced these pledges." *Op. cit.*, p. 30. Senator Albert Gore, who was Douglas's main collaborator on tax reform, writes of the oil lobby: "The oil and gas lobby, with the vast amounts of money at its disposal, is, I believe, the most diabolical influence at work in the nation's capitol. It has for years succeeded in blocking the assignment of public-spirited members to the tax-writing committees of House and Senate, and also intervened in the election of leaders and assistant leaders of both Houses." See Albert Gore, "How to Be Rich Without Paying Taxes," *The New York Times Magazine*, April 11, 1965, p. 86.

his seniority to block Clark. . . . Now on the Republican side I am sure that the same thing happens. Senator Dirksen went on Finance and I can't recall exactly who he blocked but I'm sure it was somebody.

"You will find, if you talk to them, that they want someone who they consider sound — quote, unquote. Whether we really are is another question. Someone who is sound, who is responsible, conservative, and a good *party* man. They view the Committee as one of the last strongholds against the excesses from downtown," said a Republican recruited by the conservative leaders in the Senate. "Some of my friends, my conservative friends, came to me and told me that Javits wanted to get on Finance and that I had to stop him. Man, they didn't want Javits on there." "Oil has been over-represented on the Committee," he observed. "As for business in general, as I said the Republicans put people on who are sound or responsible and they are going to tend to support the status quo on tax reforms. I think it's clear that business does have a large voice, I'd have to say that."

With such recruitment patterns, the bipartisan, conservative coalition has dominated the Finance Committee for many years. One liberal Democrat observed: "I think it was George Norris who said that the liberals would have to win every election for twelve years before there would be any liberal tax reforms because that's how long it would take to reform the Finance Committee. You know it's a conservative committee, more conservative than the Senate." [79] In his view, "all the Republicans are impossible, just impossible. Byrd and Smathers will vote with the Republicans and then they can usually pick off enough other votes. . . . It's a rotten mess. Very few are interested in the public welfare, very few."

On key votes, the members of Finance report, the split runs along liberal and conservative lines, not straight party lines, with the liberals on the low end of the count. "There's not any partisanship on the Finance Committee in the sense of Democrats against Republicans. There the issue is between the interests and the public interest, and usually it's the interests that win." A conservative member confirmed the voting pattern, if not the inference from it: "You seldom have a vote on which all the Republicans will line up on one side and all the Democrats will line up on the other. Seldom. Come to think of it,

[79] According to presidential support scores, the Finance Committee Democrats and Republicans supported the president less than any committee in the Senate in the 87th Congress. See Froman, *op. cit.*, pp. 203–04.

I can't think of one vote like that since I've been a member of the committee, not one." "On some of these welfare measures we get a liberal-conservative split. You know the chairman [Byrd] is almost always on the Republican side." A colleague sized up the situation: "Most of the time the six of us hold together solid, and on a real controversial vote we can usually get Byrd, Talmadge, and sometimes Smathers and Long." Former chairman Byrd voted with the Republicans so often "it got to be something of a joke on the Committee."

If liberal reformers on the Finance Committee have been a distinct minority, they have sometimes succeeded in getting their amendments accepted by the Senate and then, they feel, the conservative-dominated conference committee has plucked the hard-won amendments from the bill. Speaking of Paul Douglas, a conservative Senator confirmed the liberal complaint: "I don't mean to say that Paul isn't thorough but some of his amendments are on the extreme liberal side, and we pick them out pretty well. And it doesn't bother me at all, you know." With the bill purified, or picked clean, depending on your point of view, the conservative conferees return to the Senate bemoaning the adamancy of the House conferees who would not allow the Senate amendment. So say the liberals; more important, so say some of the conservatives.

A conservative admitted the liberal charge that the Senate conferees do not work hard for liberal amendments: "Time after time they will get an amendment in, either in the Committee or on the floor, and it will be dropped in conference. Happens all the time. They say once Byrd hits the rotunda he drops the amendment. . . . The old man says, 'Oh no, House wouldn't give in.' Well, of course, he doesn't fight too hard anyway." Byrd used to "drop amendments on his way to conference. He's not for them. . . ." And he revealed the relationship between roll call votes and the conference committee when he said of floor strategy:

> Well, I'll go over to Long, or Smathers, or someone and tell them which amendments they had better accept without a vote so they can be junked in conference. I did this on the tax bill last year (1964). If you know an amendment will pass you don't want a roll call because that makes it harder to drop in conference. Get a voice or division then you can drop it easier.

With the conservatives admitting that they "pick them out pretty well," and that they sometimes follow the strategy of avoiding roll call votes so popular amendments which they do not like can be removed in conference, the accuracy of the liberal protests is hard to refute. "You can shadow box all you want on the floor, but the conference writes the legislation," a conservative said. A liberal who complained that his amendments never emerged from conference probably agreed: "My God, yes. I don't keep a diary, I sometimes wish I did, so I have to rely on memory, but many, many times. The Finance Committee is more conservative than the Senate, and the conferees are the most conservative members!"

With an issue as controversial as tax reform and with conflicting opinions about the motives and activities of the antagonists, conflict in the Senate has tended to exceed generally accepted norms about the proper conduct of legislative business. Paul Douglas once charged the Finance Committee with falling into "loose procedures on these bills rushed through at the end of the session," only to have Finance Committee Chairman Harry Byrd file an unprecedented statement defending the Committee against the charge and noting that Douglas voted against all the last-minute bills except one that affected Illinois.[80] An even more delicate exchange took place on the Senate floor when Senator Joseph Clark offered an amendment dealing with tax deductions for business expense allowances. Byrd offered to take the amendment to conference but Clark pressed for a roll call vote on the amendment anyway. Their colloquy shows that on the tax issue the celebrated comity of the Senate can break down.

> *Mr. Clark.* Mr. President, if the opponents are prepared to yield back the remainder of their time, I am prepared to yield back the remainder of my time. The yeas and nays have been ordered, so I call for a vote.
> *Mr. Byrd of Virginia.* Mr. President, it is customary . . . .
> *Mr. Bennett.* Mr. President, if the chairman of the committee is willing to take the amendment to conference, it is customary, at least in the Senate, to trust the conferees.
> *Mr. Clark.* I trust the conferees implicitly. I should simply like to show the other body to what extent the Senate is in favor of my amendment; therefore, I must insist on the yeas and nays.
> *Mr. Byrd of Virginia.* I thought I was being helpful.
> *Mr. Smathers.* I recommend, then, that the Senator from

---

[80] Senate Finance Committee, S. Rept. No. 2109 to accompany H.R. 8952, 87th Cong., 2d Sess., 1962, pp. 31–32.

Virginia withdraw his willingness to accept the amendment
and that the yea-and-nay vote be in order. I, for one, would
support the principle, but I would not support the amendment as it is now drawn.

Mr. Byrd of Virginia. I have been both the chairman of
the committee and a member of the committee for 26 years.
I do not ever recall a similar situation, when the chairman
was willing to take an amendment to conference; and then
the sponsor of the amendment demanded a yea-and-nay
vote.

Mr. Clark. The debate has indicated clearly that a number of Senators do not agree with the chairman. I should
like to see what the vote will be.

Mr. Byrd of Virginia. Then I withdraw my offer to accept
the amendment and take it to conference.[81]

Clark lost the vote.

Senate liberals lost more in 1959 than the vote on the Clark
amendment. The debate on these losses reveals the crucial importance of the conference committee in making final determinations on
key policy proposals. The conservative majority on the Finance Committee was attacked numerous times on the Senate floor for failing
to defend the Senate bill — specifically, liberal amendments that they
opposed — as strongly as they should. The liberals, it is true, had little
success, but much can be learned about the relationship between the
Senate and the House from the liberals' largely futile efforts.

On the first bill, H.R. 7523, the Tax Rate Extension Act of 1959,
Mills promised the House that no Senate amendments would be
accepted.

Russell Long opened the attack on the conference report. Five
amendments, two of them Long's, had been passed in the Senate, and
Long objected strongly to the fact that before the House-Senate conferees had met for forty minutes a Senate conferee moved to accept
the House position on the amendments.[82] Not only that, claimed
Long, but the Senate conferees were representative of the Senate
neither in numbers (four Democrats and three Republicans although
the Senate was two-thirds Democratic) nor on the substantive issues
involved. Speaking of an amendment offered by Eugene McCarthy
that repealed the dividend credit (long a target for tax reformers)

81 *Congressional Record*, June 25, 1959, p. 11899.
82 *Ibid.*, p. 12047.

and of his own amendments liberalizing various parts of the social security program, Long said:

> After the Senate labored from 9:30 on Thursday morning until 1:30 on Friday morning, it finally agreed to two amendments, here on the floor. One of those amendments was submitted by the Senator from Minnesota [Mr. McCarthy]. His amendment was a very significant one. It provided for taking away certain tax advantages in the case of those who hold corporation stock. The Senate previously had voted for a similar amendment, as a result of which the House version of the bill was watered down, and only about half as much advantage was given to corporate stockholders as the House version of the bill would have given them. In this instance, the Senate voted by a substantial majority to take away the advantage which remained to corporate stockholders, bondholders and others.
>
> *Mr. Douglas.* The vote was 47 to 31.
>
> *Mr. Long.* Yes; and in the Senate that is a very one-sided vote.
>
> It is significant to note that although that amendment was agreed to by a vote of 47 to 31, in the conference committee the chairman of the committee, the Senator from Virginia [Mr. Byrd], and the three Republican conferees on the part of the Senate — the Senator from Maryland [Mr. Butler], the Senator from Delaware [Mr. Williams] and the Senator from Utah [Mr. Bennett] all voted against the amendment. The three Democratic conferees on the part of the Senate — the Senator from Oklahoma [Mr. Kerr], the Senator from Delaware [Mr. Frear] and the Senator from Louisiana [Mr. Long] voted for the amendment. But on that important and significant amendment, the Senate conferees were divided 4 to 3 against the position which had been taken by the Senate.
>
> The Senate had adopted another significant amendment; it was in the nature of a rider which was offered by me. In the conference committee, the chairman of the Senate committee had voted against the amendment, and the Senator from Delaware [Mr. Williams], the Senator from Utah [Mr. Bennett], and the Senator from Maryland [Mr. Butler] also voted against the amendment, although the Senator from Oklahoma [Mr. Kerr], the Senator from Delaware [Mr. Frear], and the Senator from Louisiana [Mr. Long] voted for it. So on the second major amendment, the Senate conferees also voted 4 to 3 against the position which had been taken

by the Senate — and which had been taken by the Senate
on a yea-and-nay vote.[83]

Despite his revelation that at least one Senate conferee did not
feel bound to defend the Senate position (at least not as firmly as
Long would have liked), the Louisiana Democrat did not explicitly
charge that the Senate conferees had failed to represent the Senate
majority. He argued, rather, that all the House conferees had to do
to know they could win was look at how the majority of the Senate
conferees had voted on the amendments at issue, and wait for the
Senate to recede.[84] However, at least one Senator, Robert Kerr, saw
in Long's remarks the implication that the Senate conferees "without
undue effort to represent the position of the Senate, either participated in a farce, encouraged one, or permitted one." [85] Kerr stressed
the other side of the picture, namely, the House conferees *had* been
adamant, and Senator Byrd took the same tack in defense of the conference report. Byrd also noted that one of the House conferees even
refused to sign the conference report because not all of the Senate
amendments had been dropped.[86]

After an extended debate, and many denials that any criticism of
the Senate conferees was implied in the statement that Senate conferees, as provided in the rules of the Senate, should represent the
majority view of the Senate, the conference report was adopted on a
57–35 roll call vote. The point had been made, however, that on some
issues the conferees of the Senate should be chosen on grounds other
than seniority, and that regardless of the need to extend the taxes before the expiration date, some members of the Senate felt strongly
enough about the amendments to make a floor fight for them. This
caused a greater storm over the closed rule in the Senate than there
had been in the House, with Long and others arguing that if the
Senate capitulated on this issue they would, in effect, be letting the
House invoke a closed rule on the Senate. None of the arguments —
maintenance of the institutional integrity of the Senate, the Senate
rule providing that conferees represent the Senate majority, the claim
that rejection of the conference report would not imply repudiation
of the conferees, or the claim that the McCarthy amendment would
both close a tax loophole and gain over $300 million in revenue — led

[83] *Ibid.*, p. 12047.
[84] *Ibid.*, p. 12049.
[85] *Ibid.*, p. 12057.
[86] *Ibid.*, p. 12068.

to the rejection of the conference report, but the Senate had come close to disintegrating over the issue.

The handling of the conference report on H.R. 7523 in the House also offers some insight into the politics of conference committees. The Senate amendments had support in the House as well as in the Senate. One amendment, in particular, had strong support from Western members of the House. Edith Green (D., Ore.) inserted a letter to Mills signed by twenty-five House members urging the House conferees to accept the amendment repealing the 10 per cent tax on transportation they felt discriminated against the West. The conference report merely cut the tax to 5 per cent effective in 1960. Thus to members who were worried about the revenue loss if excise taxes were cut Mills could say that H.R. 7523 as reported from conference had no impact on revenues in FY 1960 (the tax on local telephone service was repealed but not until 1960), and the House could take another look at the fiscal situation next year and decide whether it wanted to extend the tax. And to those who wanted the transportation excise removed, Mills could say that half of it would be removed as of the next year. The rationale behind this balancing act was articulated by the ranking Republican on Ways and Means, Richard Simpson (Pa.), who recalled the "act of total forbearance on the part of the membership of the House in offering any amendments to this urgent legislation because of the recognized need of the Federal Government for the revenue involved." [87] With Mills claiming that the bill reported from conference was essentially the same as the bill passed by the House, the conference report was adopted — in sharp contrast to the Senate — by voice vote with little conflict.

Conflict between the Senate majority and the Finance Committee conferees was not the dominant element in 1959, however. On the contrary, several weeks later the same Senators who had been critical of the conference report on H.R. 7523 heaped praise on Byrd and the other conferees for successfully defending a Senate amendment on another bill in conference despite their opposition to it when it was offered in the Senate.[88] The year ended on a peaceful note. Still, liberals in the Senate had assaulted the tradition of choosing conferees from the senior members of the committees, they had prepared memoranda defending their position, and they had served notice that the continuation of the old norms regarding conference committees

[87] *Ibid.*, p. 12104.
[88] *Ibid.*, September 12, 1959, pp. 19260–62.

were dependent, for them, upon the outcomes of the conference committee discussions. Senators Long and McCarthy had lost amendments in conference, but only after an unusually disruptive conflict in the Senate.

The next year, Senate liberals put on another major drive behind Senate-approved, conference-dropped amendments. The 4 per cent dividend credit was again repealed by the Senate, and again the House conferees prevailed in conference. Tax deductions for certain business expenses were outlawed in the Senate, and the conference agreed to have the complex question studied by the Joint Committee on Internal Revenue Taxation and directed the Treasury Department to report on its activities to curb the abuses. Major liberalizations in social security were made in the Senate and unmade in conference. Not surprisingly, vigorous protests were made in the Senate; not surprisingly, the conservative majority won.

The business expense deduction amendment, offered by Senator Joseph Clark, was, according to Russell Long who refused to sign the conference report, "torpedoed" in the conference committee by the Treasury Department. Long recognized the problems of distinguishing a legitimate business expense from entertainment expenses that, it was claimed, were being deducted by certain businessmen, but he argued that Senator Clark should have been allowed to defend his amendment in the conference just as the Treasury Department officials were present to raise objections to it.[89] Clark, who revealed that he had received covert assistance from some Treasury employees who were "shocked" by the Department's position,[90] deplored the conference committee decision on expense account spending, but to no avail. Clark was supported by William Proxmire who, on the basis of a study by the Library of Congress, argued that the Senate has always been free to amend House revenue bills. Proxmire stated that the oil depletion allowance, one of the most odious provisions to liberal tax reformers, originated as a Senate amendment to a tax bill, and he argued the Senate should not now give up its amendments in the face of House inflexibility.[91] Byrd explained that the Clark amendment was put to three votes in the conference and not one House conferee had supported it, so the Senate was forced to recede.[92]

89 *Ibid.*, June 27, 1960, p. 14528.
90 *Ibid.*, p. 14529.
91 *Ibid.*, pp. 14536–37.
92 *Ibid.*, June 28, 1960, p. 14701.

Of equal consequence was the McCarthy amendment repealing the dividend credit. In essence, the argument against repealing the dividend credit holds that if taxes are levied on dividend income, double taxation is created because the profits of corporations are also taxed. The counter argument is, of course, that the taxation of corporate profits is a tax on a legal entity, and the taxation of dividend income is a tax on individual income. In addition, as Senator McCarthy argued, excise taxes are paid out of income that has already been taxed and, if the rule of double taxation were followed, excise taxes would be as inequitable as taxing dividend income.[93] Regardless of what position is taken on this issue, the relevant fact is that Long and others again raised questions about the composition of the Senate conferees, a majority of whom had voted against the McCarthy amendment. As Senator Douglas said:

> What happens — and I hope my senior colleagues will not take this amiss — is that when these bills go to conference, the members of the conference committee representing the Senate are chosen from among the senior members of the Finance Committee. All those Senators are very estimable and very able gentlemen. I like them personally. I have great respect for them as individuals. I am sure they act conscientiously. Nevertheless, it is true that on tax matters there is very little difference between the opinions of the senior Republican Members and the opinions of the senior Democratic Members. Party lines mean very little on tax matters.[94]

Kerr of Oklahoma immediately made a point of order against Douglas's remark. Douglas declared that he did not mean to question the character of any member of the Senate but that on tax matters the senior members of the Finance Committee hold similar views. "Five hearts beat as one," in his words.[95] Douglas was forced to take his seat but the chair never did rule on Kerr's point of order. Douglas was not deterred and went on to make his point again, this time coming very close to charging the Senate conferees with duplicity:

> They are all honorable gentlemen, but their views on tax matters tend to be substantially similar, and, in some cases,

[93] *Ibid.*, p. 14703.
[94] *Ibid.*, p. 14705.
[95] *Ibid.*, p. 14706.

virtually identical. Then the conference committee comes
back saying that it has been overpowered by the House and
has been compelled to yield the provisions which the Senate
had voted.
This has been going on for some time. The consequences
are fairly evident. What it means is that as long as the bipartisan coalition which controls the seats of power in both
the Democratic and Republican Parties in the House and
in the Senate dominate the conference committees, the will
of the Senate can be negated.[96]

In the House, Chairman Mills explained that although he had
voted against the dividend credit when it was enacted in 1954, he did
not feel that the House, without hearings, could accept a Senate
amendment to repeal the provision (he also pointed out that the
McCarthy amendment had carried by only one vote, 42–41).[97] The
need for tax reform in the House was discussed but the conference
report was adopted by voice vote, compared to the 61–32 roll call in
the Senate. By and large, the 1960 movement for tax reform was concentrated in the Senate with the House unwilling to accept any controversial tax changes that were not originated in the House.

Tax reform is not the only issue on which the Senate majority has
been in conflict with the Finance Committee conferees. Russell Long
once accused the Senate conferees of discarding a 1960 amendment
on tariffs before they got to conference:

> The Senator from Indiana had his position sustained, at
> least in part, when his amendment was passed in a revised
> form, yet the Senate conferees *threw the proposal in the
> trash basket on the way to see the House conferees.* Not
> a single Senate conferee voted for the Senator's amend-
> ment. The result is that some Senator walks into the Cham-
> ber, with only a few Senators present, and moves that the
> Senate agree to the House position in conference, without
> that conference ever having really considered the Senate
> amendments.
> My good friend from Utah simply moved to accept the

[96] *Ibid.*, p. 14707.
[97] *Ibid.*, June 27, 1960, p. 14546. One Senate amendment, passed 87–0 by the
Senate, did survive the conference. Court decisions had resulted in allowing
much more percentage depletion for clay and other material than Congress
originally intended and Senator Gore's amendment to correct this situation passed
with little controversy. The Supreme Court also ruled on the question and
reached the same conclusion contained in the Gore amendment.

House position and to reject the Senate position. That is all there was to it.

Mr. President, I did not vote with the distinguished Senator from Indiana. However, I think the Senator is entitled to more consideration. His amendment should not be discarded on the way to the conference. . . .

Senators should not come back from conference and say, "We did not even try. There was not a single vote among the Senate conferees, even on the first ballot." [98]

Long felt that the Senate conferees could have retained some of the Senate liberalizations of the Social Security Amendments of 1960 if they had been more determined in conference, and he and Clark again deplored the fact that Senate conferees in some cases have opposed amendments added by the Senate and then have found it difficult to defend these amendments against the opposition of the House.[99] This was, by now, an oft-told tale.

THE JOINT COMMITTEE ON INTERNAL REVENUE TAXATION *

The Ways and Means Committee and the Senate Finance Committee are linked by a unique bicameral institution, the Joint Committee on Internal Revenue Taxation (JCIRT), the oldest joint committee in Congress. Originally conceived by the House in the Revenue Act of 1926 as the "Joint Commission on Taxation," it was to be composed of five House members, five Senators, and five members appointed by the president representing the general public. Its job was to investigate the operation, effects, and administration of the internal revenue law with the purpose of simplifying the statute. Better phraseology and administration of tax law, not policy innovations, was the Commission's task.[100] To this end, the Commission received authorization to spend $25,000 for expenses; quarters were to be provided by the Treasury Department.[101]

The Senate drastically altered the House plan. Making liberal use

[98] *Ibid.*, June 17, 1960, p. 13078. (Italics added.)
[99] *Ibid.*, August 27, 1960, p. 17992.
* This section first appeared in John F. Manley, "Congressional Staff and Public Policy-Making: The Joint Committee on Internal Revenue Taxation," *Journal of Politics*, XXX (November, 1968), 1046–67.
[100] House, Committee on Ways and Means, H. Rept. No. 1 to accompany H.R. 1, *The Revenue Act of 1926*, p. 23.
[101] *Congressional Record*, December 11, 1925, pp. 696–97.

of its authority to amend revenue bills passed by the House, the Senate provided for a Joint Committee on Internal Revenue Taxation made up solely of congressmen: five Senators and five Representatives. Surrey writes that the JCIRT was created in response to the Couzens Committee, which had revealed tax evasion aided by misconduct by Internal Revenue Bureau employees,[102] revelations which stemmed from the work of a select committee headed by Michigan Senator James Couzens. The new Joint Committee, *through its staff*, was designed to: (1) obtain information from taxpayers to assist in the framing of future revenue legislation; (2) gain a "closer insight" into the problem of the administration of the tax laws (a euphemism for preventing corruption in the Internal Revenue Bureau); and (3) gather data bearing upon revenue legislation. The House receded on the Senate amendments and the Joint Committee, a combination watchdog and law-simplifying organization, was set up and staffed.

In some fields Congress may need more staff assistance but in the area of revenue legislation the Joint Committee staff provides the legislature with a professional, independent, and highly reliable source of information. The few studies that mention the staff invariably cite its competence, expertise, and influence with congressmen. Popular articles in *Business Week* and in *The Wall Street Journal* have stressed the quality of the staff,[103] and Blough has observed that the members of the tax committees place "heavy reliance" on the chief of staff and that the staff plays a "highly important" role in tax legislation.[104] A Ways and Means Committee member contends that: "Between the Joint Committee staff and the House Legislative Counsel, Congress has developed a more competent staff for drafting tax legislation than has the Treasury." [105]

Congressional experience with the staff has been so favorable that the Joint Committee has been taken as the model for changes in the legislative process. In the 1965 hearings before the Joint Committee on the Organization of Congress, for example, Senator McClellan used the JCIRT to support his proposal to establish a Joint Committee on the Budget. This arrangement, he felt, would give Con-

102 Surrey, *op. cit.*, p. 1170.
103 "Where Tax Bills Run the Gauntlet," *Business Week*, June 11, 1966, p. 106. Arlen J. Large, "Help on the Hill," *The Wall Street Journal*, June 25, 1965.
104 Blough, *op. cit.*, p. 64.
105 Thomas B. Curtis, "The House Committee on Ways and Means: Congress Seen Through a Key Committee," *Wisconsin Law Review*, 1966 (Winter, 1966), 8.

gress the same type of technical assistance in the appropriations field that it enjoys in the revenue field, and that the Budget Bureau provides the executive branch.[106] The National Taxpayers Conference and the Tax Foundation stated that the JCIRT could be a precedent for a similar organization to deal with expenditures, and Senator Boggs used it as the prototype for a fully staffed Joint Committee on National Strategy.[107]

What does the Joint Committee staff do for the tax committee that leads people to think that a similar device would be useful in different contexts? Are members of the Senate Finance and House Ways and Means Committees happy with the work of their staff; if not, why? What does the staff do for these committees, and does it live up to congressional expectations?

The most obvious, and in some ways the most important, function of the Joint Committee staff is linkage: the continuity of the tax legislative process, apart from informal contacts between leading members of the committees, arises from the central role of the staff in both the House and Senate deliberations on tax bills. In the executive sessions of the Ways and Means Committee the staff is not merely on tap for the members but it is actively engaged in the examination of policy proposals made by the members, the administration, interest groups, and lobbyists. After explicating for Ways and Means how individuals and groups will be affected by changes in the Internal Revenue Code the staff, and most prominently the Chief of Staff, crosses the rotunda and explains the bill to the Finance Committee, going through the same basic routine on the detailed bill instead of the tax message with which Ways and Means normally begins. For many years, until Russell Long became chairman of Finance in 1965, about the only professional staff available to the Finance Committee was the joint staff.[108]

---

[106] Joint Committee on the Organization of Congress, 89th Congress, 1965–66, *Hearings*, p. 477. McClellan's proposal has passed the Senate many times but to date leaders of the House Appropriations Committee have responded negatively.

[107] *Ibid.*, pp. 1983, 1985, 800–801.

[108] In justifying his successful request for more staff Long contended: "Under our Government the legislative branch is not supposed to be a lackey or the tool of the executive and is not to take the word of the executive on matters but should be able to acquire information itself." He admitted that the Joint Committee staff does a good job but when they are working for Ways and Means the Finance Committee has only a secondary claim on their services. Long also argued that Finance has much nontax work to do and needs help which the joint staff cannot provide. The staff situation of the Finance Committee was so bad

In performing its tasks for the Ways and Means Committee and the Senate Finance Committee the staff is expected to follow certain norms, including objectivity, bipartisanship, and neutrality. As a body of professional tax experts the Joint Committee staff is supposed to be objective in its handling of data, bipartisan in its handling of member requests, and neutral on public policy questions. "Our job," according to Chief of Staff Laurence N. Woodworth, "is to see that members of Congress get the facts on both sides so they can make their own decisions." [109] "If I can come away from those meetings," he has said, "knowing that the committee has made its own decisions in the light of this knowledge, then I'm satisfied." [110] The staff's job, according to Ways and Means Chairman Wilbur Mills, is "to bring facts together for our use, to do the spadework for us." [111] A former Republican staff assistant noted the bipartisan nature of the staff: "When I tell Woodworth or those guys something I expect confidence and I get it." Recruited without regard to party affiliation ("I'm very proud of the fact that Mr. Stam [former Chief of Staff] never asked me my party politics and as far as I know never asked any other member of the staff") the staff, as one aide put it, acts "as a coordinator for the Ways and Means Committee. We serve Curtis and Byrnes [Republicans], Boggs and Mills [Democrats], in addition to Senator Byrd." Woodworth on occasion helped write the majority report on a bill and then helped the minority write its dissenting views.

Because of the controversial nature of tax policy, the well-known complexity of the Internal Revenue Code that puts a high premium on technical advice, the difficulty of facing choices without forming opinions, and the strategic role of the quartermaster corps in the conduct of any war, it is not surprising that the staff, which obviously affects the decisions made by the policy-makers, has been criticized for failing to live up to the above norms. Some policy-makers feel the norm of neutrality on public policy has been broken by the staff, especially while Colin F. Stam was Chief of Staff.

---

under Byrd, Long reports, that with only two telephone lines to the Committee, members had great difficulty getting through to the staff. When they did reach the staff, their questions could not be answered. When he became Chairman he discovered a third line so the Chairman could call the Committee but before this he sometimes had to call the Ways and Means Committee to find out what the Finance Committee was doing on his bills. See *Congressional Record*, April 20, 1966 (daily edition), p. 8239.

[109] Quoted in *Business Week, op. cit.*, p. 106.
[110] Quoted in Large, *op. cit.*
[111] *Ibid.*

"It has been estimated," Bailey and Samuel note, "that Stam exercised more influence on the preparation of tax legislation than any other single person in the federal government." [112] Little known outside of Washington, Stam accumulated so much influence with the Ways and Means Committee and the Senate Finance Committee that only Harry Byrd, of twenty people interviewed by Kenworthy for his perceptive study of Stam, was willing to have his views of the technician attributed to him.[113] Stam did not control tax policy, in Byrd's opinion, but he "has made very many vital decisions. He has made recommendations that have carried great weight with both committees." [114] Another piece of evidence in support of Stam's key role in the tax legislative process is the tribute to Stam by a Republican member of Ways and Means in 1953 in defense of the policies of former Chairman Dan Reed:

> He [Reed] had the assistance of the best tax expert anywhere in the United States, and I refer to Mr. Colin Stam, who is the chief of staff of the Joint Committee on Taxation. . . . *These two gentlemen, Mr. Reed and Mr. Stam, have as much capacity to decide what is best in the tax field as anyone in this country.*
>
> Mr. Reed and Mr. Stam agreed on a program, not that they were trying to force it upon anybody, but they advanced it as a suggestion.[115]

And a Republican Senator commented:

> He'd been here so long that he wasn't like other staff men. He was the only staff man I knew who could tell a Senator to go to hell without getting his face slapped. Not that he did it, understand, but there wasn't any of this subjugation or kowtowing which you sometimes see in the staff, no "sir" business. He was here when I first came in . . . and he cut quite a figure then.[116]

[112] Bailey and Samuel, *op. cit.*, p. 342.
[113] E. W. Kenworthy, "Colin F. Stam," *Adventures in Public Service*, ed. Delia and Ferdinand Kuhn (New York: Vanguard Press, 1963), p. 109.
[114] *Ibid.*, p. 115.
[115] *Congressional Record*, July 10, 1953, p. 8493. (Italics added.)
[116] After an apprenticeship with the Internal Revenue Bureau Stam joined the Joint Committee staff in 1927, became Chief of Staff in 1938, and ran it for a quarter of a century until his retirement in 1964. He suffered a stroke and died in January, 1966.

Controversy is inevitably associated with influence in Washington, and Stam had influence in the tax field despite his view of himself as a technician who merely supplied analyses and counsel to the decision-makers.[117] Not everyone would agree with the citation on his Rockefeller Public Service Award given "in recognition of distinguished service to the government of the United States and to the American people." Specifically, Stam's activity as the chief of the joint staff has been severely criticized by liberal Senators concerned with making changes or, as they see it, reforms in the internal revenue laws.

These Senators thought that Stam's expertise was sullied because it buttressed, in the main, the views of their conservative antagonists who were in effective control of both committees. Certainly Stam was not the linchpin in the conservative coalition which Senate liberals feel has controlled tax policy for many years, but he was a conservative who identified with the conservative leaders of Finance and Ways and Means, and his key position and acknowledged mastery of the Code were used to frustrate liberal attempts to "purify" the tax laws — at any rate, so said the liberals.[118]

"This fellow Stam was an autocrat, he played everything close to his vest, and I always felt that he was an ally of big business." A Senate staff aide agreed with this view of Stam and complained about the assistance available to liberal Senators: "First, they never offered help. They'd never come in and say here's an important bill, let's go over it. Two, they were nominal in their assistance. And you couldn't trust it so we just went out and got our own." One disenchanted Senate liberal, who once asked Stam to leave the committee room, declared:

> I just never got anything out of him at all. He wouldn't do any work for me. He was here twenty-five or thirty years and he never deviated from the line of Millikin, George, Harry Byrd. You could ask Stam if something was black and he'd say, "Well, there are several shades of blackness. . . ." On a tax bill he'd say, "This came up in the committee in 1862 and they thought . . . or in 1904 the committee did this," and when he was all done he hadn't said a goddamn

---

117 Kenworthy, op. cit., p. 115.

118 Huitt reports similar complaints about Stam. See Ralph K. Huitt, "Congressional Organization and Operations in the Field of Money and Credit," *Fiscal and Debt Management Policies*, William Fellner et al. (Englewood Cliffs, N.J.: Prentice-Hall, 1963), pp. 452–53.

thing except, "Therefore, we ought to take the bill as it's written."

He concluded, "I never did think Stam was reliable."

It appears, then, that the impact of the staff's work leaned toward the conservative side under Stam's leadership — in spite of norms of neutrality and objectivity to the contrary. What the staff does to some extent affects what the committees decide, and even the conservative members of Finance admit that in Stam they had an important friend. "Colin Stam's personal philosophy," a Senator praised the staff chief, "was that the tax law should be used for raising revenue and not for social reform. If that makes him a conservative then I suppose he's a conservative. I think this is Larry Woodworth's philosophy too, and it's certainly mine." A Republican Senator confirmed the liberals' charges when he observed that on Finance the minority, plus the Byrd Democrats, had all of the staff they needed because Stam was a conservative. "Gore and Douglas and a few others were the ones who didn't have any staff," he chortled, "our coalition had the staff." In defense of Stam he ticked off a number of famous conservative Senators saying, "Stam's career was woven into theirs. He did nothing more than discharge the responsibilities given him by his employers." A Joint Committee staff member supported the breakdown of staff neutrality under Stam and admitted that his former boss broke the rules: "Quite frankly, on occasion, I think Mr. Stam, who used to identify himself pretty much with what the majority leadership of the committee felt, would really go too far in supporting their position. He'd become too committed."

As reformer dissension shows, politics and policy preferences have affected the role of the staff, its standing with its principals, and its relationship to the formulation of public policy. An institutional device such as the Joint Committee staff may be a mixed blessing to the participants in the policy-making process; it may, depending upon such variables as the policy orientation of a Colin F. Stam, support one viewpoint over another. For one group of Senators the staff under Stam was merely doing its job for the majority; for the minority of tax reformers he was a bête noire. Their complaints about him testify to the high quality of the job he did for those with whom he identified; his expertise could — and apparently did — advantage some and disadvantage others.

Because of the difficulty of remaining neutral in the policy-making process, these policy consequences of the staff may seem almost inevitable. Men in Washington form preferences, the political system is designed for the airing and resolution of preferences, and it may be unrealistic to ask any man to be a policy eunuch, especially one who must operate amid the competing demands that surround the tax legislative process. But the history of the joint tax staff since Woodworth replaced Stam necessitates caution in accepting this conclusion. Perfect conformity to the norms of neutrality and objectivity is probably impossible, but the degee of attainment and deviation varies with different individuals. And, experience shows, there is no reason to conclude that the staff cannot both serve and please diverse masters.

When Woodworth took over as Chief of Staff in 1964 he was aware of the liberal criticism of Stam and he took steps to restore the staff to its position as a useful aide to all members of the Senate Finance and Ways and Means committees. He assured Senate liberals that the staff was ready to assist all members, regardless of policy considerations and, in effect, would not play politics on revenue bills. Woodworth's campaign worked; the critics of Stam have lauded his successor. "I'd say the staff is 500 percent improved over what it used to be," said one liberal Senator. Hired by Stam in 1944, Woodworth has been more skillful than his mentor in retaining the confidence of the factions that make tax policy. Whether he can always avoid all commitments to individual policy positions or avoid alienation of members when the staff research does in fact enhance one position at the expense of others remains to be seen, but he has been doing precisely that. "I honestly have no idea whether he's a Democrat or a Republican," one long-time associate of Woodworth's said. "He's about as straight down-the-middle as you can get." [119] By functioning "straight down the middle" Woodworth has been able to play his role as he — and the congressmen — think it should be played.

Criticism of the joint staff was found on only the Senate side of the Capitol. The Ways and Means Committee is populated with Democrats whose voting behavior is as liberal as the Finance Committee reformers, but there are crucial differences in style between the two groups. With one possible exception, there are really no reform-minded liberals like Paul Douglas or Albert Gore on the House Committee, although some House members would no doubt vote for the same reforms — if pressed. "Ways and Means," said one Democrat interviewed on tax reform, "is the strangest of all the House commit-

[119] Quoted in *Business Week, op. cit.,* p. 111.

tees — and the hardest to understand. Judging by the voting records of its members . . . the liberals *ought* to have darn near a working majority. But their public *voting* records and their 'operating' records in the committee, behind closed doors, are two different things." [120] This extreme judgment ignores the legitimate constraints operating on Committee members, but it is a fairly common perception of the Committee. A union lobbyist quoted by Stern gave a similarly dim view of the Committee and noted the dilemma facing liberal labor lobbyists with Ways and Means:

> These guys like to play games with the fat cats on tax issues. And they get away with it by voting with us often enough on other issues so the labor guys back home won't get sore at them. . . . I'm lucky if I can cover a couple of basic points on our "must" list with these guys. We can't hold their feet to the fire on *everything*.[121]

The general attitude was probably summed up by a liberal Ways and Means Democrat who dismissed criticism of Stam: "I think that's just a characteristic of some liberal Senators. They have to have something to complain about and if it's not the staff it's something else. I think complaining is their common denominator."

In summary, the Joint Committee staff, as seen by the policymakers, has had mixed results as a link between the two tax committees of Congress. Possessed of so much expertise that one House member was led to exaggerate that "they are the legislators, we are the politicians," the staff has played its role appropriately under one head and inappropriately, in light of the norms that the members and staff espouse, under another. Having gone through the process on the House side the staff is equipped to inform the Senate Finance Committee on the technical — and political — problems involved in various sections of the bill. But the staff can affect the kinds of decisions made in the legislative process; as such, it is endowed with influence and, potentially, controversy. To retain influence and avoid controversy is delicate business. Under Stam the expertise of the staff resulted in some disaffection; under Woodworth the expertise of the staff, in no way diminished, has been used in a more neutral — or less offensive — way.

Under Woodworth, the JCIRT staff still serves as a major contact

[120] Philip M. Stern, *The Great Treasury Raid* (New York: Random House, 1963), p. 284. (Italics his.)
[121] *Ibid.*

point between the two tax committees and the interest groups and lobbyists active in taxation. The anecdotes that travel the Washington grapevine, the public record, and the perceptions of those involved in the policy-making process support the observation that contacts between the staff and interested parties are frequent, legitimate, and important.

As one anecdote is told, Colin Stam carried so much weight with the formal policy-makers that a lobbyist who had difficulty seeing him bought a dog and walked it around Chevy Chase Circle in hopes of encountering the staff chief on his nightly dog-walking strolls. Apocryphal, perhaps, but the circulation of the story testifies to the importance of the staff to interest groups. "Nobody's been up to my neighborhood to see me yet," Woodworth has been quoted as saying,[122] but this may be because no one has had difficulty seeing him at the office.

Normally, access to the staff is not difficult. Both Stam and Woodworth have held quasi-hearings at which lobbyists would present their views on tax matters. Many lobbyists have heard a member of Ways and Means or Senate Finance say, "See Stam" or "See Larry." A tax attorney told how congressmen have used the staff to winnow tax proposals, and how the staff, contacted first, can reverse the procedure and assist a lobbyist:

> The congressman says to the lawyer, "Go see Stam and then let me get a report from Stam." If Stam thinks there is no merit in the idea, the congressman will usually drop it. If Stam thinks there is merit, the congressman is likely to sponsor it.
>
> An attorney will call on Stam to tell him what he would like to do and see whether it is in the cards. Stam may say, "Don't waste your time," or "You might be able to interest so-and-so in that." If Stam himself is interested, he will explain the proposal to the congressman in friendly terms, without necessarily urging it, and so help put it across.[123]

"Stam's staff," one Ways and Means member said, "is very influential and that's why they are lobbied so much."

By receiving and analyzing tax proposals the staff increases the tax committee's contacts with interested parties, which is an important part of the congressional job, and at the same time it helps the mem-

---

[122] Large, op. cit.
[123] Kenworthy, op. cit., p. 119.

bers cope with the tremendous number of demands for changes in the Code. Many times, in fact, these demands are stimulated by Congress itself as part of its legislative procedure. Prior to the passage of the 1954 Revenue Act, for example, the staff mailed tax questionnaires to thousands of individuals and groups. Over fifteen thousand replies were received and over two dozen national associations studied various tax proposals before passage of the Act, the first major revision of the Code since 1939. So much of the work had been done by the staff that one member argued that the Committee, after six weeks' labor, still did not understand the bill reported to the House:

> The staffs of the Joint Committee on Internal Revenue Taxation and the Treasury Department together have spent over two years preparing recommendations for the bill. Extensive hearings were held, and some 15,000 replies to questionnaires were reviewed preparatory to making recommendations to be included. In contrast to this, the committee deliberated on the bill for only six weeks. In my opinion, such a complete overhauling as this bill proposes to make involving the most complicated laws which the Congress has ever written, would require at least one year to fully understand. . . .[124]

Another example of the contacts between interest groups and the staff occurred in 1956 when the House considered a bill dealing with the renegotiation of government contracts. In this case the Committee did not make policy as much as it legitimated the recommendations of the staff and business organizations. Thomas Jenkins said of the bill:

> Mr. Speaker, this bill is the result of an exhaustive study by the staff of the Joint Committee on Internal Revenue Taxation. This study was conducted pursuant to statutory directive and lasted for many months. *Industry had a complete opportunity to present its problems to the staff.*[125]

Jenkins acknowledged that it may have been unfortunate that Ways and Means did not hold hearings but: "On the other hand, I believe that Mr. Stam and the joint committee staff did a magnificent job in developing these needed improvements in the act." [126] Small wonder that interest groups and individuals pay attention to the staff.

---

[124] *Congressional Record*, March 17, 1954, p. 3430.
[125] *Ibid.*, July 13, 1956, p. 12726. (Italics added.)
[126] *Ibid.*

The testimony to the important role of the staff that is found in the public record reflects the staff's activities in countless private meetings with lobbyists and in the executive sessions of the Ways and Means Committee. When the members of Ways and Means begin marking up a tax bill the staff becomes an integral part of the process. According to Thomas B. Curtis, when the doors are closed the staff represents the views of the people with whom it has been in contact:

> The role of the Joint Committee staff is even more important during executive sessions when administration officials are the only outsiders present. Then the staff must represent the views of all other "interests" whose positions are often discounted by the sometimes parochial outlook of Treasury and Internal Revenue Service officials and experts.[127]

The staff, in other words, brings to the discussion the results of the meetings and communications with people on the outside, thereby keeping the Committee informed on the views and arguments of those who will be affected by the Committee's decisions.

Thus, in 1965, when the Committee was considering President Johnson's proposed cut in excise taxes, the question arose whether the announcement of excise tax reductions would induce consumers to postpone buying certain items until the tax was removed, thus, in effect, creating a buyer's strike. Woodworth reported that the Joint Committee staff had contacted different industries to see if they thought a refund of any tax paid on such goods was needed to ward off a drop in sales. It first appeared, he stated, that the electrical appliance industry favored the refund idea, but consultation with the national organization of electrical manufacturers revealed that the only appliance to which the refund should definitely apply, due to the closeness of the summer selling season, was air conditioners. He also informed the meeting that many manufacturers were not too anxious to pass the tax cut on to consumers by way of lowered prices, and providing for a tax refund would increase the pressure on them to do so. This, together with the administrative burdens of handling the refund, argued against applying refunds to articles other than air conditioners. Ways and Means, guided by the information gathered by the staff from interested parties, decided to make the refund applicable to air conditioners.

[127] Curtis, *op. cit.*, p. 7.

A favorable response from the staff does not assure the same reaction from the tax committees, but the complexity of tax legislation and the concomitant need of congressmen for expert guidance increase the likelihood that the decision-makers will follow the advice of the fact-finders. This does not mean that congressmen are captives of their staffs. By and large, the staff probably reflects the views of the members more than it determines those views, but the staff can and does play an important role in the process.

CONCLUSION

This account of House-Senate relations in tax, trade, and social security legislation may leave the impression that relatively heavy emphasis is placed on the role of pressure goups, lobbyists, and constituent demands. This is intended. Only the rare special tax provision is not nursed through the legislative process by a pressure group or lobbyist. Social security legislation is less amenable to special provisions than the Internal Revenue Code, but pressure groups, lobbyists, and constituency representatives are only slightly less prominent in the trade legislation considered by Ways and Means than the tax legislation.

The emphasis on the importance of extracongressional demands and the role of extracongressional participants is not intended to refute the perceptive generalizations of Bauer, Pool, and Dexter. Congressmen are relatively free to decide which demands they listen to; members of Congress do affect the nature of communications they receive; the effectiveness of pressure groups probably has been exaggerated by political scientists; the existence of groups on both sides of an issue sometimes leads to stalemate; groups are sometimes cut off from influence with offended congressmen; and enough incompetent lobbyists have been met to reject the view of congressional decisions as the product of skillful insiders who rarely miss a trick.[128] As Latham writes:

> Legislators have to be approached with a certain amount of deference and tact; they may be pressured, but some forms of pressure will be regarded as too gross. The Congressman, like men everywhere, comes to his position bearing in his head

[128] Bauer, Pool, and Dexter, *op. cit.*, pp. 403–43. See also Oliver Garceau and Corinne Silverman, "A Pressure Group and the Pressured," *American Political Science Review*, XLVIII (September, 1954), 672–91.

a cargo of ideas, principles, prejudices, programs, precepts,
beliefs, slogans, and preachments.[129]

But groups, lobbyists, and constituency interests are important in
the legislative process. For the lobbyist who offended the Ways and
Means Committee staff man by coming in, sitting on his desk, and
using the phone, one can find Clark Clifford easing a tax provision
through which helps DuPont. For the lobbyist who appears to his
clients to have great connections but who in fact has none, one can
find a Ways and Means member commenting on the number of
lobbyists at a fancy party for a departing Committee staff member
turning around to see his son, a recently registered lobbyist, coming
into the room. For the lobbyist who has little respect in Washington,
one can find Secretary of the Treasury Henry Fowler a few weeks
before taking over at Treasury lobbying on behalf of the automobile
industry for a cut in the auto excise tax. For the interest group headed
by an incompetent, one can find the American Petroleum Institute
guided by former Ways and Means member Frank Ikard. For the
interest group with little access, one can find the House leadership
clearing appointments to the Education and Labor Committee with
the AFL-CIO. For the leading protectionist lobbyist who works assisted only by a secretary, there is the American Medical Association,
not noticeably underfinanced.

The interesting point about demands that can be met by the congressional tax committees is not whether they are accompanied by
illegitimate "pressure" but that the members of these committees are
in the business of responding to demands. Their craft is dealing with
demands, their material is the Internal Revenue Code, their tools are
amendments, and their workshop is the executive session. They can
disagree with and refuse some — even many — demands but their
relationship with some of the representatives making demands is so
intimate that "demands" is a misnomer. If the Ways and Means
Committee and the Finance Committee did not act favorably on
some of the questions put before them they would not be doing their
job as they see it. Ways and Means operates according to a somewhat different blueprint than the Finance Committee or the Senate,
but they are both in the same profession, they have the same problems, the same alternatives, and the same realities to face. Ways and
Means members, largely because of different institutional factors,

[129] Earl Latham, "The Group Basis of Politics: Notes for a Theory," *American
Political Science Review*, XLVI (June, 1952), 391.

frequently react differently than the Senate, but this is the raison d'être of the conference committee.[130] It is therefore hardly surprising that conference committees rarely fail to decide on *some* solution that both houses can accept.

The members of Finance and Ways and Means reveal themselves in their work. Mills calls the Internal Revenue Code a "house of horrors," [131] because primarily its high rates cannot be applied uniformly to an almost infinitely diverse set of situations. Confronted by the arguments that an amendment to the Code will help save a business and the jobs of the people it employs (e.g., the American Motors amendment); that they can help promote contributions to charity by granting tax deductions to such contributions; that the general economy will be helped if investments are increased and that special tax rates will help increase them; that people with children have additional expenses and would profit from special tax exemptions; and countless equally appealing arguments — how is the member of Congress, whose job it is to be helpful, likely to respond? If the Senate is a little more helpful than the House what is likely to happen to special tax provisions in conference? The general principle of tax equity seems rather remote when members of Congress are involved with these kinds of demands; in fact, it appears to be unreasonable not to help as long as Treasury can stand the revenue loss. And, with a $200 billion budget, congressmen are likely to think that Treasury, despite its protestations, can stand the loss.

[130] In this connection, the use of face-savers in conference is interesting. For diverse reasons, one group of conferees may have to recede on important amendments. To blunt the criticism that may follow, or to give the conferees something to use in reply (no matter how meager), face-savers are often used. These include planned hearings, special studies by the staff, vague promises that the other body is now aware of the problem and will act in the near future, and the like.

[131] Mills, *op. cit.*, p. 51.

CHAPTER SEVEN

The Committee and the Executive: Interest Aggregation

> *Alternative lines of political action, notably through the Congress, are available to groups dissatisfied with their treatment by the chief executive. The more extensively they use these alternatives, the less effectively he is able to play his role.*
>
> David B. Truman [1]

The decline of legislatures is a familiar theme in contemporary writings about politics. Everywhere, it seems, once-proud legislative institutions, in the face of difficult governmental problems, have been superseded by executives and professional civil servants who exchange deference to legislators for de facto control of policy. Obeisance to the legislature as the first branch of government is a hardy part of democratic ritual but in fact if not in form many legislatures are subordinate to the executive branch of government.

The American Congress, many feel, has inexorably followed the downward path of the mother of parliaments. Most students of American government would probably agree that compared to most national legislatures the decline of Congress has been slower, but as an empirical generalization few would disagree with Huntington's observation that, "Congress has conceded not only the initiative in originating legislation but — and perhaps inevitably as the result of losing the initiative — it has also lost the dominant influence it once had in shaping the final content of legislation." [2]

[1] *The Governmental Process* (New York: Alfred A. Knopf, 1951), p. 400.
[2] Samuel P. Huntington, "Congressional Responses to the Twentieth Century," *The Congress and America's Future*, ed. David B. Truman (Englewood Cliffs, N.J.: Prentice-Hall, 1965), pp. 23–24.

Different observers have drawn strikingly different conclusions from the "fact" of Congress's decline as a policy-making body. Huntington, for example, presents the view that Congress either cannot or should not attempt to regain its lost power, and that it should adapt itself to the reality that legislation simply cannot be handled by a representative body. Constituent service and administrative oversight, according to Huntington, are functions that Congress can perform and, in practice, they already preoccupy most congressmen. He concludes: "Explicit acceptance of the idea that legislation was not its primary function would, in large part, simply be recognition of the direction which change has already been taking." [3]

Alfred de Grazia diametrically opposed this view a year after the appearance of Huntington's essay. In a book he edited containing numerous essays on the decline and hoped-for rise of Congress, de Grazia proposed, among other reforms, limiting the president to one six-year term. He summed up his general approach to the decline of Congress in his call for a declaration of legislative supremacy: "A charter of Legislative Authority should declare the principle of legislative supremacy of Congress and the position of Congress with respect to the executive branch, and this Charter should be disseminated widely within and outside of government." [4]

This chapter does not join the discussion of what Congress should do to improve its position in the federal government. Its purpose is more prosaic: to examine the relationship between the Ways and Means Committee and the executive branch and, in so doing, to explore the empirical foundation on which calls for congressional reform are based. Obviously, generalizations as broad as the "decline of Congress" can neither be fully confirmed nor denied by a study of one congressional committee, but they can be challenged. Because the jurisdiction of Ways and Means is so broad, the policy-making role of the executive and of Congress can also be qualified by different issue areas; and because the timespan of this study includes a number of different political situations at the federal level, additional qualifications may be made depending on the effect of factors such

[3] *Ibid.*, p. 30. Some might argue that the decline of Congress in domestic policy-making has been much less than in foreign affairs. Huntington agrees but argues "even here its primary impact is on the timing and details and legislation, not on the subjects and content of legislation" (p. 24).

[4] Alfred de Grazia, "Toward a New Model of Congress," *Congress: The First Branch of Government*, ed. Alfred de Grazia (Washington, D.C.: American Enterprise Institute, 1966), p. 16.

as which party controls Congress and the presidency. Power comparisons between Congress and the executive branch are so broad, so nebulous in their simplicity, and subject to so much qualification that, as empirical generalizations, they are of doubtful validity. This conclusion is qualified because it is based on the matters considered by the Ways and Means Committee, but the accuracy and utility of generalizations might be questioned that do not describe the vital policies handled by that Committee.

Why certain policy outcomes emanate from the legislative process also will be explained. The policy consequences of such factors as recruitment to the Ways and Means Committee, bipartisan decision-making processes in the Committee, the Chairman, and the impact of the House and Senate on the policies adopted (or rejected) by Ways and Means have been discussed. But the crucial competition between Ways and Means and the executive branch in the representation of interest group–lobbyist demands has not been analyzed; a great deal of the policy made by the federal government involves this competition and can be explained in terms of this competition. From the nineteenth century when Sam Ward, the "King of the Lobbies," had his Capitol Hill office in the rooms of the Appropriations Committee, to the Senator who said of lobbyists in the 1920's "they are becoming as numerous as the lice of Egypt," to the queues outside the Finance Committee hearings on import quotas in the fall of 1967, interest groups and lobbyists have been an essential part of the legislative process.[5] Few committees draw their attention like Ways and Means, and this is the context within which the Committee's relations with the executive branch have to be placed to be understood. Washington is still full of people who suffer the "optical delusion" that the Capitol dome is an old-fashioned nursing bottle,[6] and at one time or another many are involved in the decisions of Ways and Means.

The relations between Ways and Means and the executive branch in trade, tax, and social security legislation are extremely variable over time and in different issue areas. But the Committee seems to have maintained itself as a strong autonomous force in the policy-making process, particularly in the areas of taxation and social security, and less so in trade. After looking at four main points of contact between

[5] The reference to Ward and the quotation are taken from E. Pendleton Herring, *Group Representation Before Congress* (Baltimore: Johns Hopkins Press, 1929), pp. 31 and 21, respectively.

[6] *Ibid.*, p. 30.

the Committee and the executive, the politics of executive-legislative relations is analyzed as it involves the interest groups and lobbyists who deal with the Committee. Compensatory representation, it is argued, is an important link between Ways and Means and the executive, and this concept provides the analytical focus for a discussion of the decline of Congress.

THE ROLE OF CONGRESS

If a prerequisite for congressional reform is dissatisfaction within Congress with its shrinking power to determine general policy, and if the members of the Ways and Means Committee are typical of congressional opinion on this matter, the outlook for change is bleak.[7] The Ways and Means Committee members see themselves as policy-makers, if not policy-initiators; they see their job as requiring them to pass an independent judgment on proposals that are only "bureau-cratically sound"; and they are quick to cite evidence of their policy-making role that implies that if the power of Congress as a whole has seriously eroded, the power of the Ways and Means Committee has been retained.

To probe perceptions of the Committee's relations with the execu-tive, twenty-three members were asked to estimate the degree to which the Committee changes the important parts of executive de-partment proposals. All but two replied "very much," and most mem-bers went on to discuss the Committee's superior role in policy-making. "Ways and Means," one said, "is a kind of bastion of congressional dominance. There's a strong feeling that we are a committee that can rely on itself, stand on its own feet, and not be dependent on handouts from the administration." Another typical response was:

> Oh yes, sure, very much, more than any other committee, I think. We just don't take it. They don't even send up tax bills, we write them. We sit in there hour after hour, we spend unending hours going over every part, time after time after time. It's not the easy way, I'll tell you that. God, it takes time!

One key member was asked directly about the decline of Congress. He replied, "I don't think that's true in our case. We have never

---

[7] For a general treatment see Roger H. Davidson, David M. Kovenock, and Michael K. O'Leary, *Congress in Crisis* (Belmont, Calif.: Wadsworth Publish-ing Co., 1966), chap. 3.

rubber-stamped anything they have sent up yet. It is always a *Committee* bill, there are always amendments."

Even Democrats who identified strongly with the administration, and whose administration support scores were generally high, tempered their party identification by identifying *first* with the Committee. One such member noted that the Committee profoundly changes executive department proposals: "They sit in there with us and sometimes we kick their teeth in. Time and time again we kick their teeth in. It's on the secretarial level too, and on the tax bill they had to just sit there and recede from their position, then help us write what we wanted." "On the trade bill," he said, "we just rewrote it." Less aggressively, another Democrat cited a major tax bill to support his claim that the Committee is an independent body: "The best example of that is the Revenue Act of 1964. There would never have been a Revenue Act of 1964 if the Committee had not gone through it and taken out all of those so-called tax reforms."

Republican members of Ways and Means also emphasize the important policy-making function of the Committee. One said, "I don't know of any committee that changes the bill more than the Ways and Means Committee does." He claimed that most of the changes in the 1964 Revenue Act came from the Republicans: "Some chairmen and some committees don't change administration bills at all. But Mills is fairly independent. He opposed some of our suggestions but not too many." "Very few bills the administration sends up," claimed another, "are in a condition to go through. They don't dig into it as much as we on the Committee do. Medicare is a good example. There were entire sections that we worked over." A Republican colleague agreed: "We aren't a rubber stamp for anyone. If we were medicare would not have the trouble it's having." Granting initiation to the executive, another Republican added, *"But we write the legislation."*

Ceding initiation to the executive branch is important. During the summer of 1966, for example, there was much debate over whether a tax increase was needed to dampen inflationary pressures in the economy. Many economists argued in favor of raising taxes, others discounted its importance, *but everyone waited to see what President Johnson would do, not what the Ways and Means Committee would do.* Congress was not irrelevant because in an election year a tax increase would not benefit the Democratic party, but clearly in this case, as in the case of almost every major bill reported by Ways and Means (under Democratic administrations), it is up to the president to move first. He sets the agenda for Congress (sometimes with a nudge from senior legislators who assure him they can get the bill through); he determines, with important exceptions (e.g., tax reform in 1969), what major policy proposals Congress will look at, and when.

Granting the power of initiation to the president, however, is not equivalent to granting him a preponderant share of influence on policy: it is often possible for Congress to be secondary in time but primary in influence. Congress responds to the executive but sometimes it responds with a flat "no"; more frequently, it amends the executive proposal; less frequently, it so amends proposals that there is a qualitative change in the original and Congress, in effect, becomes the most important policy-making body. It is important that the president had the first move on taxes in the summer of 1966 but it is also important that the tax increase was not proposed until 1967 and not enacted by Congress until the summer of 1968, with significant conditions attached regarding cuts in federal spending.

Anticipated response is one of the many imponderables standing in the way of generalizations about which branch of government is dominant in the legislative process. Committee members are, of course, aware of the influence they have through anticipated response. Faced by the necessity of getting a number of majorities behind what the president proposes, the departments "downtown" try to anticipate what Congress will support, how much disposable bargaining material to include in a proposal, which congressmen have to be pacified before a bill is sent up, which can be safely ignored, and what arguments to use with whom. One example of this occurred when the Treasury Department proposed a circuitous way of nibbling at the controversial oil depletion allowance. A pro-depletion Democrat asked Secretary Douglas Dillon why he did not ask for a direct cut. Dillon replied that he knew such a request would stand no chance. "That's the way it is between us and the executive. We respect each other and we all know that we have different fish to fry," remarked the member.

In response to a question about changing executive department requests one member said, "There's a lot of compromise. Now they have been getting smart and letting us know, or at least letting the chairman know, what they are going to propose. They'd be stupid to send something up without the chairman's knowledge — they want his support." "I think," declared a Democrat, "they come into the Committee, get the sentiment of the Committee, find out what we will accept, and then draft up their proposals." He felt that he himself does not have much influence on policy but that the Committee does: "Mills knows what's going on." One of the two Committee members who said Ways and Means does not change executive branch proposals very much feels the proposals are shaped according to Committee wishes in the first place. In his words:

> I don't know how to answer that. You have to realize that before it is even sent up they are in consultation with the leading members of the Committee. So before we take it up it has already been gone over. This was true even with the tax measure. I'd say very little change but remember that they anticipate, they consult before it even comes up.

Executive department officials confirm the importance of anticipating the Committee's reaction to various proposals. A Treasury Department official found it hard to say how his department makes out with Ways and Means: "Do we get 75 per cent of what we send up? Well, maybe. Of course, we modify our proposals to meet what we think the Committee will accept — not entirely, of course. Then, we don't expect to get everything we put in the message. It's hard to say, actually." "We take into account what is likely to get passed before we ever send a proposal," another Treasury official said; "we'd be crazy not to do so."

The Department of Health, Education and Welfare, like Treasury, also considers the policy orientation of Ways and Means in making its proposals. In 1967, according to one HEW man, the Department felt that Ways and Means would probably accept about a 10 per cent increase in social security benefits, and that the Senate would probably increase the House figure by some amount, so they proposed 15 per cent, got 12.5 per cent from Ways and Means, the full amount from the Senate, and 13 per cent in conference. In this case, HEW also saw the Committee make major amendments in the public welfare laws ("On the welfare amendments, I'd say 10 per cent was administration, 80 per cent Ways and Means, and 10 per cent Senate"), changes that the Department opposed but could not stop.

The Treasury Department has also lost notable contests in Ways and Means. H.R. 10, a bill sponsored by Brooklyn Democrat Eugene Keogh dealing with the tax treatment of retirement plans of self-employed, largely professional people, was reported by the Committee in 1966 over the unequivocal opposition of Assistant Secretary Stanley Surrey. Surrey opposed H.R. 10 on the grounds that he could not justify a tax break to dentists, doctors, lawyers, and others in a year when the excise tax reduction was postponed and the administration needed all the revenue it could get. Surrey tried to get Treasury's position included in the Committee report that accompanied the bill to the House but Keogh objected. Laurence Woodworth, the head of the Joint Committee staff, pointed out that the report has always been considered a "sales pitch" for the bill and that executive department opposition is never noted. This remark set Rep. Thomas B. Curtis off. While a member of Ways and Means, Curtis championed full and open debate on all matters, and he was critical of the tendency of committees to hide things from the House. He told Surrey that Treasury ought to be able to get one of the members to file supplementary views pointing out Treasury's position. Surrey asked Curtis if he would do this, and the Missouri Republican agreed. Supplementary views were filed by Curtis (who supported the bill) in which a letter from Surrey noted the reasons why H.R. 10 should not be passed.[8] It passed.

Many other cases of Committee autonomy could be cited — medicare in 1965 may be recalled — but perhaps of greater importance is the question of what patterns of relationships exist between the Committee and the executive branch — and why. Some hints that Ways and Means is more apt to change tax bills and social security bills than trade bills were gathered in the interviews. A Treasury Department official, for example, is of the opinion that the Committee "spent a lot of time on the 1962 Trade bill but in the end it did not differ substantially from the administration's proposal. . . . Now on the 1964 Revenue Act they gutted the reform proposals. Ways and Means has the staff on tax to write the bill themselves, but they don't on trade and social security." Also significant is the comment by a tax specialist with the Joint Committee on Internal Revenue Taxation: "I don't really think the Committee changes a trade bill as much as it does tax bills. Part of the reason of course is that we are here for tax matters and there's no expert staff on trade." "The gist of the idea that comes from the executive, the basic approach," a trade specialist said, "is not changed too much. It's not tampered with. What the Committee does is make a lot of formal changes but it doesn't change the substance too much." (In contrast, a couple of

[8] Committee on Ways and Means, *Contributions by Self-Employed Individuals to Pension Plans, etc.*, 89th Cong., 2d Sess., 1966, H. Rept. 1577 to accompany H.R. 10, pp. 14–19.

Ways and Means members claimed the Committee rewrote the 1962
Trade Act and changed it a good deal.)

To examine the possibility that the Committee's relations with the
executive branch may vary by issue area, trade, tax, and social security
legislation will be studied separately. The legislative-executive relationship depends heavily on the policy area under discussion and, for a
number of reasons, Ways and Means has been more dominant in the
field of taxation than in the other two. In essence, the primary explanation suggested for this pattern of decision-making involves the
interest groups and lobbyists who operate in each of the three areas,
and the response of the Committee and the executive to the demands
of their clienteles.

TRADE LEGISLATION. "The self-assigned task of the committees was
the writing of a bill in which the rates of duty were so adjusted as to
equalize the differences of costs of production at home and abroad,"
Schattschneider described the task of the Ways and Means Committee in drafting the 1930 Smoot-Hawley tariff act.[9] "What is the important part of this bill? The important part of this bill, Mr. Chairman, is the part that permits the President of the United States,
through the special negotiator provided in the bill, to try to accomplish the elimination of duties and other impediments to the flow of
our trade within the free world. That is the most important part of
it," Wilbur Mills described the 1962 Trade Expansion Act.[10] These
statements point up how the making of United States trade policy
has shifted from Congress to the executive since 1930, and also indicate that the function of Ways and Means has undergone a drastic
change. What part have interest groups played in this change and,
concomitantly, what is the new role of the Committee vis-à-vis the
groups it used to deal with directly?

Five years after Smoot-Hawley became law, the 1934 Reciprocal
Trade Act transferred the job of determining tariff rates from Congress to the executive branch of government, which ushered in an era
of liberal trade policy compared with historical American protectionism. One significant reason for this transfer of authority is of paramount significance for this discussion: the overwhelming burden, as
Schattschneider demonstrates, of writing a tariff law involving thou-

[9] E. E. Schattschneider, *Politics, Pressures and the Tariff* (Hamden, Conn.:
Archon Books, 1963), p. 67.
[10] *Congressional Record*, June 28, 1962, p. 11992.

sands of individual items that affects scores of different interests. "To preserve itself, Congress must simplify or delegate," Schattschneider writes, and in the case of the tariff Congress simplified by delegating the main task to the executive.[11] On taxes the argument is that the issue is so "complex" (i.e., susceptible to special demands) that the bill can only be written in the Committee; on tariff rates, the argument is that the issue is so complex that Congress cannot write it at all.

Since 1934 a bipartisan consensus has been shaped behind the notion that tariff-making, which is today more of a foreign policy question than a revenue-raising question, is and should be primarily the business of the executive. Eisenhower's first term was an especially important period:

> The renewal of the Reciprocal Trade Act in 1954–1955 was a sign, not only of the end of isolation and an end to one historic definition of Republicanism, but also a sign of the end of the New Deal era, in the sense that New Deal policies had lost their distinctiveness and had been incorporated into the common American heritage. A Republican administration felt free to adopt as the most cherished item of its legislative program a Roosevelt measure which transferred tariff-making from the legislative to the executive branch. In 1962, protectionism was a rear-guard action to limit a transfer of still-greater powers to the president, but the issue of principle had long since been settled in favor of executive tariff-making.[12]

Without downgrading the importance of Eisenhower's action, however, one can detect the signs of Republican acceptance (in fact, if not in ideology) of executive tariff-making among congressional protectionists, not only among more liberal Republicans, as early as the 80th Congress.

When the Republicans gained control of Congress in 1947 they did not launch a frontal assault on the program by attempting to write specific tariff schedules, as they had done in 1929–1930. Rather, they worked within the existing system of executive-centered rate determination and sought to relieve disaffected businessmen by improving their access to the decision-makers in the executive branch, and

[11] Schattschneider, *op. cit.*, p. 25.
[12] Raymond A. Bauer, Ithiel deSola Pool, and Lewis A. Dexter, *American Business and Public Policy* (New York: Atherton Press, 1963), p. 466.

by enhancing Congress's role as the final arbiter of rate disputes. The administration of the program, in other words, was the focal point of the Republicans; they made no direct effort to change a single rate.

In 1948 the Ways and Means Republicans, many of whom strongly opposed the reciprocal trade program, reported a one-year extension of the Reciprocal Trade Act. The bill, attacked by the Democrats as protectionism in disguise, gave important new fact-finding authority to the Tariff Commission at the expense of the President's Committee on Reciprocity Information. In addition, the Tariff Commission was empowered to determine the point at which a tariff would endanger domestic industry; if the president negotiated an agreement outside of this limit Congress could veto it by concurrent resolution within sixty days. The thrust of the bill, in short, improved the access of groups that felt they had no real voice in determining the substance of trade agreements, and it made Congress a court of last resort if the president rejected the peril-point findings of the Tariff Commission.[13]

These were important new changes in the administration of the program. Democrats like Robert L. Doughton, who had introduced the original 1934 bill, warned that these changes would inundate Congress with lobbyist demands, as in 1930, and that the Republican alterations were destructive to the program. "The opponents of the present law," Doughton said, "fear adverse public reaction if they kill the Trade Agreements Act with a single electric shock by refusing to extend it in any form. They have found it expedient to accomplish the same result with an overdose of chloroform." [14]

Doughton might have been right in his assessment of the motives behind the Republican bill, but his reference to adverse public reaction is important, and it is even more important that by 1948 the consensus was that the primary burden of tariff-making should fall on the executive. Certainly the bill sought to upgrade the role of Congress in the process, but as an appellate court for interest groups, not as its former rate-making self. Intentions and real desires aside, the fact is that the Republicans did not attempt to return to the days of Smoot-Hawley. Republican opposition to the 1934 innovation had declined to the point where, when they had the chance, they did little more than attempt to give industry satisfaction by altering the operation of the program as conducted by the executive.

13 *Congressional Record*, May 26, 1948, pp. 6493–6541.
14 *Ibid.*, p. 6502.

Similar evidence of de facto acceptance of the role of the executive in trade policy can be found two years before Eisenhower by looking at what the Republicans proposed when, under an open rule, they had the opportunity in 1951 to change the program. Once again they sought to give relief to complaining industries by changing the operation of the existing machinery, not by replacing it with a basically new system.

Dan Reed of New York opened debate for the Republicans. In his opinion Congress should not delegate authority to the executive to make new trade agreements, but if such authority were granted the bill should be amended in four ways that were unanimously recommended by the Republican members of Ways and Means: (1) the 1948 peril-point procedure (with some changes) should be reenacted; (2) tariff concessions should not be made to communist states; (3) Congress should pass guidelines for determining relief under the escape clause; and (4) the Act should be extended for two years, not three.[15] Much evidence shows that many Republicans adamantly opposed the Reciprocal Trade Act (e.g., Simpson argued that Congress should not have delegated the authority in the first place), but no one seriously proposed that Congress should reclaim the problem of dealing with trade policy directly. Having chased the interest groups from the halls of Congress to the halls of the executive branch in 1934, no member of the House suggested clearing the way completely for their return to the Hill, although several members would have liked to remove some of the obstacles.

In 1953 arch-protectionist Cleveland Bailey of West Virginia and Wilbur Mills debated the old free trade versus protection issue in these — strikingly new — terms:

> *Mr. Bailey.* The gentleman made the statement that the groups opposed to reciprocal trade would destroy in one year all that has been built up since 1934. I would like the record to show that the groups which are waging this fight are not interested in destroying the basic idea of reciprocal trade. We are interested in equal justice under law. We would like to have the same protection and the same privileges that have been accorded to other groups that have been enjoying the benefits of reciprocal trade. . . .
>
> *Mr. Mills.* I understand the gentleman's position. The gentleman would not, I presume, desire to go back to the old

[15] *Ibid.*, January 31, 1951, pp. 805–08.

system of Congress writing tariffs. I do not think he would. I think what the gentleman wants is an administration of the program in the light of the needs which exist in the area which he represents.[16]

And in 1962 when the House debated the first major expansion of the president's trade authority since 1934, Republican Committee member Curtis said during the floor debate:

> I have been devoting my efforts over the period of years on the Ways and Means Committee to try to get the procedure straightened out so that we, the Congress, *do the job that we are supposed to do which is to see that our industry and our labor and our agriculture are not counted out when the executive exercises its powers in the making of trade agreements and trade treaties that there are procedures whereby their interests are evaluated.* I think what is in this bill, inadequate as it is in other ways, is so far superior to what we have had in the past. All I can say is that this can be a great move forward. This can be the beginning of some really new trade policy depending upon how the Executive carries out the powers that have been granted to him. . . .[17]

Thus the modern history of the Committee's relationship with interest groups in foreign trade legislation is marked by the transference of group demands to the executive branch and, at the same time, efforts by the Committee to protect rights of affected people to be heard. The Republicans, especially responsive to charges that the executive pays little heed to legitimate claims for safeguards against foreign competition, substituted for congressional tariff-making the goal of reordering the executive process to make it more attuned to the voices of import-sensitive business interests. Republican efforts along these lines, often opposed by the Democrats, have not always been without appeal. Indeed, one major argument on behalf of the 1962 Act is that it provided efficient ways to control the adverse effects of lowered duties. Adjustment assistance for affected workers is one example, but Mills also sold the bill on the following grounds:

> Mr. Chairman, we have tried in this bill, we have tried as best we could through the process of legislation, to establish machinery to prevent to the maximum extent possible the

16 *Ibid.*, June 15, 1953, p. 6536.
17 *Ibid.*, June 28, 1962, p. 11999. (Italics added.)

making of mistakes. What do we do in this bill? I wish every Member, if he has not done so, would turn to the report on the bill beginning on page 14. Look through the procedures. Begin there. Read the pre-agreement safeguards. Read the general provisions relating to trade agreements. Read the postagreement safeguards. Read on through that — the Presidential action. . . .

Mr. Chairman, these safeguards I have talked about are in several parts. First of all, we have very elaborate machinery for people to be heard with respect to the pre-negotiation phases of this program. There are full opportunities for hearings for all interested parties. There is every opportunity after the President makes a decision as to what he might include in the list for negotiation, for interested industries and others to appear before this group and explain why their industry should not be included. There are those who have said in letters to me that this particular industry or that particular industry has been selected for sacrifice. Mr. Chairman, there is nothing further from the truth than that. . . . Every individual concerned with this legislation will have an opportunity both at the Tariff Commission and before this Interagency Committee appointed by the President to tell why his particular commodity should not be included for a reduction in duty.[18]

Tariff policy is no longer a question of raising revenue or of protecting domestic manufacturers. It is the executive's instrument of foreign policy. With this change in the issue the Committee's job has changed from resolving a plethora of demands for protection from foreign competition to building safeguards into the executive branch process. It is a change so vast that the proverbial man from Mars would understand it as readily as Willis Hawley would if the former chairman were to appear suddenly in his old domain. Lobbyists go where decisions are made, and although Ways and Means still gets its share of trade lobbyists the group struggle has shifted to the bureaucracy. With its passing from Congress there were a few wet eyes — but not enough votes to reverse the process.

TAX LEGISLATION. On October 17, 1963, *The Washington Post* headlined: "Sen. Douglas Attacks 'Interests' In Denouncing Tax Bill Changes." Make Paul Douglas a senator in the days of Smoot-

[18] *Ibid.*, p. 11991.

Hawley, substitute the word "trade" for "tax," and the same head-lines could have appeared in a 1929 edition of *The Post*.

Tax law, infinitely complex, is infinitely reducible to small decisions that affect a few people, as the trade issue used to be. Ways and Means no longer carries the main burden of writing tariff law; social security legislation is comprehensive in scope and galvanizes fewer interest groups than taxes; tax law attracts more interest groups with pinpoint aims than any other legislation that the Committee considers. Almost every provision in the intricate Internal Revenue Code affects some economic or business interest in some way, and the Committee has not delegated its authority over the writing of tax law to the executive. Given the sensitive nature of the issue and the retention of congressional control over it, the criticism of the Code has centered around Congress.[19]

Once such general questions as whether taxes should be reduced as a way of stimulating the economy are settled, the Ways and Means Committee is faced with numerous smaller questions that are of great importance to interest groups, their representatives, and individual congressmen. A word changed here, a provision added there, can be of great value to an industry, an individual firm, or even to one man, as in the case of the "Mayer amendment" (which saved MGM president Louis B. Mayer about $2 million). With no widely accepted tax philosophy to guide them in responding to special requests, the Committee members respond in the same way that the Committee did on trade legislation: positively. Thus, for example, a depletion allowance granted to oil is gradually extended to include other minerals — so far that the Code spells out which items are *not* entitled to a depletion allowance.[20] A staff man who was leaving the Committee was told that he was entitled to one request when he got

[19] The literature on the unfairness of the Code, and how interest groups get special provisions, is voluminous, but see the following as examples: Albert Gore, "How to Be Rich Without Paying Taxes," *The New York Times Magazine*, April 11, 1965, p. 28 ff.; Julius Duscha, "The Tax Bill as Amended by the Lobbyists," *The Reporter*, XXVII (October 25, 1962), 26–28; William L. Cary, "Erosion of the Tax Laws," *Harvard Business Review*, XXXIII (September–October, 1955), 103–11; Philip M. Stern, *The Great Treasury Raid* (New York: Random House, 1962). By far the most important analytical treatment of the reasons behind special provisions and the difficulties facing tax reformers is Stanley S. Surrey, "The Congress and the Tax Lobbyist — How Special Tax Provisions Get Enacted," *Harvard Law Review*, LXX (May, 1957), 1145–82. Surrey analyzes fourteen general factors which help explain why Congress is responsive to narrow tax interests.

[20] Stern, *op. cit.*, p. 33.

on the outside, and to make it a good one. Whether he can collect from the Committee or not is unimportant; that he was told this indicates the nature of the tax-making process.

However, one crucial difference exists between taxes and trade: tax policy is primarily a domestic question. Beseiged by interest groups in trade legislation the members could shift the burden to the executive branch. To some extent the Committee does this by providing that the implementation of tax law be spelled out in regulations issued by the Internal Revenue Service, but this process has not gone nearly as far toward executive control of tax policy as it has in the area of trade.

Nor does a shift toward executive control of taxation, given the special constitutional role of the House in raising revenue, seem likely. Surrey writes of Article 1, section 7:

> The House Committee on Ways and Means jealously guards this clause against possible inroads by the Senate. It also protects its jurisdiction over revenue legislation from encroachment by other House committees. When Senators and other congressmen must toe the line, the executive is not likely to be permitted to occupy a superior position. . . . The Congress, consequently, regards the shaping of a revenue bill as very much its prerogative. It will seek the views of the executive, for there is a respect for the sustained labors of those in the executive departments and also a recognition, varying with the times, of the importance of presidential programs. But control over the legislation itself, both as to broad policies and as to details, rests with the Congress. *Hence a congressman, and especially a member of the tax committees, is in a position to make the tax laws bend in favor of a particular individual or group despite strong objection from the executive branch.*[21]

On major tax legislation Congress has repeatedly demonstrated its independence of the executive branch. Senator Alben Barkley resigned as Senate leader over a Roosevelt veto of a tax bill in 1944; the veto was overridden. President Truman's tax difficulties with the 80th Congress have already been discussed, but Truman's tax problems with Congress were not confined to 1947–1948. In 1951 the Korean War led Truman to propose a $10 billion tax increase (his first request had been for $16 billion). After four months of labor on the

[21] Surrey, *op. cit.*, pp. 1154–55. (Italics added.)

bill, Ways and Means reported a $7.2 billion increase. The Senate
Finance Committee took three months to report a $5.5 billion bill.
After the House rejected the first conference report (Republicans
protesting big spending, liberal Democrats calling it a "soak-the-poor"
bill) a bill was passed raising $5.7 billion in revenue and Truman
"reluctantly" signed it.[22]

One of the most interesting aspects of the 1951 Revenue Act was
what happened to Truman's loophole-closing proposals: reduction of
the oil and gas depletion allowance from 27.5 per cent to 15 per cent,
cuts in other depletion allowances, taxation of income from state and
municipal bonds, reform of capital gains taxation, and others. Ways
and Means made some minor changes in these areas but the Committee decided against reducing the depletion allowance. In fact, the
allowance for coal was doubled from 5 to 10 per cent, the 5 per cent
rate was extended to several new items (sand, gravel, clam shells,
etc.), and a rate of 15 per cent was applied to borax, fuller's earth, re-
fractory and fire clay, quartzite, perlite, diatomaceous earth, metal-
lurgical and chemical grade limestone, and tripoli.[23] The Senate, of
course, added other "sweeteners" to the tax increase bill, and the bill
passed after a tax reform move by Senators Hubert Humphrey and
Paul Douglas failed on the Senate floor.

President Eisenhower had different (but no less serious) problems
with Ways and Means than Truman. Ways and Means Republicans
like Dan Reed were quite willing to differ with Eisenhower over tax
reduction and the excess profits tax, and the Committee Democrats
contested Eisenhower's 1954 proposal to grant a credit and exclusion
to dividend income. The Democrats proposed tax reductions for
lower-income groups by increasing the personal exemption from $600
to $700 (at a cost of over $2 billion), and when Eisenhower opposed
this plan his bill was attacked as being too beneficial to the rich at
the expense of the poor.[24] The Republicans had the votes to defeat
the Democratic amendments in 1954, but in 1955 the Senate had to
save the administration by rejecting the House-passed $20 tax credit,
and in 1959 Eisenhower "was forced to accept what was much the
smaller half of the loaf he had sought" on a major bill dealing with
interest rates on bonds.[25] Constant conflict between Eisenhower and

[22] *Congressional Quarterly Almanac*, 1951, pp. 409–30.
[23] *Ibid.*, p. 415. Truman's proposals for tax reforms in 1950 were as well
received by Ways and Means as the 1951 reforms.
[24] *Ibid.*, 1954, pp. 481–82.
[25] *Ibid.*, 1959, p. 273.

Congress over revenue legislation was not, of course, the rule in the 1950's (in part because the administration proposed few major bills in the tax field). By and large the Eisenhower years were tranquil for the Ways and Means Committee on taxation; neither Congress nor the executive was dominant in tax policy because no new policies were forthcoming. The elections of Kennedy in 1960 and Johnson in 1964 changed this. Ways and Means played a key role in the 1967–1968 conflict over President Johnson's proposed 10 per cent surcharge, but Congress also made major substantive changes in the 1962 and 1964 Revenue Acts. The 1962 Act was summed up accurately by *CQ*:

> The final version of the bill, H.R. 10650, embodied many provisions that drew the praise of President Kennedy and Secretary of the Treasury Douglas Dillon. But the final product also was *vastly different* from the tax proposals that the President first presented to Congress on April 20, 1961.[26]
>
> The investment tax credit that was enacted varied in detail and in basic approach from the proposal that President Kennedy presented in April, 1961.[27]

This evidence shows that Congress is as active in the making of tax policy as it is passive in trade policy. Ways and Means, assisted by a tax staff that is equal to the expertise of the Treasury Department, does not make fundamental changes in every administration tax bill. Many important changes, in fact, are made by the Senate and not by Ways and Means, as a study of the 1962 Revenue Act would show. But the history of tax legislation substantiates the claim of Committee members that they, not the executive branch, have the most say in tax policy. At the very least, the role of Ways and Means and of Congress generally in the area of taxation shows that some matters are not too complex politically to be handled in the legislative process. If this is the case with taxes, the quiet death of periodic proposals to give the president stand-by tax reduction authority, subject to a congressional veto, becomes understandable, and no major changes in either the process or the policy may be expected.

SOCIAL SECURITY LEGISLATION. The Ways and Means Committee has conflicted less with the executive branch of government in the

---

[26] *Ibid.*, 1962, p. 478. (Italics added.)
[27] *Ibid.*, p. 483.

social security area than in taxes — except for medicare. Congressional resistance to President Truman's national health insurance program doomed the program — attacked as "socialized medicine" by congressional Republicans and the American Medical Association — from the start. Less ambitious programs were proposed yearly in Congress during the Eisenhower years, but in 1960 the Forand hospital care bill, opposed by the administration, was defeated in Ways and Means by a two-to-one vote. HEW Secretary Arthur Flemming proposed an alternative program in 1960 that had the administration's blessing, but it had little chance in Congress: Barry Goldwater saw it as "socialized medicine," Ways and Means member Burr Harrison (D., Va.) saw it as a "Townsend plan–Rube Goldberg scheme," George Meany preferred a social security approach, and the Ways and Means Committee Republicans called for more study.[28] Kerr-Mills, a federal-state health care program of the same genre as the administration plan, did become law in 1960. It satisfied no one (except perhaps Kerr's state of Oklahoma and other states who shared in $72 million of "freed money" under Kerr-Mills).[29]

After the enactment of the original Social Security Act in 1935 and the 1939 Act, no major liberalizations were made in the program until 1950. Beginning in 1950, however, the basic appeal of the program to Congress and to the electorate was demonstrated by the enactment of a bill every election year six times running. Two of the six bills are of special interest here because they were initiated not by the administration but by the Ways and Means Committee. Indeed, the 1956 and 1958 Acts were passed by Congress over the reluctance of the executive branch.

Ways and Means, after the 1954 Social Security Act which made major liberalizations in the program in accordance with the recommendations of President Eisenhower, reported and passed in 1955 another major social security bill. Eisenhower had warned against expanding the program in his State of the Union message but the Committee, without increasing benefit payments, drafted a bill making disability benefits payable at age 50 instead of 65, and lowering the retirement age for women from 65 to 62. "Both proposals were enacted, with modifications, although the Administration opposed them." [30] The Senate did not act on the bill until 1956. The Senate

[28] *Ibid.*, 1960, p. 155.
[29] *Ibid.*, p. 163.
[30] *Ibid.*, 1956, p. 392.

Finance Committee — more conservative than Ways and Means in this period — struck out the disability program and applied the age 62 retirement provision to widows only. Both were restored on the Senate floor and accepted, with little enthusiasm, by Eisenhower.

Two years later Ways and Means again took the initiative on social security. The 1958 Social Security Amendments were enacted although, according to the Chief Actuary of the Social Security Administration, "The Executive Branch of the Government had made no major recommendations for legislation." [31] The administration did succeed, under threat of a veto, in getting the Senate to cut back the House-passed increases in federal public assistance payments to the states, but in 1958 Congress was willing to pass this major piece of legislation without waiting for presidential support or even the report of the Advisory Council on Social Security Financing.[32] The 1958 Amendments, plus a 1958 unemployment compensation bill reported by the Committee as a far more liberal measure than the Eisenhower administration supported (but which was cut back on the House floor), show that in the area of social security Ways and Means both took the lead and was more liberal on substance than the Eisenhower administration.

The social security record of Congress after the Democrats took control of the presidency in 1961 was mixed. In 1961, Ways and Means scaled down the administration's social security requests, but in 1962 the Committee liberalized federal payments in three public assistance programs over the opposition (weak opposition, according to Mills) of the administration. Medicare was stymied until 1965, but then the Committee reported a bill with major congressional-sponsored liberalizations. In 1967, Ways and Means passed a $3 billion bill that was less than the administration had requested but a sizable liberalization nonetheless. The Committee also, of course, initiated major new changes in the public welfare program over administration opposition.

It is difficult to generalize about executive-legislative relations in social security legislation. A great deal depends on which party has control of Congress and the presidency. For example, one might speculate that a major reason behind the 1956–1958 House action was the political advantage to the Democrats of taking the lead away

---

[31] Robert J. Myers, "1958 Amendments to the Social Security Act," *Transactions of the Society of Actuaries*, XI (March–April, 1959), 6.
[32] *Congressional Quarterly Almanac*, 1958, pp. 156–59.

from the Republican administration on a popular issue. The fact that
the executive branch asks Congress for things it knows it will not get
is a discount factor that must be considered and that may transform
the meaning of congressional action to the executive compared with
the view of someone outside the process. And there is no way to measure the extent to which the executive proposes legislation because
the Committee or other congressional participants have expressed
interest in doing this or that.

Yet it is clear that the Ways and Means Committee and the Congress generally have not been docile registers of decisions reached in
the executive branch on social security matters. The administration
and the Department of Health, Education and Welfare have their
constituents and attendant policy orientations, just as congressmen
have theirs. On many social security questions a shared interest
between Congress and the executive has been the dominant characteristic of the policy-making process, but on many other questions Congress has passed an independent judgment on the issues at stake in
social security. This conclusion argues against exaggerating the decline
of Congress as an autonomous influence, at least in the making of
national social security policy.

EXECUTIVE-LEGISLATIVE INTERACTION

Separate institutions sharing authority and responsibility have obvious communications problems. How are the two branches linked,
how do they organize their interaction, and what are the main points
of contact between them? The Committee members identify first
with the Committee and have "different fish to fry" than the executive departments. How do the two branches work together and resolve
the problems inherent in a checks and balances system of government?

Four main forms of Committee interaction with the executive
branch may be examined: (1) contacts between the Committee's
staff and Treasury staff; (2) the Chairman's relationship with the
bureaucracy and the president; (3) the decision-making style of the
Committee, which allows the executive department officials direct
access to the closed sessions of the Committee; and (4) ad hoc meetings between the members and executive department representatives.

1. The complexity of tax law presents a formidable problem to the
Committee and helps explain the informal but firmly rooted practice
of consultations between the Committee's tax experts, the staff of the

Joint Committee on Internal Revenue Taxation, and the "technicians" of the Treasury Department.

The Joint Committee staff, which serves as an important link between the Senate and the Ways and Means Committee, also links the Committee with the Treasury Department. For many years Joint Committee staff experts, under Stam and continuing under Woodworth, have met with their counterparts in the Treasury Department and the Internal Revenue Service in what are known as staff "subcommittees." These subcommittees discuss various tax proposals and the technical problems involved in formulating the language necessary to put them into effect. Ideas generated by Treasury Department economists and others are discussed in these meetings. "What we do in these meetings is kick ideas around, we brainstorm ideas," one participant said. "Staff subcommittees," a Treasury official noted, "discuss the technical questions, the really hard kind. If it's a simple thing like rates the staff subcommittee won't take it up."

This informal link between formally separated institutions is a conduit of information between the Committee, which may learn what the Treasury Department is thinking about, and Treasury, which learns what the Committee is likely to accept or reject. Neither group has the authority to bind its superiors on policy matters, of course, but policy is discussed and the participants do exchange their impressions as to how the policy-makers will probably respond to different alternatives. The Joint Committee staff, for example, warned the Treasury Department in 1963 that the Committee would not go along with the controversial proposal to limit itemized deductions to 5 per cent of the taxpayer's adjusted gross income, a drop of about 15 per cent from existing practice. The Treasury Department tried for it anyway and the staff's prediction proved correct — the issue was not even put to a vote.

Although neither staff group makes policy there may be a difference between the positions of the two groups. If Blough is correct, the Secretary of the Treasury is under strong pressure to support the position of his staff because the congressional committees would resent it if he overruled an agreement at the staff level.[33] On the other hand, the Joint Committee staff, subject to many masters, does not claim to speak for Ways and Means (even though they prognosticate

[33] Roy Blough, *The Federal Taxing Process* (New York: Prentice-Hall, 1952), p. 108.

about it) and would not be undermined if the Committee did not conform to what they predicted. Given the inattention of the Committee to what goes on at the staff subcommittee level Blough's observation must at this point remain unconfirmed, but it may be true that the Secretary of the Treasury feels more bound by his staff's position than congressmen.

The flow of information from the staff meetings to the members of the Committee should not be assumed. Most Committee members probably could not care less about what takes place in these meetings and not even Chairman Mills watches them too closely. In fact, he deliberately chose not to be informed about the reform proposals contemplated in the 1963 tax message because he did not want to be identified with them too early or too strongly. Mills, who has alternative sources of information, does not have to rely on the staff mechanism.

The major significance of the staff subcommittees, then, appears to be to the staff members themselves. First, the meetings ensure that by the time the Treasury Department sends its tax message the Joint Committee staff is well versed in the complexities of the proposals and is therefore equipped to explain them to the members. Second, the predictions of Committee response made by the Joint Committee staff have been relayed to the top officials of the Treasury Department and become one more element in their calculation of what they should propose to Congress. Third, having worked closely together throughout the process the two staffs are better able to draft the necessary language after the Committee makes a decision and to present the issues during the Committee's deliberations on the bill.

After the preliminaries are over and Ways and Means is in executive session, the Joint Committee staff, having spent hours in consultation with Treasury Department experts, is prepared to explain arcane tax proposals to the members. Because Ways and Means allows Treasury officials to attend and participate in its executive deliberations both staffs can explain the Treasury Department's proposals to the Committee. If the Secretary of the Treasury is especially well versed in tax matters, as was Douglas Dillon on the proposal that became the Revenue Act of 1964, he will carry a large part of the burden of presenting the Department's case, and the Treasury staff will serve as a backstop to him. But the Joint Committee staff, playing the role of *Congress's* staff, ensures that the Committee hears all sides of the issues and thus affects the decisions that are made. One staff man told how he helped a Committee member against Treasury:

> Really, as far as I was concerned it was six of one and half a dozen of the other. Treasury was opposed to it but I pointed out that on the other hand these considerations could be taken into account and the Committee said since this is the case let's pass it. Later, after the Committee had done this, O'Brien [Thomas O'Brien, D., Ill.] met me in the hall and he really went out of his way to thank me. He was very grateful and really all I had done was stated as near an objective opinion as possible.

When there is disagreement among the experts the Committee members are inclined to rely on their staff, not Treasury's. The general feeling is that the Joint Committee staff, which generates its own studies and data independent of the Treasury Department, has demonstrated that its studies are more reliable than the executive's. For example, on the basis of calculations about federal finances made by its staff, Ways and Means in 1966 rejected the administration's request for a $332 billion temporary limit on the national debt and recommended instead a $330 billion ceiling. The $2 billion cut was predicated on the joint staff's studies that showed that federal receipts would probably exceed the amount estimated by Treasury, the deficit would consequently be less than expected, and therefore a lower ceiling could be justified. The Committee's faith in its staff was not misplaced: a week after the House passed the bill Treasury Secretary Fowler acknowledged before the Senate Finance Committee that the Department, though squeezed, could live with the House figure.[34]

Finally, the staff liaison on tax legislation is unique. No comparable arrangement exists on social welfare bills or trade bills, partly because of the lack of Committee staff in these areas. Ways and Means had a professional assistant on trade when it considered the 1962 Trade Expansion Act, Al McCauley (now a lobby-lawyer), but he had not seen the bill before it was introduced. He was consulted by the administration but he did not help draft it and his role in this issue was different from Woodworth's on taxes. Informal contacts between

---

[34] Hobart Rowen, "Fowler Accepts House Debt Action," *The Washington Post*, June 14, 1966. Before the Rules Committee, with Woodworth sitting behind him, Mills backed the Committee's action in these words: "I'm prone to believe that the staff itself may be more accurate than the Treasury."

people like McCauley and the executive branch are plentiful, but only in taxation has the process become highly institutionalized.

2. If, as one observer remarked, "Mills is the guts of taxes," it is reasonable to expect that he is at the center of the Committee's contacts with the executive branch. In some ways, and not only on tax matters, Mills is not only at the center — he is the center.

In May 1966, for example, the administration made front-page news when it proposed to liberalize trade with certain communist nations in Europe, including the Soviet Union. The next day Mills made news when he killed the measure simply by refusing to introduce it and announcing that he opposed it "at this time." [35] Eugene Keogh, who had already announced his intention to retire from Congress at the end of 1966, subsequently introduced the bill but it was clear that without Mills's support the bill had no chance whatsoever. On this kind of issue Mills is virtually a divine right monarch.

Influence such as this, built on respect, commands respect. It helps explain why the administration never launched a serious effort to pry medicare out of the Ways and Means Committee over Mills's opposition; the feeling was widespread that Mills could beat them on the floor of the House — a feeling shared, and perhaps propagated, by Mills himself. One Democrat, who was usually counted as a vote against medicare, said that he told Presidents Kennedy and Johnson that he would vote to report the bill to the House but that it would do no good; without Mills the bill would be doomed. With such messages to the White House, little wonder that Mills was often courted but never completely challenged on medicare.

Although Mills decided against being informed on the tax reform proposals of 1963 (which does not mean he was caught by surprise), he is usually well attuned to what the administration is planning in areas of interest to Ways and Means; more important, his negative response on the trade proposal and his position on medicare are atypical — usually he has been generally in favor of what the administration sends up and has had a hand in determining its content. He was intimately involved in the planning of the 1962 Trade Act and his assurances that he could get it through the House — bold program though it was — might have been an important factor in President Kennedy's decision to try for it. He discussed the question of tax rates with the administration before the 1963 tax cut proposal was

[35] "Rep. Mills Dooms Wider Trading with the Reds," *The New York Times*, May 13, 1966, p. 6.

made. Once he decided to support medicare or, rather, work out a bill of his own, he worked closely with Wilbur Cohen and other medicare experts in the administration. His was a key voice in the 1962 decision against a "quickie" tax cut that was being urged by Walter Heller and others. He worked closely with the administration on the revenue act that was passed in 1962, and he was in close touch on the 1965 bill reducing excise taxes. Mills, in short, is a primary link between the executive branch and the Committee, which is evident in the mild complaint by one senior Democratic member that he is not kept informed about what the executive has in store for the Committee: "It comes through Wilbur or not at all." A Treasury Department official confirmed:

> Mills is kept informed on what we are doing. We might inform other members if we are thinking of things that we know interest them — on lumber we might inform Ullman, on cattle Watts, on oil Thompson. I'm in touch with those members who introduce a lot of bills more than with those who do not. Generally speaking, Mills is the only one who is kept informed on the broad policy questions — now he may inform the other Democrats, I don't know.

Other evidence points to Mills's central position. During the 1962 debate over the advisability of a quickie tax cut, Sorensen relates, Mills's skepticism was an important addition to the negative side of the argument. Kennedy, in an unusual move, had Mills attend a session with his economic advisers, which clearly shows Mills's unique position in the 1960's vis-à-vis the White House.[36] Other indications include a magazine interview with Mills that was read carefully at the White House, Mills's reaction to a Kennedy tax speech that was noted (no commitment), and that Mills was perceived as the "key to House approval" of the tax reduction bill and as an "invaluable ally, respected by his colleagues, well-informed on his work and a cautious head-counter." [37] "No committee chairman," Sorensen writes, "had a firmer grip on his committee." [38] And no member of the Ways and Means Committee, he might have written, receives more attention or was in closer touch with the executive branch than Mills.

"Wilbur Mills," said John Kennedy, "knows that he was chairman

[36] Theodore Sorensen, *Kennedy* (New York: Harper & Row, 1965), pp. 425–26.
[37] *Ibid.*, pp. 430–32.
[38] *Ibid.*, p. 432.

of Ways and Means before I got here and that he'll still be chairman after I've gone — and he knows I know it. I don't have any hold on him." [39] Kennedy had no absolute hold on Mills, but on several vital questions Mills and the Kennedy administration worked harmoniously together. Relations between Mills and the Johnson administration were less good. At one point during the 1967–1968 contest over the tax surcharge the White House refuted stories that Mills had been neglected by giving the press a tabulation of times Mills and the president had conferred.[40] Such developments, which delighted newspaper reporters and filled columns for weeks, were probably secondary in importance to the fact that in 1967 the issue was a tax *increase* made necessary by the Viet Nam war. The surcharge issue illustrates, however, that given certain circumstances Mills may be a key man blocking administration policy instead of running interference for it. As Kennedy knew and Johnson learned, the president in the final analysis has little hold on House members like Mills.

3. The decision-making style of the Ways and Means Committee is unique. Throughout the entire mark-up process, which often takes the Committee months on a major bill, executive department representatives not only attend the closed sessions but are an integral, active part of the discussions. Other congressional committees allow bureaucrats into their executive sessions but no committee, as far as is known, gives them as much access as Ways and Means. They are even present when the Committee votes.

On taxes, trade, or social security issues, representatives of the relevant government agencies are present while the Committee considers the legislation. On medicare in 1965, for example, Assistant HEW Secretary Wilbur Cohen, who helped draft the original social security law thirty years before, Robert Myers, chief social security actuary, Robert Ball, head of the Social Security Administration, and others attended the sessions regularly and actually participated more than some members of the Committee. Reflective of the intimate working relationship between the Committee and the executive branch is that after the Committee completed work on the medicare bill Cohen, Myers, and Ball — not the members of the Committee — held the press conference on the bill in the Committee's Longworth Building hearing room.

[39] *Ibid.*, p. 426.
[40] Lee M. Cohen, "President Striving to Keep Record Clear on Tax Issue," *The Washington Star*, October 15, 1967, p. A1.

In 1963, when Ways and Means spent months on the administration's proposed tax cut, the Secretary of the Treasury, Douglas Dillon, bore the primary burden in the executive sessions, not his underlings. One member commented:

> You know Dillon really surprised me during the recent tax bill hearings. He was there all the time and I began to wonder, my God, doesn't the Secretary of the Treasury have better things to do than sit up here and go through all this technical crap with us? But I think he really enjoyed showing us how much he knew — in fact he was almost rude to Surrey at times. Surrey would start to answer and Dillon would shut him up. Dillon got a lot of satisfaction out of showing us how much he knew about the Code.

Dillon was there so much that this member began to think, perhaps in jest, that the Secretary was using Ways and Means as a "hideout."

Not every cabinet head attends as much or involves himself as much as Dillon did. Dillon, with many years' experience in fiscal matters, probably enjoyed the fray. In contrast, Anthony Celebrezze, who came in as Secretary of HEW after being mayor of Cleveland and who had no special training in social security, was less adept and relied more heavily on others, in particular the team of Cohen, Ball, and Myers.[41]

No matter who represents the various departments in the executive sessions, Committee members agree in principle that it is a good idea to let outsiders participate in Committee decision-making. Seventeen members of Ways and Means were asked about this, and eleven of them replied that the practice has advantages over completely closed meetings. Four members feel that it would be better not to allow them in the room, and two gave mixed replies. The four members who would prefer operating a different way said the presence of the executive department representatives inhibits the Committee's discussions, and one felt that voting would be quite different away from the executive eye. Yet the general feeling on this matter did not seem very strong; when asked if he ever mentioned his discontent to Mills, one member said no, it does not bother him enough to make it an issue.

[41] Having executive agency officials in the room is no new practice. The Committee operated the same way in 1935 when the Social Security Act was drafted. See Edwin E. Witte, *The Development of the Social Security Act* (Madison: University of Wisconsin Press, 1963), p. 92.

Some Committee members resent the presence of executive department advisers, some members like having them in attendance, but even the critics of the practice admit that it helps prevent the Committee from making mistakes. One Democrat revealed that he has tried to get Mills to eject them when the Committee votes, but another Democrat finds it a source of satisfaction. When Mills wants some executive people to come up it is the "first, second, or third men and all their assistants. On other committees they come in, make a statement, then beat it. Not on Ways and Means. They become *part* of the Committee." As part of the Committee they do not leave when the other part votes. They, in the words of one member, "live with us."

Analytically, the most interesting aspect of the Committee's decision-making style is that it has advantages for all concerned.

Suppose, for example, the Committee met in isolation and attempted, on its own, to draft a major tax bill. The problem of absenteeism might be surmounted but the problem of making mistakes would remain. With the Joint Committee staff this problem might not be too severe, but the chances of error would seem to be less with experts from the Treasury Department also in attendance. Moreover, the existing arrangement pits the Joint Committee staff against the Treasury's staff and, although this is not normally a conflictual relationship, it does act as a double check on decisions. At present, the Committee's staff and Treasury experts combine to explain tax problems to the members and to explore the ramifications of amending the massive Internal Revenue Code. Expertise confronts expertise and the Committee members often find the presentation of the Committee's staff supportive, or capable of being supportive, of their own position. If the Committee had only the Joint Committee staff present it would receive information through only one channel, although with some difficulty, Treasury Department data and, more important, the Department's position on issues could be piped into the room.

Without the bureaucrats the members would be forced to confront decisions and problems not by passing them through the bureaucratic filter but by taking them up directly. Instead of the conversation flowing from the members to the executive people and back, the members would talk to — or at — each other much more than they do now. Partisan pressures being what they are, one of the latent functions of having others present may be that they serve as the focal point of antagonism since they are, after all, the chief protagonists of new policy departures. In this type of situation Mills regulates exchanges between the members and the executive department spokesmen as well as member vs. member exchanges, which may help explain why policy disputes rarely end up in shouting matches between Republicans and Democrats.

Obvious advantages also accrue to the executive branch. Of paramount importance, nothing happens in the Committee that they do not know about and — probably — do not have a hand in. Their information about the Committee's feeling on the legislation is almost perfect (not everything happens in the Committee). Joseph Barr, an assistant to the Secretary of the Treasury, could under the prevailing practice return to his office after an executive session on the 1963 tax bill and dictate a memorandum on the day's events for circulation within the Department. Instead of relying on the varying talents of friendly congressmen the executive officials can defend their positions in person, detect soft spots, and move to shore them up. In all these ways — not to mention knowing how the members vote — inclusion in the executive session enhances the position of the administration.

Ways and Means works so closely with some executive department employees that Robert J. Myers, the Social Security Administration's head actuary, is identified on some Committee publications as "Actuary to the *Committee.*" Myers, as a professional technician, works in a confidential relationship with the Committee and is expected, by everyone concerned, to supply honest cost estimates on social security legislation regardless of how it may affect the Department's case.[42] A second HEW employee expressed his relationship with Ways and Means in these words:

> It's a peculiarly undefined role. I serve as a technician and many times I don't know whether I'm appearing as a spokesman for the administration or Department or not. In fact, they'll tell me to put on my Committee hat and tell them. Literally, this is true. "Put on your Committee hat and tell us. Is this good, what are the facts?"

This man addressed the question of possible overdependence by the Committee on HEW and that HEW, with its technical expertise,

[42] This is not to say that Myers's estimates are without political importance. Mills in 1965 used a late memorandum from Myers to criticize the Republican medical care proposal. Byrnes had not seen the latest estimates before Mills used them on the floor. *Congressional Record*, April 7, 1965 (daily edition), pp. 6970–71.

may have undue influence on the Committee's decisions. As he sees it, the practice of letting HEW experts in the closed meetings is a mark of the Committee's self-confidence, not of its reliance on the Department:

> The Committee uses us just like staff and I think this is a mark of the self-confidence of the Committee. It's less a matter of technical subject matter, technical needs, than it is the self-confidence of Ways and Means. "Sure Wilbur Cohen is present but what the hell do we care, we can do what we want." They know they can do what they want, with or without us. They don't care who comes to the executive session. They know that when Wilbur Cohen comes in he'll bring anyone who is helpful, and they know we know that we can't tell what goes on. So what do they care? Self-confidence.

When asked if Ways and Means has the staff to check HEW's presentation, he replied, "And how!" The Committee, in addition to the expertise supplied by its own staff, makes extensive use of social security experts from the Library of Congress and the House Legislative Counsel's Office, and in this man's judgment the Committee is well fortified to do a thorough job on HEW proposals.

4. Administration officials illegally lobby members of the Ways and Means Committee, frequently give different information to different members, and make deals with members, one Committee member has claimed.[43] Curtis's charges were directed at the fourth nexus between the Committee and the executive branch: informal, ad hoc, unpublicized tete-à-tetes, the lack of data on which is surpassed only by their probable importance.

Under Kennedy and Johnson the Democrats were occasionally invited down to the White House for talks, but far more common were intermittent meetings on the Hill. "Dillon and other people come up and brief me a lot but it's almost always on an individual basis and not as a group. He'll say I understand you have some problem with this or that and we'll discuss it. It's all on an individual, personal basis." Also the recipient of this kind of attention, a second Democrat suspects "they don't brief us as a group because they don't want everyone to know what they tell us individually." A third member noted a relationship between contacts with the Treasury Department and opposition to its proposals: he was briefed, and coaxed, a lot in 1963 because he gave Treasury a hard time on some items.

Treasury officials also bear witness to the practice of discussing Committee business with the members on an informal basis. "We'll inform other members of the Committee if we are considering something we know they have a special interest in, but Mills is kept informed the most and, obviously, influences our pre-message deliberations." "No, we never have formal meetings with the members to brief them. Of course, by the time we are done we've probably seen all the Democratic members individually." Although general briefings sometimes occur, usually the Treasury Department stalks the members one-by-one.

Under Kennedy and Johnson Republican Committee members were lobbied less by the administration than the Democrats but they were not completely ignored. Relations with Treasury were better than those with HEW and the Commerce Department for one Republican because Surrey came to his office to discuss a bill with him. Surrey was trying to talk him out of the bill but the member was impressed nonetheless, in part because he felt that liaison with the Eisenhower administration was bad. Eisenhower vetoed one of his bills without any advance notice.

On very rare occasions such visits may induce a Republican to leave his colleagues and vote with the administration:

> I didn't vote with my Committee colleagues on the Interest Equalization bill either. I told Byrnes why. I've always been concerned with the balance of payments and I thought this bill would help the problem. It won't solve it but I still think I cast the right vote. I talked with Roosa [Robert V. Roosa, former Under Secretary for Monetary Affairs] from the Treasury Department. Everyone, including the members on our side, agrees that he is honest and one of the best informed men on this problem, and I think he is right.

The legal walls separating the Ways and Means Committee from the executive are scaled in these four ways. But explicit interaction between the branches is affected by ingrained and self-imposed attitudes that orient the members to the administration and vice versa. Some Democrats, for example, are predisposed to agree with the policy proposals of the president and, when they disagree or vacillate, to be sensitive to executive arguments. In some cases, such as medicare, they could not have gotten on the Committee unless they were so inclined. Party identification is not strong enough to obliterate differences between the majority members of the Committee and the administration, of course, but it does moderate these differences and on many crucial questions the Democrats lined up solidly behind the president with little or no presidential effort.

The role of the Republican Committee members, on the other hand, was to oppose the administration. They are recruited to the Committee because generally speaking they have proved themselves to be good conservatives, insensitive to the blandishments of the bureaucracy, and responsive to pressures at odds with a Democratic president.

Still, the Republicans on the Committee are not monolithic on all issues; there is, at times, the possibility of the executive splitting off some Republican votes. The late Howard Baker (R., Tenn.) was more likely to vote with the Democrats than his party colleagues, and in fact Baker did break with the Republicans on occasion. Herman Schneebeli (R., Pa.) has shown similar inclinations, and during the administration's abortive effort to pass the tax surcharge in 1967 two Republican members were visited by Treasury representatives. These two members happened to learn that they were to see the same Treasury official and went to see Mills first to discuss with him what was going on. It is not easy for a Democratic administration to get Republicans under normal circumstances, let alone when Mills takes a contrary position.[44]

COMPENSATORY REPRESENTATION

In 1960 twenty-seven hundred large corporations were polled on their views about depreciation reform. Of the two thousand replies received, 63 per cent were unhappy with current tax allowances and 32 per cent were reasonably satisfied with existing law.[45]

What makes this poll interesting is that it was conducted by the Treasury Department. In effect, Treasury polled part of its constitu-

[44] For a Republican to vote with the Democrats may entail some cost. Other Republican members may be alienated or upset, as in the case of one member who saw Baker's defections as legitimate but hard to accept. The same member who was upset with Baker once expressed his intention to oppose one of Schneebeli's bills because he did not like its content but also because he wanted to show Schneebeli that if he was going to get close to the Democrats he could not expect the rest of the Republicans to be with him all the time.

[45] *Congressional Quarterly Almanac*, 1961, p. 459.

ency just as congressmen sometimes poll their constituents, thus vividly pointing up that the Treasury Department, like all the executive departments, is as much involved in the business of representation as the Congress.

Although the policy-making functions of Congress have not declined as much as Huntington implies, he did identify one major factor determining which branch of government plays the most important role in the legislative process. Of the executive branch, Huntington wrote:

> Here truly is representative government along classic lines and of a sort which Congress has not known for decades. One key to the "decline" of Congress lies in the defects of Congress as a representative body.[46]

Representation of interests lies at the heart of the question of which branch of government has most to say about policy decisions reached at the national level, an observation at least as old as Arthur Bentley's classic study of groups first published in 1908.[47]

Congress and the executive branch are involved in the delicate and competitive business of arriving at policies that can be passed into law and administered effectively. With this perspective, many aspects of Congress fall into place. For example, if congressmen perceive less pressure in the area of foreign trade than expected, the reasons may be that psychologically they filter pressure out, the groups that visit them are on the same side of the issue, no single group is powerful enough to defeat them, etc. But another reason may be that their psychological filters are not as strong as their responsibility for making specific policy decisions is weak. Pressure in Congress is probably a mix of how you see it and whether you are in the position of making policy.

If the view of representation is broadened to include the executive

---

[46] Huntington, *op. cit.*, p. 17. For a similar argument see Roger H. Davidson, "Congress and the Executive: The Race for Representation," in de Grazia, ed., *op. cit.*, pp. 365–402.

[47] Arthur F. Bentley, *The Process of Government* (Bloomington, Ind.: Principia Press, 1935). Bentley writes: "If group interests tend in a certain direction, and are checked in their course through Congress, they will find their way through the presidency. If the group interests take permanently a form which makes Congress an inadequate agency for them, then the presidency will consolidate its power. If on the other hand the shifting of the interests or the change in Congress makes the latter agency adequate, then the presidency's power will readjust itself accordingly" (p. 351). See also Bertram M. Gross, *The Legislative Struggle* (New York: McGraw Hill Book Co., 1953), p. 149.

branch as well as Congress, some insight may also be gained into the common observation that congressional decision-making proceeds through bargaining and compromising. What this observation omits is that Congress does not always bargain and compromise executive branch proposals. Sometimes Congress passes these proposals virtually unchanged; at other times, Congress bargains and compromises them so much that they are virtually unrecognizable in their final form compared to the initial executive branch recommendations. The interesting question is why some proposals initiated downtown go through Congress unscathed, others are changed a great deal, and some do not go through at all. One hypothesis links the two branches of government through the medium of representation: *the amount of bargaining and compromising of executive branch policy proposals in Congress varies inversely with the amount of bargaining and compromising that occurs between interest groups and the executive branch.* A demonstration of this hypothesis might explain why Congress or the executive branch appears to be the dominant influence in national policy-making, and why the policy-making role of Congress varies in the tax field compared to trade legislation.

One of the primary functions of Congress is providing compensatory representation for those interests that are not represented, for whatever reasons, in the executive branch. Tax policy — an area in which Congress retains a good deal of autonomy, in which Congress is particularly sensitive to encroachments on its prerogatives, and in which it provides itself with an expert staff to help in making decisions — offers a policy area within which hypotheses about the executive branch, interest group, and congressional relationship may be profitably explored. The Revenue Acts of 1962 and 1964 show how the representation process works on Ways and Means, and how this process affects policy outcomes.

TAXES. Interest groups and lobbyists are, of course, intimately involved in the tax-making process from start to finish. In the initial stages of a tax bill the Treasury Department (as well as the Joint Committee staff) is in close touch with those who will be affected by what Treasury proposes to Congress. A Treasury Department official described this stage of the process:

> We call in people who will be affected, get their views, sometimes modify or drop proposed ideas. We try to get their opinion on what we think might be a good idea. Repre-

sentatives of industry and other people who are affected by what we consider are consulted — sometimes we call them in, sometimes they get wind of it and contact us. It's quite informal.

A second Treasury official, when asked if a record is kept of who Treasury consults before completing its proposals, said that no record is kept, but added, "Just take a look at the provisions and who they affect and you can be pretty sure we've met with the major spokesmen."

These meetings are important. Early in the interviews conducted for this study a staff man on Ways and Means casually observed that, "When people come in to see me I often tell them to see if they can't get what they want from the Treasury before it sends up its recommendations because if they can chances are good that they will have no trouble from the Committee." Concurring with this view, the Treasury employee who said they meet with nearly all the concerned groups declared, "This stage is important, I agree, because if we agree with the lobbyists you can be sure the Committee won't change it."

What happens to a tax bill in Congress, therefore, is affected by the nature of interest aggregation in the Treasury Department. If Treasury is able to aggregate group demands, the Committee will not have to; if, however, Treasury is not or cannot be responsive to group demands the policy-making role of Congress will be enhanced.

1962 REVENUE ACT. The first major action of the newly elected Kennedy administration in the tax field was the April 1961 proposal to grant business a 15 per cent tax credit on investments in new production equipment. This proposal, designed to stimulate economic growth, was prepared by a small group of economic consultants meeting with Stanley S. Surrey. Contrary to later practice, the Treasury Department did not discuss its 1961 proposals with leaders of Ways and Means, the Finance Committee, or with Colin Stam, head of the Joint Committee staff.[48] The investment credit was made part of a delicately balanced tax package that Treasury hoped would automatically appeal to both labor and business, a hope that was disappointed.

---

[48] David J. Stern, "Congress, Politics, and Taxes: A Case Study of the Revenue Act of 1962" (Ph.D. Dissertation, Claremont Graduate School, 1965), p. 48. The account presented here relies heavily on Stern's case study.

Coupled with the investment credit in the administration's proposal were two proposals intended to draw support from liberal
groups: withholding of taxes on interest and dividend income, a tax
reform long sought by liberals; and reforms in the taxation of foreign
income of American-owned businesses ("tax havens"), another target of tax reformers. "Politically, it was hoped that business-conserva-
tive groups would swallow withholding and the foreign income sections in their haste to reap the benefits of the tax credit, while liberals
would acquiesce in the credit in order to secure the other two." [49]
Treasury also proposed repeal of the dividend credit and exclusion, a
suggestion that died quietly in the Ways and Means Committee.

The tax package recommended by Treasury was not well received.
Business interests much preferred changes in the tax law governing
depreciation of capital assets, and organized labor attacked the investment credit as a windfall to business. Treasury, for its part, agreed
with the need for depreciation reform and in fact granted some
liberalization to the textile industry in the fall of 1961, while holding
out the promise of wider reforms in the future. Privately, many businessmen desired the investment credit, but they maintained public
opposition to it to be free to oppose other parts of the administration
program.[50]

Under these conditions, the way was open to the Ways and Means
Committee to formulate a bill that would quiet enough opposition to
pass the House, which meant drastic changes had to be made in the
proposed legislation. By a straight party-line vote the Committee in
January 1962 adopted a scaled-down credit provision of 8 per cent
compared to the original 15 per cent request, and extended the credit
to industries not covered by the administration proposal. "Party
loyalty was probably the major factor behind the Administration's
success," [51] but it was certainly a qualified success. Just prior to floor
consideration, the credit was lowered to 7 per cent.

Withholding on dividends and interest (with certain exemptions)
cleared the Ways and Means Committee despite the opposition of
financial institutions and Committee Republicans. Mills was strongly
for this tax reform; some concerned interests opposing this suggestion
were more worried about other parts of the bill; and although members received substantial mail from stockbrokers and stockholders the

49 *Ibid.*, p. 114.
50 *Ibid.*, pp. 162–63.
51 *Ibid.*, p. 167.

Committee seemed to feel, Stern reports, that these people could take care of themselves. Moreover, relatively little mail was received from bank depositors, partly because savings institutions had decided to hold their fire on this proposal for the Senate.[52] When the bill reached the Senate the Senators were inundated with mail protesting withholding, and the plan was dropped.

Another conflict between business and the administration that the Committee had to resolve was over controlled foreign corporations. Ways and Means received so much business opposition to this proposal that the administration considered dropping it, but the Committee did agree on a watered-down version of the recommendation drafted by Colin Stam and introduced by John Byrnes. This version incurred the wrath of the Executive Council of the AFL-CIO, however, and faced with the apparently serious threat by organized labor to oppose the bill unless the section were tightened, the Committee reversed itself and tightened the section. Labor acquiesced and awaited Senate consideration of the tax haven question.[53]

Not all of the 1961 Treasury proposals were opposed by business and labor. Treasury did work with some businesses in passing the bill and helped establish and maintain organizations interested in passing the investment credit. The opposition of business and labor shows that the Treasury Department did not design a program with wide appeal to concerned interests, and with little interest group backing behind the proposals and great opposition to the proposals the Committee changes were a foregone conclusion. In all, Treasury probably did better in Ways and Means than it might have given the weak interest group support behind its recommendations.

1964 REVENUE ACT. If, on any given proposal, the Ways and Means Committee were in perfect agreement with the demands of interest groups and individuals it would modify every Treasury-proposed tax reduction and increase in the direction of these demands. Omitting for the time being the question of the Committee's independent assessment of substantive policies, the Treasury would "win" in direct proportion to the extent that its proposals were supported by interested parties; it would "lose" in direct proportion to the opposition by interested parties. The stronger the opposition to Treasury proposals the more Ways and Means will tend to reject or seriously amend the

---

[52] *Ibid.*, pp. 168–72.
[53] *Ibid.*, pp. 172–76.

proposals; the stronger the support the less likely Ways and Means will reject or amend the proposal.

The Revenue Act of 1964 is strong though not conclusive support for these hypotheses. Treasury's proposal to cut taxes involved both revenue-losing and revenue-gaining proposals. To cut taxes by a net of $10.3 billion Treasury suggested a package that reduced taxes by $13.6 billion and recouped, through a variety of means, $3.3 billion.

All but $1 billion of the $3.3 billion was to come from one change in the revenue laws, a 5 per cent floor under itemized deductions (i.e., taxpayers who itemize their returns could deduct only that part of their deductions that exceeded 5 per cent of their adjusted gross income).

Virtually no one except Treasury supported the 5 per cent floor. In the testimony received by Ways and Means, one hundred and four groups and individuals opposed the proposal and only one (Roy Blough of Columbia University) supported it. The closest Treasury came to getting major support was from the AFL-CIO, who thought that the 5 per cent floor was not feasible and that constructive alternatives to it should be sought. The opposition ranged from the United States Chamber of Commerce to the Girl Scouts of America, the latter typical of a number of groups that felt the floor would adversely affect organizations dependent upon charitable contributions for their operations. One Ways and Means member felt so strongly about the proposal that he led in organizing opposition to it in his district.[54]

The 5 per cent floor, stillborn from the start, was not even put to a vote in the Committee.

The controversy over the 1964 Revenue Act did not center around lowering tax rates, although the Republicans on the Committee and in the House later banded together opposing the tax cut without expenditure controls. Conflict centered around the structural tax reforms associated with the tax reduction. These reforms were made an integral part of the tax bill by Treasury but, as John Byrnes observed on the first day of hearings, the opposition was so great that they might have to be put in "deep freeze if we are going to get a tax bill this year." [55] Byrnes also referred to a statement made by House Democratic Whip Hale Boggs that the reforms should be dropped to

[54] Everett F. Cataldo, "The House Committee on Ways and Means" (Ph.D. Dissertation, Ohio State University, 1965), p. 100.
[55] Committee on Ways and Means, *Hearings on the President's 1963 Tax Message*, 88th Cong., 1st Sess., 1963, I, p. 534. Cited hereafter as *Hearings.*

get the tax cut,[56] which was an ominous sign for the reforms but accurately expressed a wide reaction to them.

Ways and Means, as it usually does on a major proposal, held lengthy hearings on the 1963 tax message. The oral and written testimony it received on thirty-nine proposals classified by the Committee staff was overwhelmingly negative: of 1,188 classifiable responses to thirty-nine Treasury proposals, 71 per cent were negative, 18 per cent were positive, 2 per cent were positive but wanted to go further than Treasury, and 9 per cent were "other." On nine proposals costing revenue, a majority of the testimony favored Treasury's proposal or wanted to go beyond it.[57] The tax reforms received so much criticism from so many groups that the Committee felt that virtually no one supported Treasury's proposals. The following colloquy between Ross Bass (D., Tenn.) and the representative of the National Livestock Tax Committee reveals the environment within which Ways and Means went to work on the reforms:

> *Mr. Bass.* I can hardly recall a single witness who has come before the committee who has recommended any of the structural reforms. They all seem to oppose all of the reforms that are recommended which will recover a portion of the tax reduction and almost every witness that has been before this committee has opposed that reform which would affect his own industry.
>
> Now, do you recommend, in recommending a tax cut, any of these other reforms that do not necessarily affect your industry?
>
> *Mr. Mitchell.* Apparently, our industry is just going along, as we said, with the inclination of other industries in that situation.
>
> *Mr. Bass.* In other words, is there an area of collusion where he says, "I will support your opposition to my reform if you will support the opposition to my reform [*sic*]."
>
> *Mr. Mitchell.* We have not resorted to that tactic in this particular instance, but it might bear investigation.
>
> *Mr. Bass.* Well, I would agree with the gentleman because

---

[56] *Ibid.*, pp. 534–35.

[57] These statements about the testimony on the 1964 Revenue Act, and other data to follow, are based on an analysis of the testimony done by the staff of the Joint Committee on Internal Revenue Taxation. See Joint Committee on Internal Revenue Taxation, "Digest of Testimony Presented and Statements Submitted to the Committee on Ways and Means with Respect to the President's 1963 Tax Message," June 12, 1963, U.S. Government Printing Office.

it has been a rather constant occurrence before the committee.[58]

When Roy Blough testified in support of some of the reforms Cecil King (D., Calif.) complimented him for his "spunk in running against the tide of witnesses who have been presenting their views to this committee for 3 weeks." [59]

The Treasury Department had a hard time pleasing anyone during the 1963–1964 deliberations on tax reduction. Its proposal to liberalize the medical expense deduction for people with disabled dependents, for example, was met by an appeal from the National Federation of the Blind to liberalize the deduction more, and by the same group's support of a bill introduced by King providing an additional tax exemption for a taxpayer with a blind dependent.[60]

If Treasury's reform proposals met a negative reception, neither could any controversial tax reforms be passed apart from the tax reduction measure. A. Sydney Herlong (D., Fla.) was not challenged when he told Budget Director Kermit Gordon precisely that early in the hearings; [61] the remaining question was how far the Committee would go in retaining any of the reform proposals. And Ways and Means did not go very far.

Clearly, the Ways and Means Committee, when confronted by a Treasury Department proposal, does not simply calculate the political advantages or disadvantages associated with different courses of action, but in the case of the 1963 tax bill the Committee's judgment on various proposals remarkably resembles the direction of the testimony received from relevant interests. This is true, moreover, not only in the case of the 5 per cent floor, an unusually controversial proposal, but with the great majority of the 1963 proposals made by the Kennedy administration. To what extent the Committee members were influenced by the reaction of groups and individuals to the proposals cannot be ascertained, but there is no doubt that the Committee majority reacted the same way to most proposals as those who expressed themselves (rather forcefully) to the Committee.

---

[58] *Hearings, op. cit.*, III, pp. 1558–59. Once again the similarity between taxes and trade before 1934 is apparent. Schattschneider records that in the hearings on Smoot-Hawley interest groups followed the norm of mutual non-interference: do not oppose the tariff (tax) advantages of others, and they will not oppose yours. *Op. cit.*, pp. 135–36.

[59] *Hearings, op. cit.*, IV, p. 2246.

[60] *Ibid.*, II, p. 1253.

[61] *Ibid.*, I, p. 790.

The confluence of opinion inside and outside the Committee is particularly evident in the area of capital gains taxation. Treasury's proposals in this area consisted of both revenue-losing and revenue-gaining provisions. As shown by Table 7.1, the revenue-gaining proposals were overwhelmingly opposed before the Committee while the revenue losing proposals were, of course, supported by the testimony. Ways and Means, for the most part, made changes in the Treasury Department's recommendations in line with the testimony and reached a compromise on how much tax reduction should be given to capital gains taxpayers.

Treasury's reducing formula called for a decrease in the portion of long-term capital gains included in taxable income from 50 per cent to 30 per cent (supported by most of the groups), but at the same time it increased from six months to one year the time assets had to be held to qualify for the favorable long-term capital gains treatment (opposed by most of the groups). Ways and Means resolved this conflict by adopting a rather complicated compromise. Two categories of

TABLE 7.1
REVENUE-REDUCING AND REVENUE-GAINING PROPOSALS OF TREASURY IN CAPITAL GAINS AREA, 1963

Revenue-reducing:	Amount (millions)	TESTIMONY RECEIVED BY WAYS AND MEANS		
		Pro	Con	Other
Reduce inclusion percentage ⎱		15	2	4
Extend holding period ⎰	−430	8	10	5
Allow indefinite carryover of losses	−20	11	0	0
Totals	−450	34	12	9
Revenue-gaining:				
Tax gains accrued at time of death or gift	+300	2	53	2
Change definition of capital gains:	+250			
Stock options		7	38	2
Real estate		1	19	13
Timber income		0	179	0
Lump-sum distributions		3	72	0
Coal leases		0	7	0
Farming		1	18	2
Livestock		0	2	0
Patents		0	3	0
Installment sales		1	2	1
Life estates		0	0	1
Totals	+100	15	393	21

SOURCE: Joint Committee on Internal Revenue Taxation.

capital gains, class A and class B, were established. Class A capital gains applied to assets held more than two years and were given more favorable treatment than long-term capital gains under existing law: 40 per cent of the gain, compared to 50 per cent under present law, was to be included in ordinary income. In addition, an alternative tax rate of 21 per cent was provided where this would result in a lower tax than inclusion in ordinary income (25 per cent rate under existing law).

Class B capital gains, defined as capital gains on assets held more than six months but less than two years, continued to be treated the same way as long-term capital gains under the present law. To take care of the enormous opposition to Treasury's proposed redefinition of capital gains the Committee explicitly provided that the following assets would be treated the same way as under existing law:

1. Timber
2. Coal royalties
3. Iron ore royalties
4. Livestock
5. Unharvested crops
6. Patents
7. Certain employee termination payments
8. Lump-sum payments

In other words, Ways and Means, having changed the definition, then exempted many of those interests that expressed themselves in opposition to Treasury's proposals.

Two revenue-gaining proposals in Table 7.1, stock options and real estate transactions, received much attention from affected interests but the Committee did take action in these fields. Treasury supported the outright repeal of the stock option provision but the Committee refused to go this far. Ways and Means did act to correct some of the abuses of stock options that many business executives who testified admitted were wrong. Although the changes made by the Committee were many their net revenue effect was nil. The Committee agreed with the interested parties on the question of stock options, not with Treasury.

The Committee's handling of the real estate question is difficult to categorize but in general it appears that the Committee did deviate somewhat from the course of the testimony. Many people who opposed Treasury, however, acknowledged that some steps could be taken to correct abuses in the real estate area, and much of the opposition was qualified by suggestions for changes if the Committee decided to act. Thus the Committee's action was not as far out of line with the majority testimony as a simple count would indicate, largely because of an unusually large number of "other" positions on this question.

Treasury's major revenue-gaining proposal, the taxation of net gains accrued at time of death or gift, was supported by only two statements (Roy Blough and the AFL-CIO) and opposed by fifty-three. Ways and Means dropped it completely. The proposal to allow an indefinite carryover of net capital losses was the only Treasury proposal unanimously endorsed in the testimony. The Committee liberalized it somewhat and passed it.

In general, the pattern of decisions in the capital gains area follows closely that of the 5 per cent floor. Given intense opposition to Treasury proposals the Ways and Means Committee reaches decisions that are generally in harmony with the opponents. On some questions there is perfect agreement between the Committee and Treasury's opponents, and Treasury's proposals are dropped or changed completely. On others the fit between the Committee's decisions and the bulk of the testimony from interested parties is more ambiguous, but in no instance did the Committee side completely with Treasury against the majority view of the nongovernmental participants. On the key capital gains proposals the decisions made by the Committee were far closer to the negative testimony than to the Treasury position.

For analytical purposes the rest of Treasury's 1963 proposals are grouped into those that reduced the tax load and those that increased it. The majority testimony might be expected to support Treasury's revenue-losing proposals and oppose its revenue-gaining ones, and the decisions of Ways and Means vary with the effect of a proposal on the relevant parties. The theory is that revenue-losing proposals will be supported by a majority of the testimony and that the Committee will give Treasury as much if not more than it requests. Revenue-gaining proposals should be opposed by a majority of witnesses and the Committee should reject or seriously weaken Treasury's proposals.

Table 7.2 presents the data on nine Treasury proposals that cost the federal government revenue. On all but three the direction of the testimony is as expected (pro) but on four of the nine decisions the Committee did *not* act in accordance with the demands. That is, the

TABLE 7.2

REVENUE-LOSING PROPOSALS OF TREASURY AND WAYS AND MEANS
ACTION (INDIVIDUALS AND CORPORATIONS)

		TESTIMONY RECEIVED BY WAYS AND MEANS				
Treasury proposal	Amount (millions)	Committee testimony				Ways and Means action (millions)
		Pro	Con	Pro+	Other	
Individuals:						
1. Minimum standard deduction	310	4	13	1	3	320
2. Liberalize child care deduction	20	9	1	0	7	5
3. Tax treatment of elderly	320	8	16	0	6	0
4. Moving expenses	50	9	1	10	2	60
5. Income averaging	40	26	10	6	4	40
6. Charitable contributions	negligible	16	3	0	2	less than $2.5 million
7. Medical expenses	negligible	3	4	0	6	10
Corporations:						
8. Repeal 2% tax on consolidated returns	50	11	0	0	1	50
9. R & D costs	50	14	1	2	3	0

SOURCE: Joint Committee on Internal Revenue Taxation.

Committee increased the amount of the tax reduction contrary to
the majority of the testimony (minimum standard deduction, medical expenses) or reduced the amount below what Treasury proposed
to cut and a majority of the witnesses supported (liberalized childcare
deduction, deductions for research and development costs). These
decisions deserve special attention since they do not conform to our
original hypotheses.

MINIMUM STANDARD DEDUCTION. The minimum standard deduction
proposal was a classic "liberal" proposal, geared to those in the lower
income brackets. It removed some people from the tax rolls altogether and it gave those just above the minimum income levels a
larger reduction than that provided by the rate cuts. Table 7.3 shows
the groups and individuals who expressed themselves on this issue.
Three more positions were classified as "other." The AFL-CIO did

TABLE 7.3
TESTIMONY ON MINIMUM STANDARD DEDUCTION

Pro	Pro+	Con
National Farmers Union	AFL-CIO	U.S. Chamber of Commerce
Americans for Demo-		Council of State Chambers of Com-
cratic Action		merce
President's Commission		National Small Business Men's Assn.
on the Status of		American Textile Manufacturers In-
Women		stitute
Abraham J. Multer		Voice of People in Action
(D., N.Y.)		New York State Bar Association
		Associated Retail Bakers of America
		American Symphony Orchestra
		League
		National Association Retired Civil
		Service Employees
		Naturita Block Plant
		Dan Throop Smith, Harvard Univer-
		sity
		Irving F. Bolton, Oakland, California
		John J. Gerlach, Columbus, Ohio

not oppose Treasury's proposal but suggested going much farther: a $400 minimum standard deduction for Treasury's $300, and $200 for each dependent for Treasury's $100. On this issue the Committee took the minority or liberal side of the testimony. Considering the opposition to this proposal, the Committee's action may be viewed as a significant liberal victory.

LIBERALIZED CHILDCARE AND DISABLED DEPENDENTS DEDUCTIONS. The Committee did not reject completely Treasury's proposed liberalization of the deductions for childcare and disabled dependents costs but scaled it down from $20 million to $5 million. This relatively minor item in the bill did not draw great attention from the witnesses; the Committee's decision reflected the ambiguity of the testimony.

REVISION OF MEDICAL EXPENSE DEDUCTION. Although Treasury proposed a number of changes in the law governing medical expense deductions the net amount of the changes was negligible. With testimony almost evenly split between pro and con and including a number of "other" views, the Committee adopted a change that cost $10 million, somewhat higher than the impact of Treasury's proposal. Of the six "other" responses, however, most were in the direction of greater liberalization and when these are added to the number of "pro" responses the Committee's decision was more in line with the general drift of the testimony than indicated by the count.

LIBERALIZATION OF DEDUCTION FOR RESEARCH AND DEVELOPMENT. Ways and Means, contrary to the great majority of support for this proposal, dropped it entirely from the bill and thus saved $50 million in revenue. The effect of this saving was offset, however, by the Committee's decision to liberalize the investment credit, a decision that cost Treasury $155 million in 1964 and $195 million in 1965. Thus instead of limiting itself to promoting investment in research and development equipment, the Committee sought to promote investment generally. It is unlikely that those who favored Treasury's research and development proposal were unhappy with the outcome of the Committee's deliberations. In effect, the Committee did Treasury one better.

On the five remaining revenue-losing proposals the Committee's decisions were in perfect or near-perfect agreement with the majority of the witnesses. On the major proposal in terms of revenue, the majority view of the witnesses was opposed to Treasury. A majority of the testimony generally supported Treasury's position on the other four.

The deviant case proposed to change the tax treatment of the elderly at a cost of $320 million. It was opposed by a majority of the witnesses and the Committee dropped it completely from the bill. Table 7.4 shows the distribution of the testimony.

Although Treasury argued that its alterations of the tax treatment of elderly persons would benefit the vast majority of the elderly, the Committee, no doubt impressed by the claims of a number of groups that the change would hurt their members, made no change in existing law. In addition, the Committee, having rejected Treasury's major revenue-gaining proposal, needed to retrieve revenue, and rejection of this proposal meant saving $320 million. Adoption of the proposal would have adversely affected a number of people who were aware of the issue and would have been costly to boot; apparently for these reasons Ways and Means sided with a majority of the witnesses against Treasury.

REVENUE-GAINING PROPOSALS

The Committee, supported by an overwhelming number of interested parties, rejected Treasury's major revenue-gaining proposal, the 5 per cent floor, and substantially altered Treasury's revenue-raising proposals in the field of capital gains taxation.

In addition to these proposals, Treasury had planned to recoup some of the tax cut through a number of changes in the tax law. Table 7.5 presents data on the eight Treasury Department proposals that increased tax liabilities (this table omits from consideration Treasury's proposal for acceleration of corporate tax payments that was largely accepted by the Committee but involved no substantive change in the law).

Table 7.5 shows that the direction of the testimony on the revenue-raising proposals was closer to the Committee decisions than it was on the revenue-reducing proposals. As expected, the testimony was overwhelmingly contrary to Treasury's proposals and in every case but one the Committee decision ran counter to Treasury's proposals. Testimony on the exception, the taxation of personal holding companies, was split 50–50; interest in this item was the lowest of all; and even the United States Chamber of Commerce indicated that it would support "reasonable" modifications in the law.

TABLE 7.4
TESTIMONY ON TAX TREATMENT OF OLDER PERSONS

Pro	Con
AFL-CIO	U.S. Chamber of Commerce
American Textile Manufacturers Institute	Fraternal Order of Police
National Association of Postmasters	National Conference on Public Employee Retirement Systems
Illinois State Chamber of Commerce	American Institute of Certified Public Accountants
Golden Ring Council of Senior Citizens	Council of State Chambers of Commerce
American Public Welfare Association	Washington State Retired Teachers Assn.
National Farmers Union	International Association of Fire Fighters
Thomas G. Morris (D., N.M.)	National Conference of Police Associations
	National Association of Postal Supervisors
	Tax Section, Florida Bar
	Naturita Block Plant
	American Federation of Government Employees
	New York State Bar Association
	Frank K. Jones, Berwyn, Pa.
	William D. Loucks, New York City
	John J. Gerlach, Columbus, Ohio

TABLE 7.5
REVENUE-RAISING PROPOSALS, TESTIMONY, AND
WAYS AND MEANS ACTION

Treasury proposal	Amount (millions)	Testimony Pro	Con	Other	Ways and Means action (millions)
Individuals:					
1. 4% floor under casualty losses	90	3	8	2	50
2. Repeal allowance of un- limited charitable contribu- tions	10	2	17	1	0
3. Repeal sick-pay exclusion	160	12	18	0	110
4. Repeal exclusion of premi- ums on group term insurance	60	2	41	0	5
5. Repeal 4% dividend credit and exclusion[a]	460	13	44	4	300
Corporations:					
6. Limit surtax exemption	120	6	20	0	35
7. Revise taxation of natural resources[b]	300	7	108	16	40
8. Amend taxation of personal holding companies	10	3	3	3	15

SOURCE: Joint Committee on Internal Revenue Taxation.
[a] Revenue effect in 1964 only + $120 million due to repeal of the 4% credit in two stages.
[b] $20 million of the $300 million falls in individual category. On March 22 Secretary Dillon estimated that the natural resource proposal would gain only $185 million.

FOUR PER CENT FLOOR UNDER CASUALTY LOSSES. Under existing law, property losses (not connected with a trade or business) arising from casualty or theft were fully deductible. Treasury proposed that such losses be deductible only to the extent that they exceed 4 per cent of adjusted gross income. The Committee accepted the idea of a floor but adopted one of $100 rather than the proposed 4 per cent. It may be significant that the $100 floor was precisely what the United States Chamber of Commerce said was necessary for its support of restrictions on deductions of casualty and theft losses.

REPEAL OF ALLOWANCE OF UNLIMITED CHARITABLE CONTRIBUTIONS. Treasury proposed repeal of the provision allowing unlimited chari- table contributions deduction in certain cases. Only two witnesses supported repeal (Tax Section of the Florida Bar, and Frank K. Jones of Berwyn, Pa.), and seventeen witnesses opposed it (among them the American Council on Education). This item, which would have gained only $10 million, was rejected by the Committee.

REPEAL OF SICK-PAY EXCLUSION. Treasury's proposal to repeal the exclusion of sick pay, though opposed by the majority (pro 12, con 18), did attract a fair amount of support. Not even the AFL-CIO could unequivocally support its retention. Labor's position was that the sick-pay exclusion should not be repealed unless loopholes favorable to the wealthy were also closed. Ways and Means went along with Treasury and the majority but it compromised by making the exclusion applicable to pay received after the first thirty days.

REPEAL OF EXCLUSION OF PREMIUMS ON GROUP TERM INSURANCE. This proposal would have limited the employee exclusion for insurance premiums paid by the employer to the cost of the first $5,000 of coverage. It received virtually unanimous opposition from business, labor, and everyone else who went on record. A $60 million revenue-gainer when proposed to Ways and Means, it left the Committee with a $30,000 limit worth only $5 million to the Treasury Department.

REPEAL OF 4 PER CENT DIVIDEND CREDIT AND $50 EXCLUSION. After the 5 per cent floor Treasury's largest revenue-raising request would have repealed the provision enabling dividend recipients to exclude from income the first $50 of dividends and take a 4 per cent credit against tax on dividend income above $50. Treasury support came from such groups as the AFL-CIO and the Americans for Democratic Action, but the opposition from the business and finance community was great. Keith Funston of the New York Stock Exchange even suggested that the credit should be increased to 10 per cent and the exclusion doubled.

Ways and Means compromised in the direction of the business opposition. The 4 per cent credit was repealed in two stages and the $50 exclusion was doubled. Still, the overall effect of the Committee's decision raised $300 million in revenue (compared with $460 million had no compromise been made). Treasury did not do too badly on this proposal despite the large opposition. On this issue a minority composed of liberals plus the Treasury Department coincided to some degree with the majority view inside the Committee.

LIMITING SURTAX EXEMPTION. Under Treasury's program $120 million in tax receipts was to be raised by limiting commonly controlled corporations to one $25,000 surtax exemption for the group. In the face of opposition, the Committee amended the law so that only $35 million would be raised. Ways and Means did act in this area partly because of the somewhat fragmented nature of business opposition. Although twenty witnesses opposed Treasury, one of the six who favored it was the United States Chamber of Commerce. Committee members could claim at least some business support for acting on multiple corporations, and it could also present its decision as less than what Treasury wanted.

REVISION OF TAXATION OF NATURAL RESOURCES. The Treasury Department made four proposals that would have increased taxes in the oil and gas area by $300 million. The opposition to these proposals outside the Committee was just as strong as it was inside. Therefore, three of the four proposals were dropped completely; one was substantially changed and passed. Revenue gain: $40 million.

PERSONAL HOLDING COMPANIES. The Treasury Department recommended several changes in the taxation of personal holding companies (defined as closely held corporations whose income stems mainly from certain forms of investments). The testimony on this relatively inconsequential set of proposals involved only nine groups and individuals who split evenly into the pro, con, and other categories. By and large Ways and Means responded favorably to Treasury's proposals; in fact, the Committee changed the section to raise $15 million in revenue compared to the $10 million proposed by Treasury.

When the Ways and Means Committee had finished its deliberations on the 1964 Revenue Act the administration's tax reform proposals were, for the most part, either dropped from the bill or amended in ways desired by the groups and individuals who opposed Treasury's plans. Interest group–lobbyist support for the Committee bill was thereby enhanced and, presumably, so were the bill's chances in the House. *Congressional Quarterly* summed up the lobbyist reaction:

> A number of lobbyists told CQ that H.R. 8363 appeared to be a bill "we could live with" while others noted that one section or another was of particular interest and value to their

organization. One lobbyist for an organization not notably friendly to Democratic Administration observed that the bill "contains something for everybody and this Administration knows it." Thus, business, labor or citizens organizations unhappy about one section appeared to swallow it in order to obtain another section they particularly coveted. Tied in with this factor was the success of the Ways and Means Committee in meeting the objections of many groups to specific Presidential proposals. Many lobbyists indicated that the House bill in general appeared sufficiently close to their own recommendations to be acceptable if not perfect.[62]

A Ways and Means Republican concluded that the Committee "gutted" most of Treasury's recommendations. When asked if he and his colleagues responded to the extra-congressional opposition to the proposals he said, "Call them pressures or whatever you want, we were responsive."

The Treasury Department in 1963 was caught between two incompatible goals, which helps explain why Ways and Means rejected many Treasury proposals. Administration economists saw a tax cut, on the one hand, as a stimulus to the economy that would provide more federal revenue over the long run than would be lost by the initial reduction. This proposal, given the continued budget deficit, was highly controversial inside and outside of Congress. Tax reform, on the other hand, was also desired by the administration, particularly inside the Treasury Department, and the possibility of passing reforms separate from tax reduction was slim. Strong opposition to cutting taxes in the face of large budget deficits, however, made the tax cut vulnerable in the House and all but destroyed its utility as a vehicle for tax reforms. A choice had to be made between reduction and reform, and the choice was made in favor of reduction.

The tension between reduction and reform, which was evident during the intra-administration discussions of what kind of tax program should be presented to Congress, appeared frequently in the Ways and Means hearings. Treasury Secretary Douglas Dillon tried to keep the reduction-reform package together during the hearings but, when pressed, Commerce Secretary Luther Hodges acknowledged that of the two the need for a tax cut was greater.[63] Even Dillon was forced to concede that if some of the tax equity proposals stood in the way of a tax cut they might have to take lower priority, but he was insis-

[62] *Congressional Quarterly Almanac*, 1963, p. 491.
[63] *Hearings, op. cit.*, I, p. 563.

tent on the need to balance the proposed cut by some revenue-raising reforms, especially the 5 per cent floor.[64] Dillon told the Committee that a $13.6 billion cut in taxes, offset by no provisions raising revenue, would be fiscally unsound and he would recommend that the president veto it.[65]

But if this was the outer limit of the administration's tolerance, it left open a wide area for Committee discretion. When it became clear during the Committee's consideration of the tax message that President Kennedy, if not Dillon, was quite willing to accept a reasonable tax cut without the controversial reforms, the Committee's freedom to reject or temper the reforms was immeasurably strengthened. Thus the Committee's decisions that coincided with interest group–lobbyist testimony did so in part because the testimony was intensely negative, in part because with or without the testimony Ways and Means members would have had questions about such proposals, and in part because the administration was willing to accept a major tax cut with a modicum of reform.[66]

CONCLUSION

Questions about executive-legislative relations or, more popularly, the decline of Congress necessarily entail consideration of the representation of group and individual demands. Executive departments, no less than Congress, work within the context of group-lobbyist demands, and the fate of policy initiatives from the executive branch is intimately related to the support for these initiatives.

To the executive branch, one of the basic tasks in passing legislation is the mobilization of sufficient extragovernmental support behind proposals to create the impression in Congress that the proposals, whatever their substantive merits, are politically popular. On major policy initiatives some group support is probably necessary to gaining congressional approval, especially if there are groups in opposition to the proposals. To this end, the executive departments and the White House work closely with their allies outside of government.

---

[64] *Ibid.*, pp. 617–18.

[65] *Ibid.*, p. 692.

[66] Insight into how much Ways and Means departed from Treasury's proposals may be gained from the reaction of liberal tax reformers, most conspicuously Senator Paul Douglas who told Dillon during the Finance Committee hearings that "if this bill gets any worse, it is going to be very difficult for some of us to vote for it. It is going to be very difficult for some of us to vote for it as it is." Quoted in *Congressional Quarterly Almanac*, 1963, p. 498.

In 1963, for example, the Treasury Department took the lead in establishing the Business Committee for Tax Reduction, a prestigious group of business leaders headed by Henry Ford II whose purpose was to help pass the tax reduction bill. Interestingly enough, Treasury also helped form a smaller (and less effective) group interested in tax reductions and reforms, the Citizens Committee for Tax Reduction and Revision in 1963.[67]

Perfect agreement between Treasury and its clientele is not necessarily required, and not always attained, for the Department to receive useful support from groups such as the Business Committee for Tax Reduction. Henry Ford II testified in 1963 in opposition to Treasury's stock option proposals but, speaking as a member of the President's Advisory Committee on Labor-Management Policy, supported the tax cut.[68] Similarly, the 1962 Trade Expansion Act was backed by the American Farm Bureau Federation, which worked closely with the White House to pass the measure, but this did not prevent the AFBF from opposing parts of the bill and proposing amendments to Ways and Means.[69] The United States Chamber of Commerce helped the administration pass the 1962 Trade Act and also proposed changes in the bill (five of the Chamber's seven proposals were adopted by Ways and Means).[70]

Although it may be true that groups typically gravitate first toward the executive branch and then toward Congress, this is not always the case. All those affected by Ways and Means decisions do not have representatives in Washington following the legislative process, and Committee members sometimes act as representatives of unarticulated interests or as conduits for group interests into the executive branch. The members, on occasion, instruct the bureaucrats to contact interested parties and get their reaction to proposals. In this way the members ensure that the right of affected people to express themselves, regardless of whether the outcome is affected, is protected; in this way the members also protect themselves against potential complaints and charges of unfair procedure.

Three examples may be cited. While the Committee was discussing medicare in 1965 the pharmaceutical industry suggested some changes

---

[67] *Ibid.*, p. 491.

[68] *Hearings, op. cit.*, II, pp. 1127, 1135.

[69] Diane Monson, "Interests and Tariff Policy: A Case Study of the Trade Expansion Act of 1962" (Ph.D. Dissertation, New York University, 1963), p. 183.

[70] *Ibid.*, pp. 193–94.

in the bill to Mills. Mills bucked the letter to HEW, and Wilbur Cohen explained to the Committee why the department was willing to accept part of the industry's requests, though not all of them. Second, on the same bill Ullman suggested to Cohen that HEW ought to get the reaction of the American Association of Blood Banks to the proposal that patients pay for the first three pints of blood and medicare pay for amounts in excess of three pints. Third, on the 1965 excise tax bill Mills asked Surrey to see when the operators of the legitimate stage thought the effective date of the repeal of the amusement tax ought to be. Mills reasoned that because the theater season begins in the fall, the tax should come off before January (he added that the Senate would probably add such an amendment if Ways and Means did not). In all these cases the members acted as middlemen between groups and the executive branch.

Ways and Means draws the interest of large numbers of groups and lobbyists in all three of its major policy areas, but tax policy appears to be a particularly sensitive part of the Committee's subject matter. Virtually countless groups, individuals, lobbyists, and even entire industries have vital interests at stake in the internal revenue laws drafted by Ways and Means, and the Committee has demonstrated that in taxes it has both the professional staff and the will to determine what will be done.

The overwhelmingly practical context within which the Committee determines tax policy consists of decisions that have wide and profound effects. Ways and Means decisions can affect the financial condition of every person and every organization in the country, and the Committee considers policies as diverse as promoting financial contributions to charity and maintaining the competitive situation of the automobile industry. Within this context, appeals for tax reform may sound good in theory but, in practice, most of the Committee's problems seem to bear little relationship to such grand objectives. As Hale Boggs said during the 1963 hearings on tax reduction:

> I find it difficult sometimes to write a tax bill and take these broad generalities like anti-subsidy and then, bang! You are confronted with specific areas and problems and who do you have coming to see you about the subsidies? Business people, no one else.[71]

_____
[71] _Hearings, op. cit._, IX, p. 2349.

The case of Stanley Surrey provides additional insight into the nature of the tax-making process. In 1961 Surrey joined the Treasury Department and had the potential for promoting some of his well-known views on tax reform. He had written a controversial article on taxation in 1957 that became a prime bone of contention between him and the Senate Finance Committee. The Finance Committee hearing on Surrey's nomination consisted largely of what Surrey meant by certain passages of his article that Chairman Harry Byrd felt insulted Congress.[72] According to one former lobbyist, Surrey came to the Treasury Department with all sorts of tax reform ideas but soon learned "what some of your fellow political scientists seem to fail to understand: legislation is not made in vacuum."

How much Surrey actually learned after he became Assistant Secretary is not as important as that, as seen by some members of the Ways and Means Committee, Surrey — whatever his personal views — adapted to the pragmatic world of tax politics. One Committee member expressed the view that Surrey was still too impractical — an "academician" as he put it — but probably more typical is the comment by a liberal Democrat that although Surrey got off to a bad start he was "getting higher grades nowadays."

These views of Surrey, though certainly not conclusive evidence of the way Committee members approach policy, do fit well with the general approach of Committee members to issues such as tax reform — an approach best summed up by Mills in his comment that Ways and Means is no place for just the idealist.

In the interaction between the Ways and Means Committee and the executive branch the predominant characteristic is that of bargaining, not superordination-subordination, and many times the form of congressional supremacy and independence is not without substance. Joseph W. Barr, then Under Secretary of the Treasury and former congressman, discussed the complexity of influence relationships between the House and the bureaucracy:

> There is nothing that irritates me more than a somewhat recurring theme that I encounter periodically to the effect that the Congress is a rubber stamp. To the people who

[72] Senate, Committee on Finance, *Hearings on Nominations*, 87th Cong., 1st Sess., 1961, p. 7 ff. Among the many interesting items in these hearings, Byrd drew from Surrey the observation that Secretary Dillon would have the major responsibility for tax policy, and Senator Clinton Anderson (D., N.M.) elicited from Surrey the admission that he had an open mind on the question of depletion (pp. 8, 50–51).

make these speeches and write these articles, I have always wanted to extend an invitation to testify on a higher technical and controversial subject before the Ways and Means Committee.

Let me give you an example. About a month ago I testified before Ways and Means on Unemployment Compensation legislation. The subject is always controversial and it is admittedly complex. However, for my own information I kept a log of the Hours I spent in preparing for the testimony. I logged a total of 34 hours — usually late at night or early in the morning — preparing myself for a 3-hour session.

This may seem like supercaution, but too often I have seen intelligent, experienced witnesses demolished before these committees because they have not taken the trouble to do their homework. Just this week one of our assistant secretaries went before the Senate Finance Committee to testify for a total of 20 minutes on the Canadian auto parts legislation. This man told me that he had spent 29 hours in preparation.

I hope these illustrations will help to show why I become so irritated at the "rubber stamp" charge that is sometimes leveled at the Congress. Any reasonable man with any experience in the affairs of this Government knows better. He knows that when he takes the administration's case to the Congress — no matter what the majority his party may have — he is confronted with an independent panel of specialized experts who usually possess vastly more experience than he. Unless he is to disgrace himself, his department, and the administration, he has no alternative but to spend bone-crushing hours of preparatory homework. It is from this particular angle that the Congress looks most different from the outside than from the inside.

I have often wondered whether it was not this degree of specialization that has developed in the U.S. Congress that has made it the tough, effective legislative body that it is today. We live in a world of specialists in every phase of our lives. While the congressional system with its high degree of specialization may appear fragmented and disorderly to those who admire the symmetry of the parliamentary system, I would submit that the congressional system is peculiarly adapted to the world in which we live today.[73]

[73] Remarks made before the American Society for Public Administration, Washington, D.C., September 22, 1965. Reprinted *Congressional Record*, October 13, 1965 (daily edition), p. 25887.

Committee members, as Barr's comments make clear, look upon themselves as "we" and upon executive department officials as "they." In many important cases the members, at least the Democratic members, identify with the president's program and tend to define the Committee's job as getting the major administration bills through the Committee and the House. But the members are also members of the Committee and they have a natural attachment to the Committee that orients them — to some degree — against the executive branch. They are people to be bargained with, not directed, and their political goals are respected. The Democrats usually voted with the administration but sometimes they did not, and even when they did there was usually a quid pro quo. A former staff member summed up the general orientation of the members:

> I think every member of the Committee has a renegade streak. The majority of them favor the administration and go along but still they do have a sense of their own importance, of their position in the House, that they are not just rubber stamps. And they feel that Mills has protected the autonomy and independence of the Committee.

A study of the relationship between the Ways and Means Committee and the executive branch shows that the Committee and Congress generally are by no means subservient to executive branch policies. Ways and Means, particularly in the area of taxation, is an independent force in policy-making that is responsive to demands not aggregated by the Treasury Department, that is well-equipped to compete on equal terms with the expertise of the executive, and that stands as a formidable challenge to presidents and their programs. This conclusion, drawn from the study of one committee, is basically what Chamberlain concluded after studying ninety pieces of legislation: "These figures do not support the thesis that Congress is unimportant in the formulation of major legislation. Rather, they indicate, not that the president is less important than generally supposed, but that Congress is more important." [74]

[74] Lawrence H. Chamberlain, "The President, Congress, and Legislation," *Political Science Quarterly*, LXI (March, 1946), 50.

Conclusion

Four points of emphasis in this study bear special attention. First, the role of the Committee chairman since 1958, Wilbur D. Mills, was stressed because of his great influence in the decisions of the Committee. Chairman Mills, liked and respected by members of both parties, is a professional legislator who strives to get the Committee to write sound legislation even though at the end the members may — and often do — split down the middle. Mills is inclined toward the compromise position on many policy disputes in the Committee, and his flexible approach is a basic reason why he is an influential chairman. A skillful follower, he is simultaneously an influential leader who is permitted wide latitude in making decisions that affect the policy judgments of the Committee. On divisive issues Mills, if he refuses to seek a compromise, virtually can determine the outcome; if he leads the search for a compromise he likewise influences the outcome. As the middleman between the policy factions on the Committee the Chairman both reflects the political realities in the Committee and shapes the policies that can be enacted into law.

Second, the conservative coalition has been a prominent part of House and Committee politics for the past thirty years. Internal Committee processes and decisions can only be understood in the context of the coalitions that exist in the House of Representatives. Ways and Means has been highly successful in the House largely because it has responded to and represented the voting alignments in the House, which, coupled with the Committee's tradition of handling complex legislation in a professional way, helps explain why the Committee has maintained itself as the single most important congressional decision-maker in the areas of taxes, trade, and social security.

Third, the results of congressional and presidential elections have profound implications for the internal relations and policy decisions of Ways and Means. The Committee in the 1930's was very different from the Committee in the 1960's, and these differences affected matters of basic policy. Far from discounting the policy importance of elections, a study of Ways and Means leads to the conclusion that electoral stability or change is very significant in the subsequent policy-making process and the outputs of that process.

Fourth, this study views formal governmental institutions as being in competition with one another in the representation of group interests and demands. Occasionally a member of Ways and Means will represent the unexpressed interests of the "little man," but a great many Committee decisions affect very specific organized interests with much at stake in the legislative process. The Committee is a highly permeable group in which the Chairman serves as the main conduit for group demands and as the key compromiser of these demands.

In executive-legislative relations, Ways and Means deals most frequently with the Treasury Department, and it is in the tax field that the Committee's decisions have been most controversial. Ways and Means has not yielded control over tax policy to the executive branch; indeed, the Committee seems better able to aggregate tax demands than the Treasury Department.

By and large the stimulus for changes in tax law, prior to 1969, came from the Treasury Department, and when Treasury did not take the initiative it was likely to oppose changes in the status quo. Roy Blough remarks that this situation was not a happy one for the department:

> The testimony of taxpayers and taxpayer groups operates to place the Treasury always in a bad light. When the Treasury proposes tax increases, taxpayer groups oppose them as being harmful. When taxpayer groups propose tax decreases, the Treasury is obliged in many instances to oppose the decreases. The Treasury thus seems always to be against the taxpayer. In point of fact, of course, it is the duty of the Treasury to protect the silent general interest against the vociferous private interests that make themselves heard before the taxing committees.[1]

[1] Roy Blough, *The Federal Taxing Process* (New York: Prentice-Hall, 1952), p. 42.

Blough's reference to the "silent general interest" raises some questions.[2] There is a tendency inside (and outside) Treasury to look upon the Treasury Department as the guardian of the public interest in taxation. Speaking of the 1963 tax proposals, one Treasury Department man said:

> Our reform proposals were in the public interest but the Committee threw most of them out because they didn't fit the members' political interests. You get these lobbyists who hang around the Committee all the time. They tip their clients off on what Ways and Means is doing. Texaco lobbyists and others hang around up there. Members write a lot of things in.

In retort, a tax specialist with the Joint Committee on Internal Revenue Taxation expressed what is very likely a common view around the Ways and Means Committee, "Treasury always says that we represent the lobbyists and they represent the public interest. But really they represent one definition of the public interest, the administration's."

To view the tax-making process in terms of the Treasury Department as the lone defender of the public interest against a horde of special interests is an oversimplification.

The difference between Treasury and the Ways and Means Committee is not that one primarily represents special interests and the other primarily represents the public interest but that there is profound disagreement on the particulars of the public interest. In the tax field one raises money from some sources and not from others; it is extremely difficult to legislate general principles. "Our taxes," Louis Eisenstein states, "reflect a continuing struggle among contending interests for the privilege of paying the least." [3] Amid this continuing struggle — described by Eisenstein as a struggle to place these "distinctly disagreeable burdens . . . on the backs of others" [4] — the Treasury Department is no less engaged in a political struggle than Ways and Means. One Treasury official described the tax-making process:

> It's a constant process of reformulation. We continually revise and alter our original proposals and ideas. We may do it

[2] For a general treatment see Louis Eisenstein, *The Ideologies of Taxation* (New York: Ronald Press, 1961), chap. 9.
[3] *Ibid.*, pp. 3–4.
[4] *Ibid.*, p. 6.

> when we have the meetings with the lobbyists when we are
> thinking about what to propose. We do it all the time dur-
> ing the Committee stage. The people affected are kept in-
> formed and we try to work things out. We pay close attention
> to the public hearings and to what the witnesses for various
> groups say and we may alter our position because of this too.

To recognize the similarities between the legislative process in the executive branch and in Congress, however, is not to overlook the differences. In the scope of interests represented the Treasury Department cannot compete with Congress, which is the fundamental reason why Congress has retained its influence in the tax field. Twenty-five members of Ways and Means representing the demands of their constituencies plus the demands of four hundred and ten additional members of the House, complemented by the representational functions of the Senate, make Congress more responsive to more interests than Treasury. It is for this reason that, regardless of one's position on the merits of tax legislation, Walter J. Blum could tell Ways and Means, "I always feel safe in predicting that next year the tax code will offer more special havens than last year — and I renew my prediction now." [5] Since Blum made his prediction hardly a year has gone by without new special havens — or, if one prefers, new equities — being added to the Code. Granted the nature of the contemporary tax-making process the ease with which some participants suggest reforms that would have a salubrious effect on Mills's "House of Horrors" is transcended only by the ease (even in the face of the 1969 Act) with which it is concluded that cumulatively no number of reforms is likely to change the nature of the Code with its progressive theory and limited applications.

Finally, the legislative process analyzed here is subject to change, but Congress changes slowly. Under a Republican president the Ways and Means Democrats may initiate more legislation than normal. With a particularly strong extra-congressional interest in tax reform the Committee may even initiate important tax reforms. With the death of a Harry Byrd or the defeat of a Paul Douglas the process does undergo change. Yet the truly striking thing about Congress is the time it takes for lasting changes to occur and for Congress to play a new role in policy-making. In Congress, short-run fluctuations in the process are not always followed by long-run changes in

[5] Quoted in *Congressional Quarterly Weekly Report*, February 12, 1960, p. 222.

the content of the policies decided by the legislature. For basic policy change both the House and the Senate must be altered, and such alterations usually occur slowly.

Appendix I:
Persons Interviewed

Ways and Means Committee Members

Democrats	Republicans
Wilbur D. Mills	John W. Byrnes
Cecil R. King	Thomas B. Curtis
Hale Boggs	James B. Utt
A. Sydney Herlong	Jackson E. Betts
John C. Watts	Herman T. Schneebeli
Al Ullman	Harold R. Collier
James A. Burke	Joel T. Broyhill
Martha W. Griffiths	James F. Battin
George M. Rhodes	Barber B. Conable, Jr.
Dan Rostenkowski	George Bush
Phil M. Landrum	Stephen Derounian
Charles A. Vanik	Bruce Alger
Richard H. Fulton	
Jacob H. Gilbert	
W. Pat Jennings	
Ross Bass	
Eugene Keogh	
Clark Thompson	

House Democratic Leadership

Speaker John W. McCormack
Majority Leader Carl Albert
Majority Whip Hale Boggs

SENATE FINANCE COMMITTEE

Democrats	*Republicans*
Clinton P. Anderson	Frank Carlson
Albert Gore	Wallace F. Bennett
Herman E. Talmadge	Carl T. Curtis
Paul H. Douglas	Thruston B. Morton

EXECUTIVE BRANCH OFFICIALS

Treasury Department	*Health, Education and Welfare*
Stanley S. Surrey	Robert Myers
Donald Lubick	Charles Hawkins
Gerard Brannon	Michael Stern

CONGRESSIONAL STAFF

William Quealy
David W. West
Richard Wilbur
Laurence N. Woodworth

Appendix II:
Roll Call Votes

House roll call votes on Ways and Means bills during the 1933–1944 period were coded by the author and a research assistant. Roll calls for the 1945–1964 years were generously provided by the Inter-University Consortium for Political Research.

Selecting particular bills and votes for analysis is, of course, a subjective operation. For some purposes a relatively objective method of selecting votes, such as Riker's coefficient of significance,[1] may be useful, but the author concurs with Mayhew's assessment of the Riker index: "The problem is that roll calls are used not only to register the outcomes of struggles for victory, but also to record simple demonstrations of allegiance; to identify 'significance' with the former use may be a bit Procrustean." [2] In the absence of any satisfactory objective criteria, complete reliance was placed on the subjective judgment of the author.

The bills and issues considered to be major in Chapter Five are evident from the text. At the outset of this study it was decided that primary attention would be paid to major revenue, trade, and social security legislation. Distinguishing major from relatively minor bills in these three areas involves a certain amount of arbitrary judgment, but in every case of major legislation at least one roll call vote was taken in the House. Major revenue bills were further defined as bills dealing with broad questions of taxation, normally involving a half billion dollars or more and/or significant questions of domestic tax policy. Major trade bills were defined as the 1934 Trade Act and subsequent extensions of that Act, including the innovations passed as part of the 1962 Trade Expan-

[1] William H. Riker, "A Method for Determining the Significance of Roll Calls in Voting Bodies," in *Legislative Behavior,* ed. John C. Wahlke and Heinz Eulau (Glencoe, Ill.: The Free Press, 1959), pp. 377–84. Riker's index ranks votes according to the percentage of voters casting their vote and the closeness of the results.

[2] David R. Mayhew, *Party Loyalty among Congressmen* (Cambridge, Mass.: Harvard University Press, 1966), p. 7.

sion Act. Major social security legislation was similarly defined as omnibus legislation involving general policy questions such as the program's
nature and level of benefits and categories of coverage.

Because our primary interest in this study was party conflict over substantive policy issues, the roll calls selected for presentation when there
were two or more votes on a bill were those on which the IPL was the
lowest. Thus, given a choice between a vote on a motion to recommit
that split the parties more than a vote on final passage, the former vote
was picked for presentation.[3] By following this procedure the 1935 Social
Security bill, for example, is classified as a partisan bill because of the
voting on the Republican motion to recommit, even though the bill was
passed by the overwhelming majority of both parties. In most cases, the
floor debate reveals the central controversies surrounding a bill and selecting the key vote is not very difficult.

[3] There are two exceptions to this rule. H.R. 11990 in 1962 and H.R. 7824
in 1963, both debt limit bills, involved substantive motions to recommit offered
by the Committee Republicans. It appears that these votes posed the issue better
than the votes on final passage.

Index

Ackley, Gardner, Dr., 115
AFL-CIO, 83, 359–60, 371
Agar, Herbert, 16n
Albert, Carl, 12, 244
Albright, Robert C., 258n
Alexander, DeAlva S., 3n
Alger, Bruce, 48–49, 148
Allen, Leo, 221
Almond, Gabriel A., 11n
American Medical Association, 82, 193, 216, 340
American Petroleum Institute, 33
Americans for Democratic Action, 146, 371
Anderson, Clinton, 377n
Anderson, John, 43
Appropriations Committee, House, 1, 94
Arends, Leslie, 44
Avery, William, 222, 240–41
Ayres, William, 292n, 293n

Back, Kurt, 54n
Bailey, Cleveland, 199, 333
Bailey, Stephen K., 16n, 260n, 311
Baker, Howard, 79, 354
Baker, John W., 21n, 151n
Bales, Robert F., 9n, 100n, 101n
Ball, Robert, 348–49
Banking and Currency Committee, House, 21
Barber, James D., 9n
Barden, Graham, 142–44
Barkley, Alben, 337
Barnard, Chester I., 7, 10, 60–61, 63, 129, 131n

Barr, Joseph, 214, 351, 377–79
Bass, Ross, 38, 361
Battin, James F., 44
Bauer, Raymond A., 45n, 198n, 199n, 210n, 233n, 234–36, 248, 287n, 289n, 319
Becker, Howard S., 5, 6n
Bentley, Arthur F., 355n
Betts, Jackson, 42
Bevan, Aneurin, 96
Bingham, Jonathan, 119
Blau, Peter, 7, 10, 60–63, 78n, 91, 124, 127
Blough, Roy, 270n, 308n, 343–44, 360, 362, 365, 381–82
Blum, John Morton, 170n
Blum, Walter J., 383
Boggs, Caleb, 309
Boggs, Hale, 12, 29, 37, 79–81, 243–44, 310, 360, 376
Bolling, Richard W., 27, 34n, 35, 226
"Boll Weevils," 33
Borgatta, Edgar F., 100n, 101n
Brown, Clarence, 227–28, 289n
Brownell, Edmund B., 260n
Broyhill, Joel, 39, 43, 50, 78n, 139n
Bruyn, Severyn T., 4n
Bryce, James, 151
Buck, Frank, 177
Burke, James A., 49, 113, 219
Burleson, Omar, 33, 37–38, 242
Burns, James MacGregor, 15n
Burton, Phil, 47–48
Bush, George, 49
Business Committee for Tax Reduction, 375

Byrd, Harry F., 261–62, 296, 298–300, 302–3, 310–11, 377, 383
Byrnes, John W., 52–53, 66–68, 74, 87–90, 93–94, 102, 105, 110–11, 115, 117–21, 141, 146, 150, 197, 209, 213–14, 217, 228–31, 257, 310, 351n, 359–60

Camp, A. S., 34, 222
Cannon, Joe, 24
Capital gains, 363–65
Carlson, Frank, 179
Carr, Robert K., 1n
Carroll, John, 30, 49
Cartwright, Dorwin, 9n, 54n, 96n, 124n
Cary, William L., 336n
Cataldo, Everett F., 147n, 360n
Catlin, G. E. G., 121n
Celebrezze, Anthony, 349
Citizens Committee for Tax Reduction and Revision, 375
Clapp, Charles L., 52
Clark, Joseph, 296, 299, 300, 304
Clifford, Clark, 320
Closed rule, 72, 174, 204, 220–34, 250–52, 257
Cohen, Lee M., 348n
Cohen, Wilbur, 120, 347–49, 376
Coleman, James S., 5n, 123
Collier, Harold, 43
Colmer, William, 30, 229, 251, 254
Combs, J. M., 30
Committee on Committees, Democrats, 24–25, 57, 75, 77–78, 244–45
Committee on Committees, Republicans, 43
Committee on Reciprocity Information, 188, 332
Compensatory representation, 355–84
Conable, Barber B., Jr., 84, 85n
Conference committee, 13, 219, 249, 255, 257–63, 269–307
conservative control of, 294–307
recent House dominance in, 291–94
Congress, decline of, 322–42, 374, 379
Connery, William, 23

Conservative Coalition, 17–18, 20, 34–37, 58, 119, 145–48, 151–52, 154–58, 160–62, 170–71, 174, 180, 182, 186, 190–91, 193, 203, 205–10, 239–42, 297–307, 312–15, 380
Coser, Lewis A., 9n
Cox, Eugene, 171
Crockett, Davy, 21
Curtis, Thomas B., 50, 66, 74, 80–81, 87, 94, 102, 120, 129, 141, 197, 199, 207, 228, 255–56, 260, 264–65, 293, 308n, 310, 318, 329, 334, 352
Cooper, Jere, 86, 127, 178, 198, 200, 203, 222, 226–28n
Couzens, James, 308
Crisp, Charles, 226

Dahl, Robert A., 121n
Dahrendorf, Ralf, 8, 9n, 10n
Daley, Richard, 33, 79
Data
executive session, 13
interviews, 11–12
public record, 12–13
roll call, 13
Davidson, Roger H., 325n, 355n
de Grazia, Alfred, 323, 355n
Democratic Study Group, 37, 243
Denton, Winfield, 34
DePuy, Jacques, 12n
Dexter, Lewis A., 45n, 198n, 199n, 210n, 233n, 234–36, 248, 285n, 287n, 289n, 319
Dillon, Douglas, 327, 339, 344, 349, 352, 373–74
Dingell, John, 182, 185, 187–88, 191, 205, 207
Dirksen, Everett, 267, 269, 297
Donovan, Robert J., 42n, 171n, 195n
Doughton, Robert L., 3n, 55, 164–65, 167–69, 172–73, 177–78, 181, 184–86, 188–89, 191, 222–23, 332
Douglas, Paul, 285, 294, 296, 298–99, 301, 305, 313–14, 335, 338, 374n, 383
Durkheim, Emile, 99

Duscha, Julius, 100n, 112n, 336n
Duty-free goods, 213–14

Easton, David, 7–8, 11
Eberhart, John E., 54
Eberharter, Herman, 191–92, 205
Edelman, Murray, 290n
Edinger, Lewis J., 98n, 100
Education and Labor Committee, 59–60, 64, 87, 143
Eisenhower, Dwight D., 52, 152, 159, 190, 194–95, 197, 199, 200, 202–203, 205–206, 221, 284–85, 290, 331, 333, 338–40, 353
Eisenstadt, S. N., 62n
Eisenstein, Louis, 382
Evans, Rowland, 116n
Ewing, Oscar, 193–94

Federal role (Congressional Quarterly), 19–20, 30–31, 40–41, 45
Federal Security Agency, 193–94
Fellner, William, 312n
Fenno, Richard F., Jr., 1, 8, 51, 52n, 59n, 61n–62, 94n, 98n, 143n, 277–79
Festinger, Leon, 54n
Finance Committee, 253, 256, 260, 295–321, 324, 338, 341
Fleming, Arthur, 340
Forand, Aime, 26, 146, 182–83, 186, 191–92, 203, 205–206
Forand bill (*see* Medicare)
Ford, Gerald R., 44
Ford, Henry, II, 375
Fowler, Henry, 116, 214, 320, 345
Frazier, James B., 37–38
Frear, J. Allen, 296
Frear, James A., 164, 166
French, John R. P., Jr., 9, 124n, 132n, 142n
Froman, Lewis A., Jr., 20n, 268n
Fulbright, William, 296
Fulton, Richard, 37–38, 44, 49
Funston, Keith, 371

Galloway, George B., 32n, 54n
Garceau, Oliver, 319n
Gardner, John, 231
Garner, John Nance, 22–23, 32

Gearhart, Bertrand, 187–88
Geer, Blanche, 5n
George, Walter, 182, 296
Gilbert, Jacob, 33, 37–38
Glaser, Barney G., 5n
Goldwater, Barry, 206, 340
Goodell, Charles, 44
Gordon, Kermit, 362
Gore, Albert, 285, 296, 313–14, 336n
Gouldner, Alvin W., 61, 108
Gibb, Cecil A., 100
Green, Edith, 303
Green, William J., 32, 205
Griffiths, Martha, 94, 116–18
Gross, Bertram M., 355n
Gross, H. R., 259–60
Guffey coal bill, 168

Hamilton, Thomas, 2n
Hammond, Phillip E., 5n
Halleck, Charles, 18n, 44, 195–97, 199, 203
Hare, A. Paul, 100n, 101n
Harrison, Burr, 34, 37–38, 203
Hartke, Vance, 257
Havens, Murray Clark, 198n
Hawley, Willis, 335
Haynes, George H., 253n
Health, Education and Welfare, Department of, 12, 119–20, 328, 342, 348, 351–53, 376
Henderson, A. M., 124n
Herlong, A. Sydney, 34, 37, 38, 120, 145, 147–48, 202–203, 209, 219, 241–42, 362
Herring, E. Pendleton, 16n, 324n
Hill, Samuel B., 164
Hodges, Luther, 373
Holmans, A. E., 183, 187
Homans, George C., 4, 7, 9–10, 60–62n, 99, 126
Hoover, Herbert, 194
Horn, Stephen, 112n
House kibitzer, role of, 46
House Legislative Counsel's Office, 64, 308, 352
Hughes, Everett C., 5n
Huitt, Ralph K., 1n, 99, 312n
Hull, Cordell, 26

Humphrey, Hubert, 338
Huntington, Samuel P., 322–23, 355

Ikard, Frank, 33, 37, 320
Integration (defined), 163
Interest (pressure) groups, 12, 232–
    37, 250, 263–69, 279, 288–90,
    316–21, 324–79
Internal Revenue Service, 116n, 337

Javits, Jacob, 297
Jenkins, Thomas A., 42, 172–73, 189,
    197–99, 203, 228, 285, 317
Jennings, W. Pat, 34, 37–38, 94
Johnson, Lyndon, 66n, 99, 106, 159,
    206, 213, 259, 339, 346, 348,
    352–53
Joint Committee on Internal Revenue
    Taxation (staff), 64, 81, 117,
    249, 304, 307–319, 329, 342–
    51, 361n, 382
Jones, Charles O., 2n, 88n, 164n
Jones, Frank K., 370

Karsten, Frank, 118, 240
Keating, Kenneth, 254
Kelley, Harold H., 103, 104n, 124n
Kennedy, John F., 159, 206, 244, 339,
    346–48, 352–53, 357, 362, 374
Kenworthy, E. W., 311
Keogh, Eugene, 117–18, 139, 214,
    328–29, 346
Kerr-Mills Act, 340
Kerr, Robert, 302, 305, 340
King-Anderson bill (*see* Medicare)
King, Cecil, 55, 147, 205, 215, 362
Knox, Victor, 49
Knutson, Harold, 178, 183–86, 224
Kovenock, David M., 325n
Kravitz, Walter, 3n

Landrum-Griffin Act, 34
Landrum, Phil, 34–35, 37, 52, 241,
    242n
Large, Arlen J., 308n
Latham, Earl, 319–20
Lausche, Frank, 256
Leadership:
    instrumental-affective, 9, 100–105

Lee, Jennie, 96
Levy, Marion J., Jr., 8n
Library of Congress, 64, 352
Likert, Rensis, 100n
Lindeen, James Walter, 289n
Lindsey, John, 38, 80n
Long, Huey, 166
Long, Russell, 256–61, 267, 271n,
    291, 293n, 298, 300–302, 304,
    306–307, 309
Lowell, A. Lawrence, 19
Lowi, Theodore J., 290
Lynch, Walter, 186
Lyons, Richard L., 33n, 44n

MacNeil, Neil, 3n
MacRae, Duncan, Jr., 20n
Madden, Ray, 204
Madison, James, 253
Mahon, George, 243
Malone, George W., 296
Manley, John F., 59n, 98n, 307n
Mansfield, Mike, 253–54, 262
March, James G., 5n, 61n
Martin, Joseph W., 41, 42n, 43, 170–
    71, 172n, 173, 195, 197, 202
Mason, Noah, 43, 196–99, 224
Masters, Nicholas A., 2n, 40n, 55n, 77
Matsunga, Spark, 80
Mayer amendment, 336
Mayer, Louis B., 336
Mayhew, David R., 20n
McCarthy, Eugene, 262, 300, 302,
    304–306
McCauley, Al, 345–46
McClellan, John, 308, 309n
McCormack, John W., 12, 22–25, 29,
    32–36n, 46, 53, 99, 144, 168–
    70, 173, 225–28, 243–44
McCown, Ada C., 270n
Mead, George H., 11
Meany, George, 340
Medicare, 1, 26–29, 33, 38, 43, 45,
    48, 118–20, 146, 214–17, 228,
    238, 258, 340–41, 347
Mellon, Andrew, 185
Members bills, 79–81
Merton, Robert K., 6n, 7, 9n
Metcalf, Lee, 12, 55

Michener, Earl C., 225
Miller, Clem, 6, 21n, 151n
Miller, Warren E., 54
Millikin, Eugene, 264, 283, 296
Mills, Wilbur D., 13, 37, 52–53, 63, 68, 70–71, 74–76, 80–81, 85, 87–90, 95, 98–120, 122–25, 127–52, 163, 192, 194, 202, 204, 205, 207, 209, 211–19, 222, 229–32, 237–45, 247, 251–52, 255, 257–60, 263–64, 266–67, 271n, 290n, 292–95, 300, 303, 306, 310, 321, 326, 328, 330, 333–34, 340, 344–48, 350–51, 353–54, 358, 376–77, 380, 383
Mills and Byrnes, 52–53, 87–90, 102, 110–111, 117–118, 120–21, 213
Monson, Diane, 375n
Moore, Clayton F., 73n
Morgenthau, Henry, 170, 174
Morris, John D., 195n
Morse, Wayne, 261
Mumma, Walter, 42
Murphy, James T., 82n
Myers, Robert J., 341n, 348, 351

Naegele, Kasper D., 98n
National debt, 22, 179, 181, 229–30, 345
National Industrial Recovery Act, 163–64
Nature of parties, 15–21
Newcomb, Theodore M., 96
New York Stock Exchange, 371
Norris, George, 297
Novak, Robert, 116n

O'Brien, Thomas J., 32, 74, 205, 345
Oil depletion allowance, 26–27, 48–49, 296, 338
O'Leary, Michael K., 325n

Parsons, Talcott, 7–8, 9n, 10, 60–61, 91n, 98n, 101n, 121n, 123, 124n, 132
Participant observation, 4–7
Party conflict, 16–20, 35–38, 40–45, 59–96, 105–107, 152, 158–60, 162–247
Party leaders, 17, 22–38, 40–45, 48, 76, 88, 171, 195–97, 199–203, 216, 218, 239, 242–44, 289
Party unity scores, 16–17, 29–30, 42–43
Pastore, John, 263
Patman, Wright, 70
Patterson, James, 169n, 170n, 172n
Peabody, Robert L., 44n, 60n, 143n, 233n
Pearson, Drew, 236
Percy, Charles, 269
Pitts, Jesse R., 98n
Plunkitt, Boss, 59
Polsby, Nelson W., 21n, 60n, 143n, 233n
Pool, Ithiel de Sola, 45n, 198n, 199n, 210n, 233n, 234–36, 248, 287n, 289n, 319n
Porter, Frank, 258n, 267n
Powell, Adam Clayton, 18
Proxmire, William, 296, 304
Pucinski, Roman, 33

Quealy, William, 119

Radcliffe-Brown, A. R., 8n
Randall, William J., 222
Ranney, Austin, 16n
Raven, Bertram, 9, 124n, 132n, 142n
Rayburn, Sam, 23–27, 32–35, 38, 47–48, 55, 99, 111, 200, 202, 262, 289
Reciprocal trade, 1, 2, 22, 24, 26, 45, 57, 165, 181, 183, 187–90, 193, 197–200, 226–27, 233, 238, 267–68, 281–91, 330–35, 345–46, 354
Reed, Daniel, 50, 70, 169, 172–73, 193, 195–200, 202, 204–205, 207, 228n, 285, 311, 333, 338
Reid, Ogden, 40
Republican Conference, 203
Research strategy, 4–7
Restrained partisanship, 44–53, 63–96, 115

Rhee, Syngman, 195
Rhodes, George, 32, 79, 93, 96
Rice, Stuart A., 158n
Ripley, Randall B., 20n, 243n, 244n
Rivers, L. Mendell, 243
Robinson, James A., 220n
Rogers, Walter, 33
Roosa, Robert V., 353
Roosevelt, Franklin D., 155, 163–64, 166, 168–69, 172n, 174, 181, 185, 202, 210, 337
Rosenberg, Bernard, 9n
Rostenkowski, Dan, 32–33, 79, 139n
Rowen, Hobart, 345n
Rules Committee, 25, 35, 177, 195–96, 204–205, 222–26, 228–31, 238, 254
Ruml, Beardsley, 179
Ryan, William Fitz, 215

Sabath, Adolph, 177, 222, 224–25
Samuel, Howard D., 260n, 311
Scammon, Richard M., 51n
Schachter, Stanley, 54n
Schattschneider, E. E., 16, 189n, 266, 330–31, 362
Schneebeli, Herman, 49, 354
Scott, Richard, 5n
Seib, Charles B., 111n
Seligman, Lester G., 100n
Senate, 116, 118, 192, 214
    autonomy of House (Article 1, section 7), 252–63, 307–308, 337, 340
    House members' view of, 248–61, 266–67
    interest aggregation, 263–69, 279, 288–90
Shils, Edward A., 8n, 60n, 91n, 98n, 132n
Silverman, Corrinne, 319n
Simmel, Georg, 98, 108
Simon, Herbert A., 60n, 61n
Simpson, Richard M., 198–99, 204, 285, 303, 333
Slater, Philip E., 9n, 101n
Smathers, George, 257, 298
Smith, H. Allen, 230–31

Smith, Judge Howard W., 18n, 99, 171, 184n, 202, 226, 238, 243
Smoot-Hawley tariff, 330, 336
Social security, 2, 22, 48, 172, 190, 193–94, 227–28, 230–32, 279–81, 339–42
Sorensen, Theodore, 144n, 347
Stam, Colin, 310–17, 343, 357, 359
Stand-by tax authority, 339
Steiner, Gilbert Y., 270n
Stern, David J., 237–38n, 357n, 359
Stern, Philip M., 26n, 315, 336n
Stokes, Donald E., 54
Strauss, Anselm L., 5n, 11n
Street, Kenneth W., 189n
Surrey, Stanley, 116, 294n, 308, 328–29, 336n, 337, 353, 357, 376–77

Taft, Robert, 38
Talmadge, Herman, 298
Tariff Commission, 188, 193, 198, 283, 286, 332
Tax policy, 1, 2, 22, 49, 57, 114–18, 148, 166–68, 172, 177–80, 185–87, 190–93, 195–97, 200–204, 215–18, 223–24, 273–79, 294–307, 335–39, 342–79
Teague, Charles M., 253–54
Tenzer, Herbert, 295
Theory:
    exchange, 6–10, 60–96, 121–44
    role, 10, 61–63
    systems, 6–11
    functionalism, 8–9
Thibaut, John W., 103, 104n, 124
Thompson, Clark, 29, 33, 35, 38, 79
Treadway, Allen L., 163–64, 167–71, 173, 178
Treasury Department, 12, 116, 327–29, 342–83
Truman, David B., 20n, 233, 322
Truman, Harry S, 50, 152, 183, 185–88, 189n, 194, 202, 226, 337–38, 340
Turner, Julius, 20n

Ullman, Al, 65, 266, 376

Unemployment compensation, 202–206, 209, 239–40, 262
United States Chamber of Commerce, 82, 369–70, 372
Utt, James, 44, 49, 96, 197, 199

Vanik, Charles, 38
Verba, Sidney, 9n, 104n
Vinson, Carl, 34–35, 122, 243
Von Den Berghe, Pierre L., 10n
Voorhis, Jerry, 55, 232n

Ward, Sam, 324
Watson, Richard A., 200n, 210n
Watts, John, 102, 145, 148, 241
Ways and Means Committee, House:
  attractiveness of, 23, 53–58, 96
    effect of attractiveness on, 56–58, 68–72
  centralization in, 73–75
  complexity of subject matter, 92–95
  dependence-independence, 211–33, 246–47
  executive branch, relations with, 322–79
    interest aggregation, 324–79
  history of, 2–3
  importance of, 1–3, 22, 84–85
  recruitment to, 22–53
    Chairman-ranking member, 52–53
    Democrats, 22–38
    geographical balance, 36–37
    policy views, 26–29, 33, 38–42
    Republicans, 38–44
    safe seats, 51–52, 83
  same state "rule," 33–34
  seniority, 48–51
  state delegations, 22, 27, 32–34, 42–44, 55
  type of men, 46–52, 55–58, 295
  relations with House, 68, 71, 87, 110–13, 119
    1933–1939, 162–74
    1940–1946, 174–82
    1947–1952, 183–94
    1953–1960, 194–206
    1961–1968, 206–10
  serving constituents, 78–80, 82–84, 323
  socialization, 90–96, 140–41
    socialization maintenance, 91
  style of decision-making, 21–22, 44–53, 57–58, 63–96
  subcommittees, lack of, 73–75, 128–29
Weber, Max, 124n
West, Milton, 181
Westphal, Albert C. F., 1n
Wheare, K. C., 1
White, William Foote, 5n, 132n
Wilson, Woodrow, 2n, 151–52
Witte, Edwin E., 349n
Woodworth, Laurence N., 81, 117, 310, 313–16, 318, 329, 343, 345

Young, James Sterling, 2n
Young, Stephen, 30

Zander, Alvin, 9n, 54n, 96n, 124n